Theater: Preparation and Performance

Theater:
Preparation and Performance

Charlotte Lee
David Grote

Scott, Foresman and Company

Editorial Offices: Glenview, Illinois
Regional Sales Offices: Palo Alto, California ○ Tucker, Georgia
Glenview, Illinois ○ Oakland, New Jersey ○ Dallas, Texas

COVER: The Shoctor Theatre, Edmonton, Alberta, Canada.
Architectural design by Diamond and Myers in association
with R.L. Wilkin. Photographs by John Fulker.

ISBN: 0-673-13365-6

Acknowledgments

Unit openers: Interior views of Loew's Kings Theater, Flatbush Avenue, Brooklyn, New York. Photographs by Bill Frederking.

Glenbrook North High School, Glenbrook, Illinois, rehearsal scenes of *The Golden Masque of Agamemnon,* directed by Pat Murphy: pages 139, 143, 184, 188, 189, 242, 250. Student interpreter: pages 54, 60.

Northwestern University Mime Troupe, directed by Bud Beyer: pages 17, 28, 29, 123, 137, 224.

Picture Credits:

Positions of photographs are shown in abbreviated form as follows: top (t), bottom (b), left (l), and right (r). Unless otherwise credited, all photos are the property of Scott, Foresman and Company.

Page XI: Richard Younker
Chapter 1: **4,** Richard Younker.
Chapter 2: **12,** David S. Strickler/Monkmeyer Press; **16,** Milton Greene, from *The Marcel Marceau Counting Book* by George Mendoza, Doubleday & Company.
Chapter 4: **32,** Eve Arnold/Magnum; **34,** Robert Tolchin.
Chapter 7: **89,** Owen Franken/Stock Boston; **90,** David Strickler/Monkmeyer Press; **94,** Ray Hillstrom.
Chapter 9: **128,** Lisa Ebright, **129,** Michael P. Weinstein; **131,** Ellis Herwig/Stock Boston (both).
Chapter 11: **148,** John Vickers Archives, London.
Chapter 12: **152,** The New York Public Library.
Chapter 13: **173,** Joel Gordon; **175,** Frank Siteman/Stock Boston; **178,** Ellis Herwig/Stock Boston.
Chapter 14: **181,** Inge Morath/Magnum; **186,** Joe Schuyler/Stock Boston.
Chapter 15: **191,** Joe Schuyler/Stock Boston.
Chapter 16: **195,** Mike L. Wannemacher/Taurus Photos; **196,** Charles Harbutt/Magnum; **197,** Tyrone Hall/Stock Boston; **198,** Joel Gordon; **201,** John Boykin/*Dramatics.*
Chapter 17: **205,** Lisa Ebright; **207** and **208,** Shostal Associates; **211,** Lisa Ebright (1), J. Albertson/Stock Boston (r); **213,** Lisa Ebright (both).
Chapter 18: **215,** Lisa Ebright; **216,** Ben Nye Company, Inc.; **218,** R. D. Ullmann/Taurus Photos; **222,** William Morris Agency.
Chapter 19: **226,** Lisa Ebright, **227,** Owen Franken/Stock Boston (t); **232** and **235,** Lisa Ebright.
Chapter 20: **239,** Lisa Ebright.
Chapter 21: **247,** Lisa Ebright.
Chapter 22: **250,** John Walmsley; **251,** R. D. Ullmann/Taurus Photos.
Chapter 26: **301,** Owen Franken/Stock Boston.
Chapter 27: **303,** Ray Hillstrom; **304,** Hugh Rogers/Monkmeyer Press.
Chapter 28: **307,** Jean-Claude Lejeune/Stock Boston; **309,** Elaine Wicks, O.S.F./Taurus Photo **311,** James Holland/Stock Boston.
Chapter 29: **316,** The National Tourist Organization of Greece; **318,** Stratford Festival, Stratford, Ontario.
Chapter 30: **324–325,** Victoria and Albert Museum, London.
Chapter 31: **332,** The Newberry Library, Chicago.
Chapter 32: **336,** The Tate Gallery, London; **338,** Collections de la Comédie-Française, Bulloz.
Chapter 33: **348,** Craig Preston Sams; **349,** Peter Smith/Stratford Festival, Stratford, Ontario.
Chapter 34: **354,** The New York Public Library; **335,** Elliott Erwitt/Magnum; **357,** Ken Love.

CONTENTS

Unit I
Development of Performance Skills

CHAPTER 1
Facing the Audience

CHAPTER 2
Action for the Performer

CHAPTER 3
Improving Your Voice

CANDY
FRANKS

As we mature we become increasingly involved in trying to discover who we are and the image others have of us. We come to an awareness of who we are as we learn more about others. Literature brings us into the lives and fears and dreams of a wide variety of people in hundreds of situations and relationships. Sometimes we will read something or see something in a play that is very much like an experience we have had ourselves. It is comforting to know that we aren't the only ones who have worried about or rejoiced in certain things. We relate closely to the story or poem or play, and as the characters in the story or play or the speaker in the poem work out their problems, we too come to some decisions. We may agree or disagree with what they are saying or doing, but in that process we ask ourselves why we would or would not do the same thing, and thus we begin to clarify our own sense of values and priorities. As a performer, the experience mirrored in the literature and the way it is expressed becomes a part of you in a very special way. As the audience listens and responds, they, too, are changed a little, perhaps.

Performance and writing specifically for performers probably reached their pre-modern height in England during the Elizabethan and Restoration periods beginning about 1660. Plays and poetry by Shakespeare, Marlowe, and Ben Jonson were extremely popular. The plays often included poems and soliloquies which were delivered directly to the audience. For example, the actor playing Hamlet would face the audience while delivering "To be or not to be . . . " and very often the actor would deliberately walk to the front of the stage to be closer to the audience during the soliloquy. (Occasionally even today a Shakespearean actor will deliver a soliloquy directly to the audience.) Thus the members of the theatrical companies became adept in the art of what we now call interpretation as well as in the art of acting.

Focus on the single performer or interpreter, who was then called an "elocutionist," began as early as 1763 in England with the publication of Thomas Sheridan's book, Courses of Lectures on Elocution. *This interest soon spread to the United States, and by the end of the nineteenth century, America was blossoming with innumerable "studios" and "schools" of oratory and "expression," as it soon came to be called. The Chautauqua Movement, an educational program popular in the late nineteenth and early twentieth centuries, sent out scores of politicians, actors, poets, and teachers to towns and rural areas across the country. They read their own and others' literary products, performing during the summer months in tents or outdoors, often staying a week in each place. They never lacked for appreciative audiences.*

A look at the Broadway season will reveal that many of the long-run plays are a mixture of the traditional play format and performances by people we now call interpreters. There are numerous semiprofessional and professional groups which specialize in Readers' Theater and Chamber Theater. A sincere and skillful performance, whether by actor or interpreter, will never lose its charm for an audience.

Chapter 1
Facing the Audience

In our everyday lives whenever we speak to one another, we are communicating, by verbal sounds and nonverbal clues, our ideas, attitudes, and emotional reactions. These acts of communication are, on a simple level, a kind of performance in that we are "turning our minds and feelings outward" to share them with someone else.

In this book we will be concerned more with the formal performance, with ideas and emotions not strictly our own but rather with those that have been put down on the printed page by another—to be shared with an audience.

The Audience

An audience may be one person or a thousand. As an actor or interpreter you will seldom encounter a hostile one. People are there because they want to be and are eager to enjoy the experience you are bringing them. Of course, in the classroom your audience is technically a captive one, but each member of it will be caught up in what you are doing and saying, just as you will be when you are the audience. Your classmates' criticism will be constructive and will help you perfect your skills.

The relationship of an audience to the performer and to the literature being read or acted is a very special one—there is nothing quite like it. Every performance is important both to you and your listeners . . . and an important part of your enjoyment is trust in your audience.

The audiences you may have the opportunity to perform for are innumerable: to begin with—your class, your school, your church. Perhaps your community has its own theater group. Retirement homes for the elderly welcome young performers. Many libraries seek young people to read stories and perform simple plays and pantomimes for the youngsters in the community. Most every community, whatever its size, has an annual celebration commemorating its origins or the nation's—there are always special occasions and the special opportunity for you to perform in them. And then, if acting is what you most want to do—there is Broadway.

Whatever the situation, whatever the audience, your privileges and responsibilities are the same. Your first responsibility is to the author of the material you have chosen to interpret or perform. You must do a thorough and conscientious job of analyzing the material so that you know everything you have to work with and what it is doing there to help achieve a total effect. You must open your mind and tune your emotions to every detail in the selection, responding as completely and as deeply as you can, not only to what it all means but to *how* it means what it means. Your audience will both see and hear you, so you must be sure that what they see and hear serves the material at hand.

Skills Essential to Performance

Before you can effectively communicate what your material means and how it means what it means, you must master the techniques of voice and body control. Voice and body are the twin instruments by which you share the experiences of your written materials. Your voice and body must serve your analysis of what your material is all about.

The complete control of your voice and body will take some practice. Just because you have been talking most of your life does not guarantee that your voice is adequate to reach the back of a room so that you may be easily heard, nor that your articulation is good enough that you may be understood. Literature demands certain subtle changes in pace, volume, and other vocal aspects that you do not use in everyday conversation. The musician practices handling his or her instrument so it will respond to the touch instantly and unobtrusively. A painter learns to handle brushes and colors. An athlete practices for hours with the basketball, football, or tennis racket. An interpreter or actor must be equally adept at using his or her instruments.

The body must work along with the voice. We all develop little physical mannerisms which are a part of our personalities. Sometimes these gestures or postures can distract our audience and call attention to us—away from the literature we are trying to share. The actor must learn to move and stand as the character being portrayed; the interpreter must learn to get his or her own physical habits out of the way of material when they are not harmonious with what he or she is communicating. This control cannot be accomplished overnight. It is a continuing process. Skill in the execution of any art takes time, effort, concentration, and self-discipline. And acting and interpretation are arts.

The author is the original creative artist, but his or her art can only be expressed in printed symbols on a page. The actor and interpreter are artists when they take those printed symbols and make them come alive with all their implications, their sound values, and their full meaning. The experience which moved the author to record the event in the first place becomes vivid and moving once again as you share it with others.

Stage Fright

Some of you have probably had some experience speaking or reading or acting before an audience. Some of you probably have not, and the very thought may give you the shakes! Let's try to find out what causes those shakes, which are sometimes referred to as "stage fright." This is a misnomer because the sensation is by no means limited to the stage nor is the reason for it actually fright. Of course no one wants to look ridiculous or be a failure before his or her peers. But this will not happen if you have prepared as fully as you can and keep your concentration steadily on the material you are sharing.

Part of what some people call stage fright is, in reality, excitement. You want to succeed, and you want your audience to like what you are doing as much as you like doing it. The adrenaline starts pumping through your system the way it does before the big game or even before you go out with a new date. If you mistake it for fright, you tense your muscles, and they start to shake. Hold out your hand and tense your fingers and arm tightly. They shake. That is simply muscle tension. The following activities will help you achieve a state of controlled relaxation.

Activities

Muscular Relaxation

1. Imagine that you are a marionette with strings at each of your joints and that you are being held up by an imaginary puppeteer in the sky. Imagine that the puppeteer pulls you up and stretches you out as much as possible. Then, he lets go of the strings one at a time.

As each imaginary string is released, you are held up by the one below it. Relax everything above the joint where you are held. For example, when you are stretched out, the strings will hold you by your fingers. When the finger strings let go, the hand is limp and you are stretched by the wrist string. When the wrist string is released, everything below the elbow is released, and so on. Continue until all the imaginary strings are released, and you collapse onto the floor.

2. When the tension is localized or when you have only a little time to prepare, you may be able to shake the tension out.

Let your arms hang loosely at your sides. Shake your hands, moving from the elbow so that the wrist and fingers are completely loose. Then shake your arms, moving from the shoulder so the elbow is loosened too. Try the same thing with your legs, one at a time.

The secret is to move from the elbow or shoulder, the joint above the tense part of the body. If you wiggle your hand, for example, instead of shaking your arm above a limp hand, you only become more tense.

3. Reach for the ceiling, stretching as far and as hard as you can, then all at once relax everything above your waist and drop over from the waist. Your arms and head will hang loosely, your arms almost brushing the floor, depending on how far you easily bend over. Slowly and easily move your trunk from side to side, moving from the hip joints. Relax so your head and arms swing freely and easily. As with Activity 2, you must be careful not to wiggle your head or arms. Do the movement from the hip area, so that any movement in the neck and shoulder area is a result of gravity and inertia, not of muscle tension.

4. If you have time for a long relaxing exercise, try this one which takes about fifteen minutes.

Lie on the floor on your back, arms to your sides in a comfortable position, and close your eyes. Think about the toes on your right foot, one at a time. Mentally focus all your attention on each toe, and relax each muscle around each toe. Feel each individual muscle relax. You must do this one muscle at a time, one place at a time. If you try to do more, the relaxation is never complete.

When you have relaxed all the toes, relax the right foot, then the ankle area, then the calf, then the thigh. In your mind see and feel each muscle relax. Then repeat for the left foot and leg. Do the same thing for each hand and arm, starting with one finger and working up to the shoulder.

When all your limbs are relaxed, focus on the muscles in your back, moving up the spine, one muscle at a time, until you reach the neck and are completely relaxed.

Because most of us have never been relaxed this completely and don't know how it feels to be so completely relaxed, some may be surprised by the feelings generated. As you seriously let each muscle go, your weight will spread and press into the floor and you will begin to *feel* the floor. Your breathing and your circulation will slow down; as you relax, you need less oxygen to sustain you. You may even feel colder. If you feel a muscle twitching, then that muscle is not completely relaxed and you need to mentally go back and relax that particular muscle. If you feel yourself moving into a more comfortable position, then you have to re-relax that part of your body.

If you are successfully relaxed, you will not be able to leap up at the end of the relaxing time. Before you try to stand, wriggle your fingers and toes, and sit up carefully. Your circulation has to start moving again at normal tempo before you can stand without dizziness.

Mental Relaxation

1. Drop your head forward, letting the tension in the neck area relax. Close your eyes. Slowly rotate your head around the neck base. When the muscles seem relaxed, let the head balance on the neck, restfully. Let your mind wander throughout your body, and tell yourself exactly what you are doing, right now. Be specific, and stay completely in the present tense. For example, "I am sitting here, my right arm is hanging down, I hear the heater, I feel my left ankle itch," and so on.

This is a lot harder than it sounds. Learning to focus on the immediate present is essential to the performance on stage, but it is also essential to any sense of relaxation. Most nervousness comes from worry about something in the past or in the future; we think about all the things that might go wrong in the next minute or hour or day, or all the things that went wrong yesterday, and that makes us tense and nervous. If we can focus our minds on the immediate, *now* experience, that tension will disappear, and the performance itself later will be focused and alive as well. If you find your mind wandering into the past or future as you describe the experience, then you have lost the focus you need.

2. Close your eyes and assume a relaxed position. If possible, try this after the long relaxation exercise above, but it will be useful in any relaxed position. Imagine a full range of vision, all one color. For example, you may see an imaginary sky all in blue, or pink; any color will do. When everything you see is one color, imagine that the color begins to fly away from you so that you begin to see a gigantic circle of that color. Focus on that circle of color as it flies away; watch it get smaller and smaller until it is a dot of color and then finally disappears. What is left should be nothing. The mind is focused so far away that all conscious thoughts and feelings disappear along with the dot of color. This helps to focus your attention on a single point and to remove any of those extraneous confusions which cause tension before a performance of any kind.

Warming Up

Before you begin any performance or even before performing in classroom or practice exercises, you should be ready physically and mentally for that work. Part of that readiness is relaxation, and part is warming up the parts of your voice and body which will be used, so that they are awake and ready when you need them. You can develop your own warmups as you go into specific performances; some roles or interpretations will need some very specific warmups, in which you work on a specific problem of some kind. Dance or strenuous physical activity will require extra muscular stretching, and complex speeches will require extra vocal activity. The following is only a sample, a general warm-up, to use for general kinds of performance. It can be done in less than five minutes, and serves as a quick wake-up for the parts of your instrument in physical use in most performance.

1. Stretching:

(a) Assume you are a traffic policeman on a busy corner. Give directions to traffic from all sides. Be specific in your directions, but be big and clear. Try to involve a leg in the directions as well.

(b) Conduct an imaginary choir in an imaginary song. Gradually enlarge the choir so that it could fill your gym or other large space and enlarge your directions so that everyone in that large group can see them.

2. Breathing:

(a) Stretch your arms high overhead. Then drop over from the waist, swinging your upper body down and then up to one side like a pendulum. As you drop over, let out all the air in your lungs, and then fill your lungs with a good breath as you stretch upward. Repeat several times in both directions.

(b) Imagine that the laws of gravity are temporarily suspended, and that there is a ping-pong ball attached to the front of your teeth with a rubber band. When you blow on it, it will go away, then the rubber band will pull it back again right into your mouth. Try to blow it away five separate times, without taking in a breath. Then try it ten times (then fifteen), and soon you will get used to doing this with your diaphragm pushing the air for you in little puffs. Be sure the throat is completely loose and open while this is being done.

3. Mouth area:

(a) Pretend you are a motorboat, blowing air through your lips to make the boat sound.

(b) Pop your lips together as quickly as possible, making little popping sounds.

(c) Relax your jaw, and wriggle it from side to side, so that it is loose and flexible.

(d) While the jaw is relaxed, say "cookie, cookie, cookie" as quickly as you can.

(e) Stick your tongue out and wriggle it around. Say "lalalalala" as quickly as you can.

(f) Hum. As you do, try to make your sinus area vibrate with the sound. Then make the top of your head vibrate. Then try to vibrate your breastbone. Then try to vibrate all of them at the same time.

(g) Say a few nonsense syllables, or a simple nursery rhyme. Aim each sound at a place in the wall farthest from you in the room, and try to aim the sound right into one point on that wall. Turn your back, and try to aim the sound through your back at that same spot.

Chapter 2
Action for the Performer

There is no secret way to move or gesture on stage, although many people who have not worked in front of an audience think that there is. Whether you work as an interpreter or as an actor, you need to move as simply, gracefully, naturally, and expressively as possible.

It is not always easy to do. For many people, nerves interfere, making them self-conscious and worried about how they look. This nervousness, in turn, makes them look awkward.

For others, there are simple problems of coordination. When you do anything that you are not used to doing, your body often has trouble finding the easiest way to do it—you may trip over yourself, your hands may flop around without control, or any number of other things may make you look uncoordinated. The answer to problems of coordination lies in understanding how your body works and in practicing the actions that you are required to do until you find direct and uncomplicated ways of doing them.

Finally, for still others, expressive movement is a problem only because they have had little experience with it. For whatever reason, they have never had to express much through their actions. They may not have had the real-life experiences covering the broad range of emotional and social behavior that the performer may need for understanding.

In this chapter, we will look at some of the ways the performer may deal with these problems in order to develop relaxed, natural, and expressive movement in performance.

Balance

In any public performance, it is important that your stance is balanced. Your comfort, control, and expressiveness come from a sense of this balance. Before working on specific movements or gestures, every performer must find a comfortable position, a way of *being*, in which all the parts of the body are at perfect ease and in harmony with each other.

The following activities will give you practice in developing balance. Each activity must begin with a sense of relaxation, however. Review the relaxation activities in Chapter 1. Always be sure to work on the balance activities after warmup and relaxation practice. As you work on the activities, try to eliminate tension, especially in the neck and shoulder areas.

Activities

1. Stand in a relaxed position. Shift your feet so that they are a little farther apart than your shoulders. Lift one foot and then the other, rocking from side to side. Let this happen easily, without locking your knees or hips. Gradually shift your feet closer together until the rocking comes to rest. You will come to rest before your feet come together. Stop at that point at which your body would stop rocking if you did not force it to keep moving. Notice how your body works like a pendulum and slowly stops itself. The point at which you stop rocking naturally will give you the most comfortable width of stance for your own sense of balance.

2. To find a balanced position in relation to potential movement, repeat Activity 1, except spread your feet forward and back, so that you rock from front to back. Be careful to keep your upper body relaxed, otherwise you will lock your back into a board.

3. Combine Activities 1 and 2. Start with your feet widely separated on a diagonal line and rock easily as you bring your feet closer together until you come to rest. For most people, the feet will be just inside the width of the shoulders. One foot will be slightly forward of the other. When you find this position, it should be immediately comfortable and balanced.

4. Lie on the floor. Stretch your arms and legs as far and as wide as they will go. Relax your muscles and let your arms and legs surrender to gravity. Feel the lines of control coming together at a central point in your body. Re-extend your arms and legs, beginning the action at the center of this control point and gradually moving the action outward. This imaginary point is the center of your own activity. Each action that you do, whether in voice or physical movement, should begin from this imaginary point, and move outward as it occurs, then return inward to its balance.

5. Stand in your balanced position. Relax. Lift yourself up onto your toes and stay balanced. Slowly begin to bounce on the toes and the balls of your feet. Do not jump or lift your feet off the floor. Gradually increase the speed while maintaining a relaxed balance.

6. Imagine that you are a clock and that your arms and legs are the hands of that clock. Indicate as many different times as you can. Try it first with only your arms, showing hour and minute. Then add one leg, and show hour, minute, and second. Then, have the second hand move while showing the time. This is also a good stretching exercise for a warmup. Try to stay relaxed, and maintain a comfortable balance as your body expands to show the clock face.

Pantomime

One of the most useful ways for the performer to develop expressive movement is through the use of pantomime exercises. Although these activities can often lead to complete performance in themselves, they also can provide a solid foundation on which to build your concentration, coordination, and expressiveness. There are many different meanings for the term and many different kinds of pantomime, but all pantomime involves the use of the body as a whole to express some activity.

The body is an incredibly expressive instrument. People constantly communicate without words—in the ways they stand, sit, walk, and use their hands and arms. Those bodily expressions tell other people how we feel, how we see ourselves, and the ways in which we express our personalities before we verbalize. The performer must use that expressive power to his or her advantage.

One of the ways we use the body is to express emotion. Sometimes, specific emotions use specific actions. When you feel very excited, as at a football game, you jump up and down and wave your arms in a way that expresses the excitement of the game. Most of the time, however, it is not *what* we do physically but rather *how* we do it that reveals our emotion. For example, when your teacher asks a question in class and you raise your hand to answer, you can

raise that hand in many different ways. Each one of those ways will express a different feeling about your willingness to answer. You might stretch your arm high and wave your hand around when you really want to answer the question. When you don't know the answer but don't want the teacher to know that, you might raise your hand nonchalantly, in the hope that the teacher will think you know but will not really be inspired to call on you. You might be unsure of the answer and just barely raise your hand, so that you can be ready to pull it back down at any moment. Or, you might just casually wave your hand, flicking the wrist a little, as if to say, "I know all this, but it's hardly worth the trouble to answer." You might find a hundred other ways to raise your hand, each with a distinct meaning for the person watching you.

We do the same kind of thing with other parts of our bodies. The performer has to eventually learn to recognize and use all of these expressive, silent movements.

Activities

In each of the following activities, try to express a specific attitude toward what you are doing so that your own imaginary mood is absolutely clear.

As you do each of these, be aware of the way your entire body is involved in each action. Notice how the arms connect to the trunk and how that, in turn, affects the way your legs position and shape themselves, and how the head changes position as your attitudes change. The whole body is connected to every action, and no clear or accurate expression can be made without involving the full body. It is very easy to begin to worry about one particular portion of an action and make everything seem awkward and artificial by forgetting to connect the whole body to the action.

1. (a) Wave:
hello to a friend
hello to a relative you don't like much
goodby to a friend
goodby to a relative you don't like much
to get someone's attention after an accident
to get someone's attention you'd like to meet
to a movie star you see on the street
as many other ways as you can think of

(b) Sit so that you indicate:
boredom
interest in a conversation
sleepiness
excitement over something you're watching
you're going to tell a story
your mood after a quarrel with your parents
as many other emotions as you can think of

(c) Walk as if you are:
avoiding a beggar on the street
catching up to a friend
leaving behind someone you don't like
entering class after the bell has rung
thinking about a problem
depressed about something
bored
feeling as many other ways as you can think of

(d) Stand to show you are:
waiting confidently
waiting nervously
waiting for a late bus
behind a long line
waiting for your brother or sister to return something of yours to you
listening to your parents correct you
hearing someone praise you
embarrassed by someone
feeling any other ways you can think of

In the following activities, which will help you expand your expressive abilities, you will artificially separate one part of your body from the other parts. As you do the activities, remember that they are purely for experiment and practice and that in performance you must connect each expression to all the rest of your body.

2. From a paper bag, make a mask which covers your face entirely. Cut eye and mouth holes, but do not draw a face on the mask. Wearing the mask, repeat each of the actions in Activity 1 so that other persons watching you can understand the attitude of each event.

3. Repeat each of the activities in Activity 1 but with your back to the persons watching.

4. Make a screen behind which you can stand that will hide your head and trunk but show your feet and legs. Repeat Activity 1c and 1d.

Concentration

Pantomime, in which you work with imaginary props, will help you focus your concentration and coordination.

The important point to remember in the following activities is to treat the imaginary props as if they were real. Concentrate your action and attention so that you make each part of your action clear, accurate, and precise. Keep your imaginary items the same size, the same shape, the same weight, and so on whenever you deal with them. Always be specific.

In the play *Our Town,* for example, at the beginning of each act, one or both of the mothers makes a breakfast for her family—completely in pantomime. To do the scene well, the performers must make each part of that breakfast exactly.

Each egg, each piece of bacon or sausage, each pancake or piece of French toast, each piece of wood in the stove has to be treated as if it were really there. If, in doing those scenes, you simply made general kitchen motions, without specific control, the audience would not be able to tell what you were doing and the point of the scenes in the play would be lost.

Pantomime will also help you develop your sensory imagination. Sensory imagination is discussed fully in Unit III, where you will also find additional exercises to help you perfect this part of the pantomime process.

Activities

1. Perform each of the following household activities using only imaginary objects. Make sure that your audience can tell what object you are using and focus all your activity on using the object as if it were really there.

(a) washing dishes
(b) sweeping the floor
(c) putting a record on the stereo
(d) hanging up your clothes in the closet
(e) brushing your teeth
(f) pouring milk into a glass and drinking it
(g) building a shelf
(h) setting the table for dinner

2. Use imaginary props or scenery for the following activities:

(a) climb up and down a ladder
(b) walk up and down a set of stairs
(c) open and exit through an imaginary door
(d) snuggle into a warm bed
(e) dig a hole in your backyard
(f) change a flat tire on your bicycle or automobile
(g) get a soft drink from a coin-operated machine
(h) pick a bouquet of flowers

3. Using imaginary props and scenery, assume that there are imaginary characters in the scene with you and perform the following activities:

(a) do a lion-taming act in a circus
(b) get into a snowball fight
(c) have a tug-of-war
(d) play a ball game of your choice
(e) move a refrigerator
(f) hang a large picture

Mime

For some performers, pantomime can be a complete performance in itself. These performers develop complete characters and scenes, and sometimes

Marcel Marceau

even long plays, completely in pantomime activities. Sometimes the performers work alone, sometimes in groups. When a good mime is working, he or she can show the audience a wholly new view of the world. The mime establishes a completely imaginary world in which both performer and audience must stretch their imaginations. Remarkable things then happen for everyone—things that cannot happen in more "normal" or realistic kinds of performance.

The art of the mime is an extremely difficult and demanding one. The mime has only his body to work with and must be completely in control of it. This takes an enormous amount of training. It also requires intense study of the physiology of movement and of specific techniques which allow the mime to duplicate each performance in a controlled and repeatable manner. The mime is very much like the dancer who studies for years in order to look as if what he or she is doing is absolutely spontaneous. If you become seriously interested in mime as a performance technique, beyond its part of the general training of the performer, be prepared for long serious study and rehearsal.

Neither pantomime nor mime are charades. The exercise or the performance of either is not successfully completed as soon as someone in the audience "guesses" what you are doing. There will be a sense of pleasure in doing whatever it is that you have been doing so that your performance can be recognized.

But avoid the short cuts to that recognition when doing pantomime. Keep your concentration and imagination involved in making your actions seem real to yourself as well as to your audience. Then, the previous exercises and similar ones will help you grow as a total performer.

Improvisation

Another important and useful skill for the performer is the art of improvisation. In improvised activities and scenes, actions are performed without script or rehearsal. Like pantomime, improvisation can also be used as a part of the performer's basic equipment and it can be developed as a specialized type of performance in itself. One of the most valuable aids to improvisation is the practice it gives in concentrating and reacting to the scene as it happens. When you are improvising, you never know what may occur next so you must be alert to everything happening with you on stage. Improvisation is a skill that you can use throughout all your training, helping to sharpen your specific skills in all areas. Since improvisation does not require memorized, specific scenes, it is useful in helping solve a problem without the time it might take to find a written script specific to your particular problem area.

Conflict

All activity on stage is built around a conflict of some kind. Any play as a whole or any individual scene involves a conflict between characters or between a character and the world around that character. This conflict is the center of what is called the *plot*. Sometimes this conflict may be between two persons: in *The Miracle Worker,* for example, Annie Sullivan, the teacher, struggles to make a civilized person of the six-year-old untutored Helen Keller. That conflict provides the basic plot of the play. Sometimes the conflict is between a character and the world at large. *Our Town,* for example, has no conflict between individual characters; they all like each other. The conflict is between Emily specifically (and all the people in general) and the nature of life. As Emily grows up, marries, and dies, she gradually learns the real meaning of life which is different from what she thought it was and what she wanted it to be.

Although it is often quite direct, conflict does not necessarily mean a quarrel. But conflict does mean that someone cannot have what he or she wants as soon as he or she wants it. Thus the basic concept an actor must use in playing any role is the character's objective. Each character wants something. If he gets it without a problem, he may be satisfied but the audience will be bored. So, the playwright provides obstacles to that objective which the character must overcome. This in turn provides the conflict in the play. If two characters have different objectives they may block each other, making for a personal conflict between them. Each then has to find some way to get around the obstacle to reach his own objective, providing interest for the audience.

Each scene will have a beginning and an ending. The beginning introduces the conflict, the time when the forces at work in the scene or in the play are explained to the audience. Once the conflict is introduced we see it happening until it is solved in some way. Only when this conflict is solved can we have an ending to the plot of the scene or the play.

Conflict is especially important in improvisational activities. An improvised scene must be *about* something—have a beginning and an ending with a problem or conflict to resolve. Most improvisation involves other performers, thus it helps you learn to work with other actors and to react to them. Most of the following activities involve two or more people.

As you work on your own improvisations, always begin with a clear objective of what you want to accomplish in the scene. Your objective may be very simple or it may be very complicated. Whatever it is, adjust to the obstacles provided by the others in the scene with you as you try to reach your objective.

Activities

1. In each of the following situations, assume that you and a partner are the same age and basically the same kinds of people that you are in real life. As you do each scene, think about what you want to accomplish. Keep your attention completely on what you say and do and on what your partner says. Look for openings that will allow you to take advantage and reach your own objective. Concentrate so that no matter what happens, you continue the improvised scene without stopping. Improvise a scene around the following situations.

(a) Each of you wants to watch a different television program.

(b) Each of you wants the other to set the table for dinner.

(c) One of you wants the other to introduce him or her to someone.

(d) One of you wants to borrow the other's homework to copy.

2. Imagine that your partner wants to do something illegal. He or she is ready to commit the act immediately when you, acting as your partner's conscience, suddenly appear and try to talk him or her out of what he or she plans to do. Find a way which will *really* convince your partner not to do whatever it is that he or she has planned to do.

3. In each of the following situations, you and your partner try to solve the problem together. Scenery and properties should be pantomimed.

(a) You are trapped on a mountainside as snow begins to fall.

(b) You are walking on a deserted street at night and hear sounds behind you.

(c) You are in a locked room and smell smoke.

(d) You are going to a party and the car breaks down.

(e) Your favorite aunt is coming to visit and the house is a mess.

Improvisation can also be very useful in helping you to understand the situations in a play or in a selection that you will be acting or interpreting. Through improvised scenes you can use your imagination to put yourself into the situation that your character must deal with, thus helping you to better understand your character's feelings and actions.

When you do this kind of improvising, concentrate on creating an experience. Try to deal with the imaginary events as they happen and to act out your responses to those events. When the improvisation is finished, examine what you did, what others did, and how you responded. Then ask yourself how those events and everyone's reactions apply to the ways your character may have felt and acted.

Activities

1. With several people from the class, attend the following imaginary events. Each person improvises his or her own reactions to the event, and each person responds to what the others are doing. This is a very free-form activity, and you should be ready for almost anything to happen. Use it as a totally involving experience. **(a)** a wedding **(b)** a funeral **(c)** a graduation exercise **(d)** a fire **(e)** a party **(f)** a church meeting.

2. With several people from the class, enact each of the following imaginary events. One or two persons should enact the actual activity, while the others are part of a group or crowd that watches and reacts. **(a)** a political meeting **(b)** an arrest on the sidewalk **(c)** a wedding **(d)** an argument in the school yard.

Improvisation as Performance

Improvisation may also be used as a performance in its own right. Many small theatrical groups and some soloists, especially comedians, do improvised material. At one time in history, many complete plays were improvised. (See *commedia del'arte,* page 324.) Such performers must be both skilled and inventive.

However, improvised performances of this type are improvised only in part. The comedian, for example, usually has a mental file of jokes on a number of topics. If someone should ask him to do a routine about a girlfriend, he will usually begin with several jokes from his file. If they are successful, he will probably continue, using similar ones; if they fail to get laughs, he will switch to something else. The material is improvised only in that the detailed order and actual language has not been decided and rehearsed beforehand.

In the same way, entire scenes or plays can be improvised. The performers will agree on a basic conflict and a resolution, varying words and actions from performance to performance. In this way, the performers are free to use material they have found to be effective while remaining open to inspiration and imagination.

Activities

1. On a piece of paper each person in the class writes a description of a scene involving two people. This description should include a place and a time in which the scene takes place, who the two people in the scene are, and the conflict between them. Indicate a solution to that conflict. For example: "A parent meets a daughter arriving home an hour later than she agreed upon. The daughter convinces the parent that she should not be punished."

Fold each piece of paper and put them into a container. Then, in pairs, draw a piece of paper from the container and improvise a scene to fit the description given.

2. In a group of several people, select a fairy tale with which you are all familiar. Have each person choose a character to play. Improvise a performance of the fairy tale. Use imaginary props and scenery throughout. Begin with fairly short and simple stories; this activity is more complicated than it may seem. After you are comfortable and have gained some experience, try improvisations of longer stories with several scenes each.

Chapter 3
Improving Your Voice

We touched on some of the aspects of handling your voice in Chapter 1. Voice and body are the two-fold instruments by which we communicate with one another. They must work together if the actor and the interpreter are to serve the material that is being performed. Your control of both must become so complete that you do not need to think about them during your performance when all your energy and concentration must be centered on the selection you are communicating and on the audience to whom you are communicating it.

Just because we have used our voices since that first cry when we were born, there is no guarantee that we are using them to their full capacities. We all develop both good and bad vocal habits and need to check occasionally on what we are actually doing so that we may solidify the good habits and get rid of the less desirable ones. This chapter will offer some suggestions for improving your voice and thus your communication ability. It is a long process and cannot be achieved overnight.

If your audience cannot understand the words you are saying, you and they might as well not be there. If they have to stop and translate slurred or incorrect sounds before they can figure out what word you are saying, you will soon lose them completely. An audience simply will not bother. So we will give our first attention to pronunciation and articulation.

Pronunciation and Articulation

Pronunciation refers to the standard proper arrangement of the sounds within a word and the proper positioning of the stress. For example, there is quite a difference between "deter" (di tėr′) and "detour" (dē′ tu̇r). The dictionary is your safest guide in the matter of correct pronunciation. Sometimes there are two pronunciations which are acceptable. The first listed is usually more common but either would be correct. Learn to recognize the dictionary markings that indicate these differences as a guide to correct pronunciation of unfamiliar words.

Articulation refers to the shaping of the sounds that make up a word. The sounds are shaped by the placement of the tongue, the position of the lips, teeth, and jaws, and the corresponding action of the hard and soft palates. The action of the palates is largely automatic when the lips, teeth, and tongue are in their proper positions.

Try the following sequence of words: hay, he, hah, high, hoe, hue. Do them slowly. Notice how the lips change their position from being drawn back into something like a smile on "hay" to a small round opening on "hue." Exaggerate the positions until you get the feel of them. Now notice how the jaws open wider as you move toward "hah" and begin to close again for "hoe" and "hue."

Vowels do not usually cause us as much trouble as consonants do, however. Too often we tend to slur over the consonants or substitute one for another, especially those at the end of a word or within the word. The lips and jaws are also involved in forming consonants, but the tongue carries most of the burden. Try the sentence "The bidder bought the bitter batter" which doesn't make much sense, but is excellent for noticing the position of the jaws and lips and especially of the tongue as it operates in relation to the teeth. Start saying the sentence slowly and then work up to saying it as fast as you can without changing the "b" to "t" or slighting the vowels.

Some consonant sounds are called *plosives* because a sudden release of air completes their formation. Among them are p, b, t, d, k, and g. Try the following words and notice the spurt of air which gives them carrying power: plough, pretty, putty, purple, pat; bough, branch, bubble, baby buggy, brittle; King Kong, kick; good, gas, group, gobble, gluck.

The "s" sound is probably one of the most difficult to control. It involves proper positioning of teeth and jaws as well as lips and tongue and a propulsion of air all coordinated. Sometimes the propulsion of air needs to be toned down to keep the "s" from hissing so sharply that it becomes distracting. Sometimes the teeth or tongue or lips are not in proper position and the "s" is mushy like "sh." The stream of air should go directly over the center of the tongue and be expelled between the closely aligned edges of the upper and lower front teeth. Check your "s" sounds in these words: six, sisters, sessions, sizzling, simplicity, sincerity, seashells.

Activities

1. To keep the lips and tongue limber and to improve articulation, try each of the following drills. Say them slowly and clearly; then gradually increase speed. Go as quickly as you can while still saying *everything* clearly. Have someone listen carefully to you to make sure you actually say all the sounds, or try them yourself with a tape recorder. Speed in itself will not help unless you also speak clearly when you speed up.

(a) Amos Ames, the amiable aeronaut, aided in an aerial enterprise at the age of eighty-eight.

(b) The bleak breeze blighted the bright broom blossoms.

(c) What noise annoys an oyster? A noisy noise annoys an oyster.

(d) Six slick, slim, slippery, slimy, sleek, slender saplings.

(e) To the Millwheel said the Windmills, "When the wind wills do you still wheel?" "Yes, we still wheel when the wind wills!" To the Windmills said the Millwheel.

(f) Unique New York, unique New York, unique New York, etc.

(g) He didn't say he wouldn't, and he didn't say he couldn't or shouldn't, but he didn't.

(h) Papala mamala papala mamala papala mamala, etc.

(i) Hard-headed Hannah had a hard-hearted harp which wouldn't thrum a hymn when the harp was hot.

2. Make a list of five or ten words which will require careful attention to their formation. Put the words on the board or supply the class with written copies and ask class members to take turns pronouncing them. This will also teach you to hear the sounds when you and others make them incorrectly. Then make tongue twisters of your words.

3. Try this activity with selections from literature. Almost any selection included at the ends of chapters will offer some fine examples of lines or sentences which demand clean careful articulation. Here are three.

While words of learned length and thundering sound
Amazed the gazing mystics ranged around. . .
—Oliver Goldsmith from "The Deserted Village"

But when loud surges lash the sounding shore,
The harsh, rough verse should like the torrent roar.
—Alexander Pope from "An Essay on Criticism"

Drowned puppies, stinking sprats, all drenched in mud,
Dead cats and turnip tops, come tumbling down the flood.
—Jonathan Swift from "A Description of a City Shower"

Rate and Pauses

The speed at which you read aloud and your use of appropriate pauses will have a great deal to do with whether or not your audience can understand you. Most beginning readers and actors speak much too fast. You must remember that while you know where the selection or the scene is going, your listeners need time to translate your sounds into words and ideas.

Choosing material in which the mood is quiet is one way to keep your speed in check. But that would limit you as a performer. Care with articulation is a big help. Some combinations of sounds, as in the above examples, simply cannot be said rapidly if you are going to give each vowel and consonant their due attention. Take time to say them all clearly and you will be able to control your speed more effectively.

Pauses are a very important part of your ability to reach your audience with the full meaning, both denotative and connotative, of what you are saying.

Pauses are needed to separate clauses and sometimes even phrases so that they stand in meaningful relationship to each other and to the sentence in which they occur. This long sentence, in which Thomas Wolfe is talking about the passing of two trains, is a complicated one grammatically and can be untangled for the listener only by generous use of pauses.

> For, having lived together as strangers in the immense and
> swarming city, they now had met upon the everlasting earth,
> hurled past each other for a moment between two points in
> time upon the shining rails, never to meet, to speak, to know
> each other any more, and the briefness of their days,
> the destiny of man, was in that instant greeting and farewell.
>
> —Thomas Wolfe, from *Of Time and the River*

Try various ways of reading it until you are sure it will be perfectly clear. Then turn your attention to the connotative meaning of words, such as "immense," "swarming," "everlasting," "hurled," and so on down to the final "greeting and farewell." These need not all be set off by pauses, of course, or the sentence will be choppy, but you will be aware of a great variety of pace within this single sentence.

Pauses are especially useful for emphasis. Take a simple everyday sentence like "No, I won't do it!" If you really mean what it says, you will certainly put a pause after "No," and probably after "won't" to point up and emphasize the negative quality of your refusal. You would do this if you had never heard of rate or pause or indeed of interpretation or acting. But the temptation in performance is to rush through the sentence, allowing your listeners only time enough to catch the lowest level of logical meaning instead of the full meaning.

There are several kinds of pauses, and we need not be concerned with all their technical names and purposes. There is, for instance, the so-called *terminal pause* which, combined with inflection, signals the end of a sentence or paragraph or stanza of poetry. Listen to everyday speech around you, and train your ear to hear the difference between a terminal pause and one which lets you know the speaker has not finished the thought unit and that more is to come. There is also what we call a *suspension pause* which occurs at the end of a line of poetry and about which we will talk when we look at the structure of poetry. It can also be used as its name indicates—to create suspense.

Whatever type of pause you are using, it is more than just an interruption of the flow of speech. It must act as a link in thought and/or feeling. You need to be thinking, as the material demands, through the second or two of silence or you will lose the thread for yourself and obviously for your audience. Don't be afraid of pauses. For the first few times you use them, they will seem much longer to you than they actually are. Keep the thread of thought tight from what you have just said to what you will say next. You will soon learn to time your pauses for the most effective communication of the total meaning . . . both the *what* and the *how* of your selection.

Inflection and Pitch

Pitch refers to the normal or usual placement of the voice. Inflection is the variation of levels within your pitch range. Our voices have a normal range from low to high pitch which is dictated by several physical factors in the structure of our throats. The width of the throat opening, the thickness and length of the vocal bands, and the structure and capacity of the larynx (voice box) all play a part. We cannot change this basic structure but we can learn to use all the variations of pitch available to us.

The faster the vocal bands are vibrating as we speak and the more tension exists in them, the higher will be the resultant pitch. So nervousness, which produces tension and also tightens the throat, will cause your voice to be higher and more restricted in pitch range. Emotion such as anger can also cause this.

Most of us do not usually use our full pitch range in ordinary conversation. In fact, we tend to settle lazily into a range of only a few notes. In reading literature or interpreting a play script, this can become very monotonous and make your communication dull and colorless. On the other hand, it is not wise to force your voice into a pitch range that is not easy and comfortable for you. That produces the very tension you are trying to avoid.

Place your hand so that the palm rests lightly against your throat. Try a succession of vowels at your normal volume. You will feel a vibration at the base of your throat. The muscles from the base of your throat to the jaw should remain relaxed and flexible. With your hand still in place, try the phrase "Going

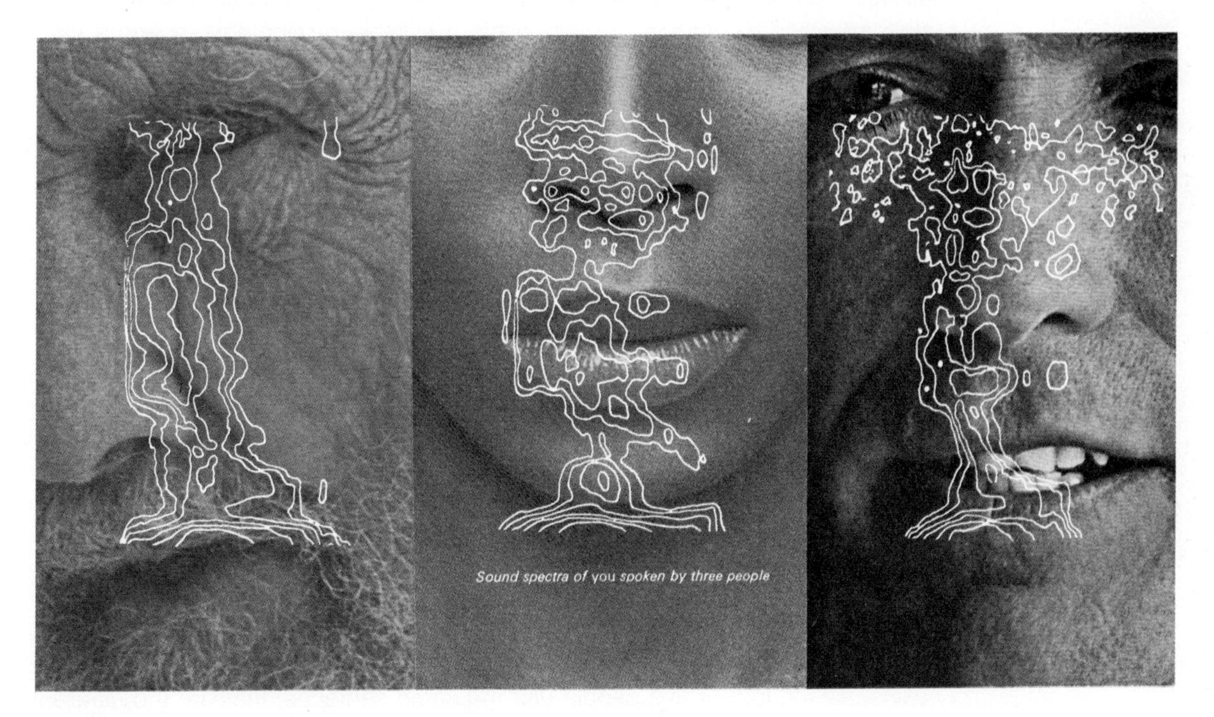

Sound spectra of you spoken by three people

up" saying the first word at your usual pitch but saying "up" on a noticeably high tone. You will be aware that you need a good full breath under the higher tone. Continue to say the phrase, attempting each time to get the last word on a still higher note. As soon as you feel the muscles in the middle and upper throat begin to tighten, stop and relax for a minute. That tightening indicates that you are pushing from your throat and causing some strain. Keep at it until you can take four or five steps above your usual pitch level.

Then try the reverse, using "going down" as your practice phrase. Keep "go-" at your usual level and "fling" the *ing* as high as you can reach without distortion. Take a full breath and consciously place "down" as low as you can manage at the base of the throat. Then try "up" and "down" to get the feel of what is happening in your throat. Be very careful to keep the throat open so that your voice drops comfortably to the lower key.

Of course, you will not stop to do this every time you wish to use a wider pitch range than you do ordinarily. But when you know how it feels when you achieve the highest and lowest range in your voice, you will soon be able to shift subtly and smoothly to accommodate tone color and imagery in your selection as well as to suggest characteristics and attitudes of *personae.*

Inflection, then, is a step or a slide up or down within a group of words. It adds vitality to your performance and is a vital factor in emphasis. It reflects both attitude and emotional response. Try the following sentence as many ways as you can think of and listen to the slight changes suggested by the different inflection patterns: *Oh, so that's it!* Say it following the diagram below using a slide inflection or change of pitch within a syllable or single word and a step inflection to set off "that."

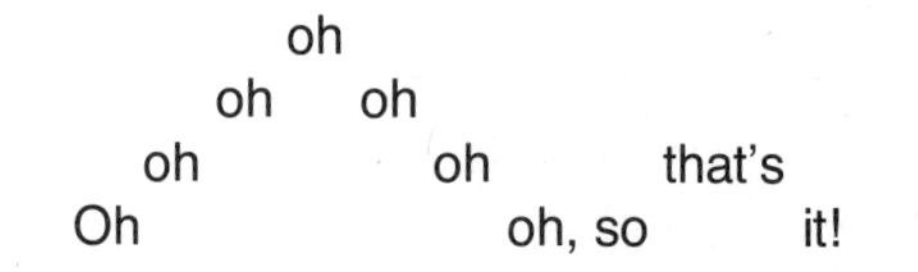

Now try the same sentence with a downward slide on the "Oh" and one step up on each of the other three words. You will be aware of quite a different implication. Here are some more sentences that will be useful for this exercise:

If you are right, then why give in?
I wasn't sure until you told me.
What in the world do you think you're doing?
I wish I could travel around the world for a year.

Activity

Make up some sentences of your own and give them to members of the class, having four or five people use the same sentence. Indicate the different emotion or attitude you want expressed, such as fear, resentment, astonishment, love, and so forth, but do not share these suggestions with any but the reader. Keep the sentences short so that you can catch all of the inflection changes. Then ask the class to interpret the emotion or attitude based on what they have heard.

Volume

All the work you do on improving your voice will be of no use if you can't be heard. Anyone who has been in an audience of any size and found to his or her distress that the speaker's voice dies somewhere in the first few rows knows the importance of volume. Volume is degree of loudness. Projection is focusing the loudness. Your primary purpose as interpreter or actor is to communicate your material, and if you cannot be heard, you cannot communicate.

Volume depends basically on good breath control and proper voice placement. The stream of air which we exhale while speaking is what carries the sounds out to our listeners. When we inhale, our concern is with the amount of air we can comfortably take in. When we exhale for speech, the concern is with control of that amount of air so that it doesn't come out in spurts or all at once like a deflating balloon.

The following exercises will help you learn how it feels to get a good full breath and where the control must come from when you exhale it.

Activities

1. Lie down on the floor on your back and spend a few seconds relaxing. When you feel the muscles of your back and waist let go, breathe normally for a few minutes and then sigh a deep contented sigh. Go back to normal breathing, placing your hands palm down on the lower part of your ribcage. Indulge in another sigh and notice how the ribcage expands as you inhale and gradually relaxes as you exhale. Repeat the process several times. Now, move your hands to rest slightly above your waistline inside the area where your ribcage curves back. As the ribs begin to expand, the area across the front of your body does the same. This is because your diaphragm, the large muscle which goes across your body at the base of your ribcage, is being pushed down as your lungs expand with the air you are inhaling. This large muscle is dome-shaped and as it is depressed it flattens and takes up more room laterally so that the abdomen expands to accommodate it. This is the basis of good breathing.

2. Now try the exercise standing up straight and easy. If your spine is straight, you will be allowing room for a full inhalation. Relax your shoulders but don't let them droop, or you will be crowding the lungs and limiting their capacity for breath. Remember how relaxed your shoulders were when you were lying down? They were even with the rest of your body, neither thrust forward nor held back or hunched up. Your shoulders should balance evenly at the top of

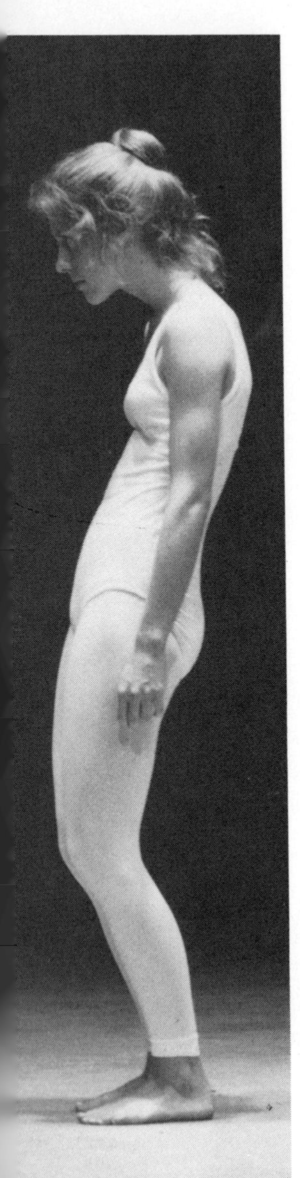

your torso, sitting comfortably on your skeletal frame.

As you sigh and inhale and exhale, put your hands on the base of your ribcage again, this time with the heels of the hands on the lower ribs and finger tips touching across the area between. A good full breath will move your hands apart so that there is space between them. Keep breathing and sighing until you can increase this space a bit.

Next put your hands at the base of your ribs where they connect to your spine. There should be some movement there, too, because your ribcage is flexible although it is attached to your backbone.

Now you know how it feels to have a good, full, easy breath. Practice it a few times every day until you develop the habit of proper breathing. When you start your performance, be sure you have just such a breath. It will relax you and make you feel in control of the situation.

3. Sometimes we take a full breath and forget to control the rate of exhaling it. Sometimes we let out more air than we need on certain sounds or simply let the muscles around the ribcage and the diaphragm go limp all at once. Then we run out of breath before we have finished a thought unit. To check your control of exhalation, hold a lighted match directly in front of your lips, as close as you can, and start to count at a normal rate of speed and with normal volume. Be careful to say each word with proper articulation. You may get no further than a count of two or three or four before you blow out the match by a spurt of air on the "t" and "w" or "th" or the "f" sounds. Light another match and try it again, speaking very softly and concentrating on the control of the muscles which you moved when you inhaled. You will feel as if you may explode but you won't. This will let you feel where the control must come from—the diaphragm and the muscles around the ribcage. Gradually increase your volume and go ahead with your counting as far as you can before you run out of breath. Try to go a little further every day.

Do not do this controlling exercise very long at a time. Stop and rest and then go back to it. You are using muscles you don't usually pay any attention to. Short periods of practice repeated often is the best plan.

Projection

Projection is closely related to volume but the two are not quite the same. Without sufficient volume you would not be able to project, but without projection, your volume may simply be noise.

Projection is part physical and part psychological. There must be enough vocal energy for the volume to be adequate for the size of the room in which you are working. Thus, all the muscles you became aware of in the exercises in breath control and volume must come into play. But projection is also the result of a mental attitude that will allow you to place your voice wherever you want it. It is a matter of focus of communication.

It is helpful in practice to think of your voice as a tangible object such as a ball. Take aim and "throw" it at a target whether it be large or small. Your target may, and probably should at least on one level, include every member of your audience, especially those farthest from you. *Playing to the balcony* is an old stage adage which works equally well for the interpreter—reach out for the farthest spot to which you want to communicate your selection.

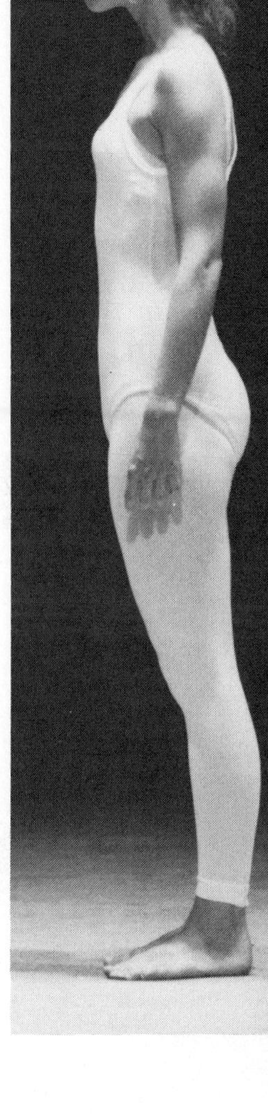

Activities

1. Thinking of your voice as a ball and using the word "no," try dropping the word into your cupped hands. After you're sure you have the feel of aiming and hitting the mark, address the "no" to a kitten or a puppy you are holding in your hands. Let the thought behind your saying the word carry to the same mark. Next move your target a little farther away, say a few feet. Speak to the pet or to someone a few feet away from you, being sure your thought goes with it. Keep moving your target farther back until you have reached the back wall. You will be aware that as you direct your thought, your eyes will probably go with it. Eye contact is an important part of effective projection. Also, of course, your volume and vocal energy increase as the distance increases.

2. Direct your call to someone outside the room. Then, mentally move to the football field, for example. You are in the stands and direct your "no" to someone on the field who, in your opinion, has just made a wrong move. It is not a private groan. It should be a command.

In working on projection you must be constantly aware of a listener or listeners; indeed, you must always be, to really reach an audience. You reach out to those listeners vocally and mentally. Even when the actor or interpreter seems to be speaking directly to someone on stage or, when the interpreter is speaking to a character or characters whom he has placed near the back of the room, you must be aware of the audience of listeners. Thus, projection requires not only vocal directness but mental directness as well. We constantly use projection in everyday situations, but sometimes a beginning performer becomes so involved with his selection or scene and all the things there are to remember about that selection or scene that the circle of concentration on communication narrows until the audience might as well not be there. When the performer allows this to happen, his listeners sense it at once and drift away to their own thoughts, and communication ceases to function.

Perhaps you are thinking that something you have been doing most of your life has suddenly become a very complicated process. Not so. This chapter was intended to call your attention to any bad habits you might have developed and to help you perfect your mastery of the vocal part of your two-fold instrument. When you are performing, your attention must be on the selection or scene you are offering to the audience. If you have been careful in your preparation and have worked to perfect the handling of the twin instruments of voice and body, the habits you will have formed in rehearsal will show themselves without much prompting from you.

Unit II
Interpretation for the Single Performer

Interpretation, like all other forms of speech, is principally concerned with communication. But, unlike the public speaker whose concern is communicating personal ideas and feelings, the interpreter's concern is communicating the ideas and feelings of others. As an interpreter, you are responsible for communicating what *someone else meant and* how *that person meant it. When you are communicating the ideas and feelings of an author, you are interpreting literature.*

The interpretation of literature involves the analysis of the material and the use of voice and body to communicate the results of that analysis. To analyze or to find out everything that is in a selection, you must first read for an overall impression, then study each detail to discover how it works with every other detail. You will, of course, put the material back together so that your audience receives the total experience. The interpreter has the same responsibility to develop an adequate, flexible voice and a flexible responsive body as does the actor. These are the instruments with which you communicate to your audience. You must learn to handle them skillfully. It will take practice and concentration.

Chapter 4
Principles of Interpretation

In the largest sense, literature is defined as all writing. The limits of good literature are not as restricted as you may think. Humorous stories, adventure stories, skillfully written sports stories, ghost stories, character sketches, nonsense verse, poetry, and drama can all be good literature.

You will like some writers very much, and wide reading will help you establish standards by which you can judge any author's success or failure. It is not necessary that you like everything. No one does. But give enough consideration to anything you dislike so you know why you don't like it. You will begin by liking what you know, and from that move to knowing what you like—and why you like it.

One test of good literature is that it deals with universal interests and experiences: things we all think about, such as remembered incidents of childhood, love, death, immortality, faraway places, war, nature, and the problems and pleasures of ordinary living.

There are many ways to write about the same thing, and the best literature is expressed in a fresh and individual way. Think of all the things you have read about a particular subject. The ones that stand out are those that said what they had to say in a way that seemed better to you than any other way you had ever heard. They had individuality.

In addition to its universal appeal and individuality, literature stirs your imagination; it makes you keep on thinking about the subject after you have closed the book. It does not tell you everything but it leads you to associations beyond what is on the printed page.

Literature is not just facts. Encyclopedias or scientific formulas contain facts. Literature goes beyond facts. The author's evaluation and expansion of the facts make the difference. He or she has carefully thought out and organized the material so that it conveys in the best possible way his or her feelings and beliefs. Each word is exactly the right word. And when the author is successful, the words are put together in such a way that each sentence gives the precise meaning the author intended it to convey to the reader. This precise meaning and all its associations may not be completely clear on your first reading. Careful analysis will reveal the clues that will make your selection clearer and richer as you work on it.

In interpretation you do not have to think of something to talk about. You need only find a piece of writing that says something you like in a way you like and

you may choose from among the best ideas of all the writers of all time.

Libraries and your own books are full of good material. But do not expect to open a book and find the perfect selection immediately. You may do a great deal of reading before you find something that you like. Start with the material in this book, or in your literature books, or with something you have previously read and liked. If you cannot find anything, look through the anthologies in your library.

Activity

Start a file of selections and add to it as you read. It could serve you well as source material for future use.

For your first reading choose a selection short enough to fit the time you need to prepare the assignment. Also part of an interpreter's job is to consider the time it takes to perform a selection. If your assignment is for five minutes, be sure your choice can be delivered within that time limit. Poetry is often brief and will fit these time limits easily. If you want to do a story that is much too long to fit your time limit, select only a few paragraphs, or a description of the setting, or a character sketch as your unit for presentation. Be sure it has a beginning, a high point, and an ending to make it satisfactory by itself.

Your first approach to any writing is sure to be subjective. You will like some authors immediately, perhaps for what they say rather than for the way they say it. Your own experience will have much to do with this. You may not know why you like one poem more than another until you have worked on it. For your first assignment it is enough that you are interested in the author's idea. If the literature deals with a universal experience, has individuality, and stirs your imagination even after you have finished reading it, you probably have made a good selection.

Beginning the Analysis

As soon as you have made your selection, you will be aware that, as an interpreter, you are relieved of another decision. You do not have to choose or organize the words for expressing the idea. The author has already done that. Your responsibility is to discover and make use of all the details he or she has given you to work with.

First decide exactly what the selection is about. You may find something you like but do not completely understand. If it appeals to you, it will be rewarding to work on until you understand it.

Read it over many times to get the entire effect. Let the material work on you before you begin to work on it. Be sure to make your selection several days before your performance so you have time to think about it.

Sometimes it helps you to know something about the author. Be careful, however, to keep your concentration on the literature itself. Do not attempt to read the author's entire biography and deathbed message into something he or she wrote at age twenty-five. Details of the author's life, times, and other writings are useful in helping you discover why he or she was interested in the subject, his or her attitude toward it, the mood he or she wanted to set, and the style in which it was expressed. Use whatever you find relevant to the selection you have chosen. But remember that the literature itself is the best place to look for clues about how to read it and what it means.

Activity

You might add to your selection file any author information you find interesting and useful.

One of the best ways to begin analysis is to look for clues to meaning in the title. Most authors spend a great deal of thought on the title in order to make it suggest—but not actually tell—what is in the story. Frequently the title provides a strong indication of both "what" and "how" the story means. "Dateline: Death" (page 42) is an excellent example. It not only tells us where the story is going but it prepares us for the controlled, journalistic style of writing which is so effective in avoiding sentimentality.

Begin at once to read aloud. After each step in analysis, read the entire selection aloud several times until the details begin to fall into place. You will discover more and more of them with each reading.

Word Meanings: Denotation and Connotation

It will be necessary to look up all unfamiliar words in the selection you intend to interpret. Do not be satisfied with an "almost" meaning. The author chose those particular words because they were the exact ones he or she wanted. They were chosen for their *denotation,* which is their exact literal meaning, and for their *connotation,* which is their implied meaning, or their cluster of associations.

Look at the words *forest, woods,* and *orchard* and how three writers have used these words to create different effects. You know what each word means. According to the dictionary, they all mean "a piece of ground covered with trees." But there is a difference in connotation. A forest is bigger than a woods, and an orchard consists of fruit trees.

Henry Wadsworth Longfellow, in *Evangeline,* used *forest* to suggest the huge uncultivated country where his poem was laid.

> This is the forest primeval.
> The murmuring pines and the hemlocks, . . .

Edgar Lee Masters writes in "The Lost Orchard":

> A lost orchard is the memory of a friend
> Wronged by life, to death, who lies
> Lifelike, but with unseeing eyes.

An *orchard* has been planted, and carries the suggestion that there were once people associated with it.

Robert Frost writes, in "Stopping by Woods on a Snowy Evening":

> Whose woods these are I think I know,
> His house is in the village, though;
> He will not see me stopping here
> To watch his woods fill up with snow.

He describes a quiet experience, brief and solitary. *Forest* is too big an area. *Orchard* is too carefully spaced and planted. *Woods* is the right word both by denotation and connotation.

As you look up the meaning of unfamiliar words, check the pronunciation carefully. You must not only understand each word but speak it so that the audience understands it too. If you do not already know them, learn the pronunciation markings in your dictionary.

If there are references in your selection to specific places or people, find out about them. These references, called *allusions,* often provide important clues to meaning and mood.

Examining Author's Method of Organization

After you are certain of the meaning and pronunciation of all the words, read the entire selection again to be sure you understand the relationship between the words and the total effect. Then consider the way the thoughts and ideas are organized. Apply all you have learned in your speech and English classes to your analysis. The author has already organized the material. But you must know how he or she has done it.

Is the organization a sequence of events in chronological order? Or does the author use flashbacks to tell you things you need to know? How does the author move from the introduction to the heart of the matter? Where and how does the author make his or her points? Are statements made and then examples used to prove a point, or have illustrations been used first and then conclusions drawn? Look carefully for connectives like "however" or "in addition." In a story, look for indications of the passage of time or change of place.

All writing will have a climax, a point of culmination of interest or excitement or mood. It is the point to which the writing has been leading. In using a short excerpt from a long selection, be sure there is at least a minor climax so that your cutting reaches a high point for your audience. There are usually numerous minor climaxes which lead finally to the main climax.

How is this climax built? Is it a steady piling up of elements? Is it a surprise? Is it a tense, shocking turn of events? Or is it a sudden release of tension into a mood of relief?

Putting the Selection Back Together

Do not be afraid to take good literature apart. As you continue to analyze it, your respect for the author's skill will grow and you will have more confidence in the material when you present it to your audience. After each step in analysis, put the piece back together, so you can see how everything works toward the overall effect.

After taking a careful look at the connotation of all the words the author uses, go back and reconsider the title to find the relationship between the two elements.

Then examine the organization and reread the entire selection to see how style and organization work together. After each step in analysis, re-read the selection out loud, keeping in mind that the audience does not want a performance of bits and pieces. Your listeners want the whole experience. The whole is more than the sum of its parts. It is the interaction of all the parts working together to create the whole. No detail or aspect should be emphasized for its own sake. Keep your attention on the total effect and use everything you learn in your analysis to achieve it.

Later we will develop more steps of analysis of specific kinds of writing so you may become aware of how to find and use everything your author has given you to work with. For your first assignment, it is probably enough to know what every word means, how the material is organized, the mood to be established, how style can help create this mood, and the overall effect you want your audience to experience.

Activity

Choose a selection from any source available to you. It should be no longer than three minutes when read aloud. It may be as short as one minute. But let it be one you would like to give again at a future time in performance. Begin your analysis by paraphrasing, or restating, (on paper) the thoughts and ideas in your selection. Then develop your analysis as discussed in this chapter.

Do not forget to look for clues to meaning in the title. And you might write down any words you are unfamiliar with, along with their denotative definitions. As you work on your selection, you will want to note the connotations of these words as well.

When you have finished your analysis, read the selection for the class, using what you have discussed in your analysis. Then spend a few minutes getting their answers to such questions as "What was the experience in the selection?" "Who is the speaker?" "Where was the climax?" "What were some of the words or phrases that were strong in connotation?" "Did you get a total impression from the selection?" "What was it?"

Then share your analysis with them to see what they missed and why. Be sure to file your work for use later.

Selections for Interpretation

This gentle poem is full of visual imagery. See the little colt as he comes close and then runs again. Two people at least are watching him. Many of the sentences run past the line-ends, but the lines as units are important. Don't ignore them. Let the five-beat lines sound like poetry. It has an easy, relaxed pulse that is right for the content.

The Runaway
by Robert Frost

Once when the snow of the year was beginning to fall,
We stopped by a mountain pasture to say, 'Whose colt?'
A little Morgan had one forefoot on the wall,
The other curled at his breast. He dipped his head
And snorted at us. And then he had to bolt.
We heard the miniature thunder where he fled,
And we saw him, or thought we saw him, dim and gray,
Like a shadow against the curtain of falling flakes.
'I think the little fellow's afraid of the snow.
He isn't winter-broken. It isn't play
With the little fellow at all. He's running away.
I doubt if even his mother could tell him, "Sakes,
It's only weather." He'd think she didn't know!
Where is his mother? He can't be out alone.'
And now he comes again with clatter of stone,
And mounts the wall again with whited eyes
And all his tail that isn't hair up straight.
He shudders his coat as if to throw off flies.
'Whoever it is that leaves him out so late,
When other creatures have gone to stall and bin,
Ought to be told to come and take him in.'

David Wagoner writes of what at first reading appears to be an exciting and enviable experience, at least from the trapper's point of view. Notice, however, that the trapper is not the persona. There are ironic lines, such as the comparison of the lady who will wear the furs to the animals being caught, and several others such as the description of the trap and the lines before "Now you know." The last part of the poem emphasizes freedom and life which the trapped animals have no chance to enjoy although they were born for it. This is a strong poem in which many elements must be kept in balance.

Trapline

by David Wagoner

Running your trapline through the woods—the miles of sets
By burrows and den-logs, at the lips of streams—
You turn bone-tired,
Sleeping a little better now than when you kept dreaming
Wolves, bears, and all that restless nonsense
You can't help
Troubling yourself about till you're cured of being alone
Like a prime skin. It was hard learning to think
At all like an animal
To outsmart even the most careless marten or gray fox.
Ermine or otter, but harder now to quit,
To act without feeling
Sorry for what you have to go through to deserve their hides:
They won't give in when they're caught, won't make it easy.
They'd rather cripple themselves
By biting away the last shreds of a paw while waiting
For you. But now you're getting used to it,
Approaching the sprung traps
Without exactly shrinking, facing those teeth and those eyes
That almost stop you cold.

Now you know
What you have to do: the handgun-shot, the knife-slash or garrotte
As businesslike as possible, then skinning
(All ways are hard
So never mind), fleshing, and salting, the quick throwaway
Of what was inside the fur, which should look ravishing
Over some lady's shoulder
As she shows all her teeth to the one who catches her.
You wash your red hands then in freezing water,

Watching it run away
Into the clear, as free and pure as it ever was
Before you touched it, while you're rebaiting
(With a ripe offering)
Your steel-spring swivel-chained offset leg-hold moneymaker
For the next go-round. This is a good life,
Isn't it?—all this
Fresh air and breathing easy, breathing over and over
As much as you like, catching your breath
As many times as you want to.

This brief poem reflects the Native Americans' close relationship to nature. The poet who is the persona has learned the wisdom of change in harmony with nature. But winter is a time when the earth sleeps and does not give us her bounty. It is a long, cold season. It is a dark time.

One Winter Thought
by Ray Young Bear

everything i have ever counted
upon
as being something
more than close,
now seems farther and it passes
me,
disregarding the value
of my feelings.
so i change like seasons—
except
my winters. they tie themselves
to me.
never the spring, summer, or fall.

The short lines help give this poem a quality of starkness. Use them carefully. Remember, also, to look for elements of rhythm and tone color.

Dateline: Death

by Suzanne Gross

The paper told where
it happened of course.
I have forgotten
the place now. It could
have been the corn-green
town where I was born
and the trestle curves
a little west to
cross the power dam:
there where I stood once,
stricken on the bank
above the rainbow,
and let explosions
in the water spin
me down and drown me.

The paper said three
children walked across
a trestle tall as
mine was. They were one
boy nine years old, one
girl of six, and one
thirteen, who was her
sister. When they had
come halfway across,
the water running
louder under them,
glittering more now
into their squinting,
they heard the diesel
horn behind them blow.

Silently all three
began to run. Then
the youngest fell, caught
her ankle hard, down
between the shaking
ties. The others leaped,
before they missed her,
safe from the roadbed.
Then, only then, one
saw her sister held
before the train, who
turned again, ran back
again, and tore at
the shackled foot. Then
she knelt on the ties
and took her sister
in her arms, blinding
her against her breast,
and said to her see,
I am here with you,
there is nothing to
be frightened of.
And the train struck them.

It may have taken
five minutes at the
most, the newspaper
said. She could not have
known the thing she chose.
She could not have known.

Remember when you learned to skate? In this breezy little poem the persona speaks to us directly with the excitement she feels as she watches the little girl's struggle. It moves rapidly through the short lines. See the child and watch her every move. You can not help an empathic response—you will find yourself responding both emotionally and physically—share it with us. The last word carries admiration with it. It will need special emphasis to bring the poem to its satisfying close.

74th Street
by Myra Cohn Livingston

Hey, this little kid gets roller skates.
She puts them on.
She stands up and almost
flops over backwards.
She sticks out a foot like
she's going somewhere and
falls down and
smacks her hand. She
grabs hold of a step to get up and
sticks out the other foot and
slides about six inches and
falls and
skins her knee.

And then, you know what?

She brushes off the dirt and the
blood and puts some
spit on it and then
sticks out the other foot

again.

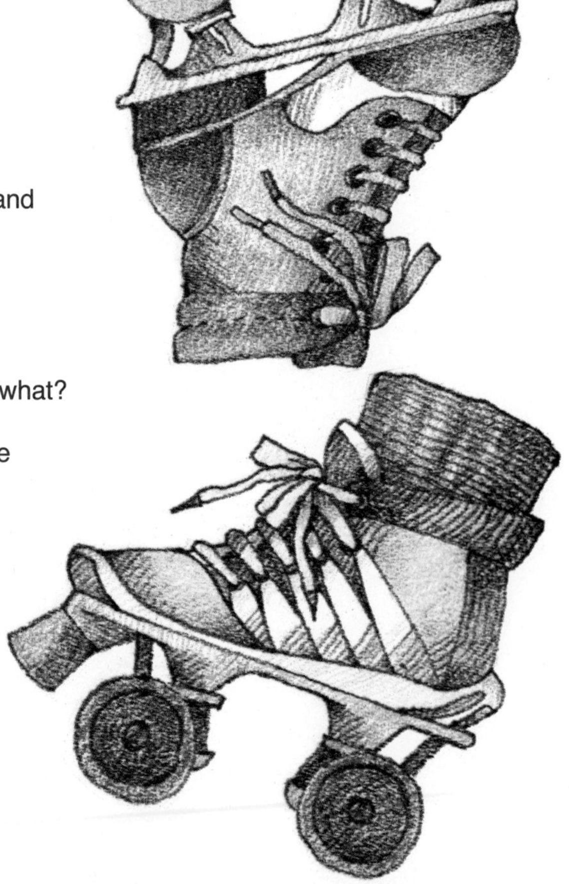

The following selection is taken from Lincoln Steffen's *Autobiography* and so, of course, the narrator is the author recalling an experience of the past. The style of writing, with its simple vocabulary and numerous short sentences, reflects a child's way of thinking. The story has several emotional climaxes. One that takes careful handling is when the man and the pony come down the street. Your audience will suspect and hope that the pony is meant for the boy but the author holds us a little longer in suspense. The real climax comes when he—and we—are sure the horse is his. As the author himself says in the last paragraph, the climaxes go from "broken-hearted misery to bursting happiness—" The dialogue must reflect real people who love each other.

A Miserable, Merry Christmas

by Lincoln Steffens

What interested me in our new neighborhood was not the school, nor the room I was to have in the house all to myself, but the stable which was built back of the house. My father let me direct the making of a stall, a little smaller than the other stalls, for my pony, and I prayed and hoped and my sister Lou believed that that meant that I would get the pony, perhaps for Christmas. I pointed out to her that there were three other stalls and no horses at all. This I said in order that she should answer it. She could not. My father, sounded, said that some day we might have horses and a cow; meanwhile a stable added to the value of a house. "Some day" is a pain to a boy who lives in and knows only "now." My good littler sisters, to comfort me, remarked that Christmas was coming, but Christmas was always coming and grown-ups were always talking about it, asking you what you wanted and then giving you what they wanted you to have. Though everybody knew what I wanted, I told them all again. My mother knew that I told God, too, every night. I wanted a pony, and to make sure that they understood, I declared that I wanted nothing else.

"Nothing but a pony?" my father asked.

"Nothing," I said.

"Not even a pair of high boots?"

That was hard. I did want boots, but I stuck to the pony. "No, not even boots."

"Nor candy? There ought to be something to fill your stocking with, and Santa Claus can't put a pony into a stocking."

That was true, and he couldn't lead a pony down the chimney either. But no. "All I want is a pony," I said. "If I can't have a pony, give me nothing, nothing."

Now I had been looking myself for the pony I wanted, going to sales stables, inquiring of horsemen, and I had seen several that would do. My father let me

---

"try" them. I tried so many ponies that I was learning fast to sit a horse. I chose several, but my father always found some fault with them. I was in despair. When Christmas was at hand I had given up all hope of a pony, and on Christmas Eve I hung up my stocking along with my sisters', of whom, by the way, I now had three. I haven't mentioned them or their coming because, you understand, they were girls, and girls, young girls, counted for nothing in my manly life. They did not mind me either; they were so happy that Christmas Eve that I caught some of their merriment. I speculated on what I'd get; I hung up the biggest stocking I had, and we all went reluctantly to bed to wait till morning. Not to sleep; not right away. We were told that we must not only sleep promptly, we must not wake up till seven-thirty the next morning—or if we did, we must not go to the fireplace for our Christmas. Impossible.

We did sleep that night, but we woke up at six A.M. We lay in our beds and debated through the open doors whether to obey till, say, half-past six. Then we bolted. I don't know who started it, but there was a rush. We all disobeyed; we raced to disobey and get first to the fireplace in the front room downstairs. And there they were, the gifts, all sorts of wonderful things, mixed-up piles of presents; only, as I disentangled the mess, I saw that my stocking was empty; it hung limp; not a thing in it; and under and around it—nothing. My sisters had knelt down, each by her pile of gifts; they were squealing with delight, till they looked up and saw me standing there in my nightgown with nothing. They left their piles to come to me and look with me at my empty place. Nothing. They felt my stocking: nothing.

I don't remember whether I cried at that moment, but my sisters did. They ran with me back to my bed, and there we all cried till I became indignant. That helped some. I got up, dressed, and driving my sisters away, I went alone out into the yard, down to the stable, and there, all by myself, I wept. My mother came out to me by and by; she found me in my pony stall, sobbing on the floor, and she tried to comfort me. But I heard my father outside; he had come part way with her, and she was having some sort of angry quarrel with him. She tried to comfort me; besought me to come to breakfast. I could not; I wanted no comfort and no breakfast. She left me and went on into the house with sharp words for my father.

I don't know what kind of a breakfast the family had. My sisters said it was "awful." They were ashamed to enjoy their own toys. They came to me, and I was rude. I ran away from them. I went around to the front of the house, sat down on the steps, and, the crying over, I ached. I was wronged, I was hurt—I can feel now what I felt then, and I am sure that if one could see the wounds upon our hearts, there would be found still upon mine a scar from that terrible Christmas morning. And my father, the practical joker, he must have been hurt, too, a little. I saw him looking out of the window. He was watching me or something for an hour or two, drawing back the curtain never so little lest I catch him, but I saw his face, and I think I can see now the anxiety upon it, the worried impatience.

After—I don't know how long—surely an hour or two—I was brought to the climax of my agony by the sight of a man riding a pony down the street, a pony and a brand-new saddle; the most beautiful saddle I ever saw, and it was a boy's saddle; the man's feet were not in the stirrups; his legs were too long. The outfit was perfect; it was the realization of all my dreams, the answer to all my prayers. A fine new bridle, with a light curb bit. And the pony! As he drew near, I saw that the pony was really a small horse, what we called an Indian pony, a bay, with black mane and tail, and one white foot and a white star on his forehead. For such a horse as that I would have given, I could have forgiven, anything.

But the man, a disheveled fellow, with a blackened eye and a fresh-cut face, came along, reading the numbers on the houses, and, as my hopes—my impossible hopes—rose, he looked at our door and passed by, he and the pony, and the saddle and the bridle. Too much. I fell upon the steps, and having wept before, I broke now into such a flood of tears that I was a floating wreck when I heard a voice.

"Say, kid," it said, "do you know a boy named Lennie Steffens?"

I looked up. It was the man on the pony, back again, at our horse block.

"Yes," I spluttered through my tears. "That's me."

"Well," he said, "then this is your horse. I've been looking all over for you and your house. Why don't you put your number where it can be seen?"

"Get down," I said, running out to him.

He went on saying something about "ought to have got here at seven o'clock; told me to bring the nag here and tie him to your post and leave him for you. But, hell, I got into a drunk—and a fight—and a hospital, and—"

"Get down," I said.

He got down, and he boosted me up to the saddle. He offered to fit the stirrups to me, but I didn't want him to. I wanted to ride.

"What's the matter with you?" he said, angrily. "What you crying for? Don't you like the horse? He's a dandy, this horse. I know him of old. He's fine at cattle; he'll drive 'em alone."

I hardly heard, I could scarcely wait, but he persisted. He adjusted the stirrups, and then, finally, off I rode, slowly, at a walk, so happy, so thrilled, that I did not know what I was doing. I did not look back at the house or the man, I rode off up the street, taking note of everything—of the reins, of the pony's long mane, of the carved leather saddle. I had never seen anything so beautiful. And mine! I was going to ride up past Miss Kay's house. But I noticed on the horn of the saddle some stains like rain-drops, so I turned and trotted home, not to the house but to the stable. There was the family, father, mother, sisters, all working for me, all happy. They had been putting in place the tools of my new business: blankets, currycomb, brush, pitchfork—everything, and there was hay in the loft.

"What did you come back so soon for?" somebody asked. "Why didn't you go on riding?"

continued

I pointed to the stains. "I wasn't going to get my new saddle rained on," I said. And my father laughed. "It isn't raining," he said. "Those are not rain-drops."

"They are tears," my mother gasped, and she gave my father a look which sent him off to the house. Worse still, my mother offered to wipe away the tears still running out of my eyes. I gave her such a look as she had given him, and she went off after my father, drying her own tears. My sisters remained and we all unsaddled the pony, put on his halter, led him to his stall, tied and fed him. It began really to rain; so all the rest of that memorable day we curried and combed that pony. The girls plaited his mane, forelock, and tail, while I pitch-forked hay to him and curried and brushed, curried and brushed. For a change we brought him out to drink; we led him up and down, blanketed like a race-horse; we took turns at that. But the best, the most inexhaustible fun, was to clean him. When we went reluctantly to our midday Christmas dinner, we all smelt of horse, and my sisters had to wash their faces and hands. I was asked to, but I wouldn't, till my mother bade me look in the mirror. Then I washed up—quick. My face was caked with the muddy lines of tears that had coursed over my cheeks to my mouth. Having washed away that shame, I ate my dinner, and as I ate I grew hungrier and hungrier. It was my first meal that day, and as I filled up on the turkey and the stuffing, the cranberries and the pies, the fruit and the nuts—as I swelled, I could laugh. My mother said I still choked and sobbed now and then, but I laughed, too; I saw and enjoyed my sisters' presents till—I had to go out and attend to my pony, who was there, really and truly there, the promise, the beginning, of a happy double life. And—I went and looked to make sure—there was the saddle, too, and the bridle.

But that Christmas, which my father had planned so carefully, was it the best or the worst I ever knew? He often asked me that; I never could answer as a boy. I think now that it was both. It covered the whole distance from broken-hearted misery to bursting happiness—too fast. A grown-up could hardly have stood it.

Chapter 5
Interpreting Narrative Literature

Plot and Action

All the things we have been talking about apply to all kinds of writing. But let us now turn our attention specifically to narration. A narrative is a story. It tells what happens to whom, and how, why, when, and where. A narrative may be either prose or poetry.

The literary term *plot,* in the simplest sense, is a series of happenings in a play, novel, short story, poem, etc. The term is also used to refer to the action as it is organized around a conflict and builds through complication to a climax followed by conclusion. Sometimes these happenings come about primarily because of outside forces. Sometimes they are the result of the kinds of persons involved. Usually these two elements are closely related since different people react differently to events and pressures.

You begin to work on a story by reading it through and asking "What happened to whom?" Next ask "How did it happen in this particular way?" As you read the selections at the end of this chapter, you will find that the answers involve you in consideration of the setting and the characters. But first study the method of organization the author has used to introduce the story, achieve a climax, and conclude.

There are many ways to organize the progress of a story. A writer may make clocks and calendars go backward or forward at any speed that suits his or her purpose. Look for the elements that help unify the progression of thought. It may be simple chronological progression using such connectives as "then," "later," and so forth. It may be a continued focus on one character or on a group such as a family. Unity may also be achieved by keeping the setting in one place or having the events happen within a brief span of time: one day, a single evening, or a weekend.

Whatever organization and unifying principle the author uses, there will be events or details as the story moves along that become important to the outcome. These are called *key situations* or *key speeches.* They are signposts that keep the story moving along the road it takes. They give us the *how* of the action and the *so what* of the plot.

Key situations, speeches, and sentences are more numerous and more important in long narratives. But even in short selections, they keep the story moving, and help build to the main climax.

Climax

A climax is the culmination of a series of events, or changes in human relationships. It may be a point of emotional pitch, the outcome of character development. It may come as a surprise with a sudden turn of events or as the inevitable outcome of whatever has gone before. In any case, it will carry with it an increase in intensity and will need to be carefully prepared for so that your voice and body will reflect and communicate that increase in intensity to the audience.

After the climax is reached, how does the author handle the ending? What kind of conclusion is used? Does it sum up all the facts, or is it a surprise conclusion?

Now go back and look at details which will help you keep the selection unified and moving toward its goal. In "One Winter Thought" (page 41) the single long sentence which comprises the first eight lines of the poem provides a nice contrast for the shorter sentences which follow and the climax in the last three lines. There are numerous other subtle unifying devices in all the selections at the end of the chapter and you will find them useful in your preparation.

Point of View

In a narrative there is a narrator who tells the story. The physical and psychical position the narrator takes in revealing plot and character is called *point of view.* Sometimes the narrator seems to be right beside the characters and sometimes he or she is viewing the scene and the actions from a distance. This may be a distance in time or place or both. Sometimes he or she enters the very mind of one or more characters or sometimes relies on their actions to indicate what they are thinking and feeling. And there are all degrees of closeness and distancing. A consideration of point of view can help you decide on your relationship to your audience as you narrate the story too.

The point of view may be objective with the narrator merely reporting events. This is rarely the case, but the narrator in "Dateline: Death" (page 42) manages this effect very well while still involving us in the characters and the things that happen.

Or the narrator may be subjective and reveal things that are going on in the minds of the characters. This is certainly the technique in *A Death in the Family* (page 72). This type of point of view allows the reader and thus the interpreter's audience to react quite fully to the character or characters whose thoughts we can share.

Or perhaps the narrator tells things that happen that the characters themselves could not possibly know, such as an event happening in a distant place or the thoughts of a character which are not shared with the other characters.

Or again, the narrator may be one of the characters involved in the plot, as in the excerpt from ". . . And Now Miguel" (page 67). In this case, you need to suggest age, sex, and mental state as the character/narrator tells the story.

When the narrator is outside the story, you handle the narration in your own person speaking directly to the audience. Do not neglect emotional tension and empathy however. When the narrator is revealing emotions and reactions of the characters, your delivery must suggest those reactions.

Point of view directly affects an author's method of organization and style of writing, and is a strong factor in unity.

Style

In addition to *what* a piece of writing means, you must also become aware of *how* it means. The "how" of the meaning is often revealed by a close study of literary style. *Style,* an important aspect of individuality, includes the choice of words an author uses, the way they are put together, and the syntax, which is the length and grammatical complexity of sentences and paragraphs. Style is an important aspect of all writing whether it is drama, prose, or poetry. We have touched on word choice briefly in our discussion of connotation. And we will talk more about syntax as we examine the various types of writing.

Style can indicate the education, background, degree of emotional tension, and general attitude of characters as well as that of the author. It helps produce a rhythm in the stress and flow of thought. Style is important in giving clues to many details in a story, play, or poem.

Setting and Description

Usually a narrative includes where and when the action takes place. The *where* and *when* together provide the *setting.* The specific place and time are sometimes relatively unimportant. But the period of history often makes the plot possible. And the *where* may also be important. Setting is revealed through description. Some immature readers feel description can be skipped because they think it doesn't have much to do with what happens. Description is important. Do not underestimate the author. If description is there, it is there for a reason.

Descriptions should be presented to your audience with the same care that you use in other parts of the story. The audience must know where and when the events take place. Moreover, a description helps you set the mood. Look at all descriptions to see what purpose they serve within the particular narrative you are working on. Then use them as important parts of the whole.

You may wish to cut some descriptions to stay within your time limit, but you must know what each contributes to the story before you do so. You may be able to condense somewhat and perhaps include important information in your introduction. If the time or place, or any detail of either, is significant in the selection you have made, and you decide to cut the description, you must tell your audience enough about it so they will find the plot believable.

Descriptions appeal to our senses and our muscles. They tell us how a person or place or thing looks, sounds, moves, and so forth. As an interpreter, you must respond fully to these sense images so that your audience will see and hear them too. If an involved narrator or a character is giving the description, your response must be keyed to his or hers.

Activities

1. Read the selection "The Day We Flew the Kites" (page 69). Then (on paper) answer the following:

a. What are the key situations and/or key speeches that reveal the *how* of the action and the *what* of the plot? What are the events that lead to the climax?

b. From what point of view is the story told? In interpreting the selection, how would you handle the narration?

2. Read Belloc's poem on page 64. Then (on paper) answer the following:

a. Is the narrator's point of view objective or subjective? What is the setting? What is the progression of events?

3. Exchange your analyses with other class members. Were most of you in agreement?

Characters

Whatever happens in a story must happen to someone or something, so there are characters around which much of the interest centers. The interpreter must know everything there is to know about the people in the story in order to present them clearly to his or her audience.

There are two sides to every character, the outside and the inside, and each affects and influences the other. The outside is the physical aspect of the person which includes age, sex, and any physical characteristics that may affect attitudes and behavior.

The inside of a character is more complex. It includes attitudes and values, emotional responses, psychological factors, and the state of tension or relaxation.

Characterization

Character may be revealed in many ways and often we have to add all the clues in description, dialogue, and style to discover the complete character. The manner in which characters speak and think indicates a great deal about them. The choice of words indicates attitudes and background. The sentence length and continuity of thought reveal the emotional state. Think back to your own speech when you are excited, and contrast it with the meandering manner of a daydream.

The title of a selection sometimes helps with character clues. Another important element is what the character says about himself or herself, others, and the setting, and we learn a great deal from what other characters say about him or her. If you need to cut some of the character description or stage directions in order to stay within time limits, you must remember everything the author has told you in the portion you cut out so you can properly suggest the character to your listeners.

Discourse: Direct

The exact quotation of a character's words is called direct discourse and the words are enclosed in quotation marks. Direct discourse demands sharp physical and mental focus. A speech is being said directly to someone. When a character speaks directly to someone else, his or her mind and eyes usually go directly to that person.

The French have a way of indicating directness that is useful for an interpreter to remember. When they mean, "think of someone," they use the phrase *penser à,* meaning "think to" or "think at." When they use *penser de,* "think of," they mean they have an opinion about something.

If you remember to "think to" your listeners, you will have no trouble with directness. When you are speaking to someone, the focus of your mind and eyes increases with the force of your thought.

To illustrate this, let's try an exercise in degrees of directness. Your small brother has something that belongs to you that you value highly. He is not handling it carefully, and you are concerned about getting it back in good condition. You watch him for a moment and then think: "I wish he would give it back to me."

Then—"In a minute I'm going to ask him to give it back to me."

Soon you speak directly to him. "May I have it back now?"

He pays no attention to you, so you speak more firmly: "Please, give it to me."

If it is quite clear that he is in no hurry, you may lose patience and say, "Give it to me."

Notice how your mind and eyes focus more sharply on the person to whom you are speaking as you become more direct.

When characters in a story are having a conversation, the interpreter suggests this directness. First, you assume the degree of mental directness appropriate for the speech. Then, you indicate by direct eye focus that someone else is present. You visualize the one being addressed, at a convenient spot on the back wall very slightly above the heads of your audience. This enables you to give the character physical and mental directness.

The insertion of direct discourse in a story requires you to be able instantly to adjust your mental and emotional state, your vocal characteristics, and your bodily tension to whichever character is speaking.

Direct discourse is a speech said directly to someone. The audience must know without question who is speaking. They must be able to identify the character at once so they don't misunderstand what is said. They must know what the character is thinking and feeling about what is said, and they must have the feeling that someone is actually being addressed.

Activity

Find a narrative in which there is direct discourse. Then select a short conversation from it and practice speaking the lines giving the character(s) physical and mental directness.

Facial expression will reflect what the character is thinking and feeling as you speak the lines. Gestures are appropriate and helpful in direct discourse. But the gesture must suit the character and the situation. All these physical aspects are the result of what is going on inside the character. They must never be put on from the outside. They must always grow out of the demands of the selection and reflect what is going on in the mind and body of the character speaking. It is the inside of the character that motivates the outside. You take your clue from this fact and respond inside yourself before you try to assume any exterior manifestations of emotion. During performance you concentrate on sharing the experience of the characters with your audience.

Complete response to the character in the situation will also be reflected in vocal quality and pace. Point of view and the style in which the character speaks will help you.

The exterior characteristics of age, sex, and physical condition will be given more specific attention in the next chapter. Now it is enough to concentrate on interior characteristics. Remember you are only *suggesting* the exterior characteristics. The individual differences within the broad classifications of age, sex, and condition are much more important.

If you have your characters identified in the minds of your audience, you can sometimes cut the "he saids" and "she saids." If the author has given stage directions, such as "he said gently" or "she shouted," you may cut them and simply follow them in your manner of delivery.

Discourse: Indirect

Indirect discourse is reported conversation, and is not enclosed in quotation marks. It includes thoughts not spoken aloud by the characters. Such phrases as "she hoped that," "I was afraid that," "we wanted to say that," and "you prayed that it would not happen" are indirect discourse. The interpreter needs to pay close attention to indirect discourse, because it reveals the characters' mental and emotional states.

In indirect discourse you use whatever emotional and mental states are indicated, as you do in subjective description. Your audience must know who the character is, what kind of person he or she is, and what his or her attitude and degree of tension are at the moment.

Activity

Find several pieces of indirect discourse, each with a different emotional tone. Or make up some of your own. See how well you can project them.

All of these matters are closely related to the why of the action and plot. Why the events take place as they do is called motivation. Usually the motivation is clear as soon as we understand the characters involved. Often motivation is subtly revealed as the characters develop. You must discover the *why* of the character's responses and actions if you are to make the plot believable. What is perfectly acceptable for one character may not be acceptable in another.

Cutting Your Selection

In cutting a story, look first for the major climax. You may wish to use only the major climax for your reading, with enough build-up to make it understandable. Or you may choose a unit with a minor climax. In either case, find the key situations that build to the climax and make it believable. Then evaluate the descriptions to see which you can eliminate or condense without destroying the effect. You may need to tell the audience some of the key situations that lead up to your selection in your introduction. You may find that a few characters can sometimes be eliminated if they are not directly involved in the action of the section you are using.

When you have decided what to cut in your story, if the book is yours, mark the omissions clearly so you can easily follow them. Mark in pencil—never in ink—because you may later change your mind. Never put marks in a book that doesn't belong to you. If it is a library book, put small pieces of blank paper fastened with paper clips over the places you want to cut.

If you skip several pages, fasten them together with a paper clip so they all turn at once. Transitions may be typed on pieces of paper and clipped to the pages where you need them. No one can tell you what to cut and what to leave in. Every story is different. You will find more satisfaction in making your own cutting and using everything you feel must be included to preserve the author's intention.

Preparation for Performance

In the final phases of preparation you will begin to work on technique in order to communicate effectively all the things you have discovered in your analysis. Only after you are sure you know what effect the selection is to create do you begin to work *consciously* to perfect your vocal and physical techniques. *These techniques must always serve the material, not vice versa.*

As an interpreter, you communicate with your voice and body, just as any speaker does. Your responsibility to be heard and understood is the same as an actor's, a public speaker's, or a discussion leader's. But you will often need greater vocal control and flexibility than does the public speaker, because you are dealing with a wide variety of styles and subject matter. You need more breath control to make the most of some authors' styles.

For instance, the following line from Walt Whitman's poem "A Noiseless Patient Spider" does not allow for a full breath within it, and the connotation and close relationship of the words indicate that the pace must be slower than that of ordinary conversation. Try it as a problem in breath control.

Ceaselessly musing, venturing, throwing,
seeking the spheres to connect them.

Activities

1. Take a full breath. Avoiding any tension, count from one to twenty. Keep your rate constant, about two counts per second. Use a normal conversational tone and be especially careful in forming the sounds as you say the numbers.

2. Repeat the above exercise, but extend your count as far as your air supply will allow. Do not strain, and stop before you have used all your breath. What was the highest count you reached?

3. Now try the same exercise, using the letters of the alphabet. When you reach **z,** start over with **a** without a break. How many times did you go through the alphabet without stopping or straining? Practice these exercises daily to lengthen your breath span and control.

The particular requirements of different types of writing will be dealt with separately in their appropriate chapters. Now it is important to remember that your voice must be capable of doing everything that needs to be done to convey the full purpose of the author. But the voice, like other techniques, must never call attention to itself. You train your voice to serve the varied demands of the literature you read. Review Chapter 3 and practice the activities and exercises there, as well as those within this chapter.

Inflection is really a part of pitch. It is the variation of levels within the pitch range. It is a step or slide up or down within a sentence or group of words. It is closely related to emphasis. Try the sentence "I don't know who you are" as many ways as you can think to say it. Put a lift on a different word each time and you will hear a wide variation in meaning and in implied attitude. Learn to listen to yourself in practice to see if you have what is called an inflection pattern. Do you tend to go up at the end of every thought unit, or to drop so low that the last word or syllable loses force? If you do, force yourself to change the inflection in practice until your voice reflects exactly what you are thinking. Your own pattern can get in the way of sharing what the literature really means. Also it can become so obvious that your listeners can't hear anything except what your voice is doing.

Rate is, of course, the pace at which you speak. Most literature must be read more slowly than the rate at which we talk informally. This is because it is complex and the audience must have time to hear it and respond to it as you go along. They can't go back and reread a line that went so fast they couldn't understand it. The chances are that any problem you will have with rate will be that of too much speed. Choose material whose mood is quiet and whose words must be said slowly in order to be formed properly. Be sure your mind is fully concentrating on all the levels of meaning and mood that you have discovered in your analysis. If your problem is speed, you will feel as if you are never going to get through, but you will. Ask someone to listen to you and keep reminding you to slow down and "taste" the words and sounds.

Activities

1. Write a short sports- or newscast of a thrilling incident or select an exciting description in a story. Read your selection aloud, using a wide variety of pitch. Now record your reading, play it back, and note your range in pitch and its relationship to meaning.

2. Repeat the above activity, making appropriate changes in pitch and rate. Compare the two recordings.

Articulation is the process of forming the separate sounds that make up words. It is very easy to get careless and slur over consonants, for instance. Try any of the familiar tongue twisters such as "She sells seashells by the seashore" and you will be aware of the nimbleness needed in your tongue and lips and jaw. All of these parts of the mouth are involved in articulation. If the sounds of the words do not come out clearly to your listeners, they must stop and translate "bean" into "being," "course" into "chorus," and "wreckers" into "records." Be sure you are forming all the sounds in every word. This will help too in slowing down your pace.

Activities

1. Practice saying the following, first, slowly, then rapidly.

a. Rubber baby buggy bumpers.
b. Peter Piper picked a peck of pickled peppers.
c. Good blood, bad blood; good blood, bad blood.
d. Five wives wearily weave bright red rugs.
e. He who laughs last, laughs best.

2. Write similar phrases and sentences of your own. Learn to say them correctly and rapidly. Share them with your class.

Volume is degree of loudness. Your voice must reach the back row of your listeners or you aren't communicating to them. But loudness is not enough. You must learn to *project* or send your voice where you want it to go. This is something we do all the time without thinking about it. When you want to speak to someone across a room, you raise your volume and send your voice to where that person is. When you want to speak privately, you drop your volume and "give" your voice to the person you are confiding in. Sometimes in a speaking situation we get so involved with ourselves and the literature, we forget this simple everyday process.

Activity

Select a prose passage, about a page in length. Read it aloud to a person seated about fifteen feet away and with his or her back to you. Have that person note any sounds not easily heard. Repeat your reading until the entire passage is clearly intelligible to your listener.

Emotional and Physical Response

As you understand your selection more fully, you will find yourself responding not just to the ideas but to the emotions they call up as well. This is an important part of your understanding. As you allow the selection to play on your emotions, you will be aware that there are accompanying muscle responses: a tightening or relaxing of the muscles of the neck, back, hands, and arms, and certainly of the facial muscles. Emotional response and physical response are interrelated.

You as an interpreter must respond as fully to all the emotions of the narrator and characters as does the actor to the characters in a play. We will talk more about this in Unit III but this is a good place to start paying attention to how the *characters* feel about what they are saying in a particular situation.

Don't be afraid of this emotional response. Without it, you cannot do full justice to the writing. If it is an honest response to the literature and a sincere desire to share with your audience, it will never become arty or theatrical. But do not try to assume an emotion you do not feel. Strive always for a genuine emotional response. A frown does not mean you are angry but rather, when you are really angry, the frown is the result of what you feel inside. The inside must always dictate what the body is doing and how it is doing it. Don't count on mere exterior manifestations. That's faking and your audience will know it!

The interplay of emotions and muscles begins with the interpreter's response to the selection. From the first time you read it, through every step in preparation and performance, let yourself get excited about it. If it is worth working on and sharing with an audience, it should move you. This does not mean you indulge in an emotional display. It means you let the author lead the way! One of the steps literature takes beyond facts is its appeal to the emotions. Emotional response of whatever degree is reflected in muscle response and bodily action. Members of the audience respond by unconscious imitation of the interpreter's muscle tone, so they are physically ready for whatever emotions or changes the piece requires. This interaction of emotional and physical response is called *empathy*.

Have you ever watched the facial expression and bodily tension of the spectators at a movie or a play? If you want your audience to be relaxed, you must pratice controlled relaxation. If you want them to be tense for a climax, you must give them the clue.

Activity

Watch family members responding to a TV program. Report to your class your family's empathic responses to the program.

The Introduction

Use a brief introduction to your reading. It helps you and the audience. Do not tell them what the selection will say. The author will do that. If you present the selection properly, you will not need to explain it. Be as direct as in public speaking. Keep the introduction short and well organized. Introductions often serve as transition from one selection to another, and the tone should always be consistent with the reading that will follow.

If your passage does not come at the beginning of a longer story or a play, you may need to sketch in what action has gone before. An introduction should accomplish three things for you and your audience. First, it gives you a chance to size up your audience. It allows you to test your voice so you are sure you are reaching the back row. It permits you to control and relax your body.

At the same time, it allows the audience to look at you. They will spend the first few seconds looking at you anyway. Don't risk wasting the opening while they are satisfying their curiosity. The introduction gives them a focus of attention while they adjust so that they can see you easily.

Second, an introduction helps you organize your thoughts so you are thinking along the lines your selection demands. It does the same thing for your audience. In a room full of people there are as many trains of thought as there are people. Your introduction will channel their attention so they are ready to start with you on the literature.

Third, the introduction helps you arrive at the mood you need for what you are going to do. You may follow a reader whose selection was extremely funny, and you may be reading something that deals with death. Your introduction should lead you and your audience from laughter into the more serious mood necessary for your selection.

In order to accomplish these three aims in your introduction, you must consider your audience. How much do they know about your author or the selection? How much do they need to know to be prepared for it? What will appeal to them and help them into the proper mood? What experiences have they had that will help them identify with the experience the author has recorded? Many suggestions for effective interpersonal relations can be used to make your introduction fit the material *and* the audience.

Finally, give careful thought to the overall impression you wish your audience to receive. It is a good idea to try to put this desired reaction into a single sentence, such as "I want my audience to be amused" or "I want my audience to understand the conflict within the character." This will help focus your attention on how the parts are related, and guide you when you prepare your introduction.

Activity

Prepare an introduction for the selection you chose for analysis in Chapter 4. Compare with those of the rest of the class.

Performance

When you perform, remember you have done all the preparation you can. Performance is not preparation. If you have prepared carefully, you know exactly what you want to achieve with your reading. Keep your mind on sharing this experience with your audience and getting the response you know the author wanted. Forget about yourself, except as the communicator between the author and the audience. This is not so easy as it sounds, but it is important. You have worked on your preparation. Now you must trust the author to hold the audience's interest, trust yourself to do justice to his or her work, and trust the audience to give their attention and interest. The audience wants to enjoy a reading. They will follow you if you give them the chance.

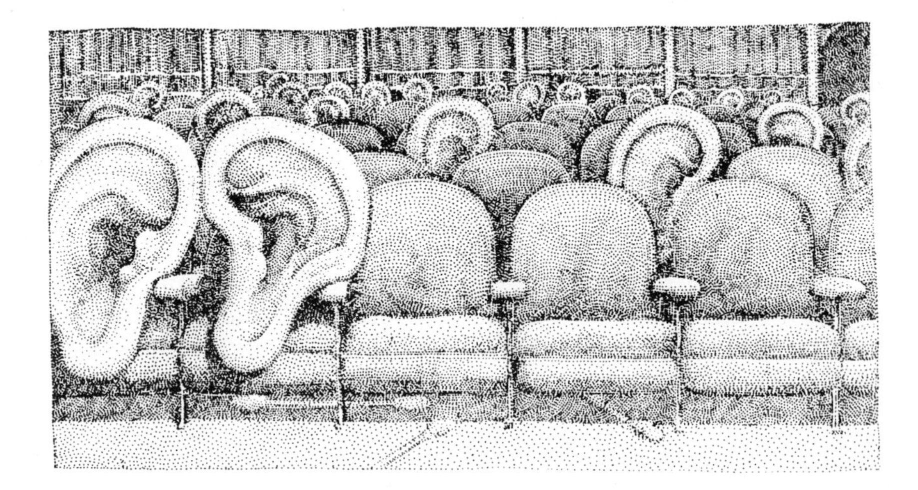

As an interpreter, you keep the book with you while you re-create the selection. You may hold the book or put it on a stand. It does not matter whether you memorize the material or not. If you want to memorize, the book still serves as a center around which you work and reminds the listeners that you are the instrument of communication between the author and them. Be careful to keep your concentration on communication and not on the act of memorization.

If you do not memorize, you must have mastered the material so well that you need not keep looking at the book for every word. An occasional glance should be enough. You must keep your eyes up and on the audience to hold their attention and gain directness of communication.

If you hold the book, learn to hold it low and casually in one hand so that you do not seem to hide behind it. The book should be tipped away from the audience so the white pages do not flash and distract their attention.

Your listeners see you before they hear you. The way you walk to the platform can set a mood. As an interpreter, you must have a flexible, controlled body so that you look at ease and have no personal mannerisms to distract the audience from the experience you are sharing with them. Be sure your body is helping you communicate the literature. The better your technique, the less obvious it is. Your audience must have its attention free to concentrate on *what* you are saying, not on *how* you are saying it.

Earlier we mentioned the relation between emotional response and muscle response and suggested that the body plays an important role in communicating the emotional force of the piece. Your posture and carriage help set the mood for your material. The audience will quickly take on your degree of relaxation or tension.

The interpreter's voice and body work together, under control of an alert and informed mind, to serve the author's purpose. Remember the members of the audience see you and hear you but what they are interested in are the *author*'s ideas and thoughts and the way *he* or *she* expresses them. It is your job to communicate all these things to the audience so they share the experience with you.

Those very large butterflies which fluttered in the pit of your stomach before you began your performance will have disappeared soon after you begin to concentrate on this sharing with the audience. If you have prepared as well as you can, enjoy your material and trust the audience to enjoy it too; the butterflies were not a sign of fear but of excitement. That's good! It makes your performance alive and vivid. The nicest compliment you can get when you have finished is "I enjoyed that story!"

Activities

1. If the selection you chose for analysis in the preceding chapter is a narrative, refine your analysis in light of the additional steps you have just studied. Then proceed with preparation for performance.

2. Find a longer narrative that interests you and try your hand at cutting.

Selections for Interpretation

In this variation of the old story about the boy who cried "Wolf!" the rhymes are strong and close. Use them for the grim humor but control them with the enjambment lines. Let the strong rhythm come through but don't let it obscure the thought progression.

Matilda Who Told Lies, and was Burned to Death
by Hilaire Belloc

Matilda told such Dreadful Lies,
It made one Gasp and Stretch one's Eyes;
Her Aunt, who, from her Earliest Youth,
Had kept a Strict Regard for Truth,
Attempted to Believe Matilda:
The effort very nearly killed her,
And would have done so, had not She
Discovered this Infirmity.
For once, towards the Close of Day,
Matilda, growing tired of play,
And finding she was left alone,
Went tiptoe to the Telephone
And summoned the Immediate Aid
Of London's Noble Fire-Brigade.
Within an hour the Gallant Band
Were pouring in on every hand,
From Putney, Hackney Downs, and Bow
With Courage high and Hearts a-glow
They galloped, roaring through the Town
'Matilda's House is Burning Down!'
Inspired by British Cheers and Loud
Proceeding from the Frenzied Crowd,
They ran their ladders through a score
Of windows on the Ball Room Floor;
And took Peculiar Pains to Souse
The Pictures up and down the House,
Until Matilda's Aunt succeeded
In showing them they were not needed;

And even then she had to pay
To get the Men to go away!

It happened that a few Weeks later
Her Aunt was off to the Theatre
To see that Interesting Play
The Second Mrs Tanqueray.
She had refused to take her Niece
To hear this Entertaining Piece:
A Deprivation Just and Wise
To Punish her for Telling Lies.
That Night a Fire *did* break out—
You should have heard Matilda Shout!
You should have heard her Scream and Bawl,
And throw the window up and call
To People passing in the Street—
(The rapidly increasing Heat
Encouraging her to obtain
Their confidence)—but all in vain!
For every time She shouted 'Fire!'
They only answered 'Little Liar'!
And therefore when her Aunt returned,
Matilda, and the House, were Burned.

At fourteen Momaday left his reservation to go to the Jemez Indian School. The journey took some time on horseback and he stopped now and then in small settlements. This is the account of one of those stops; full of action, it will involve all your muscle response.

from ***The Names: A Memoir***
by N. Scott Momaday

In another settlement there were some boys who were interested in racing. They had good horses, some of them, but their horses were not so good as mine, and I won easily. After that, I began to think of ways in which I might even the odds a little, might give some advantage to my competitors. Once or twice I gave them a head start, a reasonable head start of, say, five or ten yards to the hundred, but that was too simple, and I won anyway. Then it came to me that I might try this: we should all line up in the usual way, side by side, but my competitors should be mounted and I should not. When the signal was given I should then have to get up on my horse while the others were breaking away; I should have to mount my horse during the race. This idea appealed to me

---

greatly, for it was both imaginative and difficult, not to mention dangerous; Pecos and I should have to work very closely together. The first few times we tried this I had little success, and over a course of a hundred yards I lost four races out of five. The principal problem was that Pecos simply could not hold still among the other horses. Even before they broke away he was hard to manage, and when they were set running nothing could hold him back, even for an instant. I could not get my foot in the stirrup, but I had to throw myself up across the saddle on my stomach, hold on as best I could, and twist myself into position, and all this while racing at full speed. I could ride well enough to accomplish this feat, but it was a very awkward and inefficient business. I had to find some way to use the whole energy of my horse, to get it all into the race. Thus far I had managed only to break his motion, to divert him from his purpose and mine. To correct this I took Pecos away and worked with him through the better part of a long afternoon on a broad reach of level ground beside an irrigation ditch. And it was hot, hard work. I began by teaching him to run straight away while I ran beside him a few steps, holding on to the saddle horn, with no pressure on the reins. Then, when he had mastered this trick, we proceeded to the next one, which was this: I placed my weight on my arms, hanging from the saddle horn, threw my feet out in front of me, struck them to the ground, and sprang up against the saddle. This I did again and again, until Pecos came to expect it and did not flinch or lose his stride. I sprang a little higher each time. It was in all a slow process of trial and error, and after two or three hours both Pecos and I were covered with bruises and soaked through with perspiration. But we had much to show for our efforts, and at last the moment came when we must put the whole performance together. I had not yet leaped into the saddle, but I was quite confident that I could now do so; only I must be sure to get high enough. We began this dress rehearsal then from a standing position. At my signal Pecos lurched and was running at once, straight away and smoothly. And at the same time I sprinted forward two steps and gathered myself up, placing my weight precisely at my wrists, throwing my feet out and together, perfectly. I brought my feet down sharply to the ground and sprang up hard, as hard as I could, bringing my legs astraddle of my horse—and everything was just right, except that I sprang too high. I vaulted all the way over my horse, clearing the saddle by a considerable margin, and came down into the irrigation ditch. It was a good trick, but it was not the one I had in mind, and I wonder what Pecos thought of it after all. Anyway, after a while I could mount my horse in this way and so well that there was no challenge in it, and I went on winning race after race.

I went on, farther and farther into the wide world. Many things happened. And in all this I knew one thing: I knew where the journey was begun, that it was itself a learning of the beginning, that the beginning was infinitely worth the learning. The journey was well undertaken, and somewhere in it I sold my horse to an old Spanish man of Vallecitos. I do not know how long Pecos lived. I had used him hard and well, and it may be that in his last days an image of me like thought shimmered in his brain.

This section from a full-length book has a kind of warm humor. Its climax is a gentle one which depends for its effectiveness on full comprehension of the young boy who is too old to cry and too young to be able to laugh at the situation into which he got himself.

. . . And Now Miguel

by Joseph Krumgold

Just to look at, the morning was all right. Or even, to tell the truth, it was a nice morning. The sun was shining and the shadows were long and heavy when we came out of the house. The sky was blue and big like there was more of it around than usual, more clear sky thin as deep water all around. Over the mountains there was clouds looking like a flock of clouds grazing up there, big and little ones. And over the house, there was a couple of little ones, tramp clouds, like orphans. The Sangre de Cristo,[1] they looked closer than I ever saw them before. Or maybe that was just because of the way I felt.

I felt good that morning when we all went out to finish the shearing. I could still amost taste last night's supper in my mouth, the food and the jokes and everything. When we all walked out together, the others finishing their cigarettes after breakfast, my grandfather told me to hang up the bag for the wool. The rest of the unshorn sheep had to be herded from the fields, where they had grazed all night, into the corral. All the other hands had to go out to round them up and bring them in. So it was up to me, my grandfather said, to hang up the big sack. Me, that is, and Uncle Eli.

I was glad to do this because hanging the sack, after all, is an important job which you don't ask anyone at all to do and which I had never been asked to do before. I knew how it worked, though, from watching.

First, Uncle Eli and I, we got this iron hoop, like a hoop off a barrel only thick and solid, and this hoop we put around the top outside the opening of the sack. Then we turned over the cloth of the sack, which is burlap, we turned it over the hoop all the way around. All that's left is to take some nails, which you use like they were pins, to fasten the turned-over burlap to the rest of the sack so that the hoop is all covered over and it can't fall off.

Once you do this, it's very easy to hang the sack. All you do then is to go up on the wall of the shed where is nailed this square wooden frame and drop the bottom of the empty sack through the frame. But the opening of the sack can't go through because the hoop is bigger than the wooden square and it rests on the square letting the sack hang down its full length, six or seven feet. That's all there is to it.

But once we got the sack hung up, Uncle Eli said, "Stay up there, Miguelito.

1. **The Sangre de Cristo,** a range of mountains in New Mexico.

We'll get started and sack up these fleeces from yesterday."

So there I was up on top. Fleeces flying up from Uncle Eli. Everybody as busy and working as fast as they could, like on the day before. And soon the woolly fleeces filled up the sack to the very top. I stepped in the middle to stamp them down. And it was like the whole world gave way from right under my feet.

I dropped slowly down to the bottom of the sack. One long drop, and then a soft bump. There had not been enough fleeces to hold me up, not enough soft wool. I just went down, slow, and there was nothing to do. The sides of the bag, the burlap, was hard and rough with nothing to catch, not even with fingernails. Like going down a smooth tunnel standing straight up. There was no way to save myself. And yell, I couldn't yell. How could I yell and tell everyone what a fool I was to be falling that second into the bag which was for the wool?

I didn't yell.

I didn't breathe.

I looked up. As if I was climbing the rough cloth with my eyes, I looked up all the little crisscrosses of the cloth, and at the end I reached the top. Way up, high above me, I saw the sky, still blue like this morning but no longer big and wide. An eye, a round eye it was, way up at the end of the tunnel, still blue and with one tramp cloud, an orphan cloud.

I breathed. And then, *Madre Dios,*[2] a shadow went past the eye. It was a fleece. And right away another. Eli, without looking, he was still throwing fleeces up to me and I wasn't there. The fleeces were going right over the top of the bag. Another came and another. And no one to catch them. . . .

Someone yelled. "What are you doing with the fleeces, Eli? Throwing them away?"

"Eli!"

"What?" That was Eli. "What's wrong? Well, what do you know! Miguel! Where is he? Miguel!"

The fleeces stopped. And everywhere shouts. For me, Miguel.

I didn't say anything. I wished only that my name was something different from Miguel. Alexander, Joe, Babaloo—anyone, except me.

It was my big brother Blasito who thought of it first. "Maybe he fell into the bag?"

They screamed and yelled and laughed at how funny this was. There were also other jokes. When I looked up again it was just in time to see the face of my father come into the round blue hole way up there, above my head.

"Is this any time to start playing games, hide and seek, like you were a little boy?"

When he said this I stopped breathing again.

He put down his hand. It hung there, big fingers and a big thumb, right in front of my nose.

---

2. ***Madre Dios,*** literally translated "Mother of God" but used as a fairly common exclamation of serious surprise by Spanish Americans.

The big finger, upside down, shook at me. I put up my hands and took the hand hanging there in front of my nose. As soon as I did my father grabbed me by the wrist.

"Games," he said. "At a time like this."

He lifted me up into the bright day. He dropped me over the side. I fell into the dirt at the bottom of the bag. . . . I sat there in the dirt without moving because there was nowhere I could think of to go. When I fell I picked up a handful of dirt and now I let the dirt go out of my hand, a little bit at a time.

Whatever dirt there was left in my hand, I threw it away.

I made myself small and got up. I walked away from the shearing shed across the yard, without looking back. No one called me to look back and there was no one I wanted to see. And in this way I was able to reach the gate which led to the path that went to the house.

That's the way it was on the second day of the shearing.

The first half of this story has to do with a wonderful day. There is exhilaration and a strong sense of togetherness. The kinetic and kinesthetic imagery are as strong as are visual and thermal. After the incident itself there is a rapid time progression and the attitude of the narrator changes. So does her relationship to the others she encounters in the three very brief scenes. The climaxes of these three scenes are strong but completely interior. Be sure you are thinking as mature people in the situations which the author describes for each one. They will require careful use of empathy. They are very brief so you must be ready for them and allow your audience a few seconds to complete each one before moving on to the next.

The Day We Flew the Kites

by Frances Fowler

"String!" shouted Brother, bursting into the kitchen. "We need lots more string."

It was Saturday. As always, it was a busy one, for "Six days shalt thou labor and do all thy work" was taken seriously in those days. My father and Mr. Patrick next door were doing chores about their large yards. March was a busy time.

Indoors, Mother and Mrs. Patrick were running around in their usual Saturday

---

marathon, complicated by spring cleaning. Such a windy day was ideal for "turning out" clothes closets. Already woolens flapped on clotheslines which snaked across the adjoining back yards.

Somehow the boys had slipped away to the back lot with their kites. Now, even at the risk of having Brother impounded for beating carpets or washing windows, they had sent him to the house for more string. All of theirs had played out—heaven knows how many yards! Apparently there was no limit to the heights to which kites would soar today.

My mother looked out the window. The sky was piercingly blue: the breeze fresh and infinitely exciting. Up in all that blueness sailed great puffy billows of clouds. It had been a long, hard winter, but today was Spring.

My mother looked from the pie-baking clutter on the kitchen table to the disordered sitting room, its furniture all moved out of line for a really Spartan sweeping. Again her eyes wavered toward the window. "Come on, girls!" She fumbled in the kitchen-table drawer for a new roll of twine. "Let's take string to the boys and watch them fly the kites a minute."

On the way we met our neighbor, Mrs. Patrick, laughing guiltily, escorted by her girls.

There never was such a day for flying kites! God doesn't make two such days in a century. We played all our fresh twine into the boys' kites, and still they soared. We could hardly distinguish the tiny, orange-colored specks. Now and then we slowly reeled one in, finally bringing it, dipping and tugging, to earth, for the sheer joy of sending it up again, feeling its vibrant tug against the twine as it sought the sky. What a thrill to run with them, to the right, to the left, and see our poor, earth-bound movements reflected minutes later, in the majestic sky-dance of the kites! We wrote "wishes" on slips of paper, punched holes in them, and slipped them over the string. Slowly, irresistibly, they climbed up until they reached the kites. Surely all such wishes would be granted!

Even our fathers dropped hoe and hammer and joined us. Our mothers took their turn, laughing like schoolgirls. Their hair blew out of their decorous pompadours and curled loose about their cheeks, their gingham aprons whipped about their legs. Mingled with our puppyish delight was a feeling akin to awe. These adults were playing with us, really playing! The gulf between parent and child was greater then than now. Once I looked at Mother and thought she looked actually pretty! And her over forty!

We never knew where the hours went on that hilltop day. There were no hours, just a golden, breezy Now. I think we were all a little beyond ourselves. Parents forgot their duty and their dignity; children forgot the combativeness and small spites. "Perhaps it's like this in the Kingdom of Heaven," I thought confusedly. All our personalities stood out clearer, more individual than ever, and yet there was no sense of separateness.

It was growing dark before, drunk with sun and air, we all stumbled sleepily back to the houses. Things were just as we had left them, but Mother looked as if she hardly saw the half-rolled pastry, the stripped sitting room. I suppose we had some sort of supper. I suppose there must have been a surface tidying-up, for the house on Sunday looked decorous enough, or do I remember?

The strange thing was, we didn't mention that day, afterward. I felt a little embarrassed. Surely none of those other sensible, balanced people had thrilled to it as deeply as I; none had had ridiculous, sacrilegious thoughts about comparing flying kites with the Kingdom of Heaven. I locked the memory up in that deepest part of me where we keep "the things that cannot be and yet are" . . . and the years went on.

A good many years had passed, and one day I was flying about a kitchen of my own in a city apartment. I was trying to get some work out of the way while my three-year-old insistently whined her desire to "go park and see ducks."

"I *can't* go!" (My reasonableness was wearing thin.) "I have this and this and this to do first, and when I'm through I'll be too tired to walk that far."

My mother, who was visiting us, looked up from the peas she was shelling. "It's a wonderful day," she offered, "really warm, yet there's a fine, fresh breeze. It reminds me of that day we flew the kites." I stopped in my dash between stove and sink. So she remembered! The locked door flew open, and with it a gush of memories, and the application of her little parable. There had been much to do on that long-ago Saturday.

I pulled off my apron. "Come on," I told my little girl. "You're right, it's too good a day to miss."

Another decade passed. We were in the uneasy aftermath of a great war. All evening we had been asking our returned soldier, the youngest Patrick boy, about his experiences as a prisoner of war. He had talked freely, but now for a long time he had been silent, watching his cigarette smoke curl upward into the summer darkness. The silence seemed suddenly to throb. What was he thinking of . . . what dark and dreadful things? What was he going to tell?

"Say!" A smile twitched his lips. He looked like the little boy he used to be, the very little boy always tagging behind us others. "Say, do you remember . . . no, of course you wouldn't. It probably didn't make the impression on you it did on me. It was the first time I'd seen them."

I hardly dared speak. "Remember what?"

"I used to think of that day a lot in P.W. camp, when things weren't too good. Do you remember the day we flew the kites?"

Winter came, and the sad duty of a call of condolence on Mrs. Patrick, recently widowed. Her family had moved away many years before, but she had brought back her husband's body to our town for burial. I dreaded the call. I couldn't imagine how Mrs. Patrick would face life alone.

I found her quite gray, a little stooped, much thinner than in her vigorous, maternal middle years. But she still had those warm, brown eyes, that low, caressing voice. We talked a little of my family and her grandchildren and the changes in our town. Then she was silent, looking down at her lap. I cleared my throat. Now I must say something about her loss, and she would begin to cry.

When I looked up, I was dumbfounded. Mrs. Patrick was smiling. "I was just sitting here thinking," she said. "Henry had such fun that day. Frances, do you remember the day we flew the kites?"

Although this is a fairly long episode from a full-length novel, it is quite clear and complete in itself. Several shorter units within this excerpt could be used separately. Agee has caught the combination of shy pride, bewilderment, and sense of isolation of the small boy whose father has been killed in an auto accident. Let your muscles respond fully to help project the tensions which build and drop.

from ***A Death in the Family***
by James Agee

The air was cool and gray and here and there along the street, shapeless and watery sunlight strayed and vanished. Now that he was in this outdoor air he felt even more listless and powerful; he was alone, and the silent, invisible energy was everywhere. He stood on the porch and supposed that everyone he saw passing knew of an event so famous. A man was walking quickly up the street and as Rufus watched him, and waited for the man to meet his eyes, he felt a great quiet lifting within him of pride and of shyness, and he felt his face break into a smile, and then an uncontrollable grin, which he knew he must try to make sober again; but the man walked past without looking at him, and so did the next man who walked past in the other direction. Two schoolboys passed whose faces he knew, so he knew that they must know his, but they did not even seem to see him. Arthur and Alvin Tripp came down their front steps and along the far sidwalk and now he was sure, and came down his own front steps and halfway out to the sidewalk, but then he stopped, for now, although both of them looked across into his eyes, and he into theirs, they did not cross the street to him or even say hello, but kept on their way, still looking into his eyes with a kind of shy curiosity, even when their heads were turned almost backwards on their necks, and he turned his own head slowly, watching them go by, but when he saw that they were not going to speak he took care not to speak either.

What's the matter with them, he wondered, and still watched them; and even now, far down the street, Arthur kept turning his head, and for several steps Alvin walked backwards.

What are they mad about?

Now they no longer looked around, and now he watched them vanish under the hill.

Maybe they don't know, he thought. Maybe the others don't know, either.

He came out to the sidewalk.

Maybe everybody knew. Or maybe he knew something of great importance which nobody else knew. The alternatives were not at all distinct in his mind; he was puzzled, but no less proud and expectant than before. My daddy's dead,

---

he said to himself slowly, and then, shyly, he said it aloud: "My daddy's dead." Nobody in sight seemed to have heard; he had said it to nobody in particular. "My daddy's dead," he said again, chiefly for his own benefit. It sounded powerful, solid, and entirely creditable, and he knew that if need be he would tell people. He watched a large, slow man come towards him and waited for the man to look at him and acknowledge the fact first, but when the man was just ahead of him, and still did not appear even to have seen him, he told him, "My daddy's dead," but the man did not seem to hear him, he just swung on by. He took care to tell the next man sooner and the man's face looked almost as if he were dodging a blow but he went on by, looking back a few steps later with a worried face; and after a few steps more he turned and came slowly back.

"What was that you said, sonny?" he asked; he was frowning slightly.

"My daddy's dead," Rufus said, expectantly.

"You mean that sure enough?" the man asked.

"He died last night when I was asleep and now he can't come home ever any more."

The man looked at him as if something hurt him.

"Where do you live, sonny?"

"Right here"; he showed with his eyes.

"Do your folks know you out here wandern round?"

He felt his stomach go empty. He looked frankly into his eyes and nodded quickly.

The man just looked at him and Rufus realized: He doesn't believe me. How do they always know?

"You better just go on back in the house, son," he said. "They won't like you being out here on the street." He kept looking at him, hard.

Rufus looked into his eyes with reproach and apprehension, and turned in at his walk. The man still stood there. Rufus went on slowly up his steps, and looked around. The man was on his way again but at the moment Rufus looked around, he did too, and now he stopped again.

He shook his head and said, in a friendly voice which made Rufus feel ashamed, "How would your daddy like it, you out here telling strangers how he's dead?"

Rufus opened the door, taking care not to make a sound, and stepped in and silently closed it, and hurried into the sitting room. Through the curtains he watched the man. He still stood there, lighting a cigarette, but now he started walking again. He looked back once and Rufus felt, with a quailing of shame and fear, he sees me; but the man immediately looked away again and Rufus watched him until he was out of sight.

How would your daddy like it?

He thought of the way they teased him and did things to him, and how mad his father got when he just came home. He thought how different it would be today if he only didn't have to stay home from school.

He let himself out again and stole back between the houses to the alley, and walked along the alley, listening to the cinders cracking under each step, until he came near the sidewalk. He was not in front of his own home now, or even on Highland Avenue; he was coming into the side street down from his home, and he felt that here nobody would identify him with his home and send him back to it. What he could see from the mouth of the alley was much less familiar to him, and he took the last few steps which brought him out onto the sidewalk with deliberation and shyness. He was doing something he had been told not to do.

He looked up the street and he could see the corner he knew so well, where he always met the others so unhappily, and, farther away, the corner around which his father always disappeared on the way to work, and first appeared on his way home from work. He felt it would be good luck that he would not be meeting them at that corner. Slowly, uneasily, he turned his head, and looked down the side street in the other direction; and there they were: three together, and two along the far side of the street, and one alone, farther off, and another alone, farther off, and, without importance to him, some girls here and there, as well. He knew the faces of all of these boys well, though he was not sure of any of their names. The moment he saw them all he was sure they saw him, and sure that they knew. He stood still and waited for them, looking from one to another of them, into their eyes, and step by step at their several distances, each of them at all times looking into his eyes and knowing, they came silently nearer. Waiting, in silence, during those many seconds before the first of them came really near him, he felt that it was so long to wait, and be watched so closely and silently, and to watch back, that he wanted to go back into the alley and not be seen by them or by anybody else, and yet at the same time he knew that they were all approaching him with the realization that something had happened to him that had not happened to any other boy in town, and that now at last they were bound to think well of him; and the nearer they came but were yet at a distance, the more the gray, sober air was charged with the great energy and with a sense of glory and of danger, and the deeper and more exciting the silence became, and the more tall, proud, shy and exposed he felt; so that as they came still nearer he once again felt his face break into a wide smile, with which he had nothing to do, and, feeling that there was something deeply wrong in such a smile, tried his best to quieten his face and told them, shyly and proudly, "My daddy's dead."

Chapter 6
Interpreting Dramatic Literature

There are numerous definitions of *dramatic.* For our purposes, we will regard that literature dramatic which presents a character or characters in a situation *without* a narrator intervening between the action and the audience. Plot is revealed through dialogue and action. Everything the listeners know they learn from the actions and speech of the characters. Monologues, soliloquies, and plays in both prose and poetry are considered dramatic literature.

In dramatic monologues and soliloquies, we hear from only one character. Monologue comes from *mono* meaning "single" and the Greek verb *legein* meaning "to speak." Thus in a monologue there is a single speaker who addresses other characters who do not speak. Soliloquy comes from the Latin words *solus* meaning "alone" and the verb *loqui* meaning "to speak." In a soliloquy there are no other characters present. In this chapter, however, we will devote our attention specifically to plays.

A play is written to be presented on a stage with all the visual aids that scenery, costumes, makeup, and lighting can give and with a full cast of characters. Consequently, it presents some special technical problems to the single interpreter.

Beginning Your Preparation

Plays are constructed with acts and sometimes scenes within the acts. It is important to know how the plot of a play is developed. In the analysis of narratives you should locate all key situations and climaxes. In a drama you will find not only key speeches but key scenes and key actions as well. They all have the same function. They are signposts along the road of plot and action development. They may be a key to the plot development, or a key to character. The key actions often are handled best as narration and given to the audience directly.

Just as narration may be organized in many different ways, a play may move right along in steady chronological order, or it may have flashback scenes, or quiet scenes in which a previous episode is recalled, or any combination of these. There may be several subplots which you may or may not wish to include in your cutting. Often when there are one or more subplots, the scenes will alternate with those that move the main plot forward.

After you have examined the separate parts, look again at the play as a whole. Reread it to be sure you know how it moves and how it achieves its point, both in relation to key scenes and climaxes and to the function of the characters and their speeches. After you have examined the relationship of the parts to the whole, you may wish to do some cutting. In the case of the actor, this will be done by the director. As an interpreter, you may select a key scene or scenes for your performance or, as you become more experienced, you may do a cutting of an entire play. Eliminate the characters' names before each speech, because as the interpreter it is your duty to make those characters clear by suggestion without having to identify them each time. The same general rules for cutting a narrative apply to cutting a play.

When you feel sure of the play's organization, move to the study of the characters. First decide what each character contributes to the play. Whose play is it? Around whom does the plot revolve? The answer to the latter question may often include two or more characters. Each character in every scene is there for a reason.

We touched on character analysis when we were concerned with direct and indirect discourse in narratives. In a play, the complete understanding of a character is sometimes more difficult because there is no narrator to step in and explain matters to us. Nor does the audience have any narrative to tell them what is in a character's mind. The interpreter must communicate all these aspects with his voice and body without the help of costumes and makeup or stage setting and properties. Changes from one speaker to another are likely to be rapid. You must look for and find every possible clue for motivation, and pay particular attention to all stage directions, whether you intend to speak them aloud to your audience or use them as a guide to your own preparation and performance.

Both the interpreter of drama and the actor begin with the author's words, and both are instruments through whom the author's play is transmitted to an audience. Both actor and interpreter must be true to the author's script. Both use physical and vocal techniques to communicate all the elements of the play to the audience. Both study the complete play so the author's full intention is clear. The steps in preparation for the actor and the interpreter are nearly identical up to the final preparation for performance. Throughout this chapter we will examine both the parallels and the differences between acting and interpretation of dramatic literature.

Cutting Stage Directions

You will not need to give your audience stage directions except perhaps for entrances and exits, and the rise and fall of the curtain. These can be paraphrased, put into appropriate style, and then used as narrative inserts, which you speak directly to the audience in your own person.

Sometimes they can be mentioned in your introduction. For example, you might wish to say "As the curtain rises John, the young son, is intent on taking apart a section of the hi-fi unit which he has spread out on the floor." You may

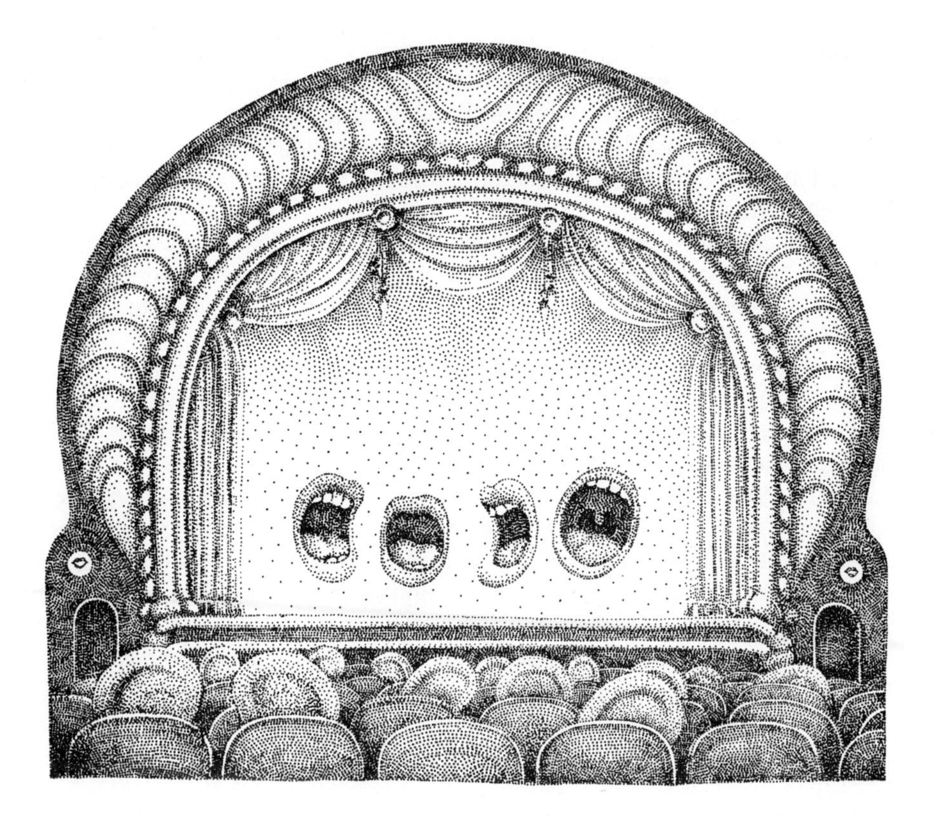

need to indicate how a character enters or exits if it is important to the scene with some simple phrase such as "She runs off in tears as the curtain falls," or "Suddenly the door bursts open and the gardener comes in carrying an up-rooted rose bush." If you keep such insertions brief, and give them directly to the audience as a narrator they will not seriously interrupt the flow of the scene.

Vocal and Physical Techniques

Both actor and interpreter turn next to a consideration of vocal and physical techniques so that everything they do with voice and body helps make the characters vivid to the audience and reflects each character's emotional reaction to the situation which exists at the moment.

Both pay particular attention to the style of dress, age, and physical condition that affect the way the character sits down and gets up, enters and leaves the room, and handles objects within the room.

One moves and stands differently in various kinds of clothes. The interpreter will probably be concerned with more than one character in the final performance. It is wise to take them one at a time until the mental, vocal, and physical pattern is set for each.

Muscle Memory

An interpreter, as well as an actor, must go through this physical phase of preparation, even though the interpreter may not take a step in actual performance. There is no reason, of course, why the interpreter shouldn't move about in performance as well as in preparation, if such movement helps communicate the author's intention.

A word of caution is needed here however. You can get so involved in moving about that you take the scene right out of the audience's minds where it ought to be and move it up on stage with you. Then they don't know where you are and in despair they sit back and watch you instead of identifying with the characters in the scene you have so carefully set in their minds. But during preparation, actually moving about as the character would on stage, adds vitality to the real performance. It is important in establishing pace and timing. It is also a valuable aid to empathy.

Let your muscles get the feel of each big open action until they are accustomed to it. Then try the scene with no specific action at all. Stand in one place but recall what you did in the previous stage of preparation. Your muscles will respond to the memory of the big action and have an important effect on the pace and emotional impact of the entire performance. This is called muscle memory. This important physical aspect should not be neglected; it is not acting, but *preparation* for vital interpretation.

Final Stages in Your Preparation

Up to this point the interpreter and the actor follow almost identical steps in analysis and preparation. Now they are ready to apply the principles of their art to a performance. It is only at this point that the differences between acting and interpretation become apparent. It is in the exterior aspects of performance that the differences appear. Actors begin to add exterior details to make their characterizations physically explicit. Interpreters now begin to eliminate physical explicitness, refining their gestures to suggest the underlying tensions.

The actors work to convince the audience that they are the characters both mentally and physically. They have memorized the lines. They use real properties. They enter and leave the stage, opening and closing doors on the set. They are fitted for costumes which help create the illusion of a period. They practice with makeup so they no longer look like themselves, but like an old man or a bearded soldier or an aging queen. They do everything they can to *be* the character physically. They respond mentally and emotionally as the character.

At this point, the interpreter begins to work toward suggestion. You may or may not memorize your material. You will find, however, that you need to have it more nearly memorized than when you are working with other forms of literature, because you must be able to handle the suggestion of character and direct dialogue without interrupting the scene to refer to the book. An occasional glance is all you can manage. You must work out all the physical and mental aspects of each character with as much care and attention to detail as the actor does. You know everything about the characters—how every one of them thinks, feels, reacts, speaks, and moves.

To help the actors achieve explicitness, an actual set is constructed, in which they play their parts. But as an interpreter you have only a book, which you always take with you—whether you have memorized the material or not—an empty stage, and sometimes a reading stand. You will not have the help of properties, scenery, lighting, costumes, and makeup. Nor will you have the actual presence of other people on the stage with you. You are the sole communicator between the script and the audience and are intent on sharing the characters' experiences, not demonstrating them. You must be technician, property person, curtain puller, costumer, director, and the entire cast of actors all by yourself. It is not an easy assignment, but it is by no means impossible. The interpretation of dramatic literature requires conscientious work on techniques. It demands steady concentration on many details at once during performance. But when the interpreter is successful, the play becomes a clear and moving experience to the audience.

Establishing the Setting

How does the interpreter fill all these requirements? First, the significant parts of the setting must be told to the audience so they will know where and when the events take place. You need not give every little detail. Judge what is important for your scene and establish it clearly for your listeners.

The important thing to remember is that the scene being set *is not* on the stage, or wherever you are standing. It does not surround you. The stage must be set *in the minds of the audience.* Therefore, you do not indicate a fireplace behind you when describing the setting. It is not behind you on the stage. The fireplace is in the room you are helping the audience create in their minds. You simply tell them what they need to know, as a narrator would do in a story. They will establish the room, the garden, or whatever setting is needed, in their imaginations and *you* keep this scene out front as you address the characters and visualize their actions.

Introducing the Characters

Having created the "visual aspects" of the setting in your listeners' minds, you introduce the character or characters in your reading. This can be done quite simply. It is helpful to establish the relationship of the characters to each other with a phrase such as "her husband" or "their daughter." Remember the audience has no program to consult to keep the names straight. You need not tell the audience very much about them as they develop in the scene. Your performance will take care of that. If there have been some important developments in plot before the scene you are to use, include this information in your introduction, as you did in introducing a cutting from a narrative. Look at some of the scenes in Unit III to see how the characters are introduced and plot developments revealed.

Once the setting is established and the cast of characters assembled in the minds of the audience, you may simply say, "As the curtain rises, so-and-so is speaking." There are many ways to phrase this information. Make sure that you understand the mood and thought of the scene; then use whatever seems suitable.

Establishing Characters' Attitudes, Emotions, and Actions

At this time the interpreter's most important function begins—that of establishing the characters' attitudes, emotions, and actions clearly. You have become accustomed to projecting the mental attitude and emotional response, and all the aspects of interior characterization from the script to the audience. You know how effective the reader's physical response is in eliciting emotional response from the audience. It is of special importance in the interpretation of drama. Whatever is going on in the mind, muscles, and emotions of the character speaking must also be going on in your mind, muscles, and emotions as you say the speech. Muscle memory will help you here, as you recall from your preparation how the character moved under whatever emotional tension he or she is experiencing. An interpretation that does not carry this full response is not a good one.

But do not confuse full response with uncontrolled response. If you become so worked up that you forget your responsibility to the audience you are not a successful performer. If you are so carried away that your eyes fill with tears and your voice becomes unmanageable you call attention to yourself and away from the character and action in which the audience is most interested.

It has been said that the interpreter does not "become" the character. This is only partially true. You do not take on the *explicit exterior* aspects of the characters you are suggesting—such as specific actions, costume, and makeup. Nevertheless, you must "become" the interior character in your mind and emotions while that character is speaking, and this "becoming" will affect your use of voice and body. Doing this for several characters in a scene requires some quick switches and thorough preparation and steady concentration.

Suggestions on Techniques

Dramatic literature requires more physical and vocal suggestion than narrative literature, because everything the audience learns comes only through the characters. There is no narrator to step in and fill in the necessary descriptions and explanations.

The audience must always know who is speaking. Therefore, vocal and physical techniques must be sharply defined to suggest exterior aspects (sex, age, and physical attributes) of the character, as well as interior aspects. The following suggestions are very general and must, of course, be varied to suit individual plays and characters.

Indicating the Sex of a Character

A male interpreter is often at a loss as to how he should suggest the voice and actions of a female character, just as a woman may have difficulty suggesting those of a male speaker.

It is not usually necessary to do more than physically shift your weight ever so slightly to differentiate between the sexes. You need not put your feet far apart for a man or bring them together for a woman. Such a performance would distract the audience, who will become fascinated by your footwork and forget all about what you are saying.

Men usually distribute their weight fairly evenly on the centers or heels of both feet. Women tend to balance forward on the balls of their feet with more pressure on the toes than the heels. Frequently one foot is slightly forward to bear most of the weight. You need not shift your feet to do this. Any movement should be imperceptible to the audience. They will only be aware of firmer muscle tone when the men speak. A feeling of broad shoulders and heavy muscles in the upper arms will help establish strength when a woman is suggesting a male character, while a man need only feel smaller-boned and finer-muscled, and the suggestion in posture will probably be enough for his audience. Here is a place where muscle memory is most helpful.

Vocally, as physically, the watchword is to underplay rather than be specific. The audience will accept the slightest change of voice if the interpreter is consistent.

A woman using the lowest octave of her voice to suggest a man speaking succeeds only in limiting her range and straining her throat, so the audience will clear theirs in sympathy. She need only relax her throat so all the overtones and undertones are given a richer quality. If she takes a good, full breath so there is strength in her voice, the attitude of the character will dictate any other vocal variations. A man need only lighten his voice and use less vigorous projection to allow his tone to come primarily from the top of the throat. He need not lift his voice above its natural pitch. He just lightens the quality.

Remember you are only *suggesting* the sex of the character speaking. The individual differences within each sex are more important.

Indicating Age

Age is one of the most relative of all aspects of character. Too often the interpreter who has not done a careful job of analysis will jump to the conclusion that anyone who isn't young is on the verge of senility. Fortunately, that is a fallacy! All old people do not have hunched backs and cracked voices. If you observe older people carefully, you will see that many of them carry themselves erect and speak firmly. Let the degree of frailty be dictated by what the author tells you about the vigor and vitality of the character. If you make the character too frail, you may not be able to build a convincing climax that requires strength and energy. The style of the speeches is also an important clue.

As a rule older people move more slowly than younger ones. They use smaller gestures with more importance attached to the hand than to the upper arms and shoulders. Try getting the feeling of weakened muscles in your arms and shoulders. Practice handling articles with this feeling until you are used to it. Your muscles will carry the memory into performance.

Older people are often less sure of their sight and balance than younger people. Their legs do not have the vigor they once had. When they walk, they tend to keep their feet closer to the ground and to shorten their steps. They often sit still a great deal, and their muscles go slack. Train your muscles specifically in rehearsal, and the suggestion will come through in performance without any acrobatics of stooping and straightening for characters of different ages.

Vocal technique will help in suggesting age. Older people tend to use a narrower range of inflection than young persons. They do not become so actively excited, and the pace of their speech is slower and the rhythm less staccato than when they were young. This can also be true of people who are not physically vibrant or who are bored or very tired.

Remember that the exterior characteristics need only be suggested. As an interpreter you are not asking the audience to believe *you are* all the characters in a scene. You are asking them to believe that *there are* such persons. It is the effect of these interior qualities on attitude that is basic to the audience's sharing of the experience. Don't exaggerate the physical aspects. Keep them subtle so that they support what is being said and how it is said rather than distracting from it.

Suggesting More Than One Character

Usually the interpreter is required to suggest several characters within a scene. Whereas an actor has other actors on stage whom the audience can see and hear, the interpreter must handle the entire cast as it moves on the stage that has been created in the audience's minds.

Once you have managed to get one character thoroughly in hand, it is not a difficult matter to add the others. In preparation you will find it wise to establish each character fully before going on to the next. In the process of analysis you will have decided which characters are important. Thoroughly develop the most important character first, mentally, emotionally, and physically. Then develop the next character with the same care. Then put the two together and work on their relationship to each other in the situation in which we find them. This process may be followed, no matter how many characters you wish to suggest.

Angle of Focus

There are a few additional suggestions for technique that may help you and the audience avoid confusion. One of these is the matter of eye focus. You will recall the suggestion that in direct discourse you select a section of the back wall to serve as an area of focus. When you are handling two or more characters, you simply select a separate area *toward* which *each* addresses all speeches. It simplifies the problem for both audience and interpreter if a specific character speaks in the same general direction no matter who is being addressed.

This technique can be clarified graphically. When you are speaking as a narrator, in establishing setting and character, you look at and speak to the audience. When you are speaking as a character you focus on a specific area behind the audience and *slightly* above their heads. You may shift your eye direction within speeches if you wish, but be sure to start and end each speech at the proper angle for the character speaking.

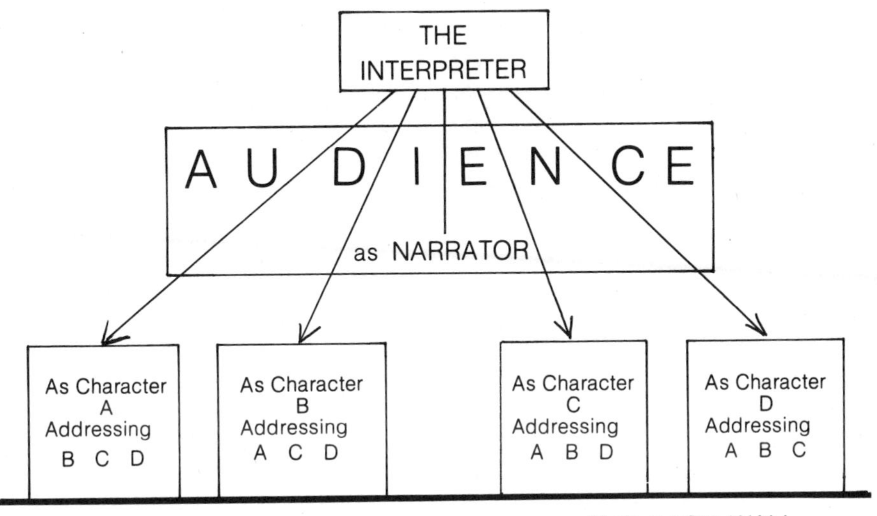

Be careful to keep the areas you assign to the various characters as close together as possible so that the continued change of direction does not become obtrusive. The angle widens as it goes away from you. To place two characters at the outside edges of the triangle makes you need to look so far from side to side that you behave like a spectator at a tennis match. Keep the angle as narrow as possible. A shift of the eyes with an appropriate change of attitude is all that is needed to indicate that another character is speaking if you use your voice and muscles to project the mental and emotional differences between the characters at the same time.

Actors must not only learn their own lines but also learn to "hear" what the other characters say so that they can respond properly. Otherwise the speeches plod along with no relation to the scene as a whole. As an interpreter handling more than one character, you must learn to "have heard." Be sure each character has heard, and is replying to the preceding speech with the motivation that causes that character to react as he or she does. This requires you to pick up the thread of the thought development in the person of the character who has heard the speech.

It requires split-second response that includes mental and emotional reaction and excellent control of physical and vocal technique. There is no shortcut to developing this ability. It takes thorough preparation of each character and the reconstruction of the situation so that each character is in proper relation to every other one.

No character can be allowed to drop out of the scene. Each must emerge complete and vivid the moment the cue is picked up. Remember a cue can be picked up by a glance or a facial expression. You need not race breathlessly from one speech to the next. A pause can be effective in indicating reaction. However, the pause must be within the character's thinking, and be so indicated by your picking up the cue physically and mentally. There must not be a sag between characters. As soon as one character finishes a speech or an action, the other character picks up immediately, whether or not he or she starts to speak. This is important in keeping the scene moving smoothly and in establishing interplay.

Suggesting Certain Properties

One other problem sometimes puzzles the interpreter—what to do about handling properties and physical contact between characters.

Remember that suggestion, not explicit demonstration, is the interpreter's goal. An action is the exterior manifestation of an inner motivation. Why and how a character acts is often more important than what he or she does. Practice the action fully in preparation, just as you do any action. Then concentrate on suggesting the tension behind the action rather than performing the action itself.

If one character hands another a letter to read, it will make a difference whether it is given eagerly or tentatively. The empathy and timing involved are important. A slight reaching out of the hand toward the area of address should be enough. When the second character takes the letter, let your audience see the manner in which it is taken rather than trying to make them believe that you have grasped a piece of paper out of thin air. Does the character snatch it quickly, or is there some hesitation? Is he or she eager to read it, or is it being done reluctantly? The answers to these and other related questions will affect facial expressions and muscle tone of the body as well as the speed of the action itself. It is the purpose served by the exchange of the letter, and not merely the actual exchange, that is important to the audience.

Likewise, you do not sit down as one character and leap to your feet to answer yourself as another character. The bending of the knees and putting the body in contact with the chair seat is not important. The muscle tone that suggests the reason for sitting down is the important factor. Does the character sink wearily into the chair or sit nervously on its edge or preside over a formal meeting? The audience will respond with empathy if the interpreter has made use of muscle memory throughout the preparation.

Even more specific physical action, such as a blow, can be suggested. An interpreter who clenches a fist and strikes at empty air is quite likely to look a little odd, to say the least. It is safer to tell the audience what is taking place. If this cannot be accomplished without breaking the scene, remember that a blow is an outward manifestation of an inner motivation. A sharper directness of eye focus, a general tensing of all the muscles and appropriate empathy, with only a slight, quick thrust of the clenched fist to point the action, will take care of the situation. You are not delivering or receiving the blow. The characters in the audience's minds are performing the action. If the emotional response is carefully suggested, the action will be clear. Moreover, the lines will usually refer to the action, so there is little chance that the audience will miss the point.

Summary
The Actor and the Interpreter of Drama

Early Preparation	Study of the author's play
	Analysis of complete play
	organization of plot
	key scenes
	key speeches
	climaxes
	relationship of parts to whole
	Analysis of characters
	relationship to plot
	relationship to setting
	relationship to each other
	Analysis of individual character or characters
	interior characteristics
	change or development of interior aspects
	exterior characteristics
	practice physical actions
	Reexamination of above in relation to whole play
	Full response to character in situation

	The Actor	The Interpreter
	Explicitness	*Suggestion*
Final Preparation for Performance	Memorizes lines completely	May or may not memorize
	Plays within physical setting	Works out narration in appropriate style to establish setting in audience's minds
	Perfects makeup and costumes	Uses muscle memory to suggest degree of tension or relaxation in the physical actions
	Perfects entrances and exits and all stage business	
Performance	Does not carry the script	Takes script to platform
	Takes his or her place in visible scene set up around him or her	Sets scene in minds of audience by narration
		Plays scene out front
	Is explicit in outer characteristics	Suggests outer characteristics
	Has full inner response	Has full inner response
	Asks audience to believe he or she is the character and that events are happening before their eyes	Asks audience to believe there is such a character and events do take place in the imagined setting
	Demonstrates the experience *before* the audience's eyes	*Shares* the experience *with* the audience

We have not included an anthology of scenes here because the scenes at the end of Unit III and those within Unit VIII are highly usable for interpretation of Drama. As a matter of fact it would be fun to try a scene both ways. You'll be surprised how one art carries over and enriches the other.

Activities

1. Select a play from which you would enjoy doing a scene. Then analyze the play according to the steps outlined in Early Preparation, (page 85).

2. Using a scene from the play you selected to analyze in the activity above, prepare it for performance according to the steps outlined above for the interpreter's Final Preparation for Performance.

3. If a tape recorder is available to you, record your scene before presenting it to the class. Following performance, each presentation should be discussed and evaluated in class.

4. Incorporating the suggestions made in the class evaluation, work independently on your scene until you feel you have done as well as you can. Perform your scene again for the class. Then, for comparison, play your recording. Discuss and evaluate the two performances.

Chapter 7
Interpreting Poetry

Poetry differs from prose in three general ways. The first difference is the importance of the sound pattern in poetry. Sounds are often important in prose, but they are a basic and integral part of poetry. *The sound pattern of a poem is made up of all the elements of its structure.*

The second difference is the high degree of condensation characteristic of poetry. The prose writer might use an entire novel to tell the story of "Beauharnois, Glengarry" (see page 107) or "Nikki Rosa" (see page 104). To achieve this condensation, the poet makes every word count, not only for denotation but for connotation as well, and takes advantage of whatever added suggestion the sound of the words can carry.

Third is the degree of appeal to the emotions. When an author creates a work in poetry instead of prose, it is because he or she is primarily interested in sharing the emotional impact of an experience. This does not mean poetry never deals with ideas nor that prose does not have emotional impact too. It means that a poet uses the sound pattern and connotative elements of the poem to go beyond the idea to an emotional experience which he or she wishes to share.

Poetry is of particular interest to the interpreter. Its extreme condensation requires close analysis and careful control of emphasis, pitch, rate, and pause. The emotional impact is best served by the interpreter's knowledge of how mind and body can work together to share an experience with an audience. The sound pattern cannot be effective until it is heard. The interpreter's voice is as essential to a poem as a musical instrument is to a musical score. Words on the printed page carry a meaning whether they are read aloud or silently, but poetry depends for its *full meaning on the blending of sound and sense.*

Types of Poetry

There are many different types of poetry. Sometimes classification is made on the basis of the structure, as with the sonnet. For our purpose, we will classify poetry on the basis of characteristics of content, as *narrative, dramatic,* or *lyric.*

It is very important to remember that content and structure cannot be separated when reading a poem. The sense and sound work together. What the poem says is only a part; and the sound pattern is another part. They must work together before you have a poem.

When the poem is basically narrative, and the chronological progression is important in the development of the experience, as in "Dateline: Death" (see page 42), you begin your analysis as you would for any narrative. Then you analyze the sound pattern and language to see how and where they reinforce the story.

A poem is termed dramatic when it presents a character in a situation without an intervening narrator to tell us what is happening. Some plays are written in poetry. In dramatic poetry, as in a play, the interpreter must be aware of what kind of character is speaking, to whom, and why. The speaker in a poem is called the *persona.*

In lyric poetry, the poet shares a highly personal emotional experience with the readers. It is comparable to a personal essay or a mood piece. The experience is of inner emotional response rather than an exterior activity.

This simple classification of poetry into types suggests your relationship to your audience when you read a poem, and helps you decide on the response you want from them.

Activity

From the poetry anthologies in your library, find at least two poems exemplifying each of the three types just discussed. Be sure your selections are ones you find appealing. Add them to your file of source materials.

First Steps in Understanding Poetry

Some people don't like poetry. They complain they don't understand it, that it has nothing to do with practical matters, and that it doesn't really make sense. That depends on what kind of sense you are asking it to make. A poem need not give information. We have learned to let the writer have his or her way about what is being said and the way it is said. This approach is doubly important in poetry, since the experience being shared is a personal emotional one. All emotional experiences are not limited to flowers, swooning ladies, and stars. Find a poem about something that interests you. There is no subject in the world about which poets have not written.

If you don't like poetry or feel you don't understand it, try reading a poem aloud, paying close attention to the sound patterns. Poetry is meant to be read aloud. You may find you have been looking at poetry the wrong way. You may even find you've never heard it read well. Poetry need not jog and jingle. But the way the words sound helps underscore mood and meaning.

Read the poem aloud over and over until the sounds catch your ear. It is always wise to let a poem work on you before you begin working on it. Remember poetry demands a great deal of the reader, just as music does of the

musician and the listener. Respond to it from your own experience, but let the poet lead the way.

Do not be discouraged when other people find all sorts of hidden meanings which you seem to have missed. A poem moves on many related levels. As your experience increases, you will find those levels. They do not cancel or contradict each other.

The way a poem goes into our minds may be compared to what happens when you toss a stone into a pool of water. The poem is the stone and the pool of water is your experience and your willingness to work at the poem until you fully understand what it means and how it means it. When you toss the stone into the water it sets up concentric circles of waves all around where the stone went in. If the pool is too shallow and the stone too big it will just splatter. If the pool is the right depth and width and the stone the right size the circles will spread out to the far edges. This will happen with a poem. Each wave that goes out from the center will add another related meaning. Just don't lose track of what is at the center of those circles. "Ozymandias," for instance, is about a ruined statute. It is also about the futility of human pride and achievement, the indifference of nature and probably of the future about our petty triumphs, and a few other things as well. Poems are full of pluses.

Finding the Poet's Clues

If each reader responds according to his or her own memories and experience, may not the poem mean completely opposite things to different people? The answer is no. A poem means what the poet wrote down. But how do we know what was intended if the associations are so personal for both the poet and us?

Part of the answer to this question is in our earlier discussion of universal experiences. A poet must choose a reference that will produce a comparable memory in the minds of the readers. Notice that we have not said *identical.* We used the word *comparable.* The best poetry grows with us. A poem may mean one thing to you when you are ten, and a great deal more when you are sixteen. A poem about rural life may mean more to one who knows the country than to one who has never seen an apple orchard or a wheat field.

However, if one reader finds a poem sad and another finds it happy, someone is obviously wrong. Perhaps the poet has failed to make the connotations clear and universal. But more likely, one of the readers has taken one line or one image and let it twist the entire poem, ignoring everything else the poet wrote. You must use *all* the clues the poet gives you.

Consideration of Meanings

One very important clue a writer gives is a well-chosen title. Not all poems have titles, but when they do, the titles have been chosen to direct our minds and support the condensation of the poetry.

An example of the importance of a title is in this sonnet by Archibald MacLeish. Read the poem first without its title.

Quite unexpectedly as Vasserot
The armless ambidextrian was lighting
A match between his great and second toe
And Ralph the lion was engaged in biting
The neck of Madame Sossman while the drum
Pointed, and Teeny was about to cough
In waltz-time swinging Jocko by the thumb—
Quite unexpectedly the top blew off:

And there, there overhead, there, there, hung over
Those thousands of white faces, those dazed eyes,
There in the starless dark, the poise, the hover,
There with vast wings across the canceled skies,
There in the sudden blackness, the black pall
Of nothing, nothing, nothing—nothing at all.

At first, this poem seems to be about a circus. We do not know who Madame Sossman, or Teeny, and Jocko, are. Ralph is identified as a lion, Jocko is the classic name for a trained monkey, and Teeny may be assumed to be an elephant. The acts are in full swing when, quite unexpectedly, the top blows off, and overhead there is the terrible blackness of "nothing—nothing at all." This would be a frightening poem if it were about a circus—but when we look at the title, "The End of the World," the poem takes on more meaning. Read it now with the title in mind. You will see the irony of the circus theme.

Discovering the Poet's Style: Word Choice

Moving from the title to the selection itself, study some details in "The End of the World." Your first task is to be sure of the denotation and connotation of the words. "Ambidextrian" must be identified. After you define it and combine it with "armless" you may be puzzled until you put it back into the side-show atmosphere of the poem's first stanza. You may need to look up "pall" in a dictionary to get the full implication of its use.

There are many other words that bear close inspection. "Quite unexpectedly" carries a load of implication. So do "dazed," "vast wings," "black pall," "poise,"

"hover," and "canceled." Try reading the poem aloud and let the sounds and the associations of the words help you.

Grammatical Structure

As soon as you are sure you understand the denotation and the connotation of the words, notice how the author has put them together. Because of the extreme conciseness of poetry, the grammatical relationship of phrases and clauses and the choice of verb forms require special attention. You will sometimes need to analyze the grammar of an involved sentence to understand the relationship of one stanza to the next.

"The End of the World" is one long sentence without even a comma until the sixth line. When it is reduced to its grammatical core we have "The top blew off," (and) there (was) nothing," although the poet has omitted the "and," "was." All the rest of the words, phrases, and clauses modify and depend on "the top blew off, (and) there (was) nothing." Even though "quite unexpectedly," is not part of the subject and predicate, strictly speaking, it must be included in the "core." The poet has indicated it's important by repeating it. So we have "Quite unexpectedly the top blew off, (and) there (was) nothing."

How is this single statement developed? In the first stanza we have specific people and animals. There are physical references in "armless," "great and second toe," "the neck of Madame Sossman," "cough in waltz-time" and "thumb." These are small, familiar things that keep our attention on the circus performance so we are shocked by the unexpectedness of "the top blew off."

After "the top blew off," our attention is "yanked" up over our heads. There is no further mention of individuals. Instead there are "those thousands of white faces, those dazed eyes," all reflecting the same shock and horror. This is followed by nonhuman references to "wings," "skies," and "blackness," then "pall," and "nothing," repeated like a bell of doom. Notice the number of commas as compared to the first stanza and the repetition of "there." The grammar helps reinforce the frozen horror as we wait for the verb that never comes.

Look at the adjectives that modify and color the nouns in the two stanzas. The only adjectives in the first stanza are *armless* and *great* and *second.* In the second stanza there are many adjectives. There are "*white* faces," "*dazed* eyes," "*starless* dark," "*vast* wings," "*canceled* skies," "*sudden* blackness," and "*black* pall."

The second stanza is a sharp contrast to the first in almost every respect. It has no connectives, no active verb forms, and no identifications. There is focus on place, which is described as "there," "overhead," and "over." After place is established, the "overhead" references shift to the more subtle words, "starless," "poise," "hover," "wings," "skies," "blackness," and "pall," and then "nothing." The poem starts with attention to specific things, shifts from the specific to the abstract, and then into nothing. It pounds the repetition of both "there" and "nothing."

The way in which the words are put together into phrases and clauses, and introduced by "as," "and," and "while" in the first stanza gives the effect of many things going on at once. We have:

> *As* Vasserot *was lighting.*
> *And* Ralph *was engaged in biting*
> *While* the drum pointed
> *And* Teeny *was about to cough*
> *swinging* Jocko

The *underlined* verb forms above add to the feeling that many things are happening, or about to happen, as in a three-ring circus. Then suddenly there is a suspension of all action in the second stanza. We have the simple past tense of "blew." "Blew off" is the last real verb in the poem. We have already noted that the poet left out "was" in the last stanza; and "hung" and "canceled" are used as participial adjectives.

Sense Imagery

Poets use a great many appeals to the senses. We mentioned the use of such appeals in our discussion of description in narratives (see page 51). Sense appeals are of great importance in poetry both as an aid to condensation and to reinforce emotional response.

You already know the relationship between bodily response and emotional response. The way we receive impressions of things and store up memories is through our senses. You can check this from your own experience. Recall a carnival, for instance. You will remember the color, the people, the lights on the rides, and sideshow tents. The music of the merry-go-round, the shouts of the barkers, and the squeals of the people on the sky rides. You remember the smell of hamburgers, popcorn, and even the dust-filled air. The taste of cotton candy, the excitement and tension of a Ferris-wheel ride, the heat inside the tents may all be part of your memory.

The appeal to our senses stirs memories. We see, hear, taste, smell, feel the weight or texture, or warmth or chill of our memories, and our muscles respond. The poet can suggest a wealth of connotation by using imagery that appeals to our senses and muscles.

There are six kinds of imagery that appeal directly to the senses: *visual,* that appeals to our sense of sight; *auditory,* to our sense of hearing; *olfactory,* to our sense of smell; *gustatory,* to our sense of taste; *tactile,* to our sense of touch; and *thermal,* to our response to heat and cold.

There are two additional kinds of imagery that appeal to the muscles. One is *kinetic* and indicates overt physical activity such as "ran," "jumped," "threw." It is closely related to the theory of muscle memory. The second is called *kinesthetic* and refers to tension and relaxation of the muscles and it is closely related to empathy. Often they occur together.

An appeal to one sense usually calls up appeals to others. As we said, when you let yourself see, in your mind's eye, the activities in "The End of the World," you will hear the noise, smell the peanuts and cotton candy, see all the glitter and pageantry that make a circus so exciting. By allowing all your senses to respond you draw on your experience and make the poem richer for yourself and for your audience. You must recognize how these appeals work and allow yourself to let the whole experience flow through your senses, into your muscles.

We have already mentioned the close relationship of emotional response and muscle response in the discussion of empathy in Chapter 5. Empathy is a most valuable tool for the interpreter in the reading of poetry. It is the surest way to share the emotional experience of the poem with your audience. And it begins with full response of your senses and muscles.

Figures of Speech

Appeal to the senses is also the purpose of figures of speech. Five of the most common literary figures of speech are: the simile, the metaphor, personification, apostrophe, and allusion. All imply comparison.

The *simile* states that something is like something else. It may look, move, sound, smell, taste, or feel like something else. The sense appeals established by the first object are transferred to the second object or person.

There are two effective similes in the stanza from Byron's "The Destruction of Sennacherib" (see page 101): "The Assyrian came down like the wolf on the fold" and ". . . the sheen of their spears was like stars on the sea . . ."

A *metaphor* is like a simile in that it uses qualities of one object to describe another object. The difference is that while a simile says something is *like* something else, as in "Your eyes are like stars," a metaphor says something *is* something else, as "Your eyes are stars." They both serve the same purpose, that of comparing one thing with another. Often a whole poem will be an extended metaphor. This is true of "The End of the World," for example.

Personification is used when a writer takes an object or an abstraction, such as night or love or death, and endows it with human qualities. Personification is a form of comparison because a nonhuman object or abstraction is said *to be* a person, so that its appearance, action, and other qualities can be described in terms of sense imagery. There are many examples in Stafford's "Things That Happen Where There Aren't Any People" (page 106).

Apostrophe is closely related to personification. It is direct address to a personification, or to someone who is absent, or to an abstraction. A poet's use of apostrophe helps you get a clear image and firm mental focus.

Another literary figure of speech is *allusion.* We mentioned allusions earlier in the discussion of connotation (see page 37). The use of allusions may be a stumbling block to an easy comprehension of some poems. Literature is full of allusions to mythology, to historic people, events, and places. It is important to understand what qualities are implied by the allusion.

Langston Hughes uses allusions to several rivers which have been important in the history of the black race in "The Negro Speaks of Rivers" (see page 291). He begins with the Euphrates which some authorities believe to have been the cradle of early civilization, to the Congo deep in the African jungle, to the Nile where the blacks were slaves, and finally to the Mississippi and Abraham Lincoln. These allusions keep the poem unified and moving and underscore the historical progression of the race.

Activities

From the poems you selected to put in your file or from this book, choose one. Then, on paper, do the following:

1. Name the type of poem you selected, *narrative, dramatic,* or *lyric.*

2. Tell what the poem is about and what clues, if any, the title gave you.

3. List the words you needed to look up, along with their denotative and connotative meanings.

4. What kinds of sense imagery does the poet use? List them.

5. Has the poet used figures of speech? What kind or kinds and how have they been used?

Exchange your paper with a classmate. Study each other's poem and interpretation. Do you agree with each other's interpretation and analysis? Discuss.

The Sound Pattern of a Poem

Up to this point we have been concerned with finding the meaning of a poem. This includes its denotative meaning, its emotional content, its connotative implications as well as its universality and individuality. Now we will turn our attention to the structure or sound pattern of the poem, remembering that content and structure cannot really be separated and that both must work together for the total effect.

The study of the structure of poetry is called *prosody.* It is an extremely complex field. We will limit our consideration to the arrangement of light and heavier stresses within the lines, the length of line, rhyme (if the poet uses it), and the contribution to the sound pattern of vowels and consonants in adjacent words.

Within each line of traditional poetry there is a fairly consistent pattern of light and heavier stresses. For centuries these have been grouped into units and these units are known as feet. The light stresses are marked with ⌣ and the heavier stress with /. The most common feet are

iamb: marked ⌣ / — as in *within* (⌣ /)

trochee: marked / ⌣ — as in *spirit* (/ ⌣)

anapest: marked ⌣ ⌣ / — as in *intercede* (⌣ ⌣ /)

dactyl: marked / ⌣ ⌣ — as in *history* (/ ⌣ ⌣)

Four other types, not quite so common but often used in modern poetry, are

pyrrhic marked ⌣ ⌣ — as in *of the* (⌣ ⌣)

spondee marked / /   as in *hot day*

amphibrach marked ⌣ / ⌣   as in *occasion*

amphimacher marked / ⌣ /   as in *unprepared*

The marking of light and heavier stresses and then grouping them into the traditional feet is called *scansion.* Scansion deals exclusively with the syllables within the line. A foot and a word need not always end together. This is true in the opening lines of "End of the World" which would be marked

Quite un | expect | edly | as Vas | serot   (spondee, iamb, pyrrhic, iamb, iamb)

The arm | less am | bidex | trian | was lighting   (iamb, iamb, iamb, pyrrhic, amphibrach)

When you begin to put the poem back together the word as a unit is, of course, the important element. And when the words override the scansion it can produce a very interesting counter rhythm. You will notice in examining the poems in this book that poets often combine types of feet in a line and often let the words override but not completely cancel the scansion.

It is important for the interpreter to consider degree of stress. All syllables marked with / will not have the same weight of stress. For the interpreter, stress is influenced by the connotation and tone color of each word in its relation to the whole poem.

You scan a poem the way you know, from your analysis of logical and emotional content, it must be read to make it mean what it means the way it means it. You need to know what basic rhythm and what variations within it the poet has used as a guide to your own handling of that phase of the sound pattern. Do not try to force a poem into a preconceived pattern. Mark it as you find it. Scansion is not the whole poem. It is only one part of the important sound pattern. Marking the light and heavier stresses is a way of making the rhythmic contribution easy to see. It is worth the little while it takes and if it has been skillfully handled by the poet it will increase your respect for and confidence in the poem a great deal.

You as an interpreter are less interested in the names and characteristics of the traditional feet than in the arrangement of light and heavier stresses to increase tone color, support a section of rich emotional appeal, or point a climax or shift in mood. An awareness of the traditional feet is handy in making the overall rhythmic pattern graphic and calling attention to useful variations.

The simplest way to begin to scan is to mark all the words of more than one syllable as they must be stressed for proper pronunciation. *Within,* for example, cannot be pronounced *within,* nor *history, history.* Every syllable must be accounted for. Next select the one-syllable words which must be accented for the meaning and mood of the whole poem. Then put light stress marks on the less important words and un-accented syllables. Group the light and heavy stresses into the traditional feet. You will see a pattern begin to emerge. In traditional poetry there will be an identical or nearly identical number of feet in each line with a predominance of one of the types we have listed.

If no such significant pattern emerges you are probably dealing with free verse. You must then look elsewhere for the rhythmic basis. In free verse it is usually found in the number of syllables, not feet, in the lines, and/or in the number of stresses per line whether or not they will group easily into traditional feet. The line is a basic rhythmic unit within the sound pattern of the poem and must not be ignored.

Let's look at the scansion of "The End of the World" to see what effect the grouping of light and heavier stresses has on the manner in which you would read it for an audience.

The End of The World

Feet per line	Syllables per line	Stresses per line	
5	10	5	Quite un | expect | edly | as Vas | serot
5	11	4	The arm | less am | bidex | trian | was lighting
5	10	5	A match | between | his great | and se | cond toe
5	11	4	And Ralph | the li | on was | engaged | in biting
5	10	4	The neck | of Ma | dame Soss | man while | the drum
5	10	4	Pointed, | and Teen | y was | about | to cough
5	10	5	In waltz | time swing | ing Jock | o by | the thumb—
5	10	5	Quite un | expect | edly | the top | blew off:
5	11	8	And there, | there ov | erhead, there, | there, hung | over
5	10	5	Those thou | sands of | white fac | es, those | dazed eyes,
5	11	5	There in | the star | less dark, | the poise, | the hover,
5	10	6	There with | vast wings | across | the can | celed skies,
5	10	5	There in | the sud | den black | ness, the | black pall
5	11	5	Of noth | ing, noth | ing, noth | ing—noth | ing at all.

Length of Lines

In traditional poetry, the line length is measured by the number of feet it contains. A two-foot line is called dimeter, a three-foot line is trimeter, a four-foot line is tetrameter, a five-foot line is pentameter, and so forth. A glance at the numbers beside our scansion tells us "The End of the World" is in perfectly regular pentameter lines. Since it has fourteen such lines it is clearly a sonnet. This means that MacLeish has adhered strictly to a classic form and yet written a very modern poem. That is quite an achievement. This consistency of line length is a strong factor of unity in the sound pattern.

A modern poet may end the lines wherever he or she wishes. Look at some of the rest of the poems in this book and notice the wide variety of line lengths which are used. You take your cue from the poet. You always use some kind of a pause at the end of every line of poetry. But a word of caution before you take this rule at its face value. There are all kinds and lengths of pauses. Most poets indicate by punctuation what kind of pause should interrupt the flow of thought. This is not always a perfect guide because some poets have nearly as much trouble with commas as you and I.

The whole unit of thought may not be complete in each line. It is only complete at the end of the sentence. You will not use a terminal, end-of-the-thought pause until you reach the end of the thought.

"The End of the World" is one long sentence which does not complete its thought until the last three words. MacLeish does indicate a distinct pause—but not a terminal one—with the dash and colon at the ends of the seventh and eighth lines, and with three commas at line ends in the second stanza. But all the rest of the lines are what we call *enjambment* lines. The word is French and means one leg on either side, or straddling. The thought straddles the line end. Such a line is also sometimes called a run-on line, but that term indicates the interpreter runs full speed into the next line. Straddling is a more exact word for our purpose.

A well-written poem gives the interpreter a good reason for a slight pause where the thought straddles the lines. Sometimes the opportunity comes when a new characteristic is being added. Sometimes it comes from the need to stress tone color or emphasize sense appeals. Sometimes the first word on the next line needs to be pointed by a pause before it. In any case, trust your poet. There was a reason for ending the line where it ends.

Handling straddling lines requires a delicate touch, a sensitive mind, and a trained ear. These are the requisites of a skilled interpreter, and your ability to control the line-end pauses will increase as you practice. The audience should not be conscious of the division into lines as you read. They are not interested in how the poem is arranged. But the rhythm in the length of the lines is an important part of the sound pattern.

You will notice, too, that all but four of the lines of "The End of the World" have ten syllables. These four have eleven syllables which is the result of their feminine line endings. A feminine ending is one which ends on a light stress. It can help soften a rhyme or give a slight suggestion of insecurity like stepping on a step that is unexpected and more shallow than the others. MacLeish has spaced them carefully to accomplish both purposes without really interfering with the regularity of the meter. All four of them are double rhymes, that is the last *two* syllables agree, and thus profit subtly from the control of the added light stress.

We have said that all the lines have five feet but they do not all have five stresses. This is because the poet has used seven phyrric feet (⌣ ⌣) in the first stanza and two in the second. Moreover, the heavier stresses increase to eight right after the poem turns. The place that it turns, the end of the eighth line is called the fulcrum. And there are six heavier stresses just before the climax which begins in the thirteenth line. This is, of course, helpful in establishing the horror of the last stanza.

Notice, too, that the last line scans into four perfect iambs and one anapest, all of which would usually produce a rising meter. Every rising foot, however, is overridden by the fact that it ends in the middle of a word which will be more important as a unit when the poem is read aloud. Thus, the effect is one of a steady beat of falling meter until the last foot.

Rhyme

Rhyme is the correspondence of sounds in the final syllables of two or more lines of poetry. The pattern of rhyme sounds makes up the rhyme scheme. Patterns are indicated by the letters of the alphabet. The rhyme scheme of "The End of the World" would look like this:

a (Vasserot) (pronounced without the t: it is French)
b (lighting)
a (toe)
b (biting)
c (drum)
d (cough)
c (thumb)
d (off)
e (over)
f (eyes)
e (hover)
f (skies)
g (pall)
g (all)

This is a perfect rhyme scheme for the classic sonnet. Rhyme can be troublesome if the poet has not handled it skillfully. It is beautifully controlled here by the numerous straddle lines and adds a very subtle element of unity to the structure. Read the rhyme words aloud and you will discover that the "o" sound of the "a" rhyme is repeated in "over" and approximated (but not quite the same) in the "d" rhyme and in "hover." Your audience will not catch this but it is fun to discover. Your audience should not be acutely aware of rhyme any more than of any other single element of the poem. You must put it all back together so that they get a total effect rather than pieces of your analysis. But everything you find will make you more confident of the success of your poet. And the more successful your poet has been the more good things you have to work with.

Activity

Scan the following lines of poetry.

Little Fly,
Thy summer's play
My thoughtless hand
Has brushed away.

Am not I
A fly like thee?
Or art not thou
A man like me?

—Blake, from "The Fly"

The Assyrian came down like the wolf on the fold,
And his cohorts were gleaming in purple and gold;
And the sheen of their spears was like stars on the sea,
When the blue waves roll nightly on deep Galilee.

—Byron, from "The Destruction of Sennacherib"

Name the kind and of number of feet each is written in. Then determine the rhyme scheme of each selection. Then read the poem aloud. The strong rhythm set up by the scansion and the regular rhymes must gradually be brought under control so that they do not overwhelm the sense but rather support it. This will take several readings.

Tone Color

You may have read that certain combinations of sounds have specific associational effects on the hearer. This is not entirely true. You need only compare *sleep* and *slap* to be aware that the vowel change does not account for the whole difference in your response. Nevertheless, the way sounds are combined can be very helpful in bringing out all levels of association. Most authorities insist it is practically impossible to separate sound from connotation.

The manipulation of vowels and consonants to reinforce meaning and mood is called *tone color.* Tone color is a large term that embraces such technical matters as alliteration (repetition of the initial sound in two or more adjacent words, as *armless, ambidextrian*), onomatopoeia (a word whose sound imitates the object or action it refers to, as *sizzle*), assonance (agreement of vowel sounds), and consonance (agreement of consonant sounds).

Attention to tone color is of great help in varying the pace of your performance and giving you and your audience time to savor the sounds and understand the connotations and respond to the appeal to the senses. Tone color is part of the sound pattern, and its effect on the emotions is deliberate. Make full use of all combinations of sounds when you read the poem aloud. Rhyme can also contribute strongly to tone color.

In general, poetry should be read slower than other forms of writing, because it is so condensed and dependent on sound reinforcement for its full impact. Your diction must be especially good to read poetry aloud. Notice how the sounds help the imagery and the shock of the eighth line of "The End of the World," when you are careful to bring out the *p* and *b* of "top blew off." Poetry should feel good in the mouth as you say it. Take the time to pronounce all the sounds the poet used.

Content and structure work together to make the whole poem. For analysis they may be looked at separately but they must always be put back together. Otherwise, you do not have a poem. Trust your poet and use everything you are given to work with.

Selections for Interpretation

This brief, gentle poem has some interesting aspects of organization and structure that will help you. The mother is addressing the first seven lines to her child but also including us in the retelling of the incident. Make the lines in italics direct to the child and let them reflect the mother's point of view. She is clearly the persona here. After line seven, the poem is directed to us and the persona's point of view changes although it is still memory. The fulcrum begins on the seventh line from the end, creating an easy balance. The climax is on the line "—and it has, it has!" It must give us both the child's excitement and the mother's joy mixed with relief.

Civilizing the Child

by Lisel Mueller

You can't keep it, I say,
it will decay.
Bury the mouse, I tell her,
it will make the tulips redder,
give the trees babies,
fatten the faces of daisies,
put manes on the grass.
Spring comes up thick from the dead, I say,
broadcasting words like seeds
until she obeys, sadly,
with her green child's trowel.
And when she runs out the next morning
to see if the pink hawthorn
has an extra blossom or two
—and it has, it has!—
I go scot-free, acquitted
by her happiness-tinged cheeks,
my judges, my blind jury.

"Civilizing the Child" by Lisel Mueller. Originally appeared in POETRY, July 1967. Reprinted by permission of the author.

This poem seems to be one long, meandering sentence with the separate thoughts connected by "and." It is remembering. But it is carefully organized and the memories follow logically one after another. Use the line lengths carefully. Take your time. Let the rhythm of each line come through.

Nikki-Rosa
by Nikki Giovanni

childhood remembrances are always a drag
if you're Black
you always remember things like living in Woodlawn
with no inside toilet
and if you become famous or something
they never talk about how happy you were to have
your mother
all to yourself and
how good the water felt when you got your bath
from one of those
big tubs that folk in chicago barbecue in
and somehow when you talk about home
it never gets across how much you
understood their feelings
as the whole family attended meetings about Hollydale
and even though you remember
your biographers never understand
your father's pain as he sells his stock
and another dream goes
And though you're poor it isn't poverty that
concerns you
and though they fought a lot
it isn't your father's drinking that makes any difference
but only that everybody is together and you
and your sister have happy birthdays and very good
Christmasses
and I really hope no white person ever has cause
to write about me
because they never understand
Black love is Black wealth and they'll
probably talk about my hard childhood
and never understand that
all the while I was quite happy

This is a very modern love poem. It is filled with activity and imagery. Let empathy help you keep it alive and moving. Use the line lengths as the poet has given them to you. The pace slows somewhat as the couple go back to work. The next sentence contains both the fulcrum and the climax. The last two lines must carry enough emotional weight to balance all the activity of the earlier lines.

August Afternoon

by Nancy Remaly

I remember the August afternoon
we washed the seats
in the '66 bug
with buckets of water, soap, and brushes.
Feeling a little like Cinderella
I crawled in on my hands and knees
and started to scrub
while soapy dirt ran
down my arms and legs
and sweat dripped off my hair.
I threw water on you
and in return I got
a dripping wet cloth in my face:
the battle was on.
Grimy grey water splashed over us
as we chased each other
with sponges and brushes.
We went back to work
drenched and laughing
only to emerge an hour later
looking old and prunish.
Then, like Jack and Jill
we carried our buckets
back to the house
and on the way
you said thanks
I love you.

In all but five lines of this poem the thought goes on past the end of the line. This is not an accident. Don't read it like prose. A slight suspended pause at a line's end gives you a chance to set off the next phrase or image or clause. Two good examples of how these pauses are used are found in the first stanza where "finally goes down" and "flat on the mud" are made more graphic by having been put down on the next line. See all the images the poet uses. The speaker is alone and enjoying it.

Things That Happen Where There Aren't Any People

by William Stafford

It's cold on Lakeside Road
with no one traveling. At its turn
on the hill an old sign sags and
finally goes down. The traveler rain
walks back and forth over its victim
flat on the mud.

You don't have to have any people when
sunlight stands on the rocks or gloom
comes following the great dragged clouds
over the huddle of hills. Plenty of
things happen in deserted places, maybe
dust counting millions of its little worlds
or the slow arrival of deep dark.

And out there in the country a rock has been
waiting to be mentioned for thousands of years.
Every day its shadow leans, crouches,
then walks away eastward in one measured stride
exactly right for its way of being. To reach
for that rock we have the same reasons
that explorers always have for their journeys:
because it is far, because there aren't any people.

In 1837 some of the French-speaking inhabitants of the British province of Lower Canada (Quebec), calling themselves *Patriotes,* took up arms with the idea of establishing a French republic on the St. Lawrence River. At first successful, they were eventually defeated by the British. In "Beauharnois, Glengarry" Margaret Atwood uses an episode from 1838 to sum up the cycle of violence that has marked the relations between French and British in Canada. Beauharnois and Glengarry are two places near the St. Lawrence. In the poem the English Canadians are seen revenging themselves on French ones for the violence of the *Patriotes,* but the locale could be anywhere in these troubled days of invasions and destruction. Lines and stanzas as units of thought are important in suggesting the speaker's real attitude. Use them as they have been written.

Beauharnois, Glengarry

by Margaret Atwood

Those whose houses were burned
burned houses. What else ever happens
once you start?

While the roofs plunged
into the root-filled cellars,
they chased ducks, chickens, anything
they could catch, clubbed their heads
on rock, spitted them, singed off the feathers
in fires of blazing fences,
ate them in handfuls, charred
and bloody.

Sitting in the snow
in those mended plaids, rubbing their numb feet,
eating soot, still hungry,
they watched the houses die like
sunsets, like their own
houses. Again

those who gave the orders
were already somewhere else,
of course on horseback.

"Beauharnois, Glengarry" by Margaret Atwood, THE AMERICAN POETRY REVIEW, Sept.-Oct. 1979. Reprinted by permission of the poet.

Robinson Jeffers uses many short, abrupt clauses within the longer sentences in this poem. Some of the words and images are harsh and almost brutal. Use them to suggest the strength and wildness of the hawk. But they are tempered by lines of compassion. Let the final two lines soar. This is a strong poem.

Hurt Hawks

by Robinson Jeffers

I

The broken pillar of the wing jags from the clotted shoulder,
The wing trails like a banner in defeat,
No more to use the sky forever but live with famine
And pain a few days: cat nor coyote
Will shorten the week of waiting for death, there is game without talons.
He stands under the oak-bush and waits
The lame feet of salvation; at night he remembers freedom
And flies in a dream, the dawns ruin it.
He is strong and pain is worse to the strong, incapacity is worse.
The curs of the day come and torment him
At distance, no one but death the redeemer will humble that head,
The intrepid readiness, the terrible eyes.
The wild God of the world is sometimes merciful to those
That ask mercy, not often to the arrogant.
You do not know him, you communal people, or you have forgotten him;
Intemperate and savage, the hawk remembers him;
Beautiful and wild, the hawks, and men that are dying, remember him.

II

I'd sooner, except the penalties, kill a man than a hawk; but the great redtail
Had nothing left but unable misery
From the bone too shattered for mending, the wing that trailed under his talons
    when he moved.
We had fed him six weeks, I gave him freedom,
He wandered over the foreland hill and returned in the evening, asking for
    death,
Not like a beggar, still eyed with the old
Implacable arrogance. I gave him the lead gift in the twilight. What fell was
    relaxed,
Owl-downy, soft feminine feathers; but what
Soared: the fierce rush: the night-herons by the flooded river cried fear at its
    rising
Before it was quite unsheathed from reality.

This free verse poem is one single long sentence with no punctuation until the final period. That does not mean it all rushes together. The lines are important units of thought in themselves. Give yourself and your audience time to see and hear and feel the empathy of all the many images. The stanzas, too, form an interesting pattern in the organization. The first stanza focuses on animals primarily, the second on fruit and seeds, the third on flying things, and the fourth brings them all together. The last line stands by itself. Be sure you give it enough impact to balance all the details that lead up to it. Be careful that the repetitions at the beginning of lines does not become monotonous. Let the tone color operate fully. The rhythm shifts gently from four to five stresses per line. Let it come through.

because this is the way things are

by Norman H. Russell

a moose is lying down in a meadow
he is crushing some grasses and flowers
some small ants running out from under him
some birds nearby eating seeds
when he leaves the grasses will stand up
after a long time and the living ants
will carry the crushed dead ants away

some green fruits turning red on the bush
some birds come to feed upon them
dropping the seeds here and there in the grass
some lice in the feathers of the birds

in the night an owl flies crookedly
softly among the trees and some birds sleep
and over a great swamp clouds of mosquitoes
and many hungry bats

all the lives going along together
every life is a full life and it is completed
every moment it is completed or finished or over
every moment it begins all over again

because this is the way things are.

"White Pass Ski Patrol" is loaded with kinetic and visual imagery. It will engage all your muscles to build the excitement of the activity and allow for the quieter moments such as those in the third and fourth stanzas. They are important for variety and to give us a chance to build into the wonderful activity of the rest of the poem. The last stanza is strongly visual but full of kinesthetic imagery as we watch the skier soar away leaving us on the ground.

White Pass Ski Patrol
by John Logan

His high-boned, young face is so brown
from the winter's sun,
the few brief lines in each green eye's
edge as of a leaf
that is not yet gone from the limb—
as of a nut which is gold or brown.

For he has become very strong
living on the slopes.
His belly and thighs are newly
lean from the thin skis.
Tough torso of the man, blue wooled.
Thin waist. White, tasseled cap of the child.

Beneath the fury of those great,
dark panes of glass, that
seem to take a man out of grace,
his gentle eyes wait.
(We feel their melancholy gaze
which is neither innocent nor wise.)

Like those knights of the winter snows—
with a healing pack
(sign of the cross on breast and back)—
serene, snow-lonely,
he patrols the beautiful peaks
and the pale wastes that slide like a beast.

Sometimes still blind from his patrol,
you'll see him pull down
from the dangerous Cascades his
heavy sledge of pain,
its odd, black-booted, canvas-laced
shape alive or dead, without a face.

Colors blooming in the sun, he
caroms down his own
path, speeds (bending knees), dances side
to side, balancing.
Under-skis glow golden in the
snow spume around his Christiana.

And as he lifts away from us,
skis dangle like the
outstretched limbs of a frog in spring.
He swings gently in
the air, vulnerable, so much
the "poor, bare, forked" human animal.

And now he slowly rises up
over trees and snow.
He begins to grow more thin, and then
vanishes in air!
as, high in the lithe boughs of pines,
the silver leaves flake silently down.

There are the shadow tracks he left
down the long, white hill
beside the lift. Wait! Look up! Cloud
trails in the bright sky!
Breathing a wake of snow ribbons,
something has just flown over the mountain!

Phyllis McGinley gives us a wealth of detailed description of many tiny delicate objects. Keep them all together in the concept of the doll house. When the restoration of the doll house has been completed (at the end of the twenty-sixth line), the woman's thoughts turn to the contemplation of this object out of the past which will now be preserved in all its quiet perfection—all her own now. The fulcrum comes on the first single line stanza. Immediately we are returned to a myriad of details but the woman's attitude changes somewhat. The experience may have come out of the poet's own life but she uses the third person to relate it. The second single/stanza line is from Keats's "Ode on a Grecian Urn" and it refers to the lovers and the musicians who play for them in the frieze on the urn. They will be "forever young" and never know the human passion that leaves ". . . a heart high-sorrowful and cloyed." Notice, too, that it, like the fulcrum, is set off by itself.

The Doll House

by Phyllis McGinley

After the children left it, after it stood
For a while in the attic,
Along with the badminton set, and the skis too good
To be given away, and the Peerless Automatic
Popcorn Machine that used to fly into rages,
And the Dr. Dolittle books, and the hamsters' cages,
She brought it down once more
To a bedroom, empty now, on the second floor
And put the furniture in.
There was nothing much
That couldn't be used again with a bit of repair.
It was all there,
Perfect and little and inviolate.
So, with the delicate touch
A jeweler learns, she mended the rocking chair,
Meticulously laundered
The gossamer parlor curtains, dusted the grate,
Glued the glazed turkey to the flowered plate,
And polished the Lilliput writing desk.
She squandered
One bold October day and half the night
Binding the carpets round with a ribbon border;

Till, to her grave delight
(With the kettle upon the stove, the mirror's face
Scoured, the formal sofa set in its place),
She saw the dwelling decorous and in order.

It was a good house. It had been artfully built
By an idle carpenter once, when the times were duller.
The windows opened and closed. The knocker was gilt.
And every room was painted a suitable color
Or papered to scale
For the sake of the miniature Adam and Chippendale.
And there were proper hallways,
Closets, lights, and a staircase. (What had always
Pleased her most
Was the tiny, exact, mahogany newel post.)
And always, too, wryly she thought to herself,
Absently pinning
A drapery's pleat, smoothing a cupboard shelf—
Always, from the beginning,
This outcome had been clear. Ah! She had known
Since the first clapboard was fitted, first rafter hung
(Yet not till now had known that she had known),
This was no daughters' fortune but her own—
Something cautiously lent to the careless young
To dazzle their cronies with for a handful of years
Till the season came
When their toys diminished to programs and souvenirs,
To tousled orchids, diaries well in arrears,
Anonymous snapshots stuck round a mirror frame,
Or letters locked away.
Now seed of the past
Had fearfully flowered. Wholly her gift at last,
Here was her private estate, a peculiar treasure
Cut to her fancy's measure.
Now there was none to trespass, no one to mock
The extravagance of her sewing or her spending
(The tablecloth stitched out of lace, the grandfather's clock,
Stately upon the landing,
With its hands eternally pointing to ten past five).

Now all would thrive.

continued

Over this house, most tranquil and complete,
Where no storm ever beat,
Whose innocent stair
No messenger ever climbed on quickened feet
With tidings either of rapture or of despair,
She was sole mistress. Through the panes she was able
To peer at her world reduced to the size of dream
But pure and unaltering.
                    There stood the dinner table,
Invincibly agleam
With the undisheveled candles, the flowers that bloomed
Forever and forever,
The wine that never
Spilled on the cloth or sickened or was consumed.

The *Times* lay at the doorsill, but it told
Daily the same unstirring report. The fire
Painted upon the hearth would not turn cold,
Or the constant hour change, or the heart tire
Of what it must pursue,
Or the guest depart, or anything here be old.

"Nor ever," she whispered, "bid the spring adieu."

And caught into this web of quietnesses
Where there was neither After nor Before,
She reached her hand to stroke the unwithering grasses
Beside the small and incorruptible door.

R. G. Vliet gives us a most detailed description of Mrs. McElroy and her house and her activities. The persona is a grown man remembering his boyhood experience. The fulcrum comes in the last four lines of the poem and you will need to be careful of balance. She was not his mother and certainly not his bride although he refers to her as both, but she obviously drew from him a special kind of enduring love and understanding. The persona acts as a kind of "camera's eye," but he has a special relationship with what he pictures for us.

Mrs. McElroy

by R. G. Vliet

The front room was always closed:
the half-pulled
shades, the listening furniture, old
novels, Latin School Cicero, lace
tea-brown
curtains waiting in the still air.

In the parlor she put another chunk
in the cast
iron stove, then sat in her rocker
with the tatted throw, among heaps
of *Christian*
Science Sentinels and *Monitors,* in company

with the pain in her hip, the constant witness
of pain
in her long hand bones: angels
of error she had daily to wrestle with.
She wore
white drawstring cap, long

blue cotton dress with flat
white
collar and white cuffs, black
apron. A cane hung from her chair.
I never saw
the ankles of her cricket-dark shoes.

continued

Her husband had been translated years ago.
A rose-wreathed
saucer sat on the table beside me
with its twice-weekly offering of apple
brown
betty. Before I split the kindling

we visited, she in the loneliness
of dwindling
time, I in the pain of a boy's
eternal present. The slop bucket
conjectured
by the kitchen door. Mrs. McElroy

hobbled through the yard, her cane
touching
this chore and that chore: slops
to be poured, mulch turned, thinning
of a strawberry
bed, tying up of brambles.

Under the mulberries, red stains
and bird
droppings. April, asparagus. Cuttings
of rhubarb thick as my wrist. Raspberries.
Loganberries.
In August I fought starlings for bushels

of bing cherries, fistfuls of damsons
for her tart
jellies. The sun still shines that shone
on her. Since then, my dear one, my mother
and my bride,
I have loved the struggling aged.

Theodore Roethke grew up in the Midwest. His father owned a large commercial greenhouse which became for the young boy a place of refuge and security. Greenhouse images and flower and root motifs run through almost all of his poems. The first half of the poem is full of frantic activity as they battle the storm. The long sentences help add to the sense of urgency and the short lines within them must be used faithfully as the poet has used them. After the fulcrum, which comes slightly after the first half of the poem, the humans, having done what they could, are not mentioned again and we give our full attention to the old rose-house which takes on strong characteristics of its own. The climax in the last two lines must receive a strong lift to retain the balance with all the details and action of the rest of the poem. Roethke is famous for his use of tone color. Let it help you support the imagery.

Big Wind
by Theodore Roethke

Where were the greenhouses going,
Lunging into the lashing
Wind driving water
So far down the river
All the faucets stopped?—
So we drained the manure-machine
For the steam plant,
Pumping the stale mixture
Into the rusty boilers,
Watching the pressure gauge
Waver over to red,
As the seams hissed
And the live steam
Drove to the far
End of the rose-house,
Where the worst wind was,
Creaking the cypress window-frames,
Cracking so much thin glass
We stayed all night,
Stuffing the holes with burlap;
But she rode it out,
That old rose-house,
She hove into the teeth of it,
The core and pith of that ugly storm,
Ploughing with her stiff prow,
Bucking into the wind-waves
That broke over the whole of her,
Flailing her sides with spray,
Flinging long strings of wet across the roof-top,
Finally veering, wearing themselves out, merely
Whistling thinly under the wind-vents;
She sailed until the calm morning,
Carrying her full cargo of roses.

Unit III
The Performer's Craft

CHAPTER 8
Sensory Imagination

CHAPTER 9
Characterization

CHAPTER 10
Working with Other Actors

CHAPTER 11
Stage Presence

CHAPTER 12
Working with the Script
Scenes for Acting Practice

To create a characterization and to successfully communicate it to an audience, performers must be skilled in three basic areas. First, they must make the best use of their bodies, in voice, gesture, and movement. This requires physical fitness, control, and practice in movement and relaxation. Many performers compare themselves to musicians, calling this part of training "learning the instrument."

Second, performers must train their imaginations in order to express imaginary characters in imaginary situations within imaginary worlds. To keep the imagination stretching, growing, and open to new situations also requires practice and exercise.

Finally, to perform the text, performers must develop and sharpen their analytical skills. They must study their material so that they know just what it is that they need to express with their bodies and with their imaginations.

You have already been introduced to these skills in earlier chapters. Unit I dealt with the imagination and the body, introducing some basic concepts about scenes and relationships between characters. Unit II built on these concepts and introduced the analytical skills used in the interpreter's performance. In this unit, you will find additional exercises and practice material, but as they apply to the actor's performance in a play. The skills overlap. Do not assume that because you are now acting you can forget about pantomime and interpretation skills.

Professional actors and actresses who have acted for years study with private teachers or in group classes, repeating regular exercises to "tune" their body, to enlarge their imagination, and to further develop their analytical skills. In general, you should go back to earlier chapters regularly, repeating the exercises and reviewing the ideas. The actor, like the musician, the dancer, or the athlete must constantly practice to stay in shape.

Several scenes at the end of this unit provide an opportunity to practice various skills. The short introduction to each scene tells something about the characters and the basic situation. Be sure to read them carefully before you start work on the scenes.

Chapter 8
Sensory Imagination

The actor works in an imaginary world, using his or her own imagination to make that world seem real to an audience. Everything on the stage is imaginary even when there are real props. The walls may look like walls but they are really scenery. You may look up to where there ought to be a wall and see several hundred people staring at you. You will pick up an empty glass that is supposed to be full of water or eat a sandwich consisting of bread alone. You will "read" letters from blank pieces of paper and scribble nonsense as if in reply. You will do hundreds of things that must look normal and realistic to an audience but which, for very practical reasons, are never absolutely real to you. To produce the sensations of an experience for yourself, as well as for the audience, requires an intensive use of your imagination.

Anything you experience during a day may become a part of a play performance. Think of all the items you pick up and put down, the things you see and hear, the places you are in, the tastes and smells you come in contact with. Be aware of the world around you. All experiences are useful in performance.

The following exercises will help you develop your imagination. Concentrate as you work on them. As you try to reproduce some particular sensation, try to remember when you did something similar in real life and remember the sensations you had then. What did things really look and feel like? Do not worry about *performing* these activities. They are not performances. Even if you are working on them in class or with a group, they are really happening inside your imagination. If you can reproduce the feelings and the sensations the activities suggest, your actions will be natural.

If you are working on the activities in class, the teacher or other students will offer criticism. For example, if you are working with a cup, someone may comment that the cup doesn't look full. To correct that, imagine the feel of a heavier cup. If you can do that, then that weight will be visible to the audience and you have created the appearance of reality.

Activities

Touch

1. Imagine that your hand and part of your arm are inside a small aquarium. Move your hand around in the tank and try to feel the following things, each in turn, filling or partly filling the tank: **(a)** water **(b)** jelly **(c)** peanuts **(d)** peanut butter **(e)** paint **(f)** mud.

2. Lay a piece of paper on the table or floor in front of you. Touch it and notice how the paper feels; rub the paper to get the full sensation. Continuing to touch and rub the paper, imagine that the paper changes to: **(a)** fur **(b)** velvet **(c)** cotton **(d)** concrete **(e)** wood **(f)** leather.

3. Select a number of real props—food, small tools, jewelry, and so forth. Arrange them on a table in front of you. Close your eyes and pick up each item. Feel it; hold it; experience all the sensations you can about each one.

4. With your eyes still closed, only pretend to pick up each item you arranged for the previous activity. Try to imagine exactly the same sensations of weight, size, and texture as when you held the real items.

5. While your eyes are closed, have a partner place a number of small and unusual items in front of you. Without opening your eyes, try to identify each item by touch alone.

6. Touch the door. Imagine that there is a fire on the other side; feel the door heating up gradually until finally it is too hot to touch. Imagine that it is winter outside and a blizzard has begun; feel the door getting colder.

Taste

7. With a real but empty cup, imagine that you are drinking each of the following liquids. Imagine the taste as you drink: **(a)** cola **(b)** water **(c)** ice-cold water **(d)** coffee **(e)** grapefruit juice **(f)** milk **(g)** buttermilk.

8. Imagine that you are eating the following foods. Concentrate on a single bite of each food. Try to duplicate all the tastes and feelings of chewing, tasting, and swallowing that one bite of food: **(a)** fried egg **(b)** hamburger **(c)** cheese sandwich **(d)** baked potato **(e)** turkey **(f)** gelatin **(g)** chocolate pie **(h)** pizza **(i)** nuts **(j)** orange **(k)** broccoli.

Place

9. Choose a place—your room, the lawn, an office—and sit there quietly with your eyes closed. Stay that way for at least five minutes and listen to all the sounds of the place. Try to hear everything going on around you. Notice how many different sounds there are to which most of us pay no attention.

10. Think of a favorite place and try to describe it as completely as possible. Include every detail you can remember about sizes and shapes and colors and textures. Try this again, but close your eyes and try to visualize the place before you start your description of it. In your imagination, try to duplicate what you saw and did in that place.

11. Recall a place different from the one you recalled before, but imagine that you are actually there. Do something that you did while you were there and see how this helps you remember other details of the experience. If you are remembering the beach, for example, spread a towel or blanket, lie in the sun, eat a hot dog, and so on. Use these actions to help your senses remember the experience.

12. Make an imaginary place and do several normal activities there. For example, imagine a kitchen and do the dishes; be sure that you try to see each dish as well as the cabinets and counters and touch each imaginary item as if it were really there. Imagine that the classroom is a room in your home and do what you would do there; treat the space as if it were really surrounding you and react to that imaginary room.

13. With a partner, go on an imaginary picnic. Make an imaginary place that includes a tree, a stream, a large rock, and lots of grass, as well as any other things you would like to include. Share the experience of the place so that both partners sense the sights, sounds, and feelings of the place.

Movement

14. Walk into an imaginary windstorm. Feel the wind pushing against you.

15. Walk around the room barefooted; imagine that you are wearing heavy boots. Walk around with imaginary shoes that are too big and then with shoes that are too tight. How do the too-tight shoes feel? How does that feeling affect all the rest of your body?

16. Go for an imaginary walk in each of the following places: **(a)** through mud puddles **(b)** on a sidewalk **(c)** on a lawn just after a rain **(d)** in a stream **(e)** over a pile of gravel **(f)** on a beach **(g)** on a newly waxed floor **(h)** on a thick carpet. How do each of these feel to your whole body as you move?

17. Imagine that you are in a room alone. Slowly the ceiling begins to move down toward you, threatening to crush you. Try to hold it back. Feel it pushing against you.

18. Imagine you are in a room and the walls begin to close in on you. Try to push them back. Feel them pressing against you as you resist.

19. Walk through a giant aquarium filled with each of the following substances. (Assume that you can always breathe, no matter what the material is.) Try to

feel the substance completely surrounding you and react to it with your entire body as you try to walk through it: **(a)** water **(b)** Ping-Pong balls **(c)** feathers **(d)** mud **(e)** grease **(f)** sand **(g)** gravel **(h)** newspaper wadded up in balls.

20. Walk, sit, stand, pick up a cup and drink from it, put the cup down, and walk out of the room while pretending to wear each of the following items of clothing: **(a)** a heavy winter coat **(b)** fur-lined gloves **(c)** gym clothes **(d)** a business suit or dress **(e)** a tuxedo or evening gown **(f)** a suit of armor **(g)** a spacesuit.

21. Do each of the following and react to the situation. Make your movement a reaction to a specific event which you see and feel in your imagination. Do not generalize.

- **(a)** tie your shoe; the lace breaks
- **(b)** burn yourself picking up a pan
- **(c)** take a shower; the hot water suddenly goes off
- **(d)** spill a cup of coffee in your lap
- **(e)** spill a glass of something on someone else's lap
- **(f)** carry your books in a bag or pack; the bottom splits open
- **(g)** sleep until you hear the alarm ring
- **(h)** trip over something while walking along the sidewalk
- **(i)** enter a room and hear a suspicious rip
- **(j)** watch your favorite TV program; the phone rings
- **(k)** read a book and hear a faucet dripping
- **(l)** eat a piece of cake and find an insect in it

22. Pretend you have a baseball. Feel it; understand its shape and size and hold it so you sense it. Toss it up and down, catching it each time. Try to feel it leaving your hand and making contact when it returns. Change it to a tennis ball and do the same thing. Bounce the ball off a wall and catch it. Make the throws and catches real to yourself.

23. With a partner, play catch with an imaginary ball. Try it with each of the following kinds of balls, giving each a specific size, shape, and weight which you both share: **(a)** baseball **(b)** softball **(c)** basketball **(d)** volleyball **(e)** beach ball **(f)** bowling ball **(g)** medicine ball **(h)** Ping-Pong ball.

24. Try to perform each of the imaginary situations while imagining the obstacles in the way.

- **(a)** Walk a tightrope to escape from a gang chasing you.
- **(b)** Improvise a scene with your partner and talk with your mouth full of imaginary food.
- **(c)** Your brother or sister has locked you out of your room. You try to get past the imaginary door to prevent the child from disturbing your possessions.
- **(d)** See an old friend across a busy street and try to get to him or her before he or she is out of sight.
- **(e)** Try to talk to a friend at a party with the stereo turned up to full volume.
- **(f)** Try to get a partner to tell you a secret whi you are riding a roller coaster.

Chapter 9
Characterization

Every actor in a play performance plays a character. Each performer is, at one and the same time, two people—himself and an imaginary person in the play. Making and sustaining this second other person so that he or she is acceptable and believable to the audience, while still remaining oneself, is one of the most complicated things required of an actor. It takes a great deal of thought, practice, rehearsal, planning, and imagination. It never happens easily, no matter how experienced an actor one may become. But in play production nothing works without the consistent, clear development of the characters. That is what plays are about: characters who interact and react with other characters.

You will remember that in Unit II we said that up to a point the interpreter and the actor follow almost identical steps in analysis and preparation—that it is in the exterior aspects that differences appear. The interpreter begins to eliminate physical explicitness, refining gestures to suggest underlying tensions. As the actor approaches performance, he adds exterior details to make his characterizations physically explicit.

One of the first problems in establishing a characterization is that the term *character* means different things to different people. First, a character in a play is simply one of the imaginary persons of the play, just as in a novel or short story. But each character in that play also *has* a character. That is where terminology begins to confuse. For instance, when people say "he's a real character," they usually mean the person is odd or unusual. If they say, "he really has character," they usually mean the person is honest, upright, moral, and self-sufficient. In the theater, we usually use the word *character* to mean the kind of personality a character has.

The most important thing to remember about each of the following concepts and activities is that character or personality must be revealed to the audience. One of the actor's jobs is to make the personality visible so that other people can see and understand it.

You see your own personality in the way you think and feel about yourself and the world. Other people see your personality in terms of what you say, what you do, and *how* you do and say those things. People evaluate your appearances and expressions. They evaluate your tone of voice and the attitudes you express. From these impressions and evaluations they interpret or "guess at" what you are thinking and feeling inside. Sometimes they are right, sometimes wrong. They are probably wrong more often than they are right. The goal of the actor is to use all of those outer characteristics in a way that helps the audience understand the inner character.

First Impressions and Stereotypes

Most people make a judgment about the personalities of others during the first moments after they meet. Audiences make the same judgments. If people have time to get to know the person they've just met, they often find that their first impressions were in some way wrong. In a good play performance, the audience should learn the same thing. The character will make a first impression; but as he or she stays on stage the audience should learn enough about the character to change that first impression.

Actors need to understand that first impression and then to use it as the play develops so that they can add subtlety and reality to the performance.

In general, first impressions are based on stereotypes or character types. These groups or categories are very general—teenagers, businessmen, school teachers, for example. And most people have a clear idea of what a "typical" member of each of these groups is like. Most people even have a stereotypical view of certain types of teenagers or businessmen or school teachers. For example, in many people's minds, teenagers are divided into subcategories such as cheerleaders, jocks, bookworms, delinquents, and so on. While it is necessary to get beyond stereotypical views if one is to develop a personal relationship, an actor can use stereotypes to help make his performance understood. The goal, however, is to always go beyond the stereotype, to play a *specific* member of a group rather than a *typical* member of a group. Each role should be unique. If it is not, then there is a serious failure in either the play or the actor, or both.

Most characterizations begin with generalities drawn from stereotypes. Costume, makeup, and basic movement and gesture begin, as well, from the typical. A good way to approach your own preparation, however, is to ask what the limits of the character are. If you are asked to play a father who is also a banker, you probably have some preconceived idea of what a banker is like. Ask yourself what the banker probably would *not* look like or act like. He would probably not wear shoulder-length hair or go barefooted or say "ya know."

Another important point to remember is that while you are making an impression on the audience, the character is also making an impression on the people in the imaginary world of the play. Ask yourself how this person wants the other characters to see him. What kind of image or what kind of personality does he or she want to project? Answering these questions will help you move from the stereotype to the individual.

Activities

1. Improvise a scene in which you are interviewing for a job. Have a partner be the employer who will interview you. Before you begin, ask yourself what impression you wish to make. Then in a short scene try to convince the employer to hire you. Apply for the different jobs listed below, asking yourself how you would change your image for each position.

Assume in every scene that you already have the proper education and experience. Whether you get the job or not will depend only on whether you make a "good" impression during the interview.

If you are playing the employer in the scene, be sure you know what you want to see in each interviewee before you start. **(a)** Bank Manager **(b)** Mechanic **(c)** Grocery Clerk **(d)** Race Car Driver **(e)** Elementary School Teacher **(f)** Salesperson **(g)** Factory Foreman.

How did you change or try to change the impression you made as you applied for each different job?

2. One of the most interesting ways to approach a role is to "play against type." This means that the actor as character does the opposite of what people would normally expect the character to do. Select one of the following character types and improvise a scene in which your partner plays himself or herself and is asking you for a favor. The first time through, react to that request as a typical character of that type might react. Then do the scene a second time, playing against the type. **(a)** Sweet Old Lady or Gentleman **(b)** Boy Scout or Girl Scout **(c)** Busy Businessman or Businesswoman **(d)** Garage Mechanic **(e)** Bratty Little Kid **(f)** Waiter **(g)** Miser.

3. A useful way to develop a set of habits or mannerisms that will suggest a character's personality to the audience is to compare the character to an animal. In this exercise, partners should first play different animals in improvised scenes. The animals can talk and speak English as well as make their own animal noises, but both partners should concentrate on playing the animal.

Then play the scene a second time as human beings whose personalities are somewhat *like* that of the particular animal. Adapt the animal attitudes and gestures to human traits so that the character *suggests* the animal.

The scene may be about any topic you and your partner agree on but should be essentially the same both times you play it. Concentrate on making the animal vivid in the first version; in the second version, concentrate on making the character clearly human. Think of voice and speaking patterns as well as physical mannerisms while you are performing.

Try the scene with both of you as the same animal. Look for variations in the portrayal of the animal, even though each partner is using the same basic material. **(a)** fox **(b)** small bird (sparrow, hummingbird, etc.) **(c)** large bird (hawk, buzzard, eagle, etc.) **(d)** bear **(e)** deer **(f)** squirrel **(g)** lion **(h)** dog (be specific as to what breed of dog you are portraying).

Objectives and Obstacles

As you learned in the improvisation chapter, a scene becomes dramatic when the objective of the character meets an obstacle that blocks that objective. What

the character does to get around the obstacle not only makes the plot of the play, it also communicates to the audience much about the personality of the character. The kinds of actions the character chooses to take, the kinds of ideas that occur to him, or the methods he uses to gain his objective all clearly show his personality.

In most plays a character's reactions to obstacles are revealed in the script. What the playwright will not tell you, however, is exactly *how* you should express those reactions. When you begin to work on a characterization, think not only of the obstacles the character must overcome and what he must do to gain his objectives, but also ask yourself why one particular idea and not another occurs to the character. Then react to each obstacle in a specific way so that the personality behind the reaction becomes clear.

Working with the concept of objectives and obstacles is also useful for the physical problems many actors face in building a characterization. Many times you will be asked to build a character who is physically different from yourself. Costume and makeup will help change your outward appearance, but you must change your gestures and body movement as well.

You may be asked to play someone who is older or younger than you are. Observe people you know who are the age you need to play. Watch how they move, how they walk, how they hold their bodies when they stand or sit. Then go one step further.

Assume that everyone would stand and walk in the same way if everyone's body worked in the same way. But for many differing reasons each person's body works in a slightly different way from every other person's. Each person's body presents a set of obstacles to the full and easy movement of all parts of the body. Those obstacles—age, illness, weight, height, genetic variations—among many others, block certain ways of doing things and force the person to move in certain ways to overcome the obstacles.

When observing people who are older, for use in a characterization, ask yourself what causes them to move in the ways they do. For example, some old people walk with shorter, slower steps than you do. Try to duplicate it in your performance. First, ask yourself why old people take smaller, shorter steps. If you are observant, you will see that, as the body grows older, many people's joints stiffen—perhaps from arthritis. Once you realize that the short steps are the result of an obstacle—the stiff joints that block leg movement—playing the age becomes easier. Use your imagination to make the obstacle, and then react to that obstacle. Apply this principle to any physical characteristic you might need for a role.

What makes a very old person's hand shake, for example? Imagine the obstacles that keep the person from holding the hand steady instead of trying to make your hand shake to show how old the character is.

This approach works whenever you have to exaggerate some physical characteristic, whether in comedies or very serious roles. If you play a giant in a children's play, imagine what the enormous arms and legs weigh and how far they are from the brain, and react to those obstacles. If the body is deformed, as was Richard III's, imagine how his humpback would get in the way of "normal" movement and then play the character trying to move like everybody else but whose movement is being blocked by the awkward lump.

If you are playing characters with illnesses, think of the cause rather than playing the symptoms. If the character sprains an ankle, think about the pain when that foot touches the ground, rather than the limp. A person with a sprain is not trying to limp; he is trying to walk, but the sprain keeps getting in the way.

Even vocal habits or voice changes can be approached in this way. If the character is hoarse, what makes him hoarse? If the voice shakes, what makes it shaky? What is blocking normal speech? Concentrate on the obstacle and then react to that obstacle. Remember that most people try to move and speak like everyone else. They do not try to limp or shake or stagger any more than they try to catch a cold. If something blocks their "normal" actions, they try to overcome that obstacle. The actor who portrays them should try to do the same thing.

Activities

1. Lie on the floor in a comfortable, relaxed position. Close your eyes to help you concentrate. Imagine a heavy weight placed on your chest. Try to breathe normally even though the weight keeps pushing on you. Try to sit up, reacting to the pressure of the weight.

Imagine that the weight is shifted from your chest to both wrists. Try to wave to someone. Open your eyes and stand, remembering the weights on your wrists. Try to do a simple activity, such as getting a drink of water or sharpening a pencil with these weights in place.

2. Perform a simple household activity, such as setting the table or putting a record on the stereo. As you are doing this, have a partner watch and signal at random times. Each time the partner signals, imagine that you lose nerve contact with your fingers for five seconds. Try to continue the activity as if nothing were wrong.

Do this with unbreakable props. Be sure to react immediately when your partner signals.

3. Read the scene from *Meet Me in St. Louis* on page 156. Each person in the scene is a member of a typical family, yet each person is quite different in character. In this scene, each person has a completely different objective. Mr. Smith wants to go to New York; except for Agnes, who changes her mind during the scene, the women do not. Each woman is opposed to the move for a different reason. Find an objective for each woman, something she wishes to accomplish by staying in St. Louis. Perform the scene.

As you rehearse and perform, ask yourself how the objective reacts to the obstacle (Father's wish to move). How does your objective affect the way you actually say your lines and play the scene? What does this objective show about the personality of your character?

"If"

A character in a play is a person in an imaginary world. As a person, the character experiences the same feelings that other people do. Each individual uses, responds to, and shows those feelings in different ways and at different times, but everyone builds from the same materials. If your performance is limited to playing only a stereotype, the character is like a machine, not a person. The actor's goal is to go beyond the machine and to find the person inside, to make each character an imaginary *person.*

One way to achieve that goal is to ask yourself, "What would I do if . . . ?" If you were a king, what would you do if someone tried to assassinate you? What would you do if you were a parent and your son refused to come home at night? And so on. This is especially helpful in improvisations. Whenever you use it, concentrate on making a real, genuine, personal response to the situation.

In a play, the playwright has answered that question; he has decided what the character will do in a certain situation. Thus, once you start dealing with a complete play, a better question to ask is, "What would I feel if this were really happening?" For example, in thinking about the scene from *Meet Me in St. Louis,* which you have already worked on, ask yourself how you would feel if you went home today and your parents told you you were moving to another city next week. You would probably feel a number of different emotions, all at the same time—confusion, fear of the new place, worry about the future, sorrow at loss of your friends, relief at escaping your enemies, hope for better things, anger that your parents didn't ask your opinion first—and a number of other feelings as well. One or two of the emotions will be stronger than the others because of your own personal experience and situation.

The same thing happens to the characters in the play. In this particular scene, everyone feels most of these same emotions, even Mr. Smith. But for each character, one or two feelings are stronger than the others, and are the ones that the character shows most clearly. For your own characterization, find the dominant emotion among the many emotions you experienced when you asked "if . . . ," and build your action on that emotion. Make the experience genuine. If the character's primary feeling is anger, ask how that anger feels inside you. What does it do to the muscles in your face, your neck, your arms? What does it do to your stomach? What does it make you want to do? Then try to duplicate those physical obstacles and objectives in the performance itself.

If the character you play is either very much like you or very much different from you, it may be dangerous to ask, "What would *I* do if . . . ," or "What would *I* feel if . . . ." It is very easy to forget that your goal is to find your own relationships to the character so that you can play the character more fully. If you forget your goal, you change the character into yourself and lose the play completely.

It is often unproductive for the student to ask, "What would I do. . . if," or "What would the character do. . . if?" because the playwright has already decided that. In performing, the more valuable question is to approach the scene from the other direction: "What if the person on stage with me is not an actor but is really doing this thing?"

Activities

1. Imagine yourself in each of the following situations. Ask "What would I do if . . . ?" for each one. Play out the situation and experience it completely. What happens to your nerves, your muscles, your thoughts, your voice, your feelings? Make all of these things clear to yourself.

This is a difficult exercise because it is easy to fall into doing what everyone expects to see, especially if you work on it in class. Do not try to make a scene or to play to or for an audience. Especially do not try to *be* anything—avoid being scared, or happy, or funny, or sad, or whatever. Try to place yourself in the imaginary situation and focus all your concentration on that experience. Use your imagination to supply as many details about the experience as possible.

What would I do if . . .

- **(a)** I were walking down the street and heard an ambulance behind me?
- **(b)** I heard my parents talking about Christmas presents in the next room?
- **(c)** my car broke down twenty miles from the nearest town?
- **(d)** I found a fly in my soft-drink bottle?
- **(e)** I found a note from my girlfriend or boyfriend addressed to someone else?
- **(f)** I were alone in the house at night and heard a strange noise?
- **(g)** I met my six-month-old nephew for the first time?
- **(h)** I saw a friend commit a crime?
- **(i)** I won a prize in a contest?

2. With a partner, improvise a scene in which you are trying to do some simple job, something you might do around the house or at school. You must both work together on the same job. Both of you have the same objective, which is to finish the job, but have your partner concentrate on being him or herself while you assume something unusual about him or her. Do not tell your partner what it is you are assuming. Concentrate on reacting to the character you *imagine* your partner to be.

What if I am doing a job and my partner is . . . **(a)** incredibly stupid? **(b)** incredibly smart? **(c)** incredibly handsome or beautiful? **(d)** incredibly ugly? **(e)** incredibly boring? **(f)** incredibly lovable? **(g)** incredibly evil? **(h)** incredibly dangerous? **(i)** incredibly rich? **(j)** incredibly poor?

What did you reveal about character by your reactions to this imaginary person?

3. The following scene is very short and can be memorized very quickly. Play the scene with each of the different characters listed below the practice scene. Consider how the choice of character relationships affects the meaning of the scene.

Practice Scene 1

A. Don't you like me?
B. What do you mean?
A. You know.
B. Why do you want to know?
A. Why won't you tell me?
B. If it means that much . . .
A. Of course it does.
B. Of course I do.

Play the scene with the following combinations of characters:

- **(a)** Parent **(A)** and twelve-year-old child **(B)**
- **(b)** Parent **(B)** and twelve-year-old child **(A)**
- **(c)** Young man **(A)** and young woman **(B)**
- **(d)** Young man **(B)** and young woman **(A)**
- **(e)** Parent **(A)** and teenaged child **(B)**
- **(f)** Parent **(B)** and teenaged child **(A)**
- **(g)** Parent **(A)** and middle-aged child **(B)**
- **(h)** Parent **(B)** and middle-aged child **(A)**
- **(i)** Boss **(B)** and job applicant **(A)**
- **(j)** Actor **(A)** and interviewer **(B)**
- **(k)** Husband **(A)** and wife **(B)** - various ages
- **(l)** Brother **(A)** and sister **(B)** - various ages

As you play the scene, imagine that the other person is really the character, and react to that character.

4. Use **Practice Scene 1** with the same characters, but this time add a specific context for each scene. For example, in any of the parent-child scenes, you could use any of the following situations: **(a)** after something has been broken **(b)** at bed time **(c)** before leaving on a trip **(d)** before the parent leaves for work

(e) when dinner has been delayed **(f)** after an argument.

For the young man-young woman scenes, you might use: **(a)** meeting for the first time on a blind date **(b)** breaking up a romance **(c)** after an argument **(d)** after one has not telephoned the other.

You may use any other situations that occur to you. In each situation ask how you would feel if this were really happening and how you would feel if your partner were really that character. How does that affect the way each character shows himself to the audience?

5. The following scene has no emotional content at all as it stands. Play the scene with the same character relationships as in Activity 3. Carefully plan and concentrate on a specific objective for your character in the scene, and play that objective so that something really does happen in the course of the scene.

Practice Scene 2

A. Hi.
B. Hi.
A. What are you doing?
B. Not much.
A. Anything interesting?
B. Not very.
A. See you later.
B. Bye.

Character Change

Characters, like people, experience change in their lives. At the same time, major parts of the personality stay the same. Some characters (like some people) may undergo major transformations, but most characters, like most people, keep the same basic attitudes and objectives. When we speak of a change in character in a play, we usually mean that by the end of the play the audience sees something different about the character which they did not see at the beginning.

You, however, know what is going to happen in the play. You have studied it and rehearsed it, so you know *all* about the character. A good performance will contain all the different parts of the character's personality.

However, the character will appear to change constantly in the performance because he is reacting to the other characters in the play. When obstacles block him from his objective, he must change his approach. If character A wants character B to give some money to a charity, for example, A may start with a straight-forward appeal. If this doesn't work, he may plead or make B feel guilty or threaten B, or even rob B. In each case, A will appear different to the audience but he will still be the same imaginary person. All that has changed has been the approach he uses to reach his objective, getting the money.

A role in a full-length play will consist of a number of these changes. Each character has things he wants to do, and every character may block others, intentionally or unintentionally. Every one of these obstacles causes a change in a character's approach and a change in the way the audience sees the character.

Activity

Play a short improvisation with a partner in which you want the partner to do one of the following things. The partner's job is to say "no," until you convince him or her to say "yes." Make it "real" so that your partner *believes* you. Concentrate on reaching your objective. Notice how many ways you have to adjust to reach that objective, and how the adjustments show the personality of the imaginary character.

(a) give you money
(b) give you money for someone else
(c) do your work for you
(d) cover for you when you do not have a good excuse for being late
(e) go out with you Friday
(f) run for office

Character and Comedies

Many of your character roles will be in plays that are supposed to be funny. Both the actions and the language of the characters are intended to make the audience laugh. This often makes problems for the actors.

Sometimes a character is purposely trying to be funny. He will tell jokes or do silly things. In this case, the character's objective is to make the other characters in the play laugh. The actor does not try to make the *audience* laugh. The audience simply laughs along with the characters on stage.

Most of the time, however, the character is accidentally funny. Look at the scene from *She Stoops to Conquer* on page 340, one of the most famous comedies in English literature. This particular scene is very funny when it is performed well. In it, Mrs. Hardcastle has had a trick played on her—she thinks she is miles away from home, stranded on the road in the middle of the night, her carriage wrecked in a pond—when in fact she is on her own back lawn. She enters soaking wet, her clothes and hat dripping, she doesn't recognize her own husband, and she lets her son convince her that robbers are attacking. All of this can be hilarious, but to Mrs. Hardcastle it is not the least bit funny. She *believes* she is miles away, she *believes* her son Tony is in danger, and she *believes* her husband (whom she has not recognized) is really a robber. And the more she believes, the funnier she becomes. The key to the performance is her belief.

Most people do not see themselves as funny. They take themselves quite seriously. When they do amusing things, they are doing what seems perfectly sensible and logical to them in the circumstances. Recall a time when you said something funny but were not deliberately making a joke. After everyone else laughed, you saw a different meaning or "heard" what you really said (which wasn't what you thought you were saying). Then you laughed too. Characters in most comedies are just like that. What they do is absolutely sensible and normal to them when they start to do it.

The key to most comic performance is to believe what you are doing. Find the character's reason for doing whatever it is that he does, just as you do in any other scene. Then play that objective. The more the obstacles block that objective, the more intensely you keep reaching for the objective. Then the scene will be funny. If you try to *be* funny, the less funny the scene will be.

Activity

Much comedy results from a person's problems with his physical world. Select one of the following problems. When necessary, provide the props you will need to do the scene. Although you try to make the prop work, no matter how hard you try, it will not work the way it is supposed to. Find an objective for the scene which does not directly concern the prop and concentrate on that objective completely throughout the scene. In each case, feel the props resist and react to that resistance. The more they resist, the more you insist on getting the job done.

- **(a)** opening a door that won't open
- **(b)** tying a shoelace that keeps breaking
- **(c)** tying a necktie
- **(d)** sharpening a pencil when the sharpener doesn't work
- **(e)** wrapping a package

Chapter 10
Working with Other Actors

Actors do not work alone. Even in a one-actor show, there are technicians and stage hands, all of whom are essential to the performance. But one-actor shows are extremely rare. Most of the time, the individual performance is only one of many that make up the complete play performance.

Coordination

While you are learning to use your voice and body, you can work alone. Much of your analysis of your part can be done alone, as well. But rehearsal and performance must be done with the other actors. And all of those actors must put all of their individual talents, skills, ideas, and analyses together to make one unified performance. In general, this process works in two overlapping ways. The actor coordinates his activity with that of the other actors and the character the actor is playing reacts to the obstacles caused by the other characters. Concentrate on the activities throughout this chapter so that you will be able to unify these processes to make the complete performance.

Activities

1. Select a partner and face one another. Extend your arms in front of you and touch the tips of your partner's fingers. One of you close your eyes. The partner with eyes open leads the other around the room, avoiding all furniture, walls, and people. Do this without making a sound. Be sure you are touching only the tips of your fingers. If you are the partner with eyes closed, concentrate on following where you are led. Focus all your attention on the tips of your fingers and follow the lead the other person gives you. Try to respond to your partner's lead as quickly as possible. Change positions so that the leader becomes the follower.

2. Repeat Activity 1 but with one person leading two people whose eyes are closed. The leader touches the fingertips of one hand of each of the followers, and keeps the followers from bumping into each other as well as into anyone or anything else in the room. Again, stay perfectly quiet so that you can respond to the movement only.

3. Work in pairs again. Start Activity 1. When you are working well together the leader will break contact. The follower should keep eyes closed and follow

the sound of the leader's voice only. The leader will repeat a single word but cannot give specific directions. Follow the sound and tone of the voice around the room.

4. Imagine that there is a mirror between you and your partner. One of you is the person and one is the reflection of that person in the mirror. Whenever the person gestures, the reflection duplicates the gestures as in a mirror image.

Start this exercise simply. Touch fingers as if you were touching the mirror, slowly moving your fingers around, up, and down the surface of the mirror. When you and your partner have begun to react to each other and to move in the same ways, step back from the imaginary mirror. Continue slowly. Concentrate on communicating across the mirror to each other so that the mirror image responds immediately. Keep the movement simple until this happens.

Once you are working well together, try more complicated movements. Always keep the objective that of working together.

5. In a large group (six or more), close your eyes and walk silently in a cleared space. Try to avoid bumping into anyone. If you bump into someone, you are glued to that person at the point of contact. If the two who are glued together bump into someone else, the three are glued together and so on, until only one person is left unglued. The groups that are glued continue moving silently with eyes closed throughout the exercise.

6. Form a large circle. A volunteer goes to the center of the circle and becomes a part of an imaginary machine. As ideas occur to them, others in the circle join on as new parts of the machine until the entire group is part of the same machine. Make all the parts move and fit together as one single machine. Make the mechanical sounds of your machine, but do not use words.

7. Play a simple game of "follow the leader." The leader varies ways of moving that all the others in the group must duplicate. Concentrate so that without delay you change as the leader changes.

8. Arrange the group in a circle. A volunteer goes to the center and closes his or her eyes. Someone in the circle is silently selected as leader and begins a simple action that everyone in the circle tries to duplicate. When all the circle is acting together, the person in the center is told to open his or her eyes. Then the leader changes the action. Everyone changes with the leader while the person in the center tries to identify the leader.

If you are a part of the circle, your objective is to react instantly to any change in action so that it is impossible for the watcher to tell who is initiating the action. Do not look directly at the leader or you will reveal who he or she is.

9. Break the group into two teams and have a tug of war with an imaginary rope. Concentrate together so that everyone sees and feels the same rope and pulls together on it. This is more difficult than it sounds; unless you give the imaginary rope reality, the illusion will be broken.

10. In a group of four to six watch an imaginary movie. React and respond with each other so that the entire group reacts to the same imaginary events on the screen. Try this first with an agreed-upon plan about what you will see, then try it again without a plan.

In a larger group, watch an imaginary sporting event. Concentrate on seeing and reacting to the imaginary game happening in front of you so that you all respond together.

11. Break the class into groups of six. With two groups, play a game of imaginary volleyball. Review the sensory exercises in Chapter 8 so that you all see and feel the imaginary ball. Then concentrate as a group so that all of you can see where the ball is hit and the speed at which it moves. Try to sustain this for a full game of seven points, then eleven points, then fifteen points. Expand the exercise to include a referee and the rest of the class as fans. Try to get the entire group concentrating completely on the flow of the imaginary game.

Reaction

One of the basic laws of physics is that you cannot have an action without having a reaction. This is equally true of acting. Although most of the individual actor's time and effort is spent deciding what actions his role calls for and how to perform them, the success and strength of a performance is usually decided by the variety and honesty of the actor's reactions to other performers. To achieve the best performance, the actor must make his actions appear natural. To reach that point of naturalness, he must not only know and understand everything possible about his role but must also be willing and able to react to the work being done by everyone else on stage.

This reaction to others takes several forms. One way in which the actor must react is by adjusting his character's objectives. When your character wants to do something and is being blocked by someone else, your character must change his approach and try a different way of reaching his objective. This means that you and your character must constantly be aware of everything other characters are doing and react to them.

A second kind of reaction is related to the timing of your own actions so that everything you do appears natural and spontaneous. More than anything else, this reaction needs split-second timing. First, you need to know the exact instant when the other character does something. Then you need to *see* and *hear* it and react at that instant. Imagine a scene in which two characters begin the scene with sympathetic understanding but end the scene with a quarrel. The change happens gradually, step by step, as each character makes the other more angry. In order to play such a scene, the actors must make each step clear by reacting to each other very precisely. As one character becomes a little bit angry, the other becomes a little bit angry. At the beginning, each matches the other's anger. By the end, they have increased the level of their anger. This kind of interplay demands instant response and reaction by each actor.

In playing such a scene, the actors must pay careful attention to one another. Each must respond at *exactly* the moment when he or she realizes what is happening. (Responses may vary from performance to performance because one actor may respond to the other a word sooner or a word later.)

For reactions to become *real action,* actors must rehearse, working together and concentrating. In performance they must really *see* and *hear* the others on stage—not just pretend to see and hear them. An actor must be aware of the look in a person's eyes and the tone of his voice, the small variations in gesture and posture and react to them as part of his own performance.

There is also the kind of reaction that most people mean when they talk about an "actor's reactions," that is, what the actor does during another actor's speech. Suppose that in the imaginary scene above that there is a third char-

Student actors: Glenbrook North High School, Northbrook, Illinois acter on stage, watching all that is happening between the two principals, but not saying much. The actor playing that third character must decide what the character is doing at any given moment. The character is interested, but the actor can't just "act interested." If he does, then the character is "acting interested" and the performance looks phony and the audience will think the character isn't really interested at all. So to react in a natural manner, the character, and the actor playing that character must *look* at something specific, *see* something specific, and *hear* something specific.

To help you in such cases, make an *interior monologue*—a full statement of the thoughts of the character you are playing—all of the things that are going on in that character's mind during the scene, whether he says anything about them or not. The interior monologue records exactly what the character sees, hears, and thinks at every moment in the scene. It gives him a motivation for his actions, a reason for doing and saying everything he does. If you as the actor assume the interior monologue of the character, then it will be easy to keep any character you are playing interested in what happens on stage.

This approach can be used in any role, but it will be especially helpful in the scene from *Blithe Spirit* (page 165). In that scene, the actors have the opposite problem. Ruth has to be on stage and *not* hear things that other people hear. She must focus on her conversation with her husband and *not hear* Elvira. To convince the audience that she cannot hear Elvira she must occupy the time it takes Elvira to make her speeches. The interior monologue, which will make Ruth's thoughts *specific,* will help the actress playing Ruth keep her involved in the action and make her reactions logical and dramatic throughout the entire scene.

Activities

1. Select a partner. In the following exercise take turns giving directions and following them. The person giving directions should think of a simple activity that can be done in the room and without words direct the partner to do it. Then direct the partner to do something else, keeping your hands in your pockets or behind your back while you are giving the direction, still without words. Try another direction, hands in pockets or in back of you, no words, no sounds. Try another—without hands, words, sounds, or the moving of your head. Finally, try to give a direction with your back turned, hands still in your pockets, or, now, in front of you, no sounds or words. If you are the partner receiving the directions, do them as soon as you think you understand them. Do not ask questions.

2. In a group of four to six, make a circle so that you can all see one another. Select a nursery rhyme or other short poem you all know. So that each person contributes to the whole rhyme or poem, say the rhyme with each person in the circle saying one line. Work together so that you all speak in the same rhythm and speed.

Repeat the exercise with each person in the group stopping at any point in the line he or she chooses. The next person picks up the line where the one before left off, trying to keep the same rhythm and tempo. Keep working at it until the entire group is together, no matter where in a line each person stops.

Begin the original exercise, but this time do not progress in one direction around the circle. When you are speaking, close your eyes. When you stop, open them and look directly at someone else in the circle. As soon as that person is aware of your look, he or she begins the line where you left off. First do this stopping at the end of lines; then, when everyone is really alert and together, try stopping at random.

3. Each class member should write a description of a scene for improvisation, as you did in Chapter 2 (page 20). In this activity, each scene description should include a place, a time, two characters, the basic conflict, and its resolution. Select a partner. One partner draws a topic and reads it. The other person should not read the topic or plan the scene in any way. The partner who drew the topic must play the active character, the one who has the initial actions. Otherwise it will be almost impossible for the other person to react and reach the resolution. The active character must try to play the scene in such a way that his partner can reach the resolution given in the scene description. If you are the receiving partner, concentrate on everything the active partner says and does, picking up any clues he gives, and adjusting as quickly as possible, wherever the scene seems to be going.

4. Return to Practice Scene 1 or 2. Add a third, silent character. Perform the scene with two partners, playing the silent third character yourself. Make an interior monologue for yourself so that your character is clearly involved in the scene.

5. Improvise a scene in which your partner has a split personality. Change your attitude toward him or her whenever he or she changes from one personality to the other.

6. *David and Lisa* is a popular play in many schools. One of the characters in this play can speak only in rhymes. Improvise a scene in which you and a partner each have this problem. As you play the scene, have a third person call out "change" at random times. Each time you hear "change," change your speech; if you are rhyming, change to regular speech; if you are speaking regularly, change to rhyme. Concentrate on keeping the scene going. Do not pause, abandoning your character in order to think of a rhyme.

Repeat the exercise, but use a melody instead of a rhyme. Each time you change from regular speech, all lines must be sung.

This is a complicated and difficult activity requiring intense concentration and quick reactions. There should be no pause or change in attitude or personality during changes in your speaking pattern.

Chapter 11
Stage Presence

Most of the discussion to this point has been about the preparation required of the actor and the interpreter before performance. The next unit will look at play rehearsals for a full dramatic production. Before beginning that unit, however, there are some elements of the art of "just being on stage" that every performer should be aware of.

As you work on the following activities remember that they are techniques that will make life on stage a little easier. They are not an end in themselves. They need to be practiced so that you can use them in performance without expending energy trying to think about them. But they will not by themselves make you a performer.

Entrances and Exits

All performance begins *before* the audience sees you. When you enter a scene on stage you must be *in* the performance before you enter into view of the audience and that performance must continue until the audience no longer has you in view. Your entrance begins off stage and your exit ends off stage.

Remember that whatever a character does, he does it for a reason. The characters in a play never go off stage or on stage. They go from one place to another and they go there for a purpose—to do something in that particular place. An entrance does not begin—it finishes something begun in another place. A character exits not because he has finished a scene—he exits to start something else.

For entrances ask yourself questions like the following about your character and the scene:

Where exactly is the offstage area?
What am I doing there?
Where did I come from? for what purpose?
Why exactly am I going into the onstage area?
What do I expect to see when I go out there?
What is the first thing I actually see?

For an exit, ask:

Where am I going?
What do I want to do there?
How far is the place I'm going to from this place?

Student actors: Glenbrook North High School, Glenbrook, Illinois

What do I expect to see off stage?

What makes me leave *at this particular time?*

When you have the answers to these questions, you will understand how your entrances and exits are part of your whole characterization and performance. Concentrate on playing the moment of entrance and the objective of the character. Some people like to play a short improvisation before each entrance to remind themselves that the role begins off stage. If you do this, be sure to time it carefully in rehearsal so that the moment your scene is ready for your entrance the actors on stage are also ready for your entrance. Whether you improvise an offstage scene or not, you need time to begin an entrance. In general, you should be in place about two minutes before you actually go on stage (one to two pages in your script). That will give you time to get organized, to think about your objectives, and to listen to the scene on stage to pick up the mood and tempo which you must fit yourself into.

Always enter and exit at speed. This means that you must begin your entrance several steps before you come into view so that when the audience sees it, your body is in motion. Finish the exit in the same way. Carry your exit several steps beyond the audience's view even though you may be off stage. This is like the follow-through motion necessary to properly hitting a baseball, golf ball, or tennis ball—if the follow-through isn't complete, the whole motion is wrong.

If you have doors to open or close, practice with them. Stage doors are notoriously unpredictable and difficult. To the character in the play they are real doors, so you, the actor playing the character, must be comfortable with them. Take a few moments before each rehearsal and performance to practice your entrances and exits. Go over the actions exactly as you will be playing them. Practice so that you can grasp a doorknob with the same hand and at the same distance each time you must do so. If you open the door with your left hand, let go of the knob as soon as the door is open and walk on past, trailing your right hand behind you. Then pick up the knob with the right hand and pull the door behind you. In this way you continue to face the direction of movement at all times. Your entrance will be ineffective if you turn your back on the audience and on the characters on stage to shut the door. Exits generally work with only one hand because you do not have to worry about staying open to anyone.

Activities

1. Improvise a short scene, one without speech, in which you exit through a real door. Imagine clearly what is on the other side of that door so that you are expecting something to happen to you once you go through the door. Only when you have that clear expectation can you exit.

If you did this in class, was the class able to tell what you had expected to find outside the door? If you practiced the scene alone, how did the expectation change the way you went through the door?

2. Without speaking, repeat Activity 1, except this time play your scene outside the door and enter into the classroom. Could the audience in the class see what you expected to find from the way you entered?

3. Without speaking, repeat Activity 2, except this time try to make the entrance the end of a scene that happened off stage. Imagine something that happened off stage that made you leave that place to come on stage through the door. Could the people watching tell what happened to you out there by the way you entered?

4. With a partner set up several items in an arrangement in the room. Leave the room while your partner moves the arrangement in some very minor way. Enter the room and find the change.

This is a simple exercise which will sharpen your awareness of the necessity of actually looking at the stage when you make your entrance. The character always expects to see something, and your entrances must duplicate that sense of actually *looking* at the people and scenery on stage.

Opening to the Audience

The whole point of a performance is to share something with an audience. The easiest way to accomplish this is to make sure that your audience can see and hear you. Most of the following techniques apply to being seen on a proscenium stage because the technical problems of being seen there are much greater than for a theater in-the-round or a large thrust stage.

The most expressive part of your body is the front. Your hands, most of the movement of your arms and shoulders, and all of your face can be seen only from the front. To get the maximum effect from your performance, you want to be visible from the front as much as possible. Being so doesn't require any particularly difficult or awkward maneuvering, nor does it mean you have to always face forward directly toward the audience. In practice, you need to make some minor adjustments in the way you stand and walk and handle things.

On the proscenium stage, the audience is seated on one side only. The side directly opposite the audience is called *upstage.* (For complete stage directions, see page 000.) To keep the body open to the audience always stand with the upstage foot slightly forward. If you are facing left to talk to someone on your left, the left foot is your upstage foot and is slightly ahead of your right foot. When you face right, your right foot is upstage and is the forward foot.

When walking forward, step first with the upstage foot. This starts your motion with an action that opens your whole body to the audience while you move. When reversing directions, step first with the downstage foot. (As soon as you turn around, of course, what used to be the downstage foot will be the upstage foot for your new direction of movement.) When you stop, end with the upstage foot slightly forward.

Whenever possible, gesture with the upstage hand and arm. This keeps the body open so that the gesture and the face are both clearly visible to the audience. A skilled performer is able to work well with either hand, whether left- or right-handed. Because the audience is often below your head height, whether you gesture with both hands or with the downstage hand, the downstage hand should stay a little lower than the upstage hand.

Handling a telephone is often a problem. Hold a telephone in the upstage hand so that the earpiece doesn't hide your face from the audience and so that the mouthpiece doesn't cover your mouth. In fact, when using any prop never block your mouth while you are talking. To do so not only blocks part of the sound, but it also prevents the audience from reading your lips. Anytime you block your mouth, a significant number of people will not understand any unusual words or anything spoken with less than perfect enunciation.

If for some reason you need to turn around, turn "across the audience." This means to turn in such a way that your face makes the turn on the downstage side. Since these kinds of big moves usually happen in very dramatic moments, the audience is helped if they can actually see the emotional reaction in your face as well as in your body.

When you need to face toward the audience, open to the audience as a whole. The easiest way to do this is to select a point of focus just above and behind the audience. That way all of the audience will be able to see your face, but you will not be looking at any particular person in the audience, which can be distracting to your own concentration.

Many young amateur actors block themselves by their posture. Most light on the stage comes at an artificial angle—from above without reflections. If your head droops, you make your own shadow across your face and the audience will not be able to see you no matter how well you have remembered to follow all the preceding suggestions. There are a number of posture and movement exercises in Unit I you can practice to prevent self blocking. Here is another way to avoid the problem. Most people when they walk focus on a spot on the ground ten or fifteen feet in front of themselves. If they are nervous or not thinking about what they are doing, they focus on a spot even closer to themselves, almost at their own feet. Every now and then they will look up for a quick glance in the distance. The actor, in contrast, should focus with his eyes on the horizon line and occasionally glance down closer to make sure of his footing when he moves. That simple change in focus will solve almost all of the problems of posture and head balance that you have when trying to adjust to stage lighting.

One of the most difficult techniques to master is looking natural when talking to someone who is upstage of you while still staying open to the audience. You will not be in this position often because most directors work carefully to avoid it except for special purposes. But it will occur often enough to cause some problems. If you have more than one or two words in the line, start the line while looking right at the person you are speaking to. Then, after the first couple of words, turn your head downstage while you continue talking. As you say the last word or two, turn again to look right at the person. Once you become accustomed to doing this, it will seem very natural. In real life, people often look away while they are talking, turning back when finished to look for a reaction. If you were to ask people watching from the audience, they would be convinced that you were looking at the other person the entire time you were speaking.

When you are working in-the-round or on a thrust stage, the problems are slightly different. In general, these problems come not from having to stay visible to one direction, but from trying to be visible to as large an area as possible. In general, the director will adjust your movements so that each actor spends about the same amount of time facing each of the audience sections.

Activities

1. With a partner find an area that you can use for a stage—an imaginary stage or a real one—so long as you both agree on where the imaginary audience will be. Have your partner sit on the audience side while you move around at random in the stage space. Without warning, your partner will give you the directions: reverse, stop, go, or turn. Try to respond immediately to the directions using the techniques described in this section but without consciously thinking about them. If the direction is "stop," you may take one extra step in order to get the upstage foot forward, but all other directions should be followed without thought or pause. It may take you some time to perform the activity correctly.

2. Improvise scenes that will allow you to practice using the following props, first in one hand and then the other: a candle, a book, a telephone, a glass of water, a cup of coffee, a flower, a handkerchief. Practice using these common props and any other specific ones you might need for a particular role so that you are completely comfortable using them with either hand.

Focusing

When an audience watches a performance, it may pay attention to an infinite number of different things. From all the activities on the stage and all the technical surroundings, an audience will select the most interesting thing to focus its attention on. Performers, in order to make the play work, must find some way to make sure that most of the audience pays attention to the most important thing in any particular moment on stage. They do this by the way in which they focus their actions and concentration.

There are a number of ways to focus a scene. Some of these are determined by the director and some by the technical design of the production. Sometimes movement is designed to set up stage groups and to focus the stage picture on a particular person or on part of the scene. The director also has the resources of scenery, costume, and lighting available to him and can use them to make some characters more vivid than others.

As a general rule, it helps to remember that most of the audience will be interested in what the actors seem to be interested in. If everyone on stage looks at a doorway while waiting for someone to arrive, most of the audience will watch that doorway as well. If you look at another actor, the audience will look at that actor along with you. At the same time, if the audience looks at you and you are looking off into blank space, many of them will look off into blank space. The first thing to learn and to remember about focusing a performance is to know what the center of attention is in the scene. Then direct your attention to that, whatever it is.

The second thing is to *really look at* that center. *See* what you are looking at. Don't look in the general direction of someone. The audience can tell the difference between focused and unfocused eyes, even in fairly large theaters and stages. When you talk to another character, if possible, look him in the eyes. Watch exactly what he does to respond and react to you. *Care* about what other characters think of what you are doing. Nothing in the world helps a performance more than that.

This holds true whether what you are doing is the center of attention in the scene or not. Sometimes because your character doesn't want to participate in whatever is happening, you may be avoiding what everyone else is doing. You must still focus your character's interest on something specific.

The performer also has to focus all his energy into the role. Warm-ups and concentration exercises just before your entrance will help your focus. Understanding and knowing what you are doing in the performance itself so that you don't have to think about what is supposed to happen next is especially impor-

Laurence Olivier in *Oedipus Rex* at the Old Vic

tant to every good performance. The character is working in a present time, a *now* of performance, and the actor should be working in that same time frame. If you don't quite know your lines, if you have to keep stopping to think of the next line, you are wasting valuable energy you could be using in the performance itself and you will be shifting your focus away from the character's actions onto your own actions (in this case, thinking about a line). If you have rehearsed and know your role, you can relax enough to let all your attention go into the performance itself.

Finally, always remember what the character wants to do. Focus your own thoughts onto the objectives; watch, listen, and react to the other characters on the stage.

Activities

1. Repeat some of the reaction exercises on pages 140-141, especially Activity 1. Focus *all* your attention on the person receiving directions.

2. Memorize Practice Scene 2 on page 133. Play it with a partner while standing or sitting very close to one another. Each time you say a line, point directly at the area on the partner's nose between his or her eyes and try to aim your eyes and your voice along your pointing finger.

Repeat the exercise at a distance of about ten feet.

Repeat the scene from opposite sides of the room.

3. Try Practice Scene 1, on page 132, and as you say each line from opposite sides of the room, throw an imaginary tennis ball directly at the center of your partner's body. Try to focus your attention and your voice so that the line is aimed directly where you throw the imaginary ball.

Repeat the scene, and this time throw each line at a different part of your partner's body: the waist, the right or left shoulder, the knees. As your partner throws you a line, try to receive the focus and catch the line as it arrives. Be careful that you don't turn this into a game of catch. Imagine throwing the line, not a ball.

4. Sit in a circle with the group. Focus on some item somewhere in the room. Try to get everyone else in the circle to focus on the same item without saying anything to anyone or without pointing. Each person will be trying to do the same thing, so it will take some time until the person with the strongest concentration pulls the interest of everyone else in the group.

Movement and Gesture

Many performers worry about the right way to move or gesture on stage. In practice, there is no such thing as "right way." Each character at each moment moves and gestures in his own way, different from other characters and sometimes different from the way in which he himself moved just moments ago. If you do the character's action with all your attention focused on that action, the movement and gesture will take care of itself.

The most important thing to remember as you examine your own action and movement is that all movement, on stage or off, has three parts: preparation, action, and release. Preparation begins with the decision to do something so that, in fact, movement results from a reaction to someone or something. Preparation or the decision to act, is the longest part of any gesture and the part that most actors tend to skip.

Preparation has several steps. There is the cause—let us say that another character insults you. You have to see, hear, and register that insult. Then comes the decision—you decide that you are going to punish that person. Then you decide you are going to hit him, and then where you are going to hit him and how hard. All of this will happen quickly, but not so quickly that if they are paying attention, the audience can't see your reactions. The physical action itself follows, but that action also has a preparation—the arm draws back, the fist clenches for a blow or the palm opens for a slap.

Then, and only then, your arm shoots out and you hit the person. You are like a spring, your whole mind and body tightening the coils until the tension is great enough to force a release. Then the action happens and the gesture occurs. The principle is the same for less dramatic gestures or for a cross on the stage. First you decide to do, then, when the decision is clear, the tension you built up while you decided is released and the movement happens.

Finally, the movement or gesture has to be completed. First, there is some kind of reaction—if you hit the person, the hand reacts to the contact and changes direction. If you are making a point—wagging your finger in front of another character—the finger hits some imaginary block, some clear point in space and bounces back up just a little. Then the gesture is released. Once it is finished, all the tension built up in the preparation is gone, and the hand or arm returns to rest. Relax and let the relaxation take your hand or arm back to where you started. If your movement was something big, like a cross, stop when you reach your goal and return to balance.

When actors have trouble with gesture, it usually means that they have lost contact with the reason for the gesture. If you ask, "What do I do with my hands?" then you are not thinking about the character. If the character isn't doing anything at the moment, the hands are at rest; the character doesn't even think about them, and you shouldn't either. When you do decide to express something physically, to actually *do* something, remember all the parts of the action, and do a complete movement or gesture. The director may adjust the size of that gesture as seen from the audience's view, but the actor must always complete all three parts of it. Then the movement will come easily.

Chapter 12
Working with the Script

Eventually actors must work with the script. They and the director must turn the playwright's words into a performance. All of the things you have learned about making a character, defining objectives, playing actions and reactions, and developing imaginary sensations and expressing imaginary worlds have now to be applied to situations in which someone else—the playwright—has already decided what should be happening.

In a play everything happens at the same time—*now.* The playwright, unlike the novelist or short-story writer, cannot tell you how character A *feels* and then two pages later tell you how character B *felt.* The audience sees what characters A and B are doing and feeling concurrently. Furthermore, any play script is incomplete because a playwright only tells you what one character does at any given moment. Everyone else on stage at the same time must figure out what they should be doing that has not been prescribed or directed by the playwright. Even what the playwright has written may be very brief. If he says, "Jane is happy," what does that really mean for the person playing Jane? Which kind of the many kinds of happy *is* Jane? Does she jump up and down? How far? Which foot first? And so on. Thus, much about most roles in a play will be left to someone's imagination to interpret.

You cannot begin to understand a script with only one reading. You need to keep rereading in order to discover all of its possibilities. When you really understand the detail that is there, you can use what you have learned to build your performance. You have an obligation to the playwright and to the audience to perform to the best of your ability the play that the playwright has written. But you have to understand what has been written before you can begin to communicate the words.

In general, you can break your analysis of the script into three parts: the context, the text itself, and the subtext. Use this kind of analysis when you study and perform the scenes that follow this chapter and for any other roles you may play. If you have worked and paid careful attention in class to this point, you have the basic tools to use. Now you are ready to use the analytical skills the actor needs to make a performance.

The Context

The context of a moment on stage is all of the world that surrounds that

A scene from the folk-opera *Porgy and Bess,* with music by George Gershwin

moment—the physical world such as the scenery, costumes, and props as well as what you and the characters know about the world outside that imaginary on-stage place; for example, historical time and place and the things that are immediately beyond the audience's view are part of context too. Context also includes whatever the other characters are doing while you are doing your moment of action. Finally, it includes all of the things that happened before and that will happen following the present moment of action.

As you read through the script, ask yourself the following kinds of questions:

Where is this place? exactly?

When is this time? exactly?

What does this place look like; what colors, shapes, and items does the character see? What does he or she hear?

What is in the next room? on the street? next door?

Where has the character come from? Where is he or she going after leaving this place?

What do those places look and sound like? How much of all of this does the character know?

What are other people like at this time and in this place?

What happened to these characters a second ago? a minute ago? yesterday? last month? last year? What will happen in the next minute, day, week, and so on? How much of this does the character know at this moment? How much does the audience know?

Each of these questions has to be asked about each moment of the performance because the answers change as the show moves through time. At each successive moment, both the audience and the characters know more than they did before. Sometimes they know different things. This is why the actor has to understand the entire play before he can make decisions about any single moment.

Text

The text is all of the lines and all of the directions the playwright gives you. Before you can understand the text, you must have a specific understanding of all the words in the text. The playwright has chosen the words with care, and you must know the exact meaning and pronunciation of all the words a character uses. Even when you think you know the meaning and pronunciation of a word, check your dictionary again just to be sure.

Knowing the definitions of individual words is not enough. You need to understand words in groups, in sentences and in speeches, in order to express the sounds and rhythms as well as the ideas. Review the section on word meanings in Unit II before you begin working on the scenes that follow this chapter.

One good way to test whether or not you really understand a line is to paraphrase it—to say it again in your own words. Then ask yourself why the character didn't use your words if they mean the same thing. In most cases, the answer will be that they *don't* mean the same thing, they mean *almost* the same thing. The difference between the statement and your paraphrase is what you need to concentrate on to be sure you completely understand the text.

Subtext

The subtext is all that part of the performance that the playwright has left for the reader's or performer's interpretation. It is implied by the text and the context but never actually stated.

Sometimes, as in the scene from *Blue Denim* on page 159, the characters not only mean what they say but they mean it more than they can actually express it in words. A character may not have the vocabulary or the sophistication to say everything he or she means. Like Janet and Arthur, characters may simply not be able to express themselves verbally. In such cases, the actor has to find the bigger, more intense feeling and somehow express that feeling while saying the more limited words.

Sometimes a character may not be telling the truth. He may be lying or keeping something secret or he may be trying to distract the other characters. Many times such hidden thoughts will eventually be explained. In the scene from *Blue Denim* for example, Janet is in love with Arthur from the very beginning, but she doesn't tell Arthur immediately that she is in love with him. However, her love for him is part of what she is thinking and feeling as she works herself up to telling Arthur about her love.

Sometimes emotions may be so strong that the characters avoid specific verbal expression, allowing tone of voice and action to carry meaning. The scene from *The Cherry Orchard* on page 350 is a famous example of this kind of expression. The scene from *Assembly Line* on page 163 is another: the women are ready to accept Marsha and express their acceptance in the way they ask her to join them for lunch. The lines are deceptively simple and quite beside the point—the characters mean to express themselves by their tone of voice, not by their words.

Finding the subtext is not easy, but without the subtext you cannot know a character's real objectives. To help you find the subtext and the real objectives of the character, ask yourself the following questions about each moment of the role:

Is this true?

What do I accomplish by doing or saying this?

What happens next? What do the other characters do to react? What could I be doing to make them react to me that way?

Why do I say this? Why do I say it this way and not some other way?

Why do I do this? Why not something else?

Why do I do or say this *right now?* Why not a minute ago? Why not in the next scene? What makes me want to do or say this?

Then compare what you decide for each moment with the moment preceding and the moment following. How do they fit together? What leads you from one moment to the next? Much of the subtext will become clearer in rehearsal where the other actors and the director will help you in determining objectives. But for the most part, the responsibility lies with yourself, with your own preparation for the role.

The Objective

As you begin to understand the context, text, and subtext, you will begin to understand what the character is actually accomplishing. This will help you decide what the character wants to accomplish. When you understand this, then you can formulate an objective that will help you decide how you want to play the scene. Review the exercises on objectives and use what you learned from them in your scene. But be sure you understand what your character actually wants so that the choice of your objective grows out of the scene instead of being artificially imposed on the scene.

Most of your previous activities have concentrated on a single objective in a scene. At any given moment a character has a particular objective. Many times these small, moment-to-moment, objectives can be combined into a single large objective for an entire scene or even for the entire play. For example, in the scene from *Blue Denim* Janet wants to tell Arthur that she loves him. But why does she want to tell him that? One obvious reason would be because she wants him to love her in return. Thus her larger objective could be, "I want to make Arthur fall in love with me." That thought shapes what she does and how she does everything else in the scene.

This big objective helps you to shape and to focus the whole role and gives you a solid foundation for all the characterization you have to build. But you must be very careful not to decide on the big objective until you understand the smaller moments. Any big objective you decide to use must include all the smaller objectives. If it does not, then you must go back and rethink everything so that each moment makes sense.

If you can successfully define a big objective for a scene or for the play, then you can begin to understand how the characters interact in the course of the scene or the play. As the character tries to accomplish the objective, he or she has to break the objective into steps. Janet, for example, cannot just say, "Arthur, fall in love with me!" It would be unlikely that Arthur would ever respond to that approach. So Janet has to hint. When Arthur reacts positively, Janet can continue her initial approach. When he reacts negatively, she must change her approach. Each one of these changes in approach is a new small objective.

As you work on a scene, try to make each objective smaller. Break actions and reactions down to the smallest possible sizes so that you play the action and thought of each moment as it happens. The final performance should be as spontaneous as one of your own improvisations. But that can only happen if you give attention to the moment of performance and the objectives, reactions, and changes of each second of the scene.

Activities

Study, analyze, rehearse, memorize, and perform the following scenes. (The scene from *A Young Lady of Property* is written for two girls; however, in class-rehearsal situations, the scene may just as easily be played by two boys.)

At the beginning of each scene is a short introduction that gives you some background about the scene to help you understand the setting and the characters' situations. These are very brief but very important, so be sure to read them. Any information not in the introduction can be found in the scene itself.

If you do these scenes as part of your classwork, it will be interesting and helpful to have several groups play the same scene; doing so will illustrate how it is possible to play a single scene different ways with different understandings. You can then discuss how each performance shows a different insight into the script and characters.

In Unit VIII there are a number of scenes from historical plays that will give you additional material to work with.

Scenes for Acting Practice

from ***Meet Me in St. Louis***
adapted by Christopher Sergel from Sally Benson's novel

The setting of this play is St. Louis, in 1904. The characters in this scene are part of the same family. Mr. Smith is a businessman whose company has offered him a better job if he will move from St. Louis to New York. Mrs. Smith is opposed to the move but will go along with her husband if he insists upon making the move. As the scene begins, Mrs. Smith has gathered the three oldest daughters in the living room. The girls have been asking, "What's the matter?" Mr. Smith enters. He has not planned on telling the girls his news just yet. (The family's youngest daughter is missing from the group, which is why Mr. Smith says, ". . . when we're all together.")

Rose, the eldest daughter, is eighteen, a beautiful young woman, and in love.

Esther is seventeen, a bit smarter than Rose but a little less sure of herself.

Agnes has just turned fifteen, undecided whether or not she wants to be a tomboy. She is very direct.

Each character has a different objective in the scene. Find that objective. Then see how it affects what each character says and how it is said.

MRS. SMITH (*seeing* MR. SMITH). Ask your father. (*All watch* MR. SMITH.)

MR. SMITH (*to* MRS. SMITH, *pausing at* L C). I thought later—when we're all together.

MRS. SMITH. But they're making all sorts of plans for the future.

ROSE. What is it, Papa?

AGNES. Tell us.

MR. SMITH. Now, just hold your horses.

MRS. SMITH. Your father has important news for you.

MR. SMITH (*as they wait*). It's—(*Then–out with it.*)—well—we're moving to New York. (ROSE *and* ESTHER *are stunned.*)

MRS. SMITH. We're moving to New York to live.

AGNES (*after a pause*). If you'll excuse me, I'll go pack my things. (*Rises and turns to go up the stairs.*)

MRS. SMITH. You're not packing anything yet. (AGNES *comes back in front of settee.*)

ROSE (*letting out a held breath*). *Move to New York!*

ESTHER (*crying*). I'll *never* move to New York. I've never seen the place and I never want to.

ROSE. Papa—why? Why?

MR. SMITH (*uncomfortably*). It's for the best.

MRS. SMITH. You mustn't blame your father. (*Sitting* D R.) It means more money and, after all, you want to go to college, and—

ROSE. Money! I hate, loathe, despise, abominate, and abhor money.

ESTHER. We don't know a soul in New York. Besides, it's a well-known fact that Eastern girls are snobs.

ROSE. And what about the World's Fair?

ESTHER. Just when it's about to begin, and just when St. Louis will be the center of attraction of the entire universe.

AGNES. I'd like to see the ocean.

ROSE. Don't be silly. It won't look a bit different from Lake Michigan, and we see that every summer.

AGNES. It will look different to me.

MR. SMITH. Of course. There are all kinds of advantages. If you'd only think about them calmly.

ROSE (*crossing to* MR. SMITH). But there are so many reasons why we *can't* go, Papa.

AGNES. I'd like to.

ESTHER. You talk like an imbecile, Agnes. I think it's important to think of what will happen to Lady Babbie. She's your cat, too, Agnes.

AGNES. Lady Babbie will come with us in a silk-lined basket.

ESTHER. And where are you going to keep her in New York—cooped up in a tenement?

AGNES. Don't they have houses in New York?

MR. SMITH. Of course they do.

ROSE. Yes, but we'd probably live in a flat—you know that, Papa.

ESTHER (*to* AGNES). There are hundreds of flats in one building, and they have landlords.

MR. SMITH. Now, wait a minute——

AGNES (*sitting on settee again*). I guess I won't pack my things, then. I like it here, all right. Besides, I don't want to miss the World's Fair.

MR. SMITH. Well, you'll just have to get used to the idea.

ROSE (*sitting on settee*). I won't go. You've no right to ask us to.

ESTHER. And I won't, either. (*Sits on settee, too.*)
MR. SMITH. There's no use discussing it. We're going to have to do it.
MRS. SMITH. Your father's word is law around here. (*Pauses.*) I talked to Katie, and she said she could never leave St. Louis—and neither will my father.
AGNES. You mean, Grandpa wouldn't come, too?
MR. SMITH. Maybe not, but——
ROSE. Papa, we can't leave here—why, all our friends and——
ESTHER. And we have plans and things to do.
MRS. SMITH. It's true, Lon. Why, everyone we love is here.
MR. SMITH. I know that, Anna. But there are other considerations and other problems. If we stay here——(*He turns* D L.)
ROSE (*begging*). Oh, *can't* we, Papa?
ESTHER. We could save money—we could eat fish and everything that's cheapest.
ROSE. And what Mama said is true—I couldn't stand it if we had to leave now. Everything would be ruined—*everything!*
MR. SMITH. *What* would be ruined, Rose?
ROSE. It would—honestly, it would!

from ***Blue Denim***
by James Leo Herlihy and William Noble

Arthur and Janet are teenagers. Janet has come to visit Arthur, and has found him in his basement retreat where he and his friend Ernie do their private talking. Trying to establish some kind of communication with Arthur, she finally gets him to dance with her to music from the radio. As the scene begins, Arthur has suddenly stopped dancing and turned off the radio.

This is a scene in which the characters say what they mean, but have difficulty communicating clearly. As the scene happens, their understanding of each other becomes more definite. As you work on the scene, concentrate on paying attention and relating your reactions to every specific thing the other person in the scene does.

JANET. What's the matter?

ARTHUR. Nothing. I told you—I'm no good at that stuff.

JANET. You'll never learn if you won't try!

ARTHUR. Too bad Ernie isn't here. He goes to dances all the time. Real ones, downtown.

JANET. I wanted to dance with you, not Ernie.

ARTHUR. I'd give anything if I could be like him.

JANET. Now why?

ARTHUR. He's really got a smooth tongue on him. I admire that. With me things get all twisted up . . .

JANET. Arthur, what sort of things?

ARTHUR. Things I wonder about—One thing, it bothers me a lot. I tried to tell Mom about it once, but . . .

JANET. But what?

ARTHUR. Aw, every time my mother looks at me I feel like she's seeing something small and pink and wrapped up in a blanket.

JANET (*moving closer to him*). Try telling me, Art.

ARTHUR. See . . . I've got this feeling I ought to be somebody—special!

JANET. Who doesn't? I want to be a poet, and what's sillier than that?

ARTHUR. Yeah, but you got what it takes. I'm just—ordinary.

JANET. Ordinary! You think I'd hang around with you if I didn't think you were going to be—special?

ARTHUR. You do?

JANET. O' course. That's why you and I can talk.

ARTHUR. I guess we do talk better than most people. All the kids at school—even Ernie . . . I mean, I figured it out, I don't really *know* anybody at all. Not even my own folks. Does that sound bats?

JANET. Not to *me!*

ARTHUR. Hunh?

JANET. It seems to me the only people who really know each other are—people in love.

ARTHUR. Maybe so.

JANET. Arthur, how d'you suppose it feels to be in love with someone?

ARTHUR. Don't ask me!

JANET (*bravely*). Because—because I think *I'm* in love. With you.

ARTHUR. You . . . ! (*Sharply*) Whadd'ya want to kid like that for?

JANET. I'm not!

ARTHUR. You are. And I thought we were talking serious.

JANET. Well, if that's your attitude, I'm sorry I told you! (*Janet starts to leave but* ARTHUR*'s voice stops her.*)

ARTHUR. Janet! Weren't you kidding? (*She turns slowly to face him, shakes her head.*) But Janet . . .

JANET. Don't worry about it. At my age it's perfectly natural to have crushes on people.

ARTHUR. Yeah, but—why me?

JANET. Frankly, I don't know. You're not the handsomest boy in the world.

ARTHUR. Thanks!

JANET. You see, I'm very objective about you, Arthur. My mistake was I told you. Norma says never let a boy know you really like him.

ARTHUR. Norma doesn't know everything.

JANET. She knows plenty!

ARTHUR (*stunned*). When did you find out? I mean, about me?

JANET (*turning to him, excited*). I can tell you the exact second. It was this morning. Remember the English test? I saw you trying to decide whether or not to copy from Billy Robinson's paper . . . Turning sideways, leaning back . . . And all you had to do was look over! But you didn't. I started to laugh. At least I thought I was—but I was starting to cry. Now, almost everything you do is funny . . . and at the same time . . . *not* funny . . . (*She turns away.*) Well—*say* something!

ARTHUR. I don't know what to say!

JANET. I guess you don't— (*She wanders away from him.*)

ARTHUR (*joining her, taking her arm*). Don't be—mad.

JANET. I'm not mad.

ARTHUR. Yes you are.

JANET. I really made a fool of myself, didn't I?

ARTHUR. No.

from ***A Young Lady of Property***
by Horton Foote

Wilma and Arabella are teenaged girls living in a small Texas town. A famous movie director has come to Houston to look for a new "star" and the girls have written for screen tests. Meanwhile, Wilma has discovered that her widowed father is interested in remarrying—"Old lady Leighton."

As you study and play the scene, notice that the girls, realizing their true objectives are completely different from their original ones, change their minds about the goal they have set for themselves. Arabella changes her mind before Wilma does and for a different reason, but both girls decide that they don't want to be in the movies after all. They never say exactly what makes them change their objectives, so to make the scene work, you, as the actors, must find the specific moment and specific reason for the change.

When Arabella arrives, Wilma is sitting on her porch. Be sure you know exactly why Arabella comes at that time with the letter and what Wilma has been thinking before she sees Arabella.

WILMA. Heh, Arabella. Come sit and swing.
ARABELLA. All right. Your letter came.
WILMA. Whoopee. Where is it?
ARABELLA. Here. (*She gives it to her.* WILMA *tears it open. She reads.*)
WILMA (*reading*). Dear Miss Thompson: Mr. Delafonte will be glad to see you any time next week about your contemplated screen test. We suggest you call the office when you arrive in the city and we will set an exact time. Yours truly, Adele Murray. Well. . . . Did you get yours?
ARABELLA. Yes.
WILMA. What did it say?
ARABELLA. The same.
WILMA. Exactly the same?
ARABELLA. Yes.
WILMA. Well, let's pack our bags. Hollywood, here we come.
ARABELLA. Wilma . . .
WILMA. Yes?
ARABELLA. I have to tell you something. . . . Well . . . I . . .

WILMA. What is it?

ARABELLA. Well . . . promise me you won't hate me, or stop being my friend. I never had a friend, Wilma, until you began being nice to me, and I couldn't stand it if you weren't my friend any longer . . .

WILMA. Oh, my cow. Stop talking like that. I'll never stop being your friend. What do you want to tell me?

ARABELLA. Well . . . I don't want to go to see Mr. Delafonte, Wilma . . .

WILMA. You don't?

ARABELLA. No. I don't want to be a movie star. I don't want to leave Harrison or my mother or father . . . I just want to stay here the rest of my life and get married and settle down and have children.

WILMA. Arabella . . .

ARABELLA. I just pretended like I wanted to go to Hollywood because I knew you wanted me to, and I wanted you to like me . . .

WILMA. Oh, Arabella . . .

ARABELLA. Don't hate me, Wilma. You see, I'd be afraid . . . I'd die if I had to go to see Mr. Delafonte. Why, I even get faint when I have to recite before the class. I'm not like you. You're not scared of anything.

WILMA. Why do you say that?

ARABELLA. Because you're not. I know.

WILMA. Oh, yes, I am. I'm scared of lots of things.

ARABELLA. What?

WILMA. Getting lost in a city. Being bitten by dogs. Old lady Leighton taking my daddy away . . . (*A pause.*)

ARABELLA. Will you still be my friend?

WILMA. Sure, I'll always be your friend.

ARABELLA. I'm glad. Oh, I almost forgot. Your Aunt Gert said for you to come on home.

WILMA. I'll go in a little. I love to swing in my front yard. Aunt Gert has a swing in her front yard, but it's not the same. Mama and I used to come out here and swing together. Some nights when Daddy was out all night gambling, I used to wake up and hear her out here swinging away. Sometimes she'd let me come and sit beside her. We'd swing until three or four in the morning. (*A pause. She looks out into the yard.*) The pear tree looks sickly, doesn't it? The fig trees are doing nicely though. I was out in back and the weeds are near knee high, but fig trees just seem to thrive in the weeds. The freeze must have killed off the banana trees. . . . (*A pause. WILMA stops swinging–she walks around the yard.*) Maybe I won't leave either. Maybe I won't go to Hollywood after all.

from ***Assembly Line***

by Marian Winters

The setting of this scene is a novelty-goods factory where a group of women work on an assembly line putting the various pieces of manicure kits into the cases. The women on the line are friends and have been working together for some time when Marsha, a new woman who has an education and cultural pretensions, gets a job on the line. Most of the play deals with the conflict among the women.

In this scene, however, attitudes have changed. The women have just witnessed their employer having a heart attack. The scene begins just after the ambulance attendants have left. Vinnie is the stock boy, a loudmouthed young man who cleans up and carries stock to the line and loads trucks.

Start the scene with a clear imaginary action—*see* the attendants enter the elevator with the employer on the stretcher.

The scene can be played two ways. Play it first with the women still antagonistic toward Marsha. Then play it a second time the way the scene fits into the complete play, with the women beginning to feel sympathy for Marsha and changing their feelings about her because of what they learn about her past. This scene exemplifies the importance of studying the subtext of a play; the characters never say exactly what they feel. The scene can be played omitting Vinnie and Mae, but it would be good practice to play them, keeping them connected to the scene while being involved in their own separate thoughts. Be sure to construct an inner monologue and objectives for each character.

JOAN. I hope he's not dead.

FILOMENA. Boy, he sure looked it.

INEZ. What will they tell to his wife?

MARSHA (*sits staring out as though remembering*). Come down to the hospital. Something has happened and we'd appreciate it if you could get down here right away. (*The girls exchange puzzled glances.*)

INEZ (*studies* MARSHA *for a moment*). How did you know everything to do?

MARSHA (*almost to herself*). I didn't. I swore I would, but I didn't.

JOAN. You did whatever you could. Maybe he'll be all right.

MARSHA (*shakes her head negatively, still staring straight ahead*). My father died like that . . . four months ago . . . In a subway station. Everybody watched and nobody knew what to do . . . Everybody was helpless . . . Like us. (*The girls are all stunned.*)

INEZ. Were you *there?* (MARSHA *shakes her head "no."*)

JOAN. Who was *with* him?

MARSHA. Strangers like now . . . only strangers . . . (*She begins to cry. The girls watch her awkwardly.*)

FILOMENA. Boy, that's rough. No wonder she was upset before.

JOAN. We were *all* upset.

FILOMENA. But for her it was different.

INEZ. Listen, you better stop that; we have only a half hour for lunch now. That was the bell for lunch. We don't have time to cry. (*Goes to* MARSHA*'s shoulder.*) Don't cry, you hear me?

MARSHA (*still sits turned away*). Yes. Thanks.

JOAN. I guess you didn't bring any lunch, huh?

MARSHA. No, but I'm not very hungry, thanks. (MARSHA *has collected herself. The girls all open lunch pails and packets and eat during the following.*)

INEZ (*calls to Marsha, deliberately harsh*). You take coffee plain or with cream and sugar?

MARSHA. Plain, but I can get my ow . . .

INEZ (*goes to paper cup dispenser. Snaps at her*). Don't be so independent, eh! You're too independent!

FILOMENA. We all always got lots of coffee left over. I got an extra sandwich. You like tuna fish? C'mon, (*Hands it to her.*) you can bring me half a tuna tomorrow.

MARSHA (*accepts it*). Thanks, Filomena.

JOAN (*hands her a tangerine*). Here . . . I've got more.

MARSHA. Thanks, very much. (*She takes it.*)

FILOMENA (*as she eats*). I wonder did he know what was happening to him? You figure he knew what was happening?

JOAN. I don't know.

FILOMENA. Like for instance, when you're drownin' you know what's happenin'! I mean you think he knew somebody was trying to help him and all?

MARSHA (*again to herself*). I hope so, in a way.

INEZ (*hands* MARSHA *coffee*). It's very hot. Be careful.

MARSHA. Thank you . . .

JOAN. I think he was unconscious right away.

VINNIE. Unconscious nothin', he looked croaked to me.

MAE. Will you quit talking about it! I'm trying to *eat!*

from ***Blithe Spirit***
by Noel Coward

Elvira was Charles's first wife. After her death, he married Ruth. Charles is a writer and while researching a book about the occult Charles holds a seance; somehow Elvira's spirit is called back from the other world. Charles (and the audience) can see Elvira, but no one else can. In the course of the play, we learn that Elvira is still madly in love with Charles and dislikes Ruth intensely. She will eventually try to kill Charles so that he can join her in spirit, but she will fail. The complications Elvira causes result in a delightful comedy.

In this scene, Ruth does not yet understand what has happened. Because she cannot see or hear Elvira, she thinks that Charles is seeing things that aren't there. They have already had a quarrel during which Charles talked to Elvira. Ruth thought Charles was talking to her instead and felt insulted. Now she is determined to find out what is wrong with her husband.

In this scene each character sees and hears something different. Make sure that as you work you concentrate on exactly what your character sees and hears. Ruth especially has to react only to Charles. When Elvira is talking, Ruth has to fill the spaces with her own thoughts.

RUTH. What's the matter now?
CHARLES. She's here again!
RUTH. What do you mean? Who's here again?
CHARLES. Elvira.
RUTH. Pull yourself together and don't be absurd.
ELVIRA. It's all those nasturtiums; they're so vulgar.
CHARLES. I like nasturtiums.
RUTH. You like what?
ELVIRA (*putting her grey roses into the vase*). They're all right in moderation, but in a mass like that they look beastly.
CHARLES (*crosses over to* R *of* RUTH, C). Help me, Ruth—you've got to help me——
RUTH (*rises and retreats a pace to* L). What did you mean about nasturtiums?
CHARLES (*takes* RUTH's *hands and comes round to the* L *of her*). Never mind about that now. I tell you she's here again.
ELVIRA (*comes to above the sofa*). You have been having a nice scene, haven't you? I could hear you right down the garden.
CHARLES. Please mind your own business.

RUTH. If you behaving like a lunatic isn't my business, nothing is.

ELVIRA. I expect it was about me, wasn't it? I know I ought to feel sorry, but I'm not. I'm delighted.

CHARLES. How can you be so inconsiderate?

RUTH (*shrilly*). Inconsiderate! I like that, I must say!

CHARLES. Ruth—darling—please . . .

RUTH. I've done everything I can to help. I've controlled myself admirably. And I should like to say here and now that I don't believe a word about your hallucination. You're up to something, Charles—there's been a certain furtiveness in your manner for weeks. Why don't you be honest and tell me what it is?

CHARLES. You're wrong—you're dead wrong! I haven't been in the least furtive—I——

RUTH. You're trying to upset me. (*She moves away from* CHARLES.) For some obscure reason you're trying to goad me into doing something that I might regret. (*She bursts into tears.*) I won't stand for it any more. You're making me utterly miserable! (*She crosses to the sofa and falls into the* R *end of it.*)

CHARLES (*crosses to* RUTH). Ruth—please——

RUTH. Don't come near me!

ELVIRA. Let her have a nice cry. It'll do her good. (*She saunters round to down stage* L.)

CHARLES. You're utterly heartless!

RUTH. Heartless!

CHARLES (*wildly*). I was not talking to you! I was talking to Elvira.

RUTH. Go on talking to her then, talk to her until you're blue in the face, but don't talk to me.

CHARLES (*crosses to* ELVIRA). Help me, Elvira——

ELVIRA. How?

CHARLES. Make her see you or something.

ELVIRA. I'm afraid I couldn't manage that. It's technically the most difficult business—frightfully complicated, you know—it takes years of study——

CHARLES. You are here, aren't you? You're not an illusion?

ELVIRA. I may be an illusion, but I'm most definitely here.

CHARLES. How did you get here?

ELVIRA. I told you last night—I don't exactly know——

CHARLES. Well, you must make me a promise that in future you only come and talk to me when I'm alone.

ELVIRA (*pouting*). How unkind you are, making me feel so unwanted. I've never been treated so rudely.

CHARLES. I don't mean to be rude, but you must see——

ELVIRA. It's all your own fault for having married a woman who is incapable of seeing beyond the nose on her face. If she had a grain of real sympathy or affection for you she'd believe what you tell her.

CHARLES. How could you expect anybody to believe this?

ELVIRA. You'd be surprised how gullible people are; we often laugh about it on the Other Side.

(RUTH, *who has stopped crying and been staring at* CHARLES *in horror, suddenly rises.*)

RUTH (*gently*). Charles!

CHARLES (*surprised at her tone*). Yes, dear—— (CHARLES *crosses to her,* R.)

RUTH. I'm awfully sorry I was cross.

CHARLES. But, my dear——

RUTH. I understand everything now. I do really.

CHARLES. You do?

RUTH (*patting his arm reassuringly*). Of course I do.

ELVIRA. Look out—she's up to something.

CHARLES. Will you please be quiet?

RUTH. Of course, darling. We'll all be quiet, won't we? We'll be as quiet as little mice.

from ***The Show-Off***
by George Kelly

Aubrey is a show-off; in fact he is a liar, a man who simply cannot help making himself seem more important by stretching the facts. Clara is his sister-in-law, and the Amy referred to is his wife. Clara has never liked Aubrey; she has put up with him because her sister loves him. In this scene, Aubrey has just finished a business conversation with a man in the living room of his mother-in-law's home. In the course of the conversation, he has told a number of whoppers, but the one which Clara is concerned about is his claim that the house is his. In reality Aubrey and Amy live in two rooms over a barber shop because Aubrey doesn't make enough money for a house of his own.

Notice that the playwright limits the way the scene can be played through stage directions that tell you how the lines should be spoken and where, on the stage, to move. If you do not use scenery, some of the directions about movement need to be adjusted. As you act the scene, find a reason for the activity. Ask yourself what the character wants to accomplish that makes him or her move to a particular place or say the line in a particular tone of voice.

During their argument Aubrey and Clara try never to raise their voices. Find objectives that account for that fact. Be sure to show the conflict between the two.

CLARA. Come here, Aubrey, I want to talk to you. (*He turns towards her, with an attempt at nonchalance.*) What do you mean by telling people that this is your house?

AUBREY. I didn't tell anybody it was my house.

CLARA. You *must* have told this man, or he wouldn't have said so.

AUBREY. What do you think I am, a liar?

CLARA. Yes, I do; one of the best I know.

AUBREY. Well, ask Amy what I said to him. She was here when I was talking to him.

CLARA (*before he has finished speaking*). I don't have to ask anybody anything!—you were lying to him here today, right in front of me.

AUBREY (*with a shade of challenge in his manner*). What'd I say?

CLARA. That you'd fixed the automobile thing up.

AUBREY. It's fixed up, isn't it?

CLARA. *You* didn't fix it up. (*There is a slight pause, during which* AUBREY, *his dignity considerably outraged, moves forward and crosses in front of her to the front of the center table, where he stops.* CLARA *moves down at the right of the Morris chair to a point near him.*) You'd have gone to jail for six months only for Frank Hyland. And telling this man that you tried to persuade Pop to stop working.

AUBREY (*over his left shoulder*). So I did.

CLARA. When?

AUBREY. I didn't say it to him. But I told Amy he ought to stop. And I think he'd be right here today if he'd taken my advice.

CLARA. He wouldn't be right here today if he'd stopped expecting *you* to keep him. (*He moves further over to the right, and she follows him.*) And now, listen to me, Aubrey; I want to talk seriously to you. You've made a lot of trouble for us since you've been in this family, and I want you to stop it. There's no reason my husband, because he happens to have a few dollars, should be going around paying *your* bills.

AUBREY (*half-turning to her*). What do you want me to do?

CLARA. I want you to stop telling *lies;* for that's about all everything you do amounts to. Trying to make people believe you're something that you're not—when if you'd just stop your talking and your showing off, you *might* be the thing that you're trying to make them believe you are. (*She glances toward the kitchen door, and then speaks to him again, in a slightly lower tone.*) Your wife's going to have a child one of these days, Aubrey, and you want to pull yourself together and try to be sensible, like the man of a family *should* be. You're smart enough—there's no reason why a fellow like you should be living in two rooms over a barber shop. I should think you'd have more respect for your wife. (*She turns and moves a few steps up towards the kitchen door.*)

AUBREY. A man doesn't stand much chance of getting ahead, Clara, when the boss has got a grudge against him.

CLARA (*turning sharply to her right, and moving to the upper right-hand corner of the center table*). Well, stop your silly talk, and get rid of that carnation, and the boss might get rid of his grudge. (*She glances toward the kitchen door again, leans across the table towards him, and lowers her voice.*) But, what I wanted to tell you was this, Aubrey—I've asked Mom to let you and Amy come in here; and she sez she wouldn't mind it only that she knows that the first thing she'd *hear* is that you'd told someone that you'd taken *her* in. And, you see, that's exactly what you've done already—to this man that brought the watch. If I told Mom that there'd be war.

AUBREY. Are you going to tell her?

CLARA (*with authoritative levelness*). I'm going to put that up to you. And the very first time I hear that you've told anybody that this is *your* house,—I'll see to it that you'll get a house that *will* be your own. (AUBREY *smiles, a bit smugly, and looks at her out of the sides of his eyes.*)

AUBREY. I guess your Mother'ud have something to say about that, Clara.

CLARA (*with a measured evenness*). Well, the only thing that needs to worry you, is what *I'll* have to say about it. (AUBREY'*s smugness begins to fade–into a questioning narrowness.*) This is my house—Pop left it to me; so that Mom'ud always have a roof over her. For he knew how long she'd have it if Amy ever got round her. And if Amy ever got hold of it, he knew what she'd do if it ever came to a choice between you and Mom.

AUBREY. What are you doing, kidding me? (CLARA *holds his eyes steadily for a fraction of a second.*)

CLARA. I'm giving you a tip—see that you keep it to yourself. (AUBREY *withdraws his eyes slowly and looks straight out, weighing this new bit of intelligence carefully in his mind.*) Be wise, now, Aubrey—you've got a chance to sit *in* here and live like a human being, and if you throw it away, you'll have nobody to blame but yourself.

"Copies of this play, in individual paper covered acting editions are available from Samuel French, Inc., 25 W. 45th St., New York, N.Y. 10036 or 7623 Sunset Blvd., Hollywood, Calif. 90046 or in Canada Samuel French, (Canada) Ltd., 80 Richmond Street East, Toronto M5C 1P1, Canada."

Unit IV
The Play and the Actor

CHAPTER 13
Auditions

CHAPTER 14
Rehearsing the Show

CHAPTER 15
Performance

CHAPTER 16
Musical Performance

Professional producers select plays to make money. It is their business to put on plays, so they are constantly looking for material. They look for the best play available to them that they believe a certain number of people will want to come to see. If the play turns out to be pretty good, and if enough people decide to see it, the play makes money and the producer goes on to other plays. If not, the producer goes out of business. It is all very unpredictable. Each producer has his own opinion of what people will like, and there are an enormous number of different groups who like different things. Thus, many different plays and kinds of plays will be done for many different audiences.

In a school, plays are selected for the same reasons, with two major differences. First, the amount of money involved is much smaller. There should be an audience somewhere in the community that is large enough to pay the costs of putting on the play. But, since no one is doing this to get rich, this audience does not automatically have to be the largest one possible. Second, the school play is a teaching program, and the play selected should teach the actors and technical workers something.

As your group decides on a play to be performed, there are several simple but important questions that should be considered.

(1) Is it worthwhile? Are the characters and events interesting and understandable? Is the writing good? Is there enough there for everyone involved to still find interesting things in it after six weeks of rehearsal?

(2) Is there an audience for it? Will enough of the people who are likely to come to the performance find the material interesting? Will it attract new people who do not normally come?

(3) Is there enough money? Royalties have to be paid, scenery built, and costumes made; how much will those cost? Do you have enough to pay for them, or can you at least expect enough from the audience or from donations to pay for them?

(4) Is there time? Can you rehearse the play in the time available? Can you get a stage for sufficient rehearsal time? Will you have time to do all the costumes and scenery that you will need? Remember that the cast also has to do other schoolwork during this same period.

(5) Will you learn from the play? Will it teach the actors new things about acting? Will it give them new insights into people? Will the technical work, onstage and backstage, be different from the work done on the last production?

(6) Will the play fit your program? If it has fifty characters, do you have fifty actors? Can you fit it on your particular stage?

(7) Is it the kind of play your group wants to be publicly associated with in your school and your community?

If you find a script that gives you positive answers to all those questions, you have a script you want to do. Then you can start the planning and get ready to audition and rehearse the show.

Chapter 13
Auditions

After the play is chosen, a cast must be selected. This is done through auditions, or try-outs. All the performers who want to take part in the play will perform some short selection for the director. Then, from all these people, the director will try to select the best arrangement of performers to fill the roles the play requires.

This is never an easy time for the actor or the director. It is especially trying for the actor, beginner or professional. No matter how they try to pretend, actors tend to regard auditions as a kind of test, which they pass if they get the roles they wanted and which they fail if they do not. This is not quite the way an audition works. It will help you to prepare for your own auditions if you can develop an understanding of the entire process.

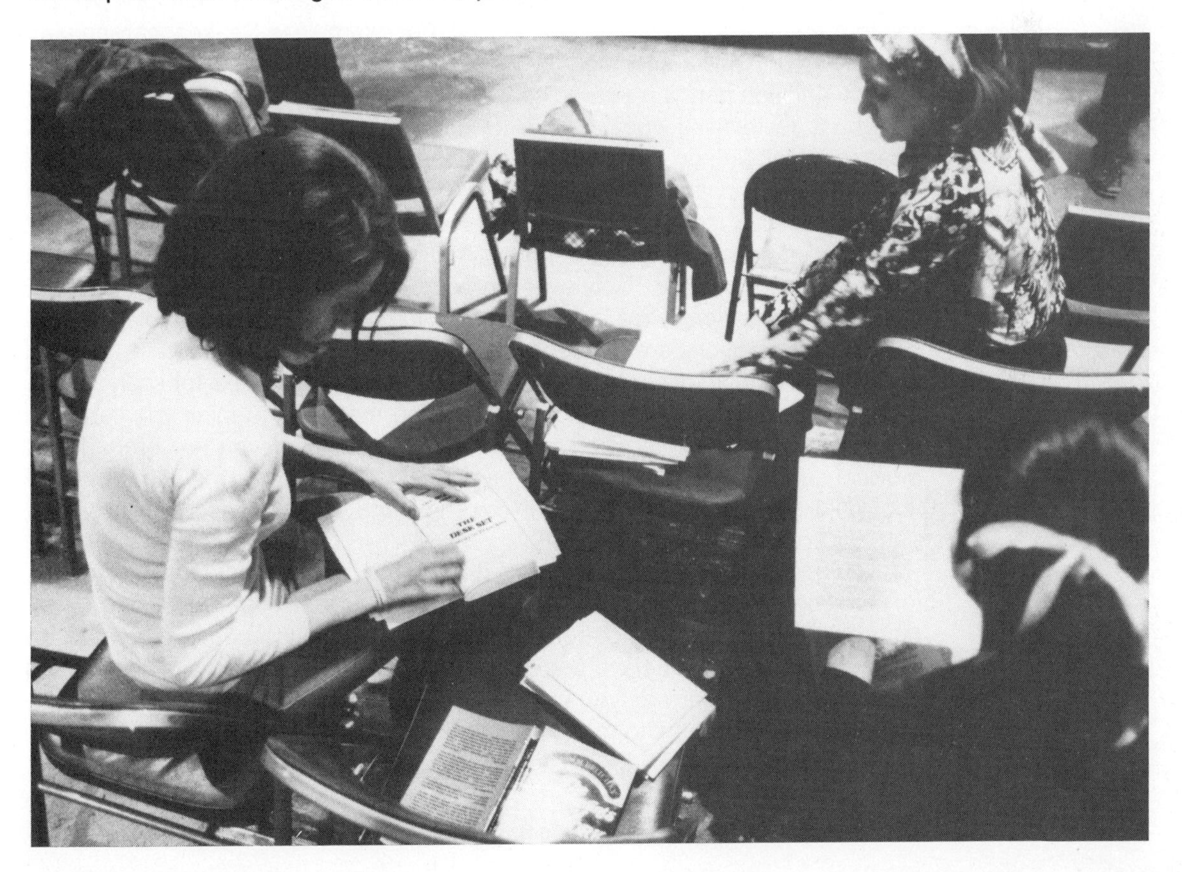

There are three basic types of auditions: the prepared scene, the cold reading, and the improvisation. A director may use one of these, or a combination of all three, depending on the requirements of a particular play script and the director's own rehearsal methods.

Prepared Scenes

A prepared scene in an audition is a short monologue that you have studied, memorized, and prepared before you came to the audition. It is supposed to be a finished scene that shows the director what you can do with a finished performance.

Directors tend to use this type only when there are a large number of people auditioning or when there are special skills needed for particular roles. In school or community groups, you will see it most often in musical auditions. There you will usually be expected to come with a song or a dance or both already prepared. It is almost always used for summer theaters, repertory companies, and college or conservatory admissions auditions, where actors will be asked to do two or three different prepared scenes to show the range of their talent. Professionals often use it in the first round of auditions, from which directors will select two or three people to read a second time from the script itself before making final decisions. Sometimes, if a play has special problems, the director will ask you to prepare a scene from the play itself. For example, a Shakespearean play or one with unfamiliar accents may be difficult to read without preparation.

If you audition from a prepared scene, remember that the director will assume that you are exhibiting what you think is your best work. Pick a scene that shows what you think you do best. It does not have to be intensely dramatic, with lots of shouting and crying, if that is not your strongest skill. It should fit what you can do. Usually these scenes are expected to be about two minutes long. They may come from any play or from other materials such as those you might use in Interpretation projects. Whatever the source, remember that you are acting a character in a performance, which happens to have a very small audience.

When the auditions are announced, examine the directions carefully. Be sure you know what kind of scenes are asked for. If the director asks for scenes from a specific play, read the script carefully to find the role you think you could do best, no matter what its size, and prepare from that. If you are preparing a musical audition, you do not usually have to sing a song from the show, but you should know what kind of music is in the show and select your song from similar material you already know.

If you become serious about acting, it is a good thing to begin to save scenes for auditions. By the time you finish high school, you might have five or six different scenes memorized, from Shakespeare to musical comedy, and a couple of songs, which you have practiced regularly and which are available to you for any audition. That way you will not have to spend hours learning new material every time you want to try out for something.

Readings

Most groups use readings as the basic part of the audition. For a reading, you are given a copy of the script and told to prepare a character and a particular scene. Then you will be given a few minutes to read the scene and think about it. These are often called cold readings because there is very little time to get emotionally and mentally warmed up. Sometimes you will read your scene with other people who are auditioning other roles in the same scene. Sometimes you will read the scene with the stage manager taking all the other parts.

A reading is not a test of your reading level. It is a chance to show something about your acting skill. You are acting a scene but with the script in your hand because you have not had time to memorize it. In your mind, try to treat it like a performance. The director uses this type because he wants to see and hear how you look in a specific part and with the other people who are auditioning. It doesn't help you or the director if you try to hide behind the script.

If the play is a new play, you may not know anything about the script before you see it. Most of the time, however, there will be copies of the script available before auditions, either from the director or in the library. It will always help to

find a copy and read it over before auditions; that way you will understand what the people in the audition scenes are talking about. Whether you have read the script or not, listen carefully to all directions. The director will always tell you what he thinks the character is like and what is happening in the scene. That will give you the goal for your own particular audition performance.

Improvisations

In many groups, part or all of the audition is done by improvisation. Many directors feel that readings do not tell them anything about potential acting skills because the actors are too tense, worrying about reading everything correctly. Because of the demands of a particular play, some directors may be more concerned with the way the actors work together or with the actors' physical abilities than with their speaking abilities. In these cases, you will be asked to improvise a number of exercises or scenes.

These improvisations will work in much the same way as the improvisations you have done in activities in other chapters. You may be given a place or a character type or a situation and asked to make a scene from that. You may be asked to pretend to be a number of different objects or personalities. You may even be asked to do some pantomime work. In any of these situations, the director will be looking for imagination, concentration, expressiveness, and the speed with which you follow directions. The most important things you can do to help yourself are to listen carefully to all instructions, to concentrate, and to react as quickly as possible to what other people are doing with you.

Casting

After the auditions, the director casts the roles in the play. This is a much more complicated process than just picking the "best" actors and putting them in the biggest roles. The director will try to match actors to specific parts to make the best possible arrangement of people available. Casting is never easy.

The director must consider everything he saw in auditions and everything he knows about the performers and match that with everything he knows about the play. He must consider not only the quality of the readings or scenes but also the size and shape of the performer, the tone of voice, the speed of reading and taking directions, and the overall sense of concentration. He must also consider the relationships with other actors; if two of the characters are a parent and a child, the director will try to cast a parent who is taller than the child, for example, no matter how well the tallest person may have read for the child's role. He will also consider past experience. Every role is in some way an audition for another role, not just because it gives you experience; the director will also remember who came late to rehearsals, who didn't memorize lines, or who wouldn't stop talking backstage in the last show. If he has a choice between two good auditions, one of whom had a good rehearsal manner and one who did not, he would be silly not to cast the one with the good record.

If the director is also a teacher, he will also consider how he can train actors by casting them in certain ways. He may decide that, no matter how beautifully you play them, you have played enough mother roles and cast someone else as Anne Frank's mother to help that person learn and grow too. This rarely happens in professional or community theaters, but it is an important part of the casting process in the schools.

Procedures

Most auditions will be announced several days to several weeks before they actually occur. Check all the information and directions so that you know where and when they will happen and what, if anything, you should be prepared to do. If scripts are available, try to get one to read at least once before the audition so that you know a little about the play.

When you arrive, you will be asked to fill out an information sheet. Usually, this will be a card or paper asking (1) your name, (2) how you can be contacted (address, phone, parents' names, etc.), (3) past experience, (4) availability for rehearsals (class and job schedules, family commitments, etc.), and (5) physical descriptions which help the director recognize and remember you (hair, height, weight, etc.). Fill out the information sheet clearly and accurately. If you are cast, it will usually serve as the file for the stage manager as well as the director. If you are not cast, it will help people find you for other shows or for other jobs on this one.

Some directors audition performers individually or in small groups. If so, there will be someone, usually the stage manager, who will schedule you and give you the basic information you need, such as a copy of the scene you will be asked to read and to whom you turn in your information sheet.

Many other directors hold large-group auditions, especially for cold readings and improvisations. If so, they will make one single explanation to the entire group about what is expected in each role and how the audition will work. Then scripts or instructions will be given out and people brought up in random groups to read or to do scenes. During each audition, the director will watch and make notes about each person.

Most directors in large-group auditions will not only allow, but will expect, you to read for more than one character. Usually, if there is sufficient time, you will be able to re-read scenes; it will depend on the director and the number of people present at any given audition.

After everyone has auditioned, the director will select the cast. Usually this takes some time. If there is a public bulletin board near the theater, a cast list will be posted there as soon as decisions are made. If not, the stage manager will call each person cast. At that time, if you get a part, you will also find out when the first rehearsal will begin and when and where to get your copy of the script.

Sometimes a director will not be able to make up his mind about several roles. In that case, he will have a call-back, which is a second audition for a

small group he would like to see again for some reason. That call-back will be run in the same way as the original auditions. If you used prepared scenes for the first audition, then you will normally do readings or improvisations at call-backs. After this second round, the cast will be selected, notified, and the cast list posted.

Some Suggestions

There is no easy way to audition. Most directors are unhappy with the audition system, but no one has found a better way to pick a cast. It is a nervous, difficult experience for every actor, and that nervousness never goes away, no matter how experienced you become. But there are some things you can do to make yourself more calm and more successful.

(1) Ask questions. If you are not sure about a direction or a description of a character, ask before you start the scene.

(2) Relax. There are relaxing exercises and some warm-ups in other chapters. Take a few moments before you begin to go through a couple of those. Do this just before, not just after, you have been called so that you are ready when your opportunity comes.

(3) Stand where you can be seen. It is surprising how many people forget

this. If there is a spot of light, be sure your face is in it. If you are on a stage, come as near the apron as you can.

(4) Make sure you have what you need. If auditioning for a musical, you may need to bring an accompanist. If an accompanist will be provided, you will have to bring clear sheet music that can be followed easily. For a dance routine, you may need a tape recorder and the tape of your music. However, it is usually better not to use props for prepared scenes; props take too much time to set up and make you seem awkward. You will always need a pencil to fill out an information sheet, and you may need to make notes of directions or ideas in the script.

(5) If you are in a large group or if you will have the chance to read more than once, help the director remember you by not changing the style of your clothing or hair. Many groups audition on several days and allow people to come back. If the director doesn't already know you, he may not recognize you the second time if you look too different.

(6) Practice auditioning. One way is just to go to auditions. You will never get roles if you never try out. Even if you think you don't have a chance, go to the audition and give it a try. Sometimes you will surprise yourself and get a part. At the very least, you will gain experience, and the next time you will know more about how to audition.

Another way is to practice readings. Once each week pick a scene in a play you have not read before and try to act it out. If you can't find a partner to work with you, read from a story or a book. Try to pick sections in which a single character is talking so that you create a character and establish an emotional attitude. Don't spend more than about five minutes preparing; it will help you get used to reading new material you haven't rehearsed.

Another way is just to read. Anything. Many young actors worry about auditions simply because they worry about the act of reading in public. The more you read the less it will bother you, and the more you can spend your time thinking about the performance.

You can also give yourself improvisation practice. Put a little bowl or box somewhere in your bedroom. Think up characters and situations and write them on little pieces of paper and put them in the box. These should be simple but varied. You might try things like "a banker finding an empty vault," "a construction worker finding peanut-butter sandwiches when he expected ham and cheese in his lunch pail," or anything else that can be written in that form. Try a few strange ones, like "a tree waking up" or "jelly being spread on a piece of bread." Put in new ones whenever you think of some. Then, every couple of days, draw one out and try to improvise a scene with it. Don't do more than one a day, and throw each one away after you do it.

(7) Always think of each audition as an opportunity, not as a test. So many different factors are involved in casting a play that getting a role or not getting one tells you nothing about your talent. The only thing you can be sure of is that you won't get a role if you don't audition. Each time you try out is another chance, another opportunity to take part in a play.

Chapter 14
Rehearsing the Show

No play, or any other kind of performance, just happens. No matter how brilliant the cast, no matter how simple the material, the show must be planned and rehearsed. The exact schedule for each production will be different, depending on the needs of individual casts and scripts. However, schedules will usually follow a general pattern.

The word *rehearsal* comes from an old word which means a "harrow." A harrow is used on farms to go over the plowed land to break up the clods the plow turned up, to aerate the soil, to uproot weeds the plow may have missed, and sometimes after planting to push soil back over the seeds. That is a good metaphor for what happens in a play rehearsal. The play is gone over a number of times, broken into smaller and smaller parts to let light and air into the details and to find and eliminate ineffective ideas, and then it is put back together again to grow into a full, interesting, unified production.

This takes time. The Russian director Stanislavski once had 108 rehearsals for a single show. Most groups, however, don't have that much time. American professionals spend about four weeks, and most school groups spend about six weeks, sometimes more for musicals or very complicated shows. Approximately two-thirds of the time will be spent taking the play apart, and the last one-third putting it back together again, depending on the director and the play.

First Rehearsal

When you are cast in a role, a first rehearsal will be announced. This will be used to get everyone acquainted with each other and with the play and to schedule the remaining rehearsals. Many directors will read through the script at this rehearsal so that everyone knows what happens and who does what in the story. Very often, the costumer will take measurements as well so that work on costumes can begin immediately. In some cases, this may be the only time everyone in the entire cast is present at the same time until a run-through of the entire play.

The director and stage manager will also go over all rehearsal rules at this time. These may vary in detail, but they can usually be reduced to three basics: (1) be on time, (2) be prepared, and (3) pay attention.

A good cast member will always be ready to start when the rehearsal is scheduled. If it starts at 7:00 P.M., the actor is waiting to start at 7:00 P.M. If he needs to warm up or to talk to someone in the cast, he comes a few minutes early so that is all out of the way when it is time to rehearse.

The good actor will always be prepared for any rehearsal. In practical terms, this includes such things as always having a script and a pencil to make notes with, knowing what is scheduled and where, and having any needed rehearsal props.

At this rehearsal, the director will probably talk about the basic themes of the play, and the designers will show some sketches. If time allows, the scenery designer will show a model of the set. Pay close attention to these, because they will help you visualize the director's instructions.

After this rehearsal, read the script again, just to be completely familiar with everything. If the scripts can be marked in, underline or highlight all your own lines. This will help you keep your place in rehearsals and help you study as well. Some people like to mark their lines in one color, such as yellow, and mark their cue lines in another, such as red. If you are doing a musical, you will probably not be able to do this, because most musical scripts are rented and have to be returned without marks.

Blocking

The next section of rehearsals will involve blocking the show. This means that the director will give directions for each actor's movement throughout the entire play.

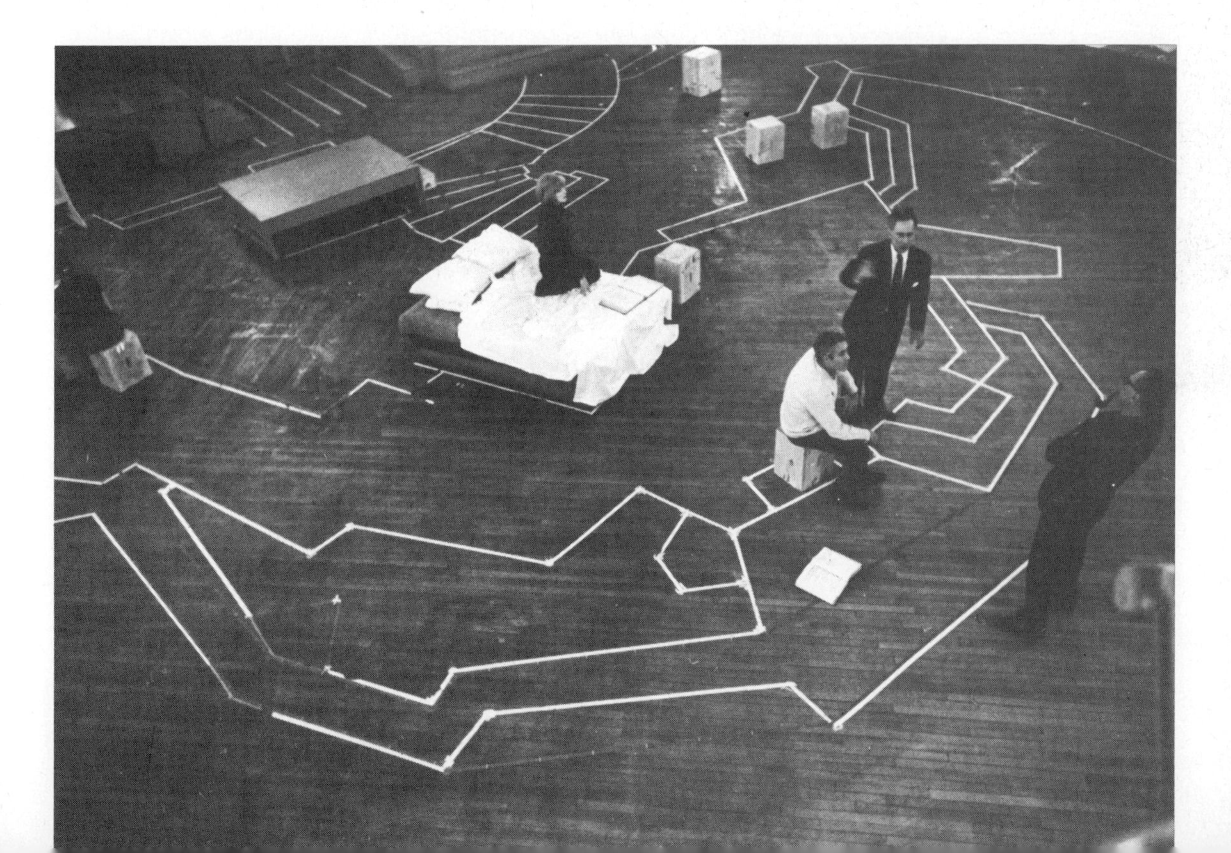

Stage blocking for Arthur Miller's *After the Fall*

When you arrive at rehearsal for a scene, the director will explain the floor plan. Whether you are on your stage or in a rehearsal room, the stage manager will have marked the floor with tape to show where the set pieces and furniture will be. Some kind of temporary furniture, usually made from folding chairs, will be set up to stand in for the final set pieces. Draw a picture of this in the script of each scene so that you remember it clearly when you study at home.

Write down everything that applies to you in a scene's directions. For the first couple of weeks, all the directions will run together, and many people tend to forget even the simplest pieces of blocking during that time. Always use pencil; directors have been known to change their minds. There are only a few common directions used and they can be easily abbreviated, so you can pack a great deal of information into the margin of a script. Any movement from one place to another is called a cross, and it is abbreviated by an X.

On a proscenium stage, there are four basic directions: up, down, left, and right. All directions will be combinations of these. When proscenium stages were first developed hundreds of years ago, the audience was on a flat floor and the stage was slanted, or raked. Thus, if you went to the audience side of the stage, you went down, and if you crossed away from the audience, you went up an incline. Although most theaters now have flat stages and raked audience seating, the terms have stayed the same. Left is always to the actor's left when he is facing the audience. Any diagonal crosses are described with the two shared directions; to cross down-right means that you move diagonally in the direction between right and down.

The proscenium stage is usually divided into fifteen imaginary areas for reference in blocking. These are shown here with abbreviations which can be used.

Stage Areas

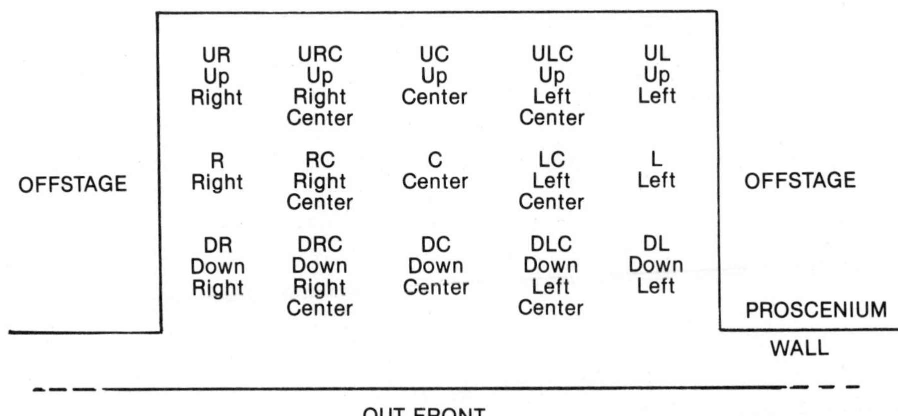

Arena Stage Areas

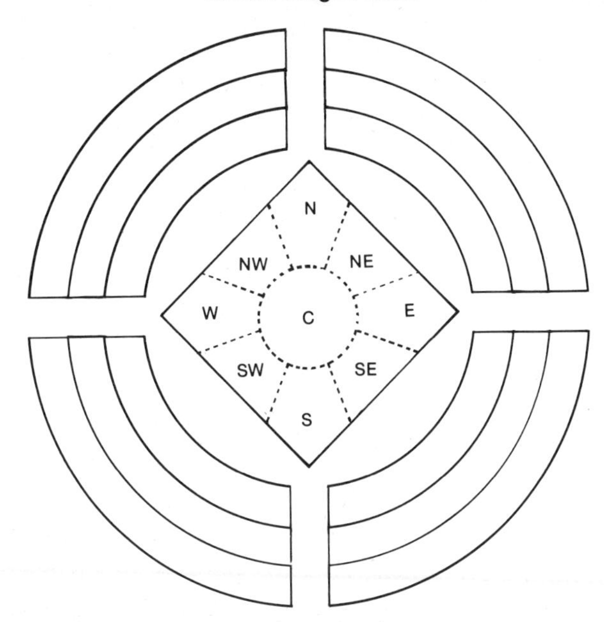

Since an arena stage has audience on all sides, it does not have an up or down direction. Directors use either the compass or the clock as the method of dividing and labeling the stage. One point, such as a major entrance way, is arbitrarily called north, or 12 o'clock, and other directions work around the area from that point. The center will always be Center.

Blocking rehearsals are usually slow. It takes time to get everyone moved around and everything written down. Probably just one scene at a time will be worked, so it may take several rehearsals to work through the entire play. This is another reason why everything needs to be written down; it may be several days before you come back to a scene to really work on it.

The director uses blocking rehearsals to give the basic shape to the show and to test his ideas. He may also expect to give the basic outline of your characterization in this time. The actors use these rehearsals to familiarize themselves with the script and to get an understanding of the imaginary world their characters will have to live in.

Thus, there is a great deal of work for the actor to do on his own during this time. This is the time when you should sit down with the dictionary and learn meanings and pronunciations for unfamiliar words. It is also the time for you to start the analysis of the character. Refer to Chapter 9 and to the beginning of the section of practice scenes to remind yourself about this process. Write notes, definitions, questions, goals, and emotional attitudes all over the script; don't be afraid to mark it up, so long as you use pencil.

Scene Rehearsals

After blocking has been worked out, you will begin a long series of rehearsals in which you will break the show into smaller and smaller units to rehearse. This is the major, most important part of rehearsals. It is the period in which you, the other actors, and the director all analyze relationships, test your ideas about the characters, and work out the details of business and emotion. It is a time of questions and changes.

The actors and the director work together, but from two different viewpoints. The actors try to make the characterizations make sense. They see the play from one person's view, from the inside. The director tries to have the play make sense to the audience and sees the play from the outside. In general terms, the actors are responsible for analysis and interpretation of character, and the director is responsible for finding the best way to make that interpretation visible. Of course, these always overlap. The director will make many suggestions and decisions about motivations and characterizations, and the actors will alter the blocking, business, and expression when they have ideas as well. But it is a shared experience. Many inexperienced actors expect the director to do everything for them and seem to forget all of the things they studied in class about

Students and director: Glenbrook North High School, Northbrook, Illinois

acting. This is a misunderstanding of the acting process. The ideas and class exercises, such as those you did in the first three units, are preparations for each actor to use personally. The director has different problems, for he is trying to put on a particular play. If he does not repeat a particular exercise in rehearsals, that does not mean that the skill is not needed. It only means that the actor is expected to deal with that on his own. Half of any rehearsal time for a play happens away from rehearsals, where each actor does all of the preparation needed to understand the role. The director must make the final decision as to what plays best, but it will be a better decision if he can select from the ideas of the entire cast rather than dictate his own ideas. If the process is shared, the play will be alive rather than mechanical.

At some point in this period, you will be expected to have all the lines learned. This deadline is absolutely critical. All other parts of the rehearsal fall apart if actors do not know their lines. Other actors cannot develop any consistency because the actor with problems is thinking about the next word, not the characterization or the scene.

The French call this period *repetition* because that is what happens. You will break the play into small scenes, and you will go over those repeatedly. Each time you repeat the scene, you will be looking for something to add to what you've already done or something different to try which will solve a problem in the scene. Each time through you will be looking for more details.

In these rehearsals, you should become aware of the other characters on stage. A play is a collection of actions and reactions. As each actor develops actions in these rehearsals, all other actors in the scene must adjust their reactions. These may force you to rethink all your planning and analysis, because no play or character is ever completely understood the first time through a reading or study session. There are always adjustments and ideas that come out only in the constant shared process of rehearsal.

Even after you have memorized your lines, continue to bring the script and a pencil to rehearsals so that you will have it to study and refresh your memory when you are offstage. You can also mark any changes that were made in a scene, to help you remember them for the next rehearsal. You will be most comfortable if you are always mentally prepared. Take a few minutes before rehearsal starts to read over the scenes scheduled and to refresh your memory. If you can't get to rehearsal early, do it before you leave home. As soon as you return home, read over the scenes you just rehearsed. Mark any changes in the script if you need to, but this reading is primarily to help you remember everything you did.

As soon as lines are memorized, the hands are free. Then you can work on the specific business of your role. Sometimes it helps to use rehearsal props or clothes. The director may supply these, or you may wish to bring them yourself. These are props or clothing like the ones you will use in the show, which you use to work out "business." If you familiarize yourself with the items, your performance will not fall apart when you use the real things at technical and dress rehearsals.

Rehearsal props and clothes are most helpful when you have to do something very unusual. For example, in a production of *Our Town,* all the women should rehearse in long skirts so that they get used to the ways they can walk or sit in them. Boys playing businessmen may want to rehearse a few times in a coat and tie. Hats, umbrellas, glasses, purses, and similar items all affect the way you play a role and should be rehearsed with whenever possible. It is also a good idea to come to every rehearsal in shoes similar to those the character will wear, so that all your crosses can be worked out smoothly.

Run-Throughs

At some point, the director will decide that it is time to start putting all the little pieces of the play back together. This is usually done by running through sections of the play. A run-through is just a rehearsal which the director does not stop or interrupt.

These rehearsals usually start as scene run-throughs. As soon as the director thinks most of the problems of a scene have been solved, he will ask you to go through it without stopping. During the run-through he will make notes, directions that he will give to you at the end of the run. When the director gives notes, listen carefully *all the time.* Even if he is not speaking directly to you, what he tells someone else to do may affect what you do in the scene. If you still have problems or don't understand something, ask questions. It will be too late once all the technical complications begin. After several scenes seem ready, you will run the full act; and after the separate acts seem ready, you will run the entire show.

During this period, you should concentrate on making connections. The director will not interrupt because he wants the actors to concentrate completely on what they are doing, to fit the pieces together in gradually larger sections until all the parts from beginning to end flow smoothly.

There will still be changes and adjustments. Quite often you will find new ideas and understandings about your role as the focus of rehearsals shifts from tiny problems to the overall show. This in turn will help you make the small adjustments which complete the performance.

During run-throughs the work is almost completely done in groups. Refresh yourself on some of the ideas and exercises in Chapter 10. Work especially hard on *listening* to the other actors so that you hear what the characters are saying, not just the actor's cue line.

One of the things you will work on will be tempo. The director will try to adjust the speed of each scene so that the dramatic action moves at an interesting pace. One of the things the actor must do is to pick up cues. This means to start your response immediately, as soon as possible after the cue given by another actor. A way to do this is to take your breath for a line while the other person is speaking. Then there is no pause while you get ready to speak.

The director will also begin to stress projection and diction. If you have been in a rehearsal room, you should begin to have some time on the stage so that you can learn to speak clearly in the larger room where the audience will be. Refer to Chapter 3 for help if you have problems.

In an ideal rehearsal, the final run-through will be suitable for an audience to see, except that there will be no technical parts of the show. Many actors find the final run-through their favorite part of all acting because they do not have to worry whether the doors will work, a light will come on, the phone will ring, or whether they will trip on the hem of a skirt. The important point to remember is, although there will continue to be minor adjustments, the essential shape of the performance has to be ready at this rehearsal, not at the first performance. After this run-through, most of the director's attention has to be given to fitting everything together, and he will not have another chance to give undivided attention to the actors.

Tech Rehearsals

Eventually, all the work done by the various technical crews will be added to the work the actors have been doing in rehearsal. If you are lucky and can rehearse on your stage for several weeks, this will happen gradually. As set pieces and props arrive, they will be worked into the rehearsals. But most

Tech rehearsal: Glenbrook North High School, Northbrook, Illinois

groups are not this lucky and can move onto the stage only a few days before performance. In either case, there will be one or more tech rehearsals.

In these rehearsals, all the technical elements—lights, sound, costumes, scenery, and props—are meshed with the performance of the actors. This is not always easy. In fact, these rehearsals tend to be the longest. If the schedule allows, they may be spread over several evenings, but if time on stage is severely limited, rehearsals may start in the morning and go all day.

The actor's primary goal in these rehearsals is to learn to use his imaginary world in a practical sense. You will go through the play from the beginning and walk on the stairs, open the doors, drink the water, and sit on the furniture. If at all possible, you will wear the costume and walk in the shoes. The director will pause from time to time to solve problems, and much of the sense of tempo and movement will be broken. This is why you worked on tempo in the run-throughs. But this practical work has to be done or the finished show will collapse.

Dress Rehearsals

After the tech rehearsals have solved the practical problems of set and costume and sound cues, you will have several dress rehearsals. These are performances without the audience. Everything is done exactly as it will be done on opening night. The only difference is that the director will give notes to the cast and crew after each dress rehearsal.

In many ways, these rehearsals put together that which was taken apart in the tech rehearsals. They allow the actor and the crews to rebuild the flow of the show, to make the performance one continuous unit. At the end of the last dress rehearsal, you will probably be as good as you are likely to be. Treat these dress rehearsals exactly as you would a performance and follow the guidelines in the next chapter.

Chapter 15
Performance

After all the rehearsals, you know how the play is supposed to go and what you are supposed to do, but you still need to do it in public. Eventually, opening night arrives.

There is a great deal of excitement about any opening night. It is an adventure, a trip into a secret hidden place. No matter how well you are prepared, the audience makes it a new territory, still unexplored. It also makes many actors quite nervous. However, if you are prepared and if you follow some simple procedures, you can cope with both the excitement and the nervousness of the first, and any other, performance.

Call

The call is the time you are expected to be in the building. Usually there will be two calls, a makeup call and a final cast call. If you have a makeup call, you should be there promptly, because the makeup room will be overcrowded if several people fail to meet the makeup schedule.

Makeup itself is discussed in Chapter 18. However, there are a few points that the actors need to remember. Makeup is messy, and costumes, if you are having more than one performance, have to be used again. Put on the makeup before you put on the costume. Once the makeup is on, you are becoming the character. No one from the audience should see you in makeup except on the stage or immediately after curtain calls.

Most groups will have a sign-in sheet posted on the callboard or in the makeup room. Be sure you check in as soon as you arrive, so that the stage manager can tell at a glance if everyone is present.

The general cast call comes just a few minutes before starting time. Everyone in the cast will gather in one place for any last-minute questions or information. You should have all makeup finished and normally should be in costume as well. This is the last business session, where information about where a prop will be found, whether a hem has been repaired, or where a lamp has been moved, is communicated. After this, you are in the show and should go directly into final warm-ups.

Once the call is released, backstage should become quiet. The house will be open and the audience will be taking their seats. You can begin focusing all your concentration on the performance. If you have not done so before the cast

call, go into a quiet room and warm up. Some of the exercises in Chapters 1 and 2 will help.

After you are warmed up, find yourself a quiet place and think over your character for a few moments. Try to make this positive. Remind yourself what the character wants to do, what he expects to see, and where he has been before the show starts.

Even the most experienced actors are nervous at this point. About five minutes before your first entrance, do a couple of the relaxation exercises in Chapter 1.

Then, about two minutes before your first entrance, move to your entrance area. If you enter after the beginning, listen to the flow of the show already in progress so that you begin to get the feel of the performance. Think about one thing, the first thing you will do when you enter. Try not to think of anything else. Once you do that first one thing, all the others that follow will happen. Then, just before your cue, prepare your entrance just as in Chapter 11. And go.

Performing

While a performance is in progress, including during intermission, the focus of everyone should be on the stage. The audience should see and hear only what is out there on the stage, what they came to see and hear. Absolute quiet is essential at all times. If you exit in a scene, begin immediately preparing your mind for the next entrance, whether it is a minute or an hour away. Don't assume the show is over just because you left the stage.

On the stage, let the show happen. If you rehearsed it, if you understand it, if you listen and react, if you pick up the cues and project just as you did in rehearsals, it *will* happen. There will be no need to force it. Relax, and do what you know how to do as well as you know how to do it.

If you are in a humorous scene, the director will ask you to hold for laughs when they come. If an actor keeps talking while the members of the audience are laughing, they will think they are missing something important and try to stop laughing. This can be deadly for a comedy. The actor has to learn to gauge the volume of the laughter. It will start with a few early people, then get very loud, and then fade off. When they start laughing, you want to take a tiny freeze until they hit the loudest moment. Start the next line just as the laugh starts to fade. This is a delicate skill and will take several performances to perfect. Many directors like to invite a few people to dress rehearsals so that the actors can practice holding for whatever laughs they get.

When you are offstage, stay out of the crew's way. They have jobs to do, which they have rehearsed the same way the actors have. The crew cannot move the scenery if actors are in the way. Keep all entrances clear, so other actors can enter and exit smoothly. If you are watching from the wings, remember that if you can see the audience, they can see you. Stay completely offstage.

At the end of the performance, the cast will acknowledge applause by taking a curtain call. This is part of the performance. The director will block it and rehearse it, usually at the last tech rehearsal or first dress rehearsal. If you are offstage at the end of the play, get in place quietly, because this is usually a very dramatic moment and any noise at all could ruin the mood of the entire show. Most curtain calls will include bows for the men and curtsies for the women, although the director may make things more complex. Look at the house when you take the bow, and smile. The audience is thanking you, and you are thanking them for telling you they liked it.

Sometimes people will come backstage to congratulate you after a show. Even if you think you did poorly or know you made a mistake, don't insult them when they say you did a good job. Say "Thank you," or "I'm glad you enjoyed it," if you can't think of anything else to say. If you say, "No, I was terrible," it makes them feel foolish and uncomfortable for thinking you were good. Always treat the audience with respect, wherever you meet them. They are the reason the performance exists.

Strike

After the final performance, the cast and crew will strike the show. This means that everything must be cleared out and cleaned up. It is described in more detail in Chapter 22. The important point to remember here is that *everyone* helps with the strike.

After each previous performance (and dress rehearsal), you should not leave the building until all your materials are ready for the next performance. Costumes should be hung up properly, props returned to the prop tables or storage, and all makeup and makeup areas cleaned and ready. If you leave the building prepared for the next performance, then each night's call is simple and easy, and you can spend all your time thinking about a good performance.

Chapter 16
Musical Performance

The musical comedy is currently the most popular type of play with America's audiences. The musical combines singing, dancing, and "straight" acting, so musical performers often need all three skills. Actors have always been expected to sing and dance, at least a little, as you may see from some of the plays in Chapter 12. However, in the twentieth century, the rise of new teaching techniques and of the intensely realistic theater separated "serious" actors from this tradition. In the musical, all the old skills come back together for the actor.

In general, a role in a musical is approached in exactly the same way as a nonmusical role. The script has to be studied, the character analyzed, and the imaginary world built and maintained. But the songs and dances put limits on what you can do in performance. Once the music begins, you cannot improvise, adlib, or change even a few seconds of business, because the music shifts everything into an artificial time scale. If you learn to cope with this artificial time scale, the musical can become an exciting performance for you, whether you are a trained singer and dancer or not.

Before we look at some specific ways to work with song and dance, remember that rehearsal is the key to the performance. No matter what you do in the performance, you are still a character with goals, with feelings, and with a personality. You must know the musical sections so well that you do not have to think consciously about them. Practice them until your body knows them so that when you are on stage, you can use your mind for the character and the character's emotions.

The Song

Interpreting a song is like interpreting poetry, except that you must deal with the music as well as the lyrics. If a song is well written, the music will help you interpret what the words mean, at least on the surface. The music will emphasize the important words and give some indication of the speed at which they should be delivered as well as the mood of the piece. Listen to the entire musical arrangement, not only your notes.

Most songs in most musicals are somewhat like soliloquies. They express how the character feels at that moment. In effect, they show the audience what is inside the character's mind, thoughts that might not be expressed in realistic dialogue. Much of the time, the singer will be alone on stage. Even when there are two people on stage, the song is rarely a dialogue but is just a soliloquy directed toward the other character. Even large groups in chorus express their thoughts as one character, for example, in the choral song "Iowa Stubborn" in *The Music Man*. The song is a rare chance for the actor to show exactly how a character feels, so try to make the song an emotional expression. Ask yourself: What does the character want to say? Why does he need to say it right now? What happens to the character's feelings once he has expressed his emotions? If you find and use the answers to these questions, the song will flow from the spoken dialogue back into the spoken dialogue and the performance will be a whole unit.

Since it takes longer to express a thought musically than it does in straight dialogue, time is suspended during the performance of a song. Therefore all gestures and movements have to be extended and sustained at unnatural

Gilbert and Sullivan's operetta, *H.M.S. Pinafore* performed by students of South Adams High School, Berne, Indiana

lengths. This does not mean that every gesture is done in slow motion, however. It does mean that it takes longer than normally to prepare a gesture, and it usually means that the gesture is held longer than normally. This requires a tremendous amount of energy and careful focus of all your physical expression into single, clear movements with four clear parts: preparation, action, hold, and relaxation. Look again at Chapter 11. This concentration is even harder for the character or characters listening than for the character singing. On-stage listeners must focus completely for an extremely long time, hold emotional reactions much longer than normally, and still look natural while doing it.

The notes of the song are important, but they are not the only thing of importance. A good performer may suggest notes rather than hit them exactly. Listen to recordings of Robert Preston, Rex Harrison, or Richard Burton in their musi-

cals. The goal is a single, dramatic, expressive moment. That moment becomes more dramatic and expressive with the added resources of the music that accompanies the words.

Dancing

Every kind of dance begins with a series of natural movements. These movements are expanded and adjusted to become *the dance,* but each starts from natural movements. Thus, it is possible for an actor to dance in many musicals without being a trained dancer.

Dances, like songs, happen for a reason. Only in very old-fashioned musicals are the dances unrelated to the plot. Today every dancer, even in dancing choruses, is a character, a person in the play. As a dancer, you will be expressing a character's emotions physically, or you will be giving the audience information about what the people in the play are doing, or both.

Dance is movement done to rhythm. The choreographer will decide what movements seem to be the best in a given situation. If you listen to the rhythm and work to match your movements to the rhythm in all the rehearsals, the result will be a dance, however simple or complex.

Rehearsals and Performance

Musical rehearsals take longer than straight drama rehearsals. There are fewer lines of dialogue in a musical, but there is a great deal more physical business, in song and dance, which must be learned until it becomes second nature.

Musical rehearsals are more confusing. There are usually at least two different directors and sometimes four. The director is responsible for everything that happens on stage, just as in a nonmusical play, but there will be a music director who teaches and rehearses the music. Often, there will also be a choreographer to plan and teach the dances. Sometimes, if there is an orchestra instead of piano accompaniment, the conductor will be a different person from the music director. All of these people have different responsibilities, and all of them will give the performers directions. Concentrate and make lots of notes. Eventually everything will fit together, but in the early stages it is very confusing.

Rehearsals will follow approximately the same schedule as for nonmusical plays, except that the musical rehearsal will be broken into smaller segments. Almost immediately you will begin work on the music and dances. Some scenes may not be blocked until part way through the rehearsals because the songs occupy so much of those scenes that they cannot be practiced until the music is ready.

Dances and songs are usually rehearsed with piano accompaniment. If there is an orchestra, you probably will not see or hear it until the tech rehearsal. This will be a problem for some because everything will sound different. Often, you will have to relearn all your musical cues to find the rhythm and the notes in the new sound of the orchestra.

Rehearsals will be very fragmented. Because there are several different directors, there may be several different aspects being rehearsed at the same time. Be extremely conscious of the schedule to be sure you are where you are supposed to be at the right time.

In performance, the show is controlled by the conductor. You must be constantly aware of his directions without ever looking directly at him. Rehearse watching out of the corner of your eye; this is a necessary skill, however peculiar it seems.

Many songs can be addressed to the audience rather than to other performers. If you are directed to do this, select a spot in the auditorium over the heads of the audience, such as an exit sign at the back of the house. Focus your energy and aim your songs or dances to that point. The audience will feel that you are singing to them all and you will avoid distractions. If the song is long, select several points around the building and vary your focus.

At the end of each musical number, the audience will usually applaud. It is no longer acceptable to take a bow in the middle of a scene, since such an act tends to destroy the dramatic characterization. However, there should be a freeze, much like the hold for a laugh but a little longer, which allows the audience to applaud. Freeze until the volume peaks, and then go into the next scene. Sometimes with groups, the conductor will cue this release so that everyone goes into the next scene at the same time. Sustain your energy during this freeze so that you hold the emotion you had at the end of the music.

Backstage areas will be even more confusing than in nonmusical shows. Most musicals have several costume and scenery changes, so the number of crew members and pieces of equipment is much greater than usual. Be very careful where you go and be very quiet. Be especially sure to keep exits clear; if there are choruses or dancers, they exit and enter in groups and need lots of room.

Activities

1. Select a simple everyday activity such as washing the dishes, putting on makeup, or building something; the activity should have a clear beginning and end. Prepare a pantomime of that activity. Then select a piece of music without words and fit the pantomime to the music. Use the rhythm and the mood of the music. Perform it for the class and discuss the differences. You have just made a dance.

2. Do the same thing you did in the previous activity but with a group of people working together.

3. Arrange the class in a circle. Select a series of simple movements such as a walk, a turn, and a jump and arrange them in any order. Go to the center of the circle and do the actions while the people in the circle clap a regular rhythm. Adjust your movement to fit the rhythm the rest of the class provides. Repeat the exercise with the group changing the tempo or the rhythm as you move; adjust to whatever change the group makes. Repeat the exercise several times, trying to express a different mood each time, such as happiness, sadness, or excitement, still using the rhythm the group provides. This will help you use rhythm in other performances.

4. Select a song that tells a story and that you can easily memorize. Use it for the following exercises:

(a) Retell the song and perform it as a spoken scene. Fill in any external movements for a character to use with the ideas.

(b) Prepare an interior monologue for the song. Ask yourself who the speaker is, where he is, and why he says what he is saying. Be very specific. You want to find an exact thought that passes through the speaker's mind *before* he says each line, or even one word, of the song lyric. Play this scene, saying only the words of the interior monologue.

(c) Play the scene again, but silently, physically expressing the interior monologue but not saying the words. Do this at your own speed. Then repeat the exercise with the music of the song, and time the physical expression of the emotions to the music.

(d) After you have done all this, perform the song, remembering all the levels of the song you expressed in **a-c** while you sing. (It may help to say the lyrics first before you sing them until you are sure you can fit all the pieces together.)

Actor / interpreter Robert Hahn signing for the deaf in the California Shakespeare Festival Apprentice Company's production of *The Two Gentlemen of Verona.* Here, he and Ken Jensen both play Launce.

Unit V
Stagecraft

CHAPTER 17
The Actor's Use of Costume

CHAPTER 18
The Actor's Use of Makeup

CHAPTER 19
The Imaginary World of Scenery and Properties

CHAPTER 20
Lighting and Sound

CHAPTER 21
Management—The Production Staff

CHAPTER 22
Preparation, Rehearsals, and Performance

Often the people who act or perform and the people who put together the artificial world of a play performance get separated. They become "actors" and "techies" who scarcely speak to one another. The audience, however, watches both actors and visual effects. Therefore each person involved in a production needs to know what all the other people are doing and why, so that each can contribute to a single impression for the audience.

The primary purpose of what is called stagecraft *is to give information to the audience through nonverbal means. This information is conveyed chiefly through visual effects, although sound effects and music are just as informative. The visual effects create impressions that tell an audience how it is supposed to react to the performers. How you can make those impressions happen properly on stage and how the actor can use and complete those impressions are the subjects of the following chapters.*

Safety

One of the most dangerous professions in the country is that of stage technician. The professional stage actors' union, Equity, devotes most of its contract negotiations to improving the safety of the performers' working conditions. There is a great potential for personal injury in any work around the stage, and that danger is greater for amateurs and students.

On a stage, everything is temporary; a stairway of a stage set cannot be as solid as the one in your home. People are working with a number of potentially dangerous tools—saws, drills, hammers—and with ladders they can fall off, wagons that can roll away, and electrical appliances that can burn or shock them. During performances and many rehearsals, people have to walk around backstage in the dark. Even worse, many different jobs are going on in the same place at the same time; some people are painting while others are sawing, and a third group is hammering. If safety is not made an important consideration at all times, people could very easily get hurt.

These simple rules will help in all theater groups.

1. Be Neat. *Most accidents happen because something is left where it is not supposed to be. Keep tools and equipment with you when you are using them and put them back where they belong as soon as you are finished. Clean up spills as soon as they happen and sweep up the entire work area before you leave.*

2. Don't Crowd. *Give yourself plenty of room to work. That way you won't accidentally bump into or hit other people, and they won't bump into or hit you.*

3. Unplug All Power Tools As Soon As You Finish Using Them. *It takes seconds to plug a tool back in if you need it. It takes no time at all for someone to accidentally bump the start button. It's worth the few seconds to save someone's fingers.*

4. Know Where the Fire Extinguishers and Fire Exits Are. *Keep exit lanes clear between you and the doors.*

5. Don't Play with the Tools. *Drills and hammers are not six-guns, screw-*

drivers are not darts, and ladders are not for shaking, no matter how much fun it is to hear a friend yell from the top rung.

6. Tell the Teacher When Anything Goes Wrong. *Don't wait until the end of the day; someone may get hurt in the meantime. The teacher cannot correct problems he or she does not know about.*

7. Look Out for Other People.

8. Know the Rules. *Every school, stage, and shop has its own hazards. Every tool has its own operating instructions. Learn them, study them, use them, and ask questions if you have any doubts at any time.*

Chapter 17
The Actor's Use of Costume

Costumes and makeup provide an audience with external clues to character. They can help to explain a character's age, economic status, social position, and occupation. They can provide information as to place, time of year, time of day, and historical period. They can even contribute to the personality and mood of a character. When costumes and makeup are carefully chosen and successfully done, they complement the preparation the performer has made. When they are poorly chosen or unsuccessfully done, they contradict the performer and make it almost impossible for the performance to work. When the performer does not understand and use them well, they are wasted and unsuccessful.

For practical purposes, we will look at costume and makeup as separate areas. However, in actual performance, they are inseparable. Both are part of the single physical impression the actor makes, and both should be planned together.

A costume is a set of clothes a character wears. Shoes, hats, and anything in between are parts of a costume. For the comfort and ease of the actor, as well as for the efficient production of the play, costumes must be practical. The actor must be able to do what he or she needs to do while wearing the costume. The dancer has to be able to dance, the tumbler has to be able to tumble without getting tangled up in the costume. The costumes should also be affordable and easy to make. The most important way to assure practicality is to know *exactly* what the script requires the individual performer to do. This can only be done by reading the entire play carefully.

One of the first qualifications for a costume is that it should help to express the outward aspects of a character. We are all aware that certain clothes are associated with people of certain ages and that some clothes are unsuitable for people of certain ages. Both old people and young people wear shoes, for example, but they wear different kinds of shoes.

Watch people around you at school, in your neighborhood, at home, and in public places and notice their clothing. Then you can begin to sort out how age makes a difference in what people wear.

Clothes are also a clue to a person's economic status and social position. During several periods in history, governments passed laws that made certain

Children's theater presenting *Oliver*

kinds of clothes legal only for certain groups of people. People could not wear a particular color, for example, unless they were of noble birth. Modern society does not have such laws, but many people still try to use their clothing to show their importance, or the importance they wish other people would believe they have.

Among people with a reasonable amount of money, new, expensive, fashionable, and exotic clothes may help to mark their importance. Persons who are generally acknowledged to have importance or influence may find it unnecessary to express this in their clothing (although they may express it in other personal possessions) and tend to be conservative. The three-piece business suit and tie, for example, have been worn in some variation by men in government and business for over fifty years. About the only thing that has changed has been the width of lapels and ties. Women in government and business tend to be somewhat conservative, too. There are of course notable exceptions among both men and women.

Good costumers and actors are constantly aware of how people present themselves in public. It doesn't matter to the actor or costumer whether people really are "important" so much as what they do to look important. Try to use

Rehearsing a school play

what you discover to help express the social and economic position of the characters in your play.

Clothing is also a clue to occupation, profession, or leisure-time activities. Everyone recognizes the obvious uniforms worn by military people, service-station attendants, nurses, plumbers, ministers, and various athletes. However, there are other kinds of less obvious "uniforms" made up of variations in ordinary clothing. Long-distance truck drivers do not dress the same as construction workers, and social workers do not dress the same as editors. People dress differently for golf than they do for bridge. Recognition and use of these less obvious uniforms are critical to the success of costume work.

Clothing also immediately tells the audience how formal or informal the characters and the play will be.

Most people dress with varying degrees of formality, depending on where they are and what they are doing. Even among the most informal of people, there will be different clothing worn to school, to work, to church, to a funeral, to a party, or to a fancy restaurant.

In general, the more formal a costume, the more restrictive it will be. Actors in more formal costuming will be limited in the manner in which they can move, sit, walk, and even talk. This will in turn limit everyone else on the stage with them and make the entire performance more formal and less active.

Costuming also tells about the time and place of the play. It can indicate time of day and time of year. In some places and within some economic classes prior to the early twentieth century, a rather formalized sequence of clothing was worn at various times during the day. This sequence is still reflected in the names of some articles of clothing—morning coats, tea gowns, evening gowns, and dinner jackets. Modern clothes tend to be more flexible, but there are still major differences for many people between, for example, formal business clothes and formal evening clothes. And obviously people wear different types of clothing at various times of year if there is a change in climate.

Costuming also conveys the historical period in which the play is set. What most people wore in 1980 was different from what most people wore in 1920, or 1880. There is a difference, however, in what people in the Far East wore in 1880 and what people in the United States wore in 1880.

You will need to do some serious study and library research if you are doing a play set in another time or place. There is no such thing as "old-fashioned" clothing or "Russian" clothing. Every time in every place is different. If you wish to have the strongest possible performance, you will have to spend some time finding out about the place and period in which the play is set and then use that information to design and make costumes for your own performance.

Activities

1. Make a photo file for reference. Select from newspapers and magazines clear photographs that show real people and their clothes. Avoid fashion magazines because they try to interest readers in clothes they *might* wear next month or next year. They almost never tell you what real people are actually wearing right now. Mount each picture on a piece of paper, and record the following information on the paper:

(a) date of picture,

(b) who is in the picture and what each person's job or profession is,

(c) what kind of activity he or she is engaged in (partying, vacationing, going to court, etc.),

(d) each person's age.

(e) If you have seen other people in similar situations wear the same kinds of clothing, note that. Very often, the reason the person is in the paper is that he or she is unusual.

Try to use only news photos. Advertising photos will be much more clear, but it is much harder to get factual data from them.

2. Advertising depends on making impressions on its audience, and uses costume to say many things the text does not say. In many ads, products are associated with certain kinds of people, and the viewer is subtly encouraged to use the product if he or she wants to be like the person in the ad. Select several pictures from magazine ads and try to answer the following questions about the types of people depicted:

(a) How much money does the person make?
(b) What kind of job, if any, does the person have?
(c) Where does the person live?
(d) How do you know all that?

Try the same thing with people in television commercials.

3. Keep a journal about your own clothing for two weeks. List what you wear, when you wear it, and why you decided to wear it at that particular time. (It's easier to do this each night before going to bed.) At the end of the two weeks, look for any recurring patterns. Were there any "uniforms" you wore to school? Was there a difference when your mood changed? What colors did you wear most and why?

Try the same thing with someone you see regularly. Record all the clothing the person wears for a couple of weeks. Then ask yourself what impressions those clothes gave you each time you saw the person.

4. Come to class one day dressed as someone else that you know, but whom the class probably does not know. Be as accurate and exact as you can; do not exaggerate for a comic effect. Discuss the information the class can see from what you wear and compare that with what you know about this person.

Costume and Characterization

Costume, like daily clothing, also reflects and reveals the personality of the wearer. When you buy clothes, for example, you consider a number of factors—style, material, price, color, labels, workmanship, fit, comfort, as well as how much it is like what everyone else wears, how much it is different, how it fits with other parts of your wardrobe, and so on—all of which affect the way you feel about the clothes. Then you buy the clothes that combine most of those things you like and feel comfortable with. Sometimes people use an expression, "that's really *you,"* to indicate that the clothes you chose do indeed reflect your personality and your personal feelings.

The characters in a play have those same kinds of feelings in their imaginary world. When planning costumes, you should always ask, "What kinds of clothes would this person buy? What's his or her favorite color? favorite material?" Be sure that you also ask, "Why?" so that you stay with the character in the play instead of turning that character into you. Asking these kinds of questions will help you remember that the costume is helping to express the personality of the character.

Costuming also tells us about the mood of the character and how his or her personality is coping with this particular day. Think for a moment about how you

decided what to wear to school today, and you will realize how much mood affects clothing and appearance. Assume the character has the same kinds of moods, and this will help determine the costume he or she should wear.

Color and accessories are very important to costuming. Bright, happy characters tend toward bright happy colors, eccentric characters put normal clothes together in peculiar combinations, bland personalities tend to use conservative items that are unlikely to attract attention, and so on.

Filling the Costume

Whether you are involved in designing costumes or not, you must understand and use the costume as a part of your performance. It is essential that every performer work with costume for some time before performance. You first need to get used to wearing the costume. This takes some time, and the more unusual the costume, the more time it will take. Second, you need to adjust the costume. Spend some time in front of a mirror playing with combinations of items in the costume. Notice what happens to the costume as you sit, stand, walk, pick up things, or gesture. Experiment a little to find ways of moving that make the costume as expressive as it can be.

Most important, *never* fight your costume. Many performers will spend weeks getting ready for a show and then panic when they get into the costume because it makes them look "different." That's the whole point of a good costume, to make you look different from the way you normally look. Study the costume.

If you don't understand why it looks the way it looks, ask the director or the designer what it is supposed to show. Work in it and with it. Let the costume help you do your performance.

Activities

1. Return to the pictures in your file. Ask yourself what kind of person each one looks like. Try to define personality and mood from the clothing worn and the way in which it is worn. Discuss exactly what gives you that impression in each picture.

2. Prepare a costume for an imaginary person and model it for the class. Wear the costume two ways:

(a) be as serious and absolutely realistic as possible; then

(b) use exactly the same pieces of clothing, but wear them in a way that exaggerates some feature of the character for comic effect.

Discuss what you wanted to accomplish, whether it worked or not, and why or why not.

3. See how many different ways you can wear a single piece of costume. Take a simple item, such as a hat or a scarf, and pass it around the group. Each person must wear it in a different way. Repeat the exercise with two items and two people working as partners. Each person must wear his or her item in a different way and then play a character who fits the personality shown. Have the two people meet some place, like a bus stop or park bench, and improvise a scene about their meeting.

4. Select one of the scenes you have already done in Unit III. Perform it again, this time in costume. Discuss the differences the costuming made in the scene. Ask how it helped you as an actor and how it helped or affected the audience. In what way is the scene different with the costume added?

Repeat the scene with a different costume but try to perform the role in exactly the same way. Discuss the differences seen by the audience and why they happened.

5. If you are interested in changes in clothing over the years or in the clothing of a particular time period in which a play you may be doing is set, do some research in the library. Your teacher and your librarian will give you suggestions on the best places to start looking.

The Costume Crew

When you produce a play, there will be a group of people who will serve as costume crew. Depending on how many costumes are needed, how many need to be sewn or altered, and how many dressers are needed, the crew will vary in size from as few as two to as many as fifteen or twenty. In general, this crew will include the following people: designer, wardrobe mistress (or master), seamstresses or tailors, and dressers.

Designer—decides what each character will wear at what time on stage. In most schools, this person will be a faculty member, but it may be a student. If costumes are made at the school, the designer will determine patterns and materials and provide drawings and instructions for the crews; if costumes are rented or borrowed, the designer will make the selections.

Wardrobe Mistress or Master—is responsible for the care and storage of finished costumes and the operation of all backstage areas having to do with costume use. Most will have several assistants, because this is a very demanding job. If costumes need to be cleaned and/or repaired, this person is responsible for getting that work done as well.

Seamstresses and Tailors—sew the costumes and make alterations.

Dressers—help backstage during the performance, especially with any quick or complicated costume changes. Generally, these are few and act as assistants to the wardrobe mistress or master.

Generally, the official crew head will be the person serving as wardrobe mistress or master. As crew head, she or he will be responsible for informing crew members of duties and schedules and coordinating all costume activities with the designer and the director.

Chapter 18
The Actor's Use of Makeup

Any temporary changes made in the shape, color, or texture of a performer's face and head is called makeup. Any of the substances used to make those changes are also called makeup. Makeup adds detail to the information given by the costume, and uses the performer's face to tell the audience the age, health, and personality of the character.

This information is given by altering the shape and color of the face. Makeup can be used to give the appearance of wrinkles for age, or to take away wrinkles for youth. It can make someone look rosy-cheeked and healthy, or sickly, pale, and near death. It can alter the features of the face and head to make a nice person look like a monster or a wise person look like a buffoon. It can also make the fat look thin and the thin, fat.

Every performer should be familiar with the uses and techniques of makeup application. Application itself is quite easy with a little practice. Thus, every performer should learn and should be expected to apply his or her own makeup, except in cases of extreme complexity.

Hair

The most important part of any makeup does not require any special applications to the face at all. Since most of the audience cannot see the fine details in your face, the first and most decisive impression to be made on them comes through the length and styling of your hair.

The hairstyles people choose to use vary from time to time, and place to place, and they vary for ages and social positions as well. There are, in fact, almost as many different ways to wear hair as to wear clothes. However, at any given time and place, there are usually a limited number of hairstyles in fashion, and people use those to show age and personality, just as they use clothes. At any time, children's hairstyles will usually be very simple and casual, so that parents can easily take care of them. Then hairstyles become more complicated, more individualized, and harder to manage as the wearers take over their own control and begin to use current fashions. After some years, usually in middle age, people get used to a favorite style, and styles become simpler again

and look more "old-fashioned." Men's hair begins to thin or recede and most people begin to get gray.

A good age makeup is more than just putting white spray in the hair. An actor with a brilliant costume and excellent facial makeup but still with his own young man's hairstyle will never look like someone's father or grandfather, no matter how much white spray he tries. Men often have to cut their hair shorter or let it grow longer than they normally wear it. For women, the variety of styles and the availability of cheap wigs simplify the makeup task. But, however it is achieved, proper hairstyling is critical to a totally effective makeup.

Makeup Materials

Makeup that is applied to the skin comes in a variety of materials and colors and may be grouped into basic categories. In your own makeup work in class or in a play, the names of each item and the shade numbers and names will vary, depending on the company whose products you use. But the principles will stay the same.

In general, makeup can be divided into two types, greasepaint and cake. Greasepaint usually comes in tubes or in sticks and is made with a creamy base so that it can be applied directly to the skin and smoothed on with the fingers. Cake makeup has water as its base, but the water is not included. The makeup comes in a flat container in a dry or nearly dry solid. It is applied to the skin with a wet sponge. There are advantages and disadvantages to each type and to each brand. In many cases, the two materials can be used together, but in general it is simpler to use either all grease or all cake makeup.

You will also need makeup brushes of several sizes, usually 1/4″ and 3/8″ (although 1/2″ or 1″ are sometimes useful). Eyebrow pencils of several shades will help too.

If you are using greasepaint, you will need powder. Some companies make powders in shades to match their foundation colors, others offer translucent or neutral shades. Powder is applied after all the greasepaint is on and is used to "set" the makeup so that it doesn't melt off or shine. To use the powder, you will need a powder puff and a makeup brush which removes the excess powder. If you are using cake, you will need sponges. Small silk or natural sponges are best.

In addition, you will need items for clean up. All makeup is designed to cover the skin. While it is fresh, it is attractive and useful, but after a while, it just makes your skin dirty. To have clean skin, you must remove *all* the makeup after the show. Greasepaint requires cold cream of some kind; cake is easily removed with cold cream, but it can also be removed with soap and water. You will need to use lots of tissue and then, when you think you are clean, go over your skin once again.

A Basic Makeup

Even when you are playing someone like yourself, you will usually need some makeup. Stage lights are extremely strong. They tend to wash out normal skin colors. Also, in many cases, normal facial features will not be very clear to people who are watching from thirty to fifty feet away, or further if you have a big auditorium. So, everyone will need a simple makeup.

To apply the makeup, follow these steps.

1. Examine the makeup you will be using. If the container has directions on it, read them. Be sure you know whether the makeup is grease or cake and that you have the tools you will need.

2. Clean your face and neck. No makeup will work properly unless the skin is clean and dry. Wear old clothes or a towel around your neck. Do not wear your costume until makeup is finished.

3. Select a foundation color that is about the same as your skin color. None will be exactly the same; choose one that is close. Apply it to your face. Smooth it out so that there are no streaks or lumps. Be sure you cover every part of the skin that will be visible, including around the eyes, the ears, and the neck areas that will show above your costume. The ideal result should be thick enough to cover your skin, but smooth and thin enough so that the face does not look as if you are wearing a mask.

To apply grease, put small dots of paint around your face, then rub them together with your fingers until they are thin and smooth. To apply cake, dip the sponge in water, and then squeeze it out until it is moist but does not drip. Rub

the sponge on the cake, then on your face. You may have to moisten the sponge occasionally. If the cake is flaky on your face, the sponge is too dry. If it is streaked or runny, the sponge is too wet.

4. Go on stage and stand under the lighting the show will use. Have the designer or head of the makeup crew check to see if the color looks good under the lights. If the color is too dark or too pale, go back, clean it off, and select a new shade. If it is OK, go to the next step.

5. Select a rouge that fits with your base color and apply it to each cheek, usually along and below the cheekbone. Do this gently, gradually adding color—it's easier to put on more than to take off some. Smooth out all the sharp edges with your fingers. Rouge is used to color and to help shape and break the masklike evenness of the base.

6. If the lighting is very strong or flat, you may want to shape your nose a little. You may wish to shade and shape the eyes. These techniques are discussed on page 219, but you would do them now if you do them at all.

7. If using greasepaint, powder now. Dip the puff in the powder and pat it straight into the makeup, slapping gently until all of the skin is covered. Since you have to close your eyes, this is a step in which you normally need help. Brush the excess powder off so that no powder grains are visible. Do not rub;

rubbing will wipe off the makeup and you will have to start over. If you use cake makeup, skip this step.

8. Line and emphasize the eyes. From a distance the eyes disappear easily, so they have to be lined. Apply a little mascara to the eyelashes, depending on how much you want them to show. Then, using a very thin brush, apply a very thin line above and below the eye, as close to the edge of the eye as you can put it. You may use mascara, black lining colors, or, if you are very pale or light haired, a dark brown liner.

9. Color your lips with a lip rouge. For males, the colors will usually be not nearly as reddish as with most female makeups, but the lips still have to be emphasized or they will disappear under the lights.

10. Go back on stage and have the designer or crew head look at the finished makeup under the lights. Be sure whoever is checking looks from about the middle of the audience, because that is the place from which you want to look natural. Make any adjustments needed, and then clean up your mess.

11. After all makeup for you is finished, put on your costume and prepare for the performance.

Shaping the Face

Makeup is also used to change the face in some way, to make it look like that of the character being played. Some of these changes are based on color. For example, you can give yourself a tan in the middle of winter by doing the basic makeup with a darker base, or you can make yourself look pale and sickly by using a lighter than normal base. More or less rouge can change the healthiness of your appearance. Changing the shape of the face is accomplished by a single, simple trick. If you understand the basic principle of this one trick, you can adapt it to almost any makeup problem.

Essentially, this is how it works. Light comes from one strong direction. When something protrudes, the space underneath the protrusion is in shadow—that is, light is blocked off, so that the underneath area looks darker. The part that protrudes furthest looks lightest.

Look in the mirror and you will see that the area under your nose, for example, is darker than the area on top of the nose. If you squint, you will see a wrinkle form around the eye. The reason you can see that wrinkle is that part of the skin suddenly juts out to catch the light and makes a shadow underneath it.

You can apply the following principle to any part of your face. To make part of it appear to stand out farther than it really does, highlight it, that is, make it lighter than the surrounding skin. To make a part appear to recede, shadow it by making it darker than the surrounding area. If you want a wide, flat nose, put lighter makeup on the sides of the nose. For a thin, sharp nose, put darker than normal makeup on the sides of the nose and lighter makeup on the bridge.

Age makeup is the most detailed use of this principle. The older the character you play, the more changes you will need to make, but they are all made in the same way.

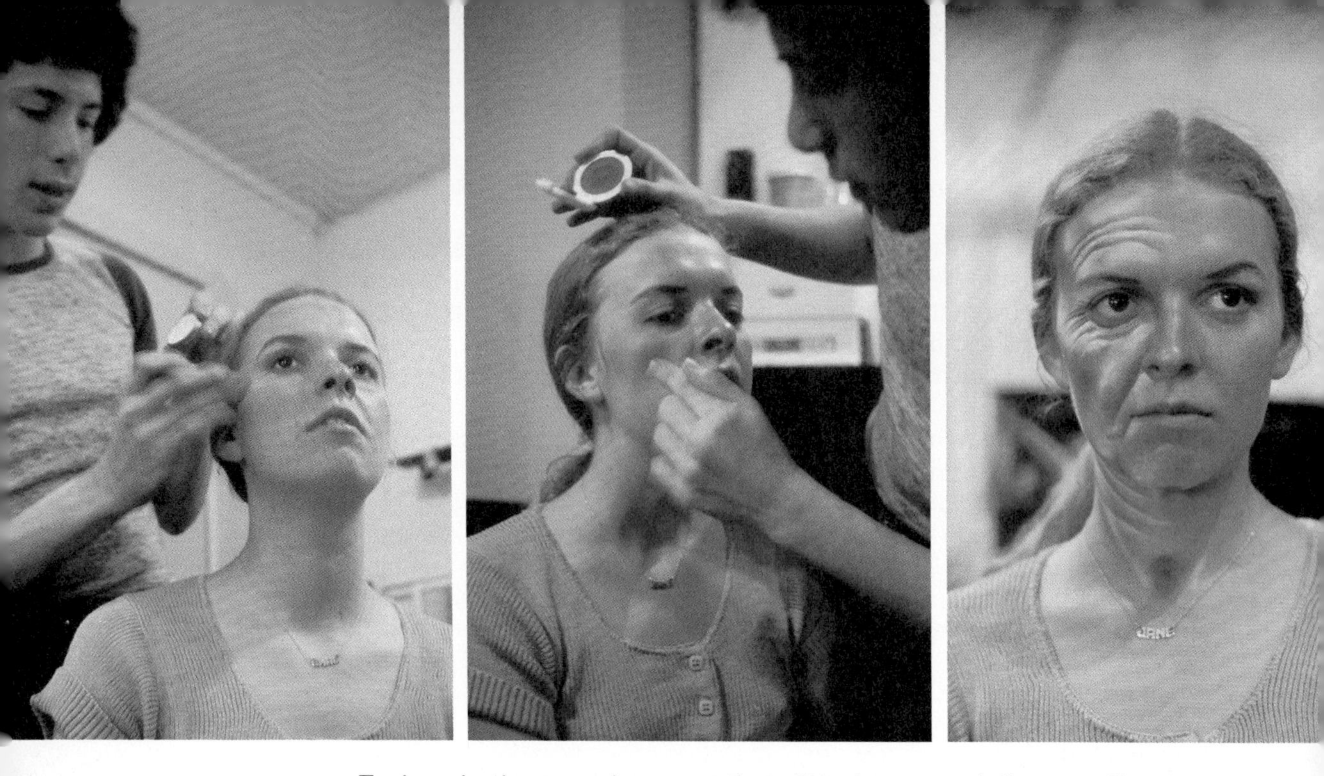

To do a simple age makeup, one that will look very much like you will probably look when you are older, follow these steps.

1–4. Same as with the basic makeup. You may want to make the base a shade lighter than your skin, especially if you are now wearing a summer tan.

5. Apply the major shadow areas. Select a darker shade of makeup, about three shades darker than your base, depending on the brand used. Feel along your temple until you find the soft spot and place a small streak of shadow there. Look in the mirror and say "oooh"; you will see a new shadow area form under your cheekbone. Apply the shadow there in two light streaks like the two sides of a triangle, below the cheekbone and downward toward the chin. Relax your face and place shadows under the chin.

6. Apply major highlight areas. One of these is above the shadow on the temple; feel for the protruding bone there, and place a color about three shades lighter than your base. Do the same along the peak of the cheekbone; notice that this bone extends far past the eye. You may feel a slight protrusion in the skull above the eye—if you do, then apply a highlight here as well.

7. Blend. With a clean finger in big areas, and with a brush in closer, smaller spots, blend the edges of the highlight and shadow so that they gradually fade into the medium shade of your face.

8. Apply the wrinkles. Start with the shadow color again and do all the shadows first, then do the highlights. The best shadow applicator, whether you use grease or cake, is the 1/4″ or 3/8″ brush. Applying wrinkles will take some practice, but you will soon learn to make fine lines that will look absolutely natural. Unless you are trying to significantly change your whole face, it is usually best to try to match the wrinkles of your own face; then when your face moves, the makeup will be natural from all sides.

First, smile. You will see a big wrinkle form from the nose to each side of the mouth. Relax. You will still see a tiny crack in your base makeup where that wrinkle was. Apply a shadow along that line. With a clean brush, smooth it upward, but leave a sharp edge on the lower side. Smile again, and you will probably find another wrinkle at the edge of the mouth. Do it the same way.

Now, squint one eye, then relax. This will identify the wrinkles that are developing around the eye. Put shadow along each wrinkle line. Repeat for the other eye.

Finally, arch your eyebrows to find the forehead wrinkles. Relax, and apply shadow very carefully to the wrinkle line revealed. These are the hardest of all wrinkles to do because they require a very fine shadow line and absolute accuracy in placement to look natural. In most age makeups, these wrinkles can be left off.

It is very important that you remember to relax completely when applying shadow. If there is any tension, the skin will stretch and you will accidentally get the shadow too wide and in the wrong place.

To apply highlights, repeat the procedures, with one difference. When you smile or squint, hold it while you apply the highlight. That way, you can be absolutely sure that you have put the highlight on what will be the highest part of the wrinkle.

When all highlights and shadows are in place, take a clean brush and very gently blend the *edges* of each toward each other. The blending is what makes it all work.

9. If your neck will show, apply shadows and wrinkles to the neck area in exactly the same manner.
10. Go back to Step 7 of the basic makeup and finish.

Special Problems

Only the most basic techniques have been described. Each show will have unique problems. Your teacher will be able to show you more details and to recommend books that will help you if you are especially interested in makeup or if problems arise. Some general hints, however, can be suggested.

When using brushes, be sure to hold them perpendicular to your face. That is the easiest way to keep the lines clear and sharp.

Sometimes you will need to darken or define your eyebrows. That's what eyebrow pencils are for. However, always use them lightly, with a series of very short, light strokes. Again, it is easier to add than to subtract makeup.

There are a number of ways to lighten hair. Liquids and sprays of various kinds are available, and it doesn't matter much which you use. It is important to remember that you have to color all the hair, not just the outside layer.

When you work in a large auditorium, makeup has to be stronger so that it can be effective for people farther away. This does not mean that it needs to be broader. The best way to cope with larger houses is to make the difference between tones stronger. For example, instead of a shadow color that is three

Cicely Tyson as Rebecca Morgan in *Sounder,* and as the 110-year-old Jane Pittman in *The Autobiography of Miss Jane Pittman*

shades darker than the base, you might need one five or six shades darker. If you are in an arena or a very small room, you have to blend carefully, but you also have need of less difference in tones. On a small stage, a difference of two shades may be best. Practice; and constantly check your makeup under the lights.

In recent years, a number of new materials have made it possible to do three-dimensional alterations in the face. Most of these revolve around latex materials, which build up three-dimensional layers of wrinkles, bags, and artificial pieces which are then glued to actors' faces. These materials are still too complicated and expensive for most schools, but they are so common in television and movies as to be taken for granted. If you have time for advanced projects, you should learn about and try to use latex for some parts of the makeup. Again, your teacher and librarian will be able to suggest where you can look for information.

Mime Makeup

Makeup for clowns and mimes is applied the same way as other makeup. However, it is designed for a different purpose. Makeup for mimes and clowns is supposed to work like a mask; it should simplify and exaggerate the features of the face. Colors are stronger, edges are sharper and less blended than in more natural makeups.

Most of these makeups start with the traditional white base. The face is covered completely and smoothly with clown white. Then, for the traditional mime

makeup, the eyes are sharply lined, the mouth emphasized with a bright, strong red, and the eyebrows darkened and slightly exaggerated. Sometimes a rouge will also be applied to the cheeks, but it will be very strong and sharply defined. In general, it is much easier to do this makeup with greasepaint than with cake makeups, because much stronger colors are available in greasepaint. This means that the final result must be carefully powdered. Many times the powder will dull the colors that have been put over the white base, so a touch-up coat may be necessary.

Clown makeup is much more varied and exaggerated. Where mime makeup serves to simplify and purify the facial structure, clown makeup is designed to make a completely artificial and unnatural face. Mime makeup tries to make one face serve every possible character or expression; clown makeup tries to define a single vivid character expression. For clown makeup, almost anything is possible.

Makeup Crew

In general, the performer should do his own makeup. The performer should also clean up his own mess. However, there will usually be at least one person on the makeup crew. If there are several people, the crew head is responsible for knowing how the makeup is supposed to look when finished, either by designing the makeup or by conferring with the director. The crew head will spend much of each makeup period going with actors to the stage to check how the makeup looks under the lights. The crew head is also responsible for seeing that brushes are cleaned, lids replaced, and makeup stored each evening. If there is a special layout or schedule to be followed, the crew head is in charge of that too.

Any other makeup crew members should assist the crew head and be available only for those parts of the makeup which the actor cannot do alone, such as powdering the greasepaint or whitening hair in the back of the head. In any case, this crew should be kept to a minimum. The makeup room is always too crowded.

Activities

1. Enlarge your photo file to include close-ups of faces. Mount and identify in the same way as you did with costuming photos. Study this file regularly to see how faces change as they age.

2. Do a simple, straight makeup for yourself.

3. Do a simple age makeup for yourself. If you do this in class, there will probably not be enough time to do a complete one, so do half a face.

4. Select one of the photos from your file, and do a makeup in which you try to look like that person.

5. Plan and do a makeup for a character in one of the scenes in Unit III.

Chapter 19
The Imaginary World of Scenery and Properties

Just as the performer's costume and makeup work together to give a visual impression of an individual character to the audience, so performer's surroundings suggest an imaginary world for the audience. This world can be very detailed or very simple, depending on the style and the requirements of the script, stage size, equipment, and budget. But in any case, it is always imaginary, and it is always designed to give the audience information about the characters, their feelings, and the events of the performance.

The basic parts of this physical imaginary world are the scenery, properties, lighting, and sound. Lighting and sound will be discussed in Chapter 20. In general, any physical items the actors stand on or in front of and which they cannot carry or move are regarded as scenery. Anything the actors carry or move around in the course of the play is a prop. Depending on the organization of each production and each group, furniture is usually considered to be a prop and to be the responsibility of the prop crew. Decorations on the scenery may also be props in some productions.

Scenery and props change from show to show. There is no one way to plan for all shows. However, there are fundamentals which will be useful in most situations. As you work on different shows, you may need to broaden your knowledge. Your teacher will be able to suggest books to consult.

Types of Stages

Scenery and properties are designed to fit a show and to fit a stage. There are three basic types of stages, and for each of these the seating arrangement of the audience is different. Each basic type of stage requires a different scenery design. Thus, depending on the kind of stage, the scenery for any given show will differ.

The oldest type of stage is the *thrust* stage, which dates back to the Greek theaters. The audience sits in a horseshoe around three sides of a stage that extends into the audience area. Some flat scenery is possible at the back of the stage, but most of the part that extends into the audience must be free of scenery since it would block the view of part of the audience.

In many theaters the audience is seated completely around the stage. This

Cross Section of a Typical Proscenium Stage

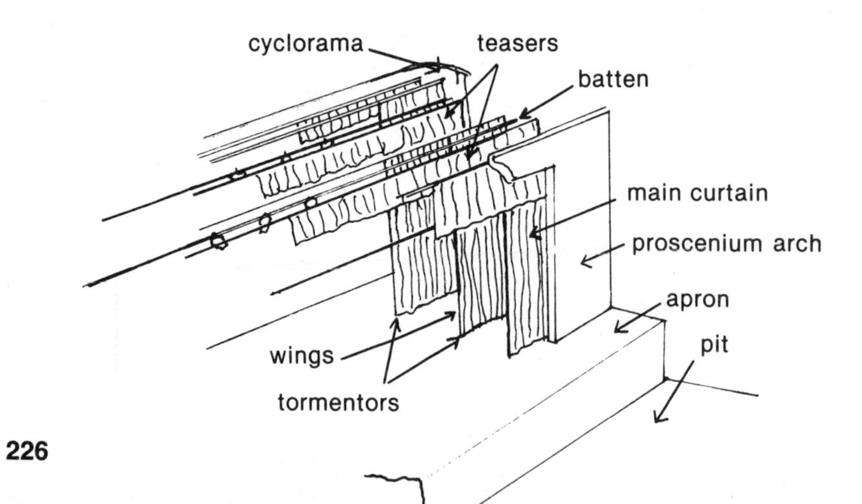

type is called an *arena* stage or *theater-in-the-round.* Since the audience is on all sides, any properties and scenery must be three-dimensional. Also, no scenery should be so tall as to block the view from any seat in any direction.

The most recent and also the most common stage is the *proscenium* stage. It is named for the proscenium arch, which is like a picture frame around one side of the stage. The audience sits on one side and looks through the opening in the proscenium arch to see the play. Scenery walls can be on three sides of the stage. Because backstage areas are hidden from the audience's view, complicated scene changes can be made more easily than with the other two types of stages.

Top: Theater in-the-round

Bottom: Thrust stage, The Guthrie Theater

Scenery and the Play

Whatever type of stage is used, scenery and props serve several functions.

First, scenery must tell the audience where the play occurs. If the play is in a room in a house, the scenery should suggest a room in a house to the audience as soon as they see it. This does not mean that it has to be absolutely realistic or that it has to be solid and complete. Arranging a sofa, an armchair, and a television set on an empty stage can suggest and identify a living room just as easily as a set of walls, doors, furniture, and ceiling pieces. But, however you arrange your scenery, it should make very clear exactly where the play occurs.

Second, the scenery must serve the practical needs of the script. If characters run up and down stairs, slam doors, and leap out of windows, the scenery should have enough stairs, doors, and windows for them to do those things.

Third, the scenery should tell the audience something about the taste, position, and wealth of the characters. We should know by looking at the scenery and props whether the characters whom we will see are rich or poor, powerful or unimportant, artistic or crude, and so on.

Fourth, it should establish a mood for the performance as a whole. Style, shape, detail, and color should all combine to give the audience a consistent feeling about the kind of show they are about to see.

Types of Scenery

Building and painting scenery is slightly different from building and painting a house. Scenery items are not the real thing. They may look like the real thing and work like the real thing, but they can rarely actually be the real thing. Scenery is a temporary representation and since it is temporary, it must always be:

strong enough to do the job,
portable enough to be moved on and off stage by hand,
cheap enough to be practical, and
standardized enough to fit together and be easily stored or reused.

There are two basic kinds of scenery units, *platforms* and *flats*. Platforms can be walked on. Flats stand vertically and look solid but usually are not. Platforms may be at various heights or levels and will often have stairs attached. Flats act as walls and will often have doorways and windows built into them. A complete set may be made from only platforms, only flats, or from combinations of platforms and flats.

Building Scenery

Platforms are usually built from wood and are much heavier than flats because they have to be much sturdier. They should have detachable legs so that they can be set at different heights from show to show and so that they can be stored easily in a small space when the show is over. The easiest way to do this is to bolt the legs into the support frame of the platform. Many groups have a set of standardized platforms with folding wooden frames that act as support legs. Recently, many have begun to use pipe, slotted steel, or other metal frames to support their platforms. Whatever method your group uses, remember that people have to walk on the platforms; build carefully and solidly.

Flats are quite different. They have to be as light as possible but still look like solid wall. The lightness is achieved in the construction. The apparent solidity is achieved by an artistic paint job.

A flat is simply a wooden frame over which a strong and sturdy material, usually *canvas* or heavy-duty *muslin* is stretched and then painted. The frame is made from either 1″ x 3″ or 1″ x 4″ wood, usually pine. The corners are joined by corner braces cut from 1/4″ plywood. All corners must be square so that any two flats will fit together when standing side by side.

Flats may be made in almost any size, although there are practical limits. Tradition says that the maximum width should be 5′9″ because scenery was once transported on the railroads and had to fit through freight car doors. You can build wider flats, but they are not very practical. Most muslin and canvas comes in pieces six feet wide or smaller, and it is very hard for any one person to move and balance anything wider than that. The height of a flat is determined by the height of your stage and the height needed for the room you want to

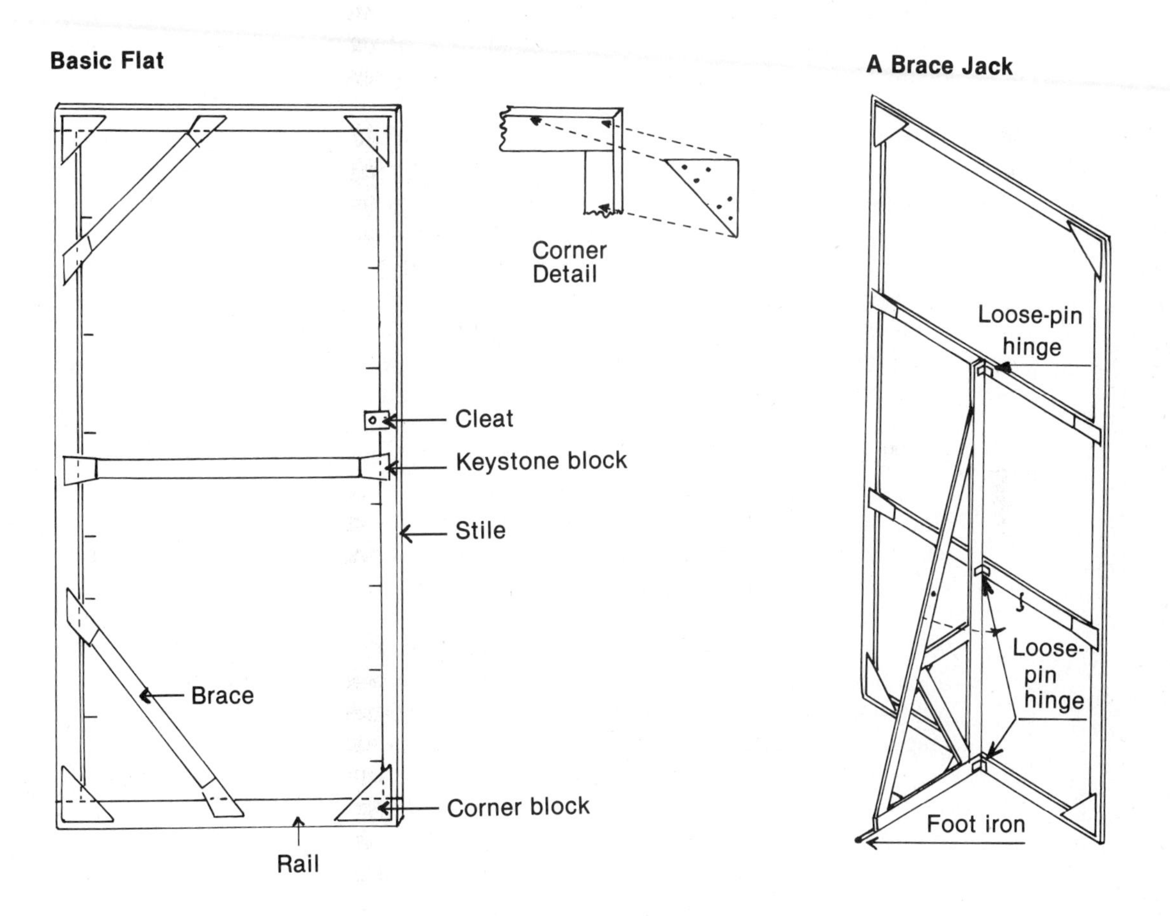

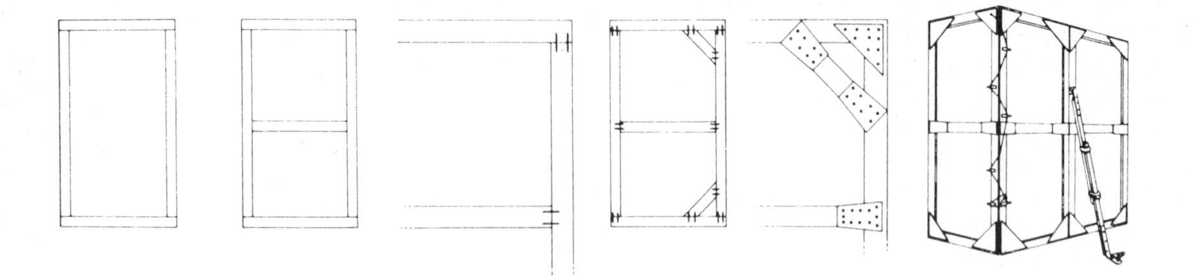

build. The taller the flats are, the harder they are to support, but flats that are eight, ten, or twelve feet are quite easy to move, stand up, or store.

After the frame of the flat is finished, turn it over so that it is lying with the corner braces down. Cut your covering material to the approximate size of the frame. Then tack or staple it lightly across one narrow end, placing the tacks near the inside edge of the wood. Next, stretch the material smooth and tight by working down both long sides of the frame. This will take at least two people and is easiest with four. Put in another tack or staple every nine to twelve inches, again near the inside edge of the wood. When both long sides are smooth and tight, tack down the last side.

Next, lift up the outside edges of the material and brush a coat of glue (white polyvinyl glue works quite well) onto the wood frame. Be sure it is applied smoothly. Then glue the material down. Work down the sides in the same way you tacked or stapled. It is often a good idea to staple along the outside edge, to hold the material tight until the glue is completely dry.

When the glue is dry, trim all the excess material away from the edge with a *mat knife.* Then remove the tacks and staples, and the flat is ready to go.

A flat looks much more awkward than it really is. If you lift and move it properly, one person can handle almost any normal-sized flat.

Flats may be braced in several ways to stand up. If you have a wood floor and traditional stage materials, you will have stage braces. These hook onto the back of the flat through a cleat and then are screwed into the stage floor by a stage screw. If you don't have wood floors or if you cannot put stage screws into the wood, a simple hinged jack will work. If you use jacks, lay a sandbag or a stage weight across the bottom brace to prevent wobbling.

The sturdiest way to put two or more flats together is with loose-pin hinges. When the flats are standing, put the hinges on the back so that the two flaps of each hinge are on separate flats. To take them apart or to move them, just pull out the loose pin. To put them back together, stand the flats up so that the two parts of the hinge meet and reinsert the pin.

Suggestions for Handling Flats

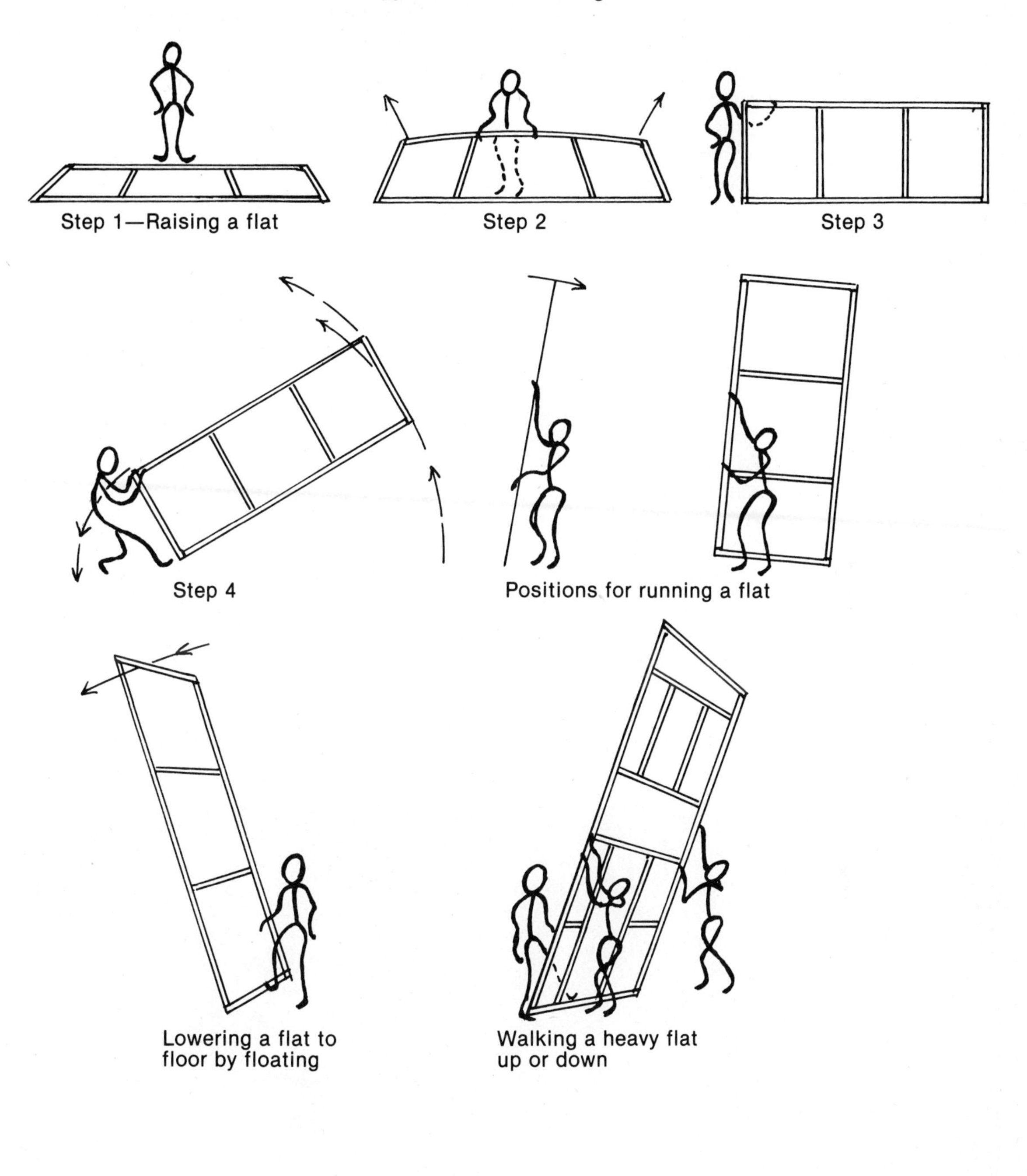

Painting Scenery

Most of the solid look of a set is provided by the paint. Both flats and platforms will need to be painted and repainted for each show. Each time you paint, you can use a different method to make the walls and floors look like anything from raw wood to marble.

For many years scene painters mixed their own paints. Many groups still do, making their own glue and size and mixing dry color pigments to make their own paint. However, since washable latex and acrylic paints were developed and are available in many colors, many groups have switched to these paints for their scenery and props.

If you are using new flats, a *priming coat* will normally be needed. This one smooth coat of a basic color, usually off-white, stretches the covering tight when it dries, seals the pores in the material so that colored paints will not soak in, and gives all flats the same base on which to build colors.

Once all the pieces that are to be the same color or imaginary material are finished, apply a *base coat*. If the surface is supposed to look smooth, this will be your only color. If there is any texturing to be done, this will usually be the middle color. Smooth surfaces which should look shiny from a distance should be painted with all brushstrokes going in the same direction. Smooth surfaces which should look flat or dull should be cross-hatched; apply the paint in long, overlapping strokes, like an X.

Any other textures can be faked by using different painting techniques. As with makeup, a three-dimensional surface is suggested on the flat scenery by mixing highlights and shadows with each color. Remember that each color has its own shades and that the shadow and highlight is different for each color. All shadows are not black or dark brown. Also, remember that the stage light comes from above so that specific shadows go below. It is important that all shadow and highlights on any pieces used under the same lighting run the same way.

Plaster walls and brick can be suggested by *spattering*. After the base coat is dry, pick two colors, one slightly darker than the other. Dip your brush in the darker one; remove the excess. Stand about two feet away from the surface, with your empty hand out, palm upward. With the bristles aimed toward the scenery, slap the brush handle against your palm. Lots of little spots of paint will be thrown at the flat. Adjust the size and spacing of the spatters by the amount of paint in the brush and the distance you stand from the flat's surface. When there is an even coat of the dark color, do the same with the lighter color.

Rough stucco and cinder block can be imitated either by spattering with sharper color contrast and larger spatters or by *scumbling.* Scumbling may be done in two ways. Take the two colors, dip one brush in the darker, one in the lighter, then with a brush in each hand, paint the surface with irregular, short, overlapping strokes which go in all directions. Or, dip a large, wadded-up rag into the darker paint and roll it irregularly across the surface in all directions. Repeat the process with the highlight.

spatter

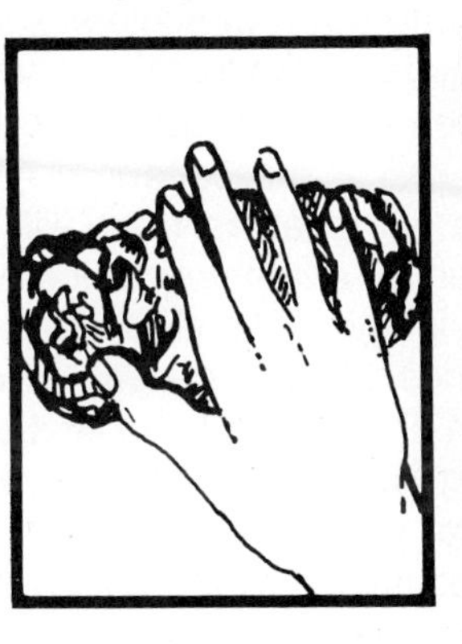

rag roll

dry-brush streaking

stenciling

Wood grain effects are achieved by *dry-brush streaking*. Dip the brush in the darker color, squeezing out the excess so that there is no drip at all. Then just barely touch the brush to the surface, brushing gently in one direction. This will give you several thin, light streaks of paint. Repeat the process with the lighter color, being sure you brush in exactly the same direction with all strokes.

Wallpaper can be simulated by painting over *stencils*. Make a pattern for your wallpaper design, separating each color in your design and making a cut-out for each color. Cut the stencils from stencil paper, cardboard, or vinyl plastic. Be sure that all the stencils are the same size and that their tops are clearly marked so that the patterns can be repeated across the surface to form your *complete* pattern. Lay one stencil on the surface, and apply paint across the opening with a sponge or a brush. Pat; do not stroke the paint. Patting keeps excess paint from dribbling underneath the stencil and ruining the design. Lift that stencil carefully and set it down in its next space. Repeat the process until the surface is painted with the first part of your design. Then repeat the process with each additional stencil and color until your wallpaper pattern is finished.

Marble is usually simulated by a mixture of scumbling, spattering, and occasionally dry-brushing. Grains, colors, and textures of marble are so varied you have to examine very carefully the marble you wish to imitate to determine colors and textures needed in your painting.

Bricks are usually imitated by first painting the entire surface of the flats with the mortar color. Then apply the basic brick color with a stencil, as you did with wallpaper. Then spatter paint over the entire surface. Finally, to make the bricks three-dimensional, lightly shadow underneath the bricks with a darker shade of the mortar color. Do this very thinly and carefully, or you will lose the even edges of the bricks or cover all the mortar.

Remember that all stage painting is meant to be seen from the audience. When you have done your surfaces, look at the scenery from a distance equal to that of the distance between the stage and the middle of the audience. If the surface doesn't show, you need to make the paint job stronger; if it still looks like a paint job, you need to tone down the colors or the size of the texturing. None of these painting techniques should fool *you* when you are up close. They should fool the *audience* when they are looking at the stage. You may use these techniques on props as well as on scenery.

When flats or platforms are put together, there will always be cracks at the joinings. These can be covered by *dutchmen*. Cut or tear a piece of muslin or canvas about 4″ wide and the length of the crack. During the base-coating process and before the base dries, lay the material over the crack, starting at the top and smoothing it down. Paint over it and let it dry with the paint holding it in place. Then finish painting the entire surface. If you have to move the flats from the shop to the stage after you paint them, carefully pull the dutchmen off and roll them up so they do not crack or wrinkle. After all the scenery is in place on the stage, glue the dutchmen back in place.

Scenery Crew

A scenery crew is responsible for building and painting the scenery. In most school groups, this crew includes almost everyone involved in a production, so it tends to be rather loosely organized. However, there should always be at least a designer and a crew head who have specific responsibilities.

The designer confers with the director and decides what the scenery will look like. Then he or she makes drawings or scale models so that everyone can see and understand what the finished product should look like. Then the designer should provide plans for any pieces the crew has to build and specific instructions for the mixing of colors used to paint the set.

The crew head is responsible for organizing, scheduling, and planning the work. In most schools, since teachers have to be present for safety reasons, this responsibility will usually be shared between a teacher and a student. In other groups, the crew head will have full responsibility. He or she should know when scenery has to be ready to go on stage and should make certain that the builders and painters know and meet the deadlines.

Prop Crew

The prop crew is responsible for preparing all the props used in the play. Usually, this crew has a crew head and several members. The crew head is responsible for organizing and planning, and the crew members assist.

This job is the most unpredictable in all theatrical production. Some props have to be made, and the crew will have to do the construction and painting. Some props will be borrowed. The crew has to find them, arrange to borrow and to move them, then take care of them, and return them in the same condition in which they were borrowed. Some props, if unavailable otherwise, have to be rented. The crew will have to find a supplier and handle all the arrangements. It is a long, time-consuming process, and it requires planning, transportation, responsibility, *and* a great deal of luck.

Stage Crew

A backstage crew handles everything in the backstage area. If there are no scenery or prop changes during the play, the "crew" may be only one person who is responsible for setting out props before the show and clearing them afterward. If scenery has to be moved and props changed, the crew may be rather large. In such cases, the crew will often have to close and open curtains, move scenery pieces, change the props at intermissions and in blackouts, and operate special effects backstage. The stage crew works directly for the stage manager and is usually composed of people from both the scenery crew and the prop crew. This group will often have special tech rehearsals in which they rehearse just as the actors do. These rehearsals are extremely important because they determine the fastest and smoothest way to do the job, making the entire production run in the best possible way. Sometimes these tech rehearsals will include the light and sound crews. If a show is complicated, the crews will often run through the entire show without the actors to practice the timing and coordination of all the technical aspects of the production.

Chapter 20
Lighting and Sound

Lighting Equipment

An audience needs light to see a performance. Stage lighting gives that light. However, it does much more than merely provide illumination. Because it can be focused and colored, stage lighting indicates the time, place, and dramatic mood of the play. These elements are reinforced by the sounds of the show.

There are six basic pieces of stage lighting equipment. By mixing the kinds of special light produced by each, various effects can be achieved.

The *ellipsoidal spotlight* gives a bright, sharp-edged light which is evenly bright across the whole area of light. It is named for its reflector, which is ellipsoidal in shape. Its lamp burns base up, and it usually has two lenses. It is sometimes called a *Leko,* the brand name of one of the most popular versions.

The *Fresnel* gives a bright, soft-edged light (bright in the center and fading gradually to the edge). It is named for the inventor of its lens. The lens is a single piece of glass with a series of circular ridges. Its lamp burns base down.

The *carbon-arc spotlight* gives a bright, sharp-edged light that is evenly bright across its area. The light comes from an electric arc that jumps from two pieces of carbon when electricity passes through them (like the machine in Frankenstein's lab). Because the carbon must constantly be adjusted, it requires an operator at all times, and is usually used only for spotlight effects.

A *scoop* gives a general, unfocused flood of light, bright in the center and

ellipsoidal

Fresnel

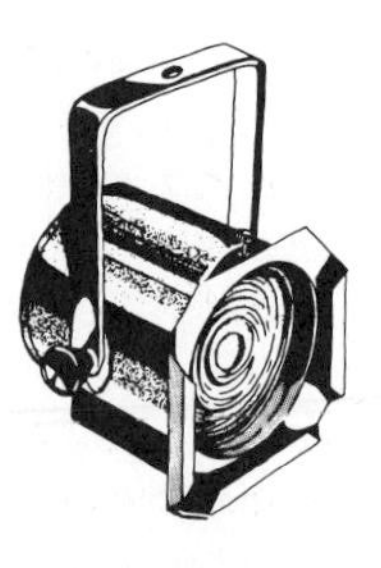

carbon-arc spot

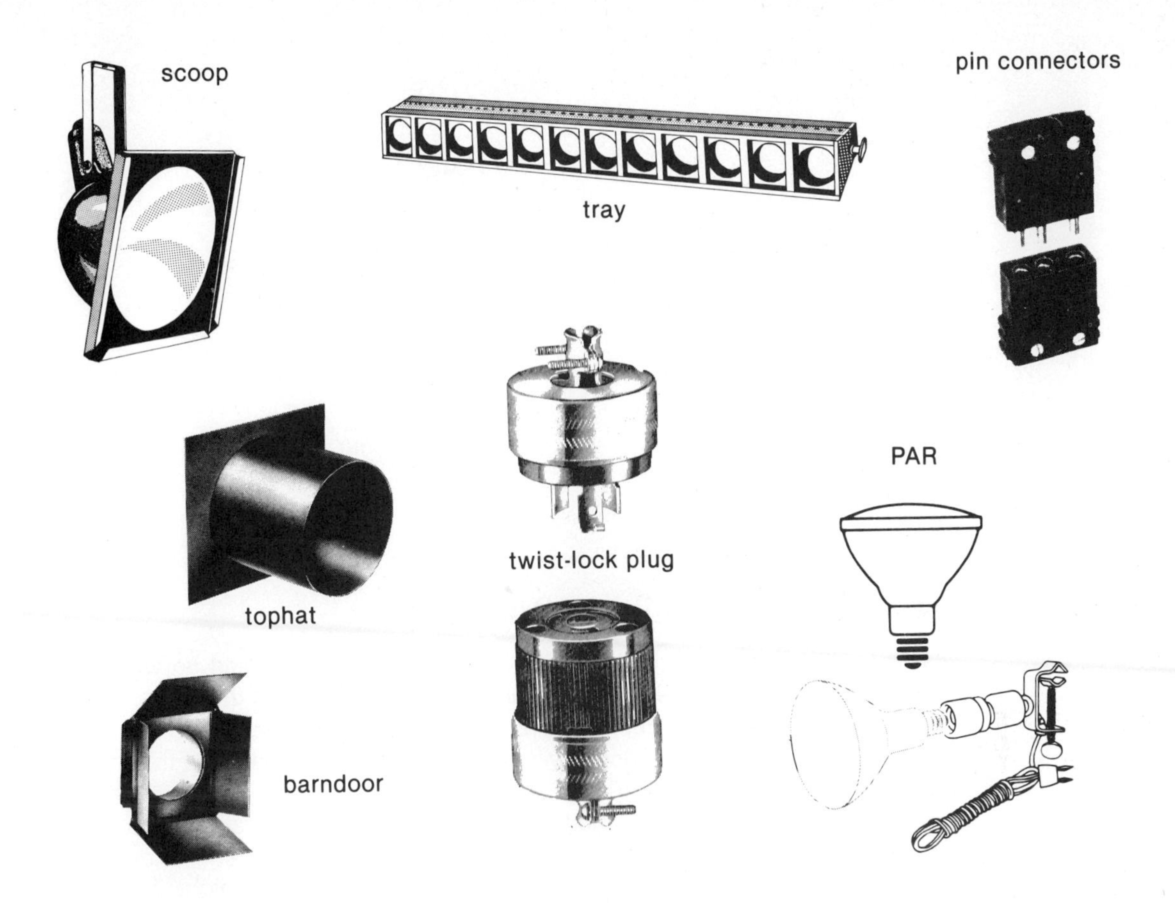

fading toward the edges. It is used when big spaces, such as a sky or scenery walls, need to be lighted in a very general way.

Trays are strips of small lamps in a long metal tray that give a general, unfocused light. The lamps are usually wired in several circuits with a different color on each circuit and the trays hung overhead for general overhead lighting. Trays can also be used at floor level as footlights, but footlights are rarely used today since they tend to spoil the effectiveness of makeup and scenery painting.

The *PAR* is a commercial flood lamp used in the home as well as on the stage. It is a lamp with a built-in reflector. It can do the same kinds of things the scoop or the trays do. Some kinds of PARs are slightly focused and may be used for spotlight effects in small areas.

Most stage lighting is movable. Lights can be hung and focused from any place in the building as long as there is enough extension cable to reach a plug. Since most lighting hangs overhead, plugs are specially designed to hold firm. Most stages are equipped with twist-lock plugs, which require twisting after being plugged in and before they make electrical contact. Household plugs are almost never used.

C-clamp and Yoke

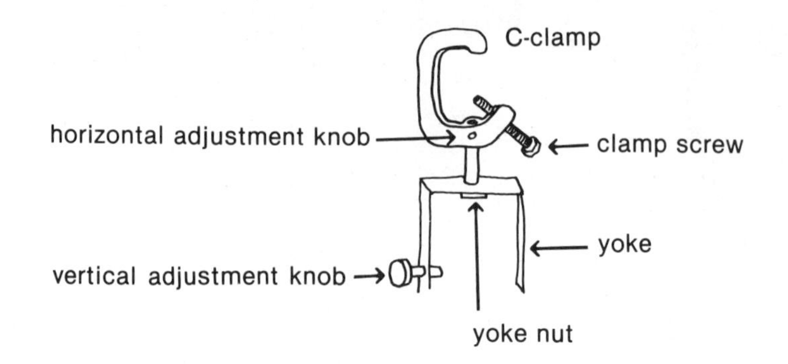

Hanging the Lighting Equipment

The lighting designer will determine which instruments should go where. If you are on the lighting crew, you will have to hang and focus the lights. It is a relatively simple process, but it requires concentration and care. You will need an adjustable wrench and a good pair of gloves, the gloves because the instruments often get hot while you are focusing them. Most lights have a *C-clamp* and *yoke* to secure them as shown; note the names of the various pieces of equipment so that you can follow instructions for mounting that equipment.

1. Before you carry the instrument, make sure the yoke nut is tight. The yoke nut is all that holds the instrument to its frame. It must be tight and should never be loosened.

2. Take the instrument to its designated position. Some stages have catwalks; others have scaffolds or ladders to enable you to reach the *lighting batten*. If you use a scaffold or ladder, be sure there is always one crew member at the bottom to steady it and to keep others from bumping into it while you are on top.

3. Loosen the *clamp screw* until the opening is bigger than the batten. Lift the instrument by the yoke and slide the clamp over the batten until the pipe is securely inside the C. With your other hand, tighten the clamp screw until the clamp is securely fastened to the batten; you will need the wrench for the last few turns.

4. Aim the lens opening in the general direction you wish to aim the light. Check that the instrument is right side up. An ellipsoidal or a scoop should have the *lamp housing* on top. The Fresnel should have the lamp housing on the bottom. If it is not, loosen the vertical adjustment knob and turn the instrument over.

5. Find the proper plug. Make sure the power is off. Plug the instrument in.

Be sure you are looking at the stage; do not ever look into the lens of an instrument. Have the power turned on. If light comes on, you are ready to focus.

6. To raise the light, loosen the vertical adjustment knob. Then lift the front of the instrument until the light is at the approximate height you wish; then tighten the knob. To move the light to the side, loosen the horizontal adjustment knob (this one needs a wrench), move the front of the instrument until light is at the place you wish, and then tighten the knob. Continue alternating these adjustments until the light is placed exactly where it should be.

7. The shape of the light may be changed in several ways:

ellipsoidals: Each instrument will have a set of shutters. These slide in and out, blocking off part of the light. Push or pull the shutters until the light is the size and shape you wish. Note that the lens works like a telescope and reverses the light, so the top shutter will cut off light at the bottom of the stage, and so on.

Fresnels: There is a little knob on the bottom of the lamp housing. Loosen this slightly and slide it back and forth. The closer the knob is to the lens, the bigger the light area; the farther back it moves, the smaller the light area.

8. Double-check all bolts and knobs to make sure that they are tight. Then have the power turned off. The instrument is focused.

Scoops, PARs, and trays can only be hung and aimed. They cannot be focused. If they require C-clamps, hang them using steps 1 through 6.

Color

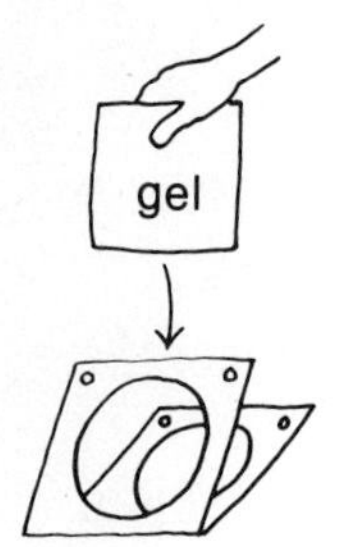

The color of a stage light is controlled by placing some color medium in front of the lens opening. The most common medium is called a *gel* because it was first made from gelatine. Most gels are now made from plastic or acetate, but the name has been retained.

Gels come in a variety of colors, usually in large sheets that have to be cut to size for the various instruments. Each color has an identifying number and most *lighting plots* will tell you what color to use on each instrument by listing the number.

The gel is cut to the size of the gel frame, a metal frame with a large circular opening matched to each size of instrument. The gel is then inserted in the frame, and the frame is dropped into the prongs on the outside of the lens. When the light is turned on, it reflects the color of the gel.

Most stage lighting requires the use of a variety of colors. The lighting designer will determine these colors after experimenting with them to determine which best bring out the colors of the scenery, makeup, and costumes.

Lighting Plots

Usually a designer will work out the lighting plot, a chart showing where the instruments should be hung and the directions for plugging and focusing them. A light plot will usually look something like this.

First, it shows where the instruments are to be hung. It is drawn to scale, and shows the approximate spacing of all instruments. Each instrument is numbered for identification.

Second, it gives you all the directions you need. These include:

1. type—kind, size, and wattage of each instrument. On the example, 1 would be a 6″ Leko (or ellipsoidal) with a 500-watt-lamp.

2. circuit (circ on the example)—This tells you what plug to plug into. Your stage should have all the plugs numbered to identify their circuits.

3. gel—the identification number of the color for gel you should use.

4. focus—directions for focusing the light.

5. remarks—any special directions or unusual information you need to finish focusing.

Some designers will give more information:

6. plug/w (means "plug with")—tells that the instrument described is plugged into the same circuit as another instrument. This is a safety device; first, so that you know exactly which lights should come on at the same time, and then, so that you can find them if for some reason you need to change the plugs.

7. patch—tells you which *dimmer* the circuit will be patched into.

Dimmers

The most important part of stage lighting is control. This control is exercised through the dimmers.

Sample Light Plot

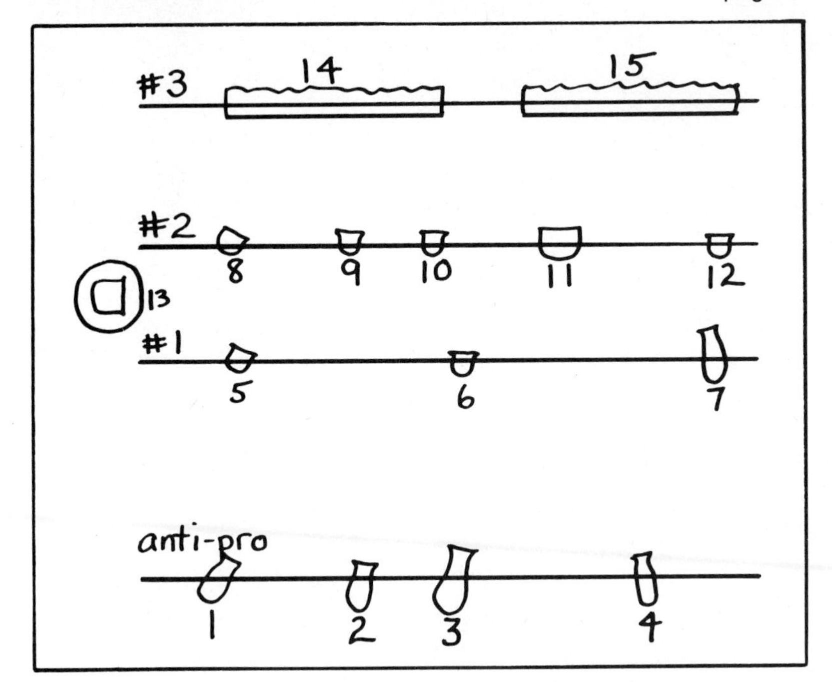

page 2

INST. #	TYPE	CIRC	PLUG/W	GEL	FOCUS	REMARKS
1	6"L500	1	4	802	DR, stage edge to RC	
2	6"L750	4	-	841	DRC, curtain line	
3	8"L750	5	-	826	DC	
4	6"L500	1	1	851	DR, stage edge-RC	cut at curt.R
5	6"F500	21	-	802	RC	medium full
6	6"F500	22	-	829	DRC, str. down	smallest poss.
11	10"S750	35	-	836	str. down	
12	6"F500	32	8	841	URC	med. full
13	8"F1000	37	-	805	str. across	open
14	tray	R40,B41,W42	15	-	tilt back to cyc	
15	tray	same as 14				

Working the lights: director and students, Glenbrook North High School, Northbrook, Illinois

There are hundreds of different kinds of dimmers manufactured by dozens of companies. Dimmer-control panels fall into three basic types, the radial, the slider, and the pre-set.

The *radial dimmer* looks like a wheel or a knob. It has a handle that is pushed up and down or around, turning an oval or circular scale.

The *slider* is flat, with a small grip that is slid back and forth across a scale.

The *pre-set dimmer* may be a radial or slider or both. It is distinguished by having two or more identical sets of controls. To make a lighting change, you make the settings on one set of controls while the power is passing through another. Then, instead of changing a number of individual dimmers as you would on the radials and sliders, you move one master control. This master control shifts the power from the old row of controls to the new one, making it possible for one person to do lighting changes that other systems need several people to do.

Whichever system your stage has, be sure you understand it before you try to work it. All of the power for the production passes through the dimmers, and you have to be right all the time.

All the controls will have a set of numbers which are the settings. Usually these go from 0 to 10, with **0** meaning **off** and **10** meaning **brightest possible** light. All your cues will be marked with these settings.

The Cue Sheet

The *cue sheet* will tell you when to change the lighting and how to change it.

In most cases, the stage manager will have a copy of the script in which all the light and sound changes are marked and numbered. The manager will watch the show and follow along with the script. As cues come up, he will signal the light or sound crew to start the cue.

The light crew will have a cue sheet. On that cue sheet all the lighting cues are listed and numbered. For each numbered cue, the cue sheet will tell you which dimmers change, what settings they change to, and how many seconds it should take you to make the change.

If you are running the lights for a production, you must follow the cue sheet carefully. The stage manager should give you warning for each cue about 30 seconds before it happens, so that you can double-check and make sure that you are ready. The manager will always identify the cue by number. When the manager says "go," start the cue immediately, and do it exactly as written on the cue sheet.

Sound

Stage sound involves two kinds of sound—music and effects. Music may be used during scenes, with songs or dances, and/or during intermissions and curtain calls. Sound effects are used throughout a production to tell the audience what is happening offstage in the imaginary world of the play. These sounds can be simple or complicated, and often involve such things as rain, thunder, crickets, automobiles passing by, and crowds of one type or another. All of these sounds must be loud enough to be heard by the audience, but they must also be balanced with the sound levels of the actors' voices so that the effect has reality.

Although some sounds can be done live—phone rings, doorbells, buzzers—most effects are more easily recorded. Because it provides easy editing and instantaneous cueing, the best method is reel-to-reel tape recording.

If you are working sound for a production, begin by going over the script carefully. Note every place where sound is required. Confer with the director to find out exactly what type of sound is needed at each place in the script and approximately how long the sound needs to be sustained.

There are a number of sound-effects records that can be rented or purchased. If these are not available, you may be able to make your own sound tape. You can carry a portable tape recorder to a parking lot or a train station or wherever you need to find a particular sound. Re-record the sounds from the portable or from the effects records onto a single reel-to-reel tape. **Be sure to put them in the order in which they'll be used.** Edit the tape by putting a piece of leader tape (nonmagnetic white tape) before each separate sound.

Make a cue sheet for sound the same way one was made for lights. The stage manager will have a script with all the sound cues marked and numbered. You should have a cue sheet that tells you the number and volume setting for each of the cues. The manager will give you the "go" signal in the same way he gives it to the light crew. When he tells you to play sound cue 1, turn on the recorder at the volume shown and play it until you reach the next leader tape. Stop there and you will be ready for the next sound cue.

When setting the volume for sound cues remember that you must match the volume of the actors' voices. Often the best sound effects are very soft—just loud enough for the audience to hear but not so loud that they distract from the scene.

Sound-effects tape must be played through speakers. If the stage has a good sound system, you can play directly through the system. If you want the sound to be specific—to come from a particular place or direction backstage—you will need one or more portable speakers. These speakers will be placed backstage and connected to your recorder. If it is necessary to use portable speakers, tape down all cables so that no one can trip over them.

Chapter 21

Management—The Production Staff

The production of any play requires the work and skill of a large number of people who may never be seen by the audience. In addition to the technical crews there must be a production staff that makes the plans, organizes the work, controls the money, finds the audience, and makes the decisions involving the work of actors and crews. This staff may be large or small, depending on the show and the organization involved. Usually, it will include the producer, director, designers, stage manager, assistants, publicity director, business manager, and house manager.

Producer

In the professional theater the producer is the person who is responsible for everything. The producer selects the play, raises the money, hires the actors and staff, supervises the budget, schedules the production, arranges for the theater, and supervises publicity and ticket sales. Other production staff members confer with and report to the producer.

In many groups, especially in community theaters, the producer's job is handled by a committee. In schools, it is usually handled by a teacher—often the teacher who is also the director. Whether the producer is one person or a committee, each production needs a head who knows what each staff is doing at all times so that all of the pieces of the production fit together.

Director

The director decides what happens on the stage. Most of the time the director works with the actors; he runs rehearsals, determines blocking, and guides the actors in their interpretations.

The director also confers with all the designers so that they understand exactly what the production requires from each of them. He determines how many sets are needed, the basic floor plan for those sets, how many costume changes will be needed for each character, and so on. He must approve the plans made by each designer before the plans go to the shops to be implemented.

Designers

Designers make the decisions and plans for the physical parts of the show. Most of these duties have been explained in detail in the foregoing chapters of this unit. Usually, a production will have several designers. Some groups, especially small ones, may combine the duties of two or three designers.

The scenery designer is responsible for planning and drawing models of all the scenery. He will decide placement, sizes of flats and platforms, colors and materials. Generally, he will also select the props.

The costume designer decides upon all costumes to be worn by the cast. If costumes must be constructed, he will provide drawings and suggest materials.

The makeup designer plans the makeup for everyone in the show. Sometimes a separate person will be assigned to hair design. Sometimes the costume designer assumes makeup and hair design as well as costume.

The lighting designer plans all the lighting effects, provides the light plot, and supervises the hanging of the equipment and the setting of the lighting cues.

The sound designer plans the sound cues, supervises their selection, and determines the best way to reproduce them. In musicals, the sound designer determines the placement of microphones and selects all sound equipment.

All of these persons regularly confer with the director and producer so that all work is coordinated.

Stage Manager

The stage manager runs the show. He is supposed to know everything about anything that happens either on stage or backstage. During rehearsals, he makes the schedules and is responsible for keeping crews and cast on schedule. During rehearsals, the stage manager will make and keep the *production book*—the single copy of the script in which *everything* about the show is recorded. All the blocking, the light, sound, curtain, and scene-change cues are marked and recorded in the production book. The production book will tell you where every prop should be and when, what costume each character wears in each scene, and anything else that could be pertinent to a successful show. During rehearsals, the stage manager follows the script. When actors need prompting or have questions about blocking, he provides the information.

In performance, the stage manager runs the show. He makes sure that the cast and crew are ready; he decides when to start the show; he calls all the cues. He is responsible for making everything work! After the show, when the cleanup has been completed, the stage manager releases the cast.

Assistants

Most production staffs will have several assistants. Nearly every group will have an assistant stage manager and an assistant director. Most crew heads will also have assistants.

The assistant stage manager does whatever is necessary to help the stage manager. If the stage manager is prompting a rehearsal, the assistant may be checking props. If the stage manager is calling cues, the assistant may be supervising scene changes. The duties will vary on the needs of the show.

The assistant director may do anything from running errands to taking notes on rehearsals to rehearsing actors in small scenes.

Publicity

The publicity director is responsible for letting the public know that there is a show and for getting the public to come to the show. All advertising—posters, newspaper and radio/television coverage, billboards—are his responsibility. Arranging for interviews or any other kind of special event which will draw attention to the show is his responsibility. An audience cannot be assembled if it is not aware of the production.

Business Manager

The business manager is in charge of finances. He keeps careful records of how much is spent and for what. He supervises ticket sales and box-office operations and reports regularly to the producer on the financial state of the production.

House Manager

The house manager arranges for and schedules the ushers, making sure that they greet the public in a positive manner. As the official host, he plans carefully for the comfort and convenience of the audience. The house manager also arranges for the programs and sees that all audience areas are clean, neat, and attractive at all times.

Chapter 22
Preparation, Rehearsals, and Performance

Work for backstage crews and staff breaks down into three basic periods. **Preparation** includes all work done before the actors begin rehearsing and before crews move onto the stage. **Rehearsal** begins as soon as everyone moves on stage. **Performance** begins with audience. Not everyone does the same amount of work in each period.

Preparation

During preparation the staff makes the basic technical decisions. The staging plans are made, materials ordered, and schedules determined. Individual crews are organized and given their assignments.

As you begin work be aware of the schedule and your deadlines. A stage production resembles a complicated jigsaw puzzle. Each piece has to fit. For stage crews that means each piece has to be ready as scheduled. Often, one crew cannot do its job until another crew has finished. If you are late, the entire show may fall behind schedule. Technical work must be completed far enough in advance of performance to be tested, corrected, and then rehearsed with.

During preparation, the scenery crew will be building and painting sets, the prop crew will be finding or making props, the costume crew will be making or fitting costumes, and so on. All preparation work will be done in many different places at many different times; it must be carefully scheduled by the crew heads and stage manager.

Rehearsals

Once the production has moved to the stage, you are in the rehearsal period. Your goal now is to make sure that everything works and then find the best, fastest, and simplest way to keep it working in performance. Rehearsal is a difficult and complicated period. Each crew must coordinate its work with that of the other crews and with the actors. This takes time, concentration, and careful attention to schedules.

For some groups, this may be a very short period. It is often difficult to reserve the stage for long periods; everything may move onto the stage at the same time and at the last possible moment. If at all possible, avoid this situation. Ideally, crews should be brought in one at a time. The prop crew usually has the earliest deadline: actors need to become familiar with the things they must use. Scenery is usually set up before the lighting is hung so that it can be focused and gelled in exactly the right places and colors. Costume and makeup crews are generally last. It is pointless to do makeup until the lighting is completed. Before bringing in the costumes the painting crews should have finished and their working areas should be clean.

The stage manager will be in charge of these rehearsals. Be well organized, know what you have to do, and do it as quickly as possible. When you are backstage, remember that you are there to do a job; know where you should be and always be quiet. Almost every sound backstage will be heard in the audience.

Once everything is on the stage, there will be one or more *tech rehearsals.* In the tech rehearsals all light and sound cues will be set, all props and costumes tested, and all scene changes planned and rehearsed. If time allows, at least one of these rehearsals will be without the actors. Several other rehearsals may include the actors and these will involve a run-through of the entire show, stopping whenever it is necessary to solve a problem. These rehearsals are usually long and difficult. Concentrate.

After tech rehearsals there may be special rehearsals for small crews. For example, a stage crew may come in an hour early to practice a difficult scene change.

Dress rehearsals are the last rehearsals before performance. A dress rehearsal should be treated as if it were a real show—only the audience is missing. The purpose of a dress rehearsal is to make certain that everything runs smoothly and that the entire show is consistent.

After run-throughs and dress rehearsals the director will call cast and crew together for last-minute corrections and directions. Listen carefully to everything said. Everyone on stage and backstage is involved in the making of a single performance. What is said at these meetings will make the performance the very best possible.

Performance

In performance each person has a specific job to do. Below are general procedures to be followed by all technical staff and crews:

1. No one should appear on stage or in front of the curtain after the house is open and the audience starts taking their seats. The audience comes to see the show. They should hear or see nothing that distracts from it. Once the curtain goes up and the house lights go down, remember a simple rule: if you can see the audience, they can see you. Stay out of sight. Be quiet.

2. The stage manager will set arrival time for each crew. Know and meet your call time which will be set so that each crew has the time it needs to make its checks on equipment and responsibilities before the house is opened.

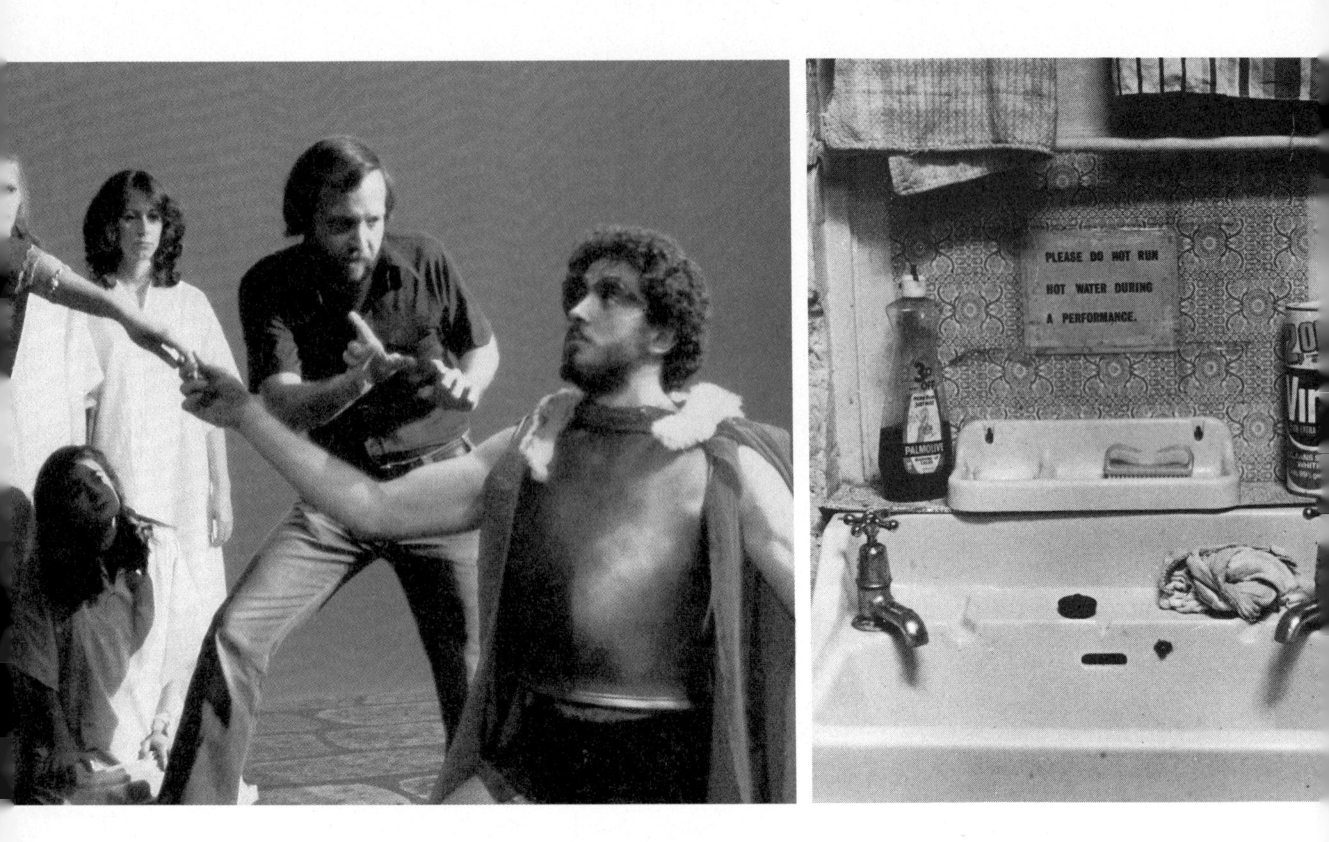

"last minute corrections . . ." (left)

" . . . every sound backstage will be heard in the audience . . ."(right)

The stage crew should set out all props and make sure that all scenery is solidly braced and in working order. Light and sound crews should check all equipment making sure that all lighting instruments are working. Costume and makeup crews should make sure everything is in place. Costumes should be checked for any last-minute repair; makeup kits should be in order.

3. Remember that the stage manager is in charge. Whatever he says, goes.

4. Know where you should be and stay there so that you can be found when needed. Don't wander off assuming you have ten minutes until the next scene change; actors have been known to skip a page! Do not get in the way of the actors or other backstage workers.

5. Always treat the audience with respect. Ushers and ticket sellers should dress attractively, smile, and be pleasant. Remember that you represent the entire group; present a positive and pleasant image. Those who are on stage or backstage and see the audience only after the show should react pleasantly to compliments. Say "thank you," even if you know you missed several cues.

6. Be accurate. Technical crews are expected to do it right 100 percent of the time. If an actor misses a line but covers it well, probably no one in the audience will notice. But if the light crew doesn't turn on the lights at the right time or if the prop crew leaves the candle offstage where the actor cannot pick it up, everyone in the audience will notice. Unfair but a fact: actors *should be* perfect, but the tech crews *have to be* perfect.

Strike

After the last performance the cast and crew will strike the show. This means that everything that was put up must be taken down. Everyone involved in the show helps with the strike. All scenery must be taken down, all lighting unplugged and removed, all costumes prepared for cleaning and storage. All areas must be left clean. When the strike is finished, the building should look as if you have never been there.

Be careful during strike. There are a lot of people doing a lot of different things, most of them in some way destructive. It is easy to get hurt. Remember and closely follow your safety rules.

Many items will go into storage so that they can be used again someday. Store them properly. Be sure that everyone understands what items were borrowed and who is to return them so that they are returned as soon as possible. Be sure that all makeup and costume items are clean before they go into storage, and be sure that all tools are put away. The house manager should check the box office and auditorium areas to be sure that there are no programs, refreshments, or other debris left about.

When everything is finally clean and everything has been put away, then, the show is over.

Unit VI
Group Interpretation

CHAPTER 23
Readers' Theater
Selection for Readers' Theater Interpretation

CHAPTER 24
Chamber Theater
Selection for Chamber Theater Interpretation

CHAPTER 25
Choric Interpretation
Selections for Choric Interpretation

There are three popular forms of group interpretation: Readers' Theater for drama, Chamber Theater for narration, and Choric Interpretation.

Very often the term Readers' Theater is used to cover all three methods of performance, but there are some basic differences among them. We will talk about them separately to help make those differences, as well as the similarities, a little clearer. Sometimes your material will profit from a combination of modes. Nevertheless, it is wise to know what it is you are doing when. We will look briefly at each of these techniques remembering that they are all part of the bigger field we have been discussing. The success of each depends upon the skill and concentration of every individual involved in the group. The same detailed analysis of the literature is necessary. And the same control of voice and body is important.

Chapter 23 Readers' Theater

You know the method of analysis and the techniques a single reader uses to interpret dramatic literature in which there are two or more characters. Go back to Chapter 6 and review the suggestions on technique. In Readers' Theater there is a separate interpreter for each part, reading only the lines of one particular character, just as an actor presents only one character in a staged play. In this regard, Readers' Theater closely parallels a conventional theater production. The interpreter and the actor use all their skill to project the complete *inner* character to the audience. The difference lies in the interpreters' use of suggestion.

There is no "one way" to do Readers' Theater. The cast and the director must always be guided by the demands of the selection they are using. Many directors place the readers on stage in groups suggesting the psychological relationship of the characters. Some use reading stands; others do not. If reading stands are used, they must not be so high that they obscure the view for the people in the front row.

The interpreters in a Readers' Theater production hold their scripts or put them on the reading stands. Some directors prefer to have their casts work without scripts, but unless your group is very experienced, it is safer to have them with you. Moreover, it helps your audience establish both scene and characters in their minds, and reminds them that what you are sharing with them is going on in the literature you have chosen. Thus, they can respond with no self-consciousness, which they might feel if the scene is a highly emotional one and they feel they are eavesdropping on someone who is actually standing before them.

Whether the cast brings the scripts on stage or not, they play out into the audience area since they are placing the scene in the minds of the audience just as they always do as individual interpreters of drama.

They sit or stand, use reading stands or not, as their director wishes. They often remain present onstage, even after their characters would have left the stage in a staged production. They wear their own clothes, though often in a prearranged style, and only enough makeup to emphasize their features under stage lights. We will study each of these elements in more detail later.

It must be remembered that empathy and muscle memory are as important to group work as to the single interpreter of drama. The members of the cast do not stand like wax figures behind the reading stands. They may feel free to move about the stand as the individual interpreter does.

The Readers' Theater Script

A well-written play will require very little change to make it a satisfactory Readers' Theater script. In fact, it may often be used exactly as it is written for stage presentation. This is certainly true of the short play, *Second Chance,* which is used at the end of this chapter and for the selections at the end of Chapter 7 and for the scenes following Unit III. If you are using a full length play you may need to do a little cutting here and there, however, because a Readers' Theater production should not run over two hours playing time, since there is very little visible action to hold attention. Your director may plan for intermissions at appropriate places to allow the audience and the interpreters to relax. These intermissions need not come at the places indicated by act conclusions, since there is no change in scenery or costumes. A curtain may be drawn, or the cast may leave the stage and return to their places after the intermission in full view of the audience.

Divisions between scenes are eliminated when they merely indicate an entrance or exit of a character. This kind of division is found in Shakespeare and in many classic and foreign plays. The passage of time or change of place may be indicated on a printed program, or by a person who remains in an inconspicuous place or even offstage during the scenes and comes forward when needed to speak to the audience in the manner of an oriental stage manager. This technique is suggested for two or three bits of business in *Second Chance* where the lines would not make the action clear. It would also be the simplest way to introduce the scene and the characters.

Rehearsal Suggestions

A Readers' Theater production takes as much rehearsal time as a fully staged performance even though setting, lights, and costumes are much simpler to manage.

Rehearsal procedure for Readers' Theater differs somewhat from that of a fully staged play since you need a minimum amount of blocking for specific actions. The first few rehearsals consist of an informal group reading of the entire play. This is important so all members of the cast come to understand the director's concept of the play and the contribution each speech and scene makes to the play. Even if you read only one speech, it is important for you to listen to read-through rehearsals.

During the first half-dozen rehearsals, the director makes cuts and additions. He may alter these as the play progresses, so mark them in pencil, but clearly enough so you can read them easily. You are concerned primarily with your own characters and lines but very soon you will need to develop the habit of really hearing others' lines so there will be clear interplay between your character and theirs. This is extremely important. You must listen, react, and reply when you are in a scene.

After a few read-through rehearsals, you will begin to rehearse on your feet. You may even spend a few sessions walking through the actions as you would for a traditional stage production. Remember this was suggested for muscle memory and empathy even when you are doing an interpretation as a single reader. As soon as you have the actions in your mind and muscles you will begin to work on actual Readers' Theater technique of performance.

At this point you become aware of one of the real problems of Readers' Theater. You have an irresistible desire to turn and address your lines to the character they are meant for. Until you've had some experience, it feels pretty peculiar to be directing your mind and voice to the audience area and have the reply to your line come from a reader who is sitting or standing on stage beside you.

To make you feel more comfortable until you are used to Readers' Theater technique, the director may divide the cast in half and let you work across the room from each other. Then you will be projecting out front, mentally and physically, but you will have an area of focus to help you. After a few such sessions, the habit of speaking, looking, and thinking out front will be easier. When you again take your place onstage, continue to visualize the characters you speak to as if they were still across the room.

The rehearsal technique of *playing across the room* is useful to get a good mental focus, help you concentrate on what the other character is saying so your lines answer him properly, and move the action along. You "hear" what is said as if it came from out front. When you reply, your mind goes out across the audience to where you have placed the other characters, just as it does when you handle an entire scene alone.

If you turn and address another reader, you pull the scene out of the audience's mind and place it onstage. You ask the audience to believe the person next to you is really Queen Elizabeth and present them with an impossible task, since she neither dresses nor looks like good Queen Bess. In Readers' Theater you are still an interpreter and you use the same techniques for creating a scene that you learned to use in the interpretation of drama.

Lines of Focus

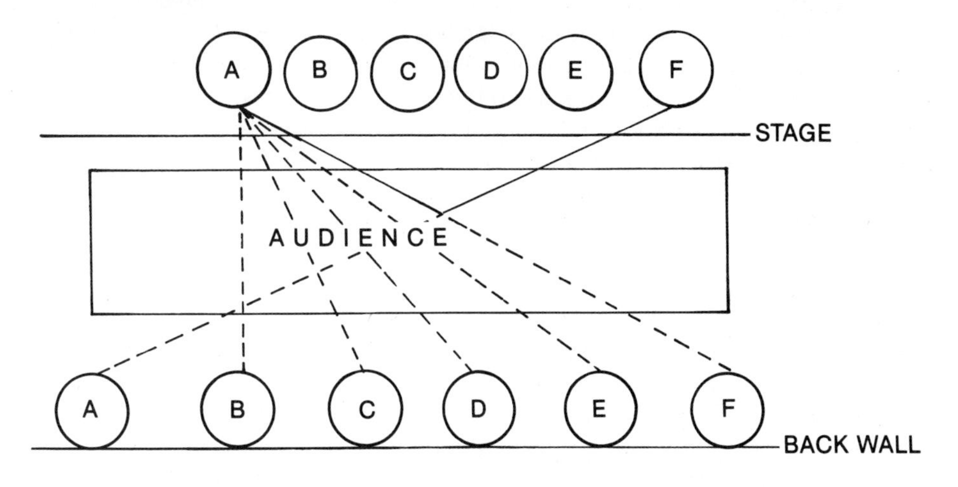

When you are speaking to other characters, it is not necessary to keep your eyes glued on a single spot on the back wall. Go back again to Chapter 6 for a brief discussion of this. Feel free to turn your eyes and body slightly as long as you keep the scene out front. Do not let the angle of your body, or the focus of your eyes, move inside the stage area nor beyond the outside of the audience area.

When we discussed angle of focus for an individual interpreter, we indicated placement of characters. Assume that there are six characters in a Readers' Theater production: A, B, C, D, E, and F. Interpreter A uses the same technique suggested for the interpreter of drama, except that his or her position at the far right of the stage does not allow so wide an angle at the right. Thus interpreter A adjusts his or her area of focus as illustrated in the diagram above. Interpreter F does the same thing to keep from going too far to the left and so on across the cast with each reader using the whole back wall to address other characters, shifting eyes and mental directness to the appropriate area within the width of the audience area. When characters address each other, their lines of focus cross somewhere in the center of the audience area.

The lines of focus from A to B, C, D, E, and F continue to the back wall for purposes of projection.

Feel free to move about, but, for practical purposes, it is wise to indicate crosses by only a few steps and to remain near your reading stand. Muscle memory from the walk-through rehearsals will help you here.

During the middle period of rehearsals, work to understand the "why" and "what" of everything your character says. The procedure is the same for Readers' Theater as for interpretation of drama, except that you concentrate on one character. But, you must know the relationship of your character to the others and make this relationship clear to the audience.

The final ten days of rehearsal you polish the details. One of these is pace. As you work on a play, you become aware that some scenes have more suspense than others, or some move faster than others. Your director helps you decide questions of pace, but you will want to take a good look at the structure of the play to see how the scenes fit so the plot moves in its proper rhythm.

Be sure that you are speaking loudly enough to be heard in the auditorium. If you cannot be heard, everything else is lost. During every rehearsal, keep your visualized characters placed against the back wall and project both your voice and your mind the full distance.

Handling Entrances and Exits

Work on the timing of your entrances and exits, although you may not actually leave the stage at the end of your scenes. Entrances and exits in Readers' Theater are made in many ways. A technique frequently used is to stand for your scenes and to sit for your exits. This is effective if you use high stools. If the play is short, all readers may stand during the entire play. Then the exits may be handled with a step back, a general relaxing of muscle tone, and a lowering of the head. Sometimes you may leave the acting area, retire to the back of the stage, and sit with other readers whose characters are offstage.

Whatever technique your director adopts is carefully timed. Take your cue from the kind of exit you would make onstage and use your power of suggestion to make this clear to the audience. If the scene has been tense and your character exits rapidly, then time your sitting or crossing to the back of the stage fast, and relax abruptly. If the scene has a slow, dim-out closing, move smoothly, and hold your muscle tone for a second before lowering your head and eyes and "dropping out of scene."

When your character enters, stand or move in quickly and firmly, or slowly and gently, as the scene demands. Stand with your muscles alert so you command attention. Widen your circle of concentration to include the entire room, place the characters to be addressed at the back of the room, and direct your thoughts, voice, and eyes to them. When your character exits, reverse the process at whatever pace is right for the character. Sit or move to the area designated as offstage, maintain muscle tone a few seconds, then relax, drop your eyes, and bring your circle of concentration to a small area around yourself. Do not turn your attention to the other characters, but keep alert for your next cue.

The way you sit "offstage" is important to the appearance of the entire production. You are not out of sight when your character leaves the scene, so when several characters are "offstage," they must be careful not to distract from the scene being done. You must sit still. Any movement will immediately call the attention of the audience away from the scene in progress. Only hams steal scenes. Real performers are interested in the play. This physical discipline is tiring. Start practicing it several weeks before performance.

Practice holding your manuscript. If you use typed pages, put them in a stiff notebook. When you are on, hold the script in one hand, with the other on the open book or notebook to keep your place, and be free for gestures. Keep the manuscript tipped toward you so the white pages won't catch the light. After you leave the scene, turn quickly and quietly to your next entrance. Then hold the manuscript in your lap. If you use individual reading stands, the problem is simpler. With a reading stand, you turn to your next scene unobtrusively, and leave the manuscript on the stand when you step back or sit down. Or take it with you so you won't miss your next cue.

If there are several pages between your scenes, clip them together. You don't want to turn pages every few minutes when you are out of scene. Mark your entrances in large enough writing, so you can see them from a distance. Some professionals put a WARN mark several speeches before their entrances so they are ready for them. Keep your attention on the play so you do not cause a break in pace. But keep your eyes down and remain mentally out of scenes you are not in.

Stage Setting

The most effective stage background for a Readers' Theater production is a simple neutral curtain. There need be no attempt to portray an actual period or location because the setting, like the action and characters, is in the minds of the audience, not on the stage. If your stage is deep, it is better to hang the background curtain at the center of the stage, so there is no expanse of empty space behind the readers. Such space tends to swallow up the voices and spoil the symmetry of the stage picture. Readers' Theater may be presented before the front curtain if there is enough room for the interpreters to work.

The interpreters stand near the front of the stage so their voices will carry readily. They may form a straight line, or a curve, or be grouped in twos or threes, depending on the area and the number of characters involved. If there are many short scenes with only a few characters, an attempt may be made to keep a balance of activity in the grouping so that half the stage does not get too much play, leaving the other half without activity for long periods.

Readers' Theater may be used even when there is no stage or curtain. It is ideal for work in the classroom. That is one of its advantages. The cast may enter together and take their places in the area used as a stage, in full view of the audience. When the play is finished, they leave. This should be rehearsed so everyone knows exactly where he or she is going, and when to sit or rise to leave. If there is no backstage area, they may enter from the front row of the audience, or the back of the house, and return to that location when the play is over. Whatever is practical is effective, as long as it is done with decorum and dignity and is in harmony with the mood of the material you are using.

Costumes and Makeup

Since the picture the audience sees is fairly static, the use of color is often attractive. Slacks and simple blouses are useful. Full skirts are easier to manage than tight ones, especially if the reader is to sit. Long dresses are more graceful than street-length onstage. Color is chosen for its harmoniousness with the draperies and with the clothes of the others. Solid colors are best, although this depends on the director's taste. Sequins and rhinestones are distracting. Jewelry is kept at a minimum. Small earrings which will not catch the light and simple necklaces are permissible. Bracelets jingle against the reading stands and interfere with handling the script.

Men often wear dark trousers with white or solid color shirts. If the play is not modern, corduroy or velour sport shirts and dark trousers are effective. They look rich under stage lights, and the colors are excellent. When the shirts are buttoned at neck and wrist and worn tucked in, they take on a surprising degree of formality that helps to suggest a period. A small strip of matching material placed over the buttons, and then buttoned through the buttonholes, will disguise the shirt's casual origin. Tie clips and wristwatches catch the light and are removed before performance.

A light base of pancake makeup keeps you from looking anemic under the lights. The eyebrows are darkened and sometimes the outline of the eye accented by a pencil line and/or eye shadow. Both men and women need this type of makeup if the lights are strong. Age lines, gray, or partly gray hair, or character makeup are not necessary, since you are not asking the audience to believe that you *are* the character.

You must not make the mistake of thinking that Readers' Theater takes less time and effort on the part of the participants than a fully staged production. You must be as well prepared as the actor. You must be completely in control of all the elements of the entire play and alert to the contribution your scenes make to the total performance. Though difficult and challenging, Readers' Theater is an effective and satisfying technique.

Selection for Readers' Theater Interpretation

Second Chance has some interesting problems for a Readers' Theater production. Avoid specific costumes even though the script suggests them. It would be awkward and distracting for Rita to keep changing her clothes. Those stage directions reprinted in boldface type are probably best handled by narration.

Be sure Evelyn is hearing the other end of the telephone conversations and reacting to what she hears. There is a clear rhythm of emotion throughout the play although the changes come rather quickly. Don't rush them but remember to pick up the characters neatly and then let the reaction show even before they speak in a new mood. Rita's exercises could be done by her as she speaks since they are brief and would add action to an otherwise physically static scene. If the British accent can be handled well, it would add a touch of humor. Otherwise an exaggerated "theatrical" manner of speaking would accomplish the same purpose. Notice that Rita abandons the accent very soon.

The cues must be picked up fairly rapidly in most cases to keep the scene moving.

It might work very well to have a narrator, who remains off and to one side out of scene, give the setting and time and then say "The characters are . . ." letting Rita and Evelyn introduce themselves.

Second Chance

by Elyse Nass

Characters:

RITA, *late sixties. Vivacious, trying to appear buoyant.*

EVELYN, *mid-sixties. But she looks tired and is letting things take their course.*

Scene:
A small, nicely furnished apartment in New York City.
Old movie posters and theatrical memorabilia are on the wall, as well as family photographs.
The time is the present.
As the curtain rises, RITA *is pacing around in a full-length caftan.*
Finally, EVELYN *knocks on the door.*

RITA (*in a British accent*). Hurry up and enter! (EVELYN *walks in. She is wearing a plain housedress.*) I never thought you'd get here.
EVELYN. Why? I live right next door. What's the matter?
RITA. Please sit down.
EVELYN. Why?
RITA. You're all out of breath, so take a seat quickly. ***(She pushes her down in a chair.)***
EVELYN. I am not out of breath. What's going on?
RITA. Now just relax. ***(She begins massaging*** EVELYN's ***temples.)***
EVELYN. Just what are you doing to my head?
RITA. Just massaging your temples to give you a sense of calmness.
EVELYN. I am calm. What's happening?
RITA. Breathe deeply—
EVELYN. Look, Rita. You better tell me what this is all about.
RITA. A calcium tablet is good for the nerves. Let me get—
EVELYN. No, I'm not taking anything. I want an explanation. Right now!
RITA. I only wanted to prepare you for the surprise.
EVELYN. Surprise?
RITA. Yes, the big surprise . . . the revelation . . . but you won't sit still for a minute . . . So here we go . . . But first close your eyes . . . (EVELYN *does so reluctantly. Now* RITA *takes off caftan and is wearing a flesh color leotard with matching tights.*) Now open them slowly—very slowly . . . (*She does so*) Ta-ta!
EVELYN (*rises, doing a doubletake*). Good heavens! What are you wearing?
RITA. It's my costume for the play.
EVELYN. That's your costume?
RITA. Yes, this is what I wear.
EVELYN. But it's so—so revealing.
RITA. It is not.
EVELYN. Oh, let me sit down. ***(She does)*** I can't believe it. So that was the surprise?
RITA. I didn't realize you'd be so shocked.

EVELYN. Well, you told me about the play. I didn't expect you to look like that. You said you were a strange British grandmother who sits around blowing bubbles and eating Barricini chocolates.

RITA. Yes, and my whole family is all around me. My grandson believes he's a frog. My daughter goes back and forth to Mars.

EVELYN. And the people around you—how are they dressed?

RITA. In various ways. Some are clothed, some are—

EVELYN. I don't want to hear anymore! I'm living next door to a weirdo for twenty-five years and didn't know it till now.

RITA. Don't be such a prude. This is a different generation we're living in. It's the "now" generation.

EVELYN. Maybe for you, Rita. (*Pause*) I don't think we'll be at the play. I mean, George and I. He might have a heart attack seeing . . . (*Pause*) Is that what you made me rush in here for? To see you like this——

RITA. I had no idea you'd be so shocked. I thought you were more up on the times. Evelyn, you better sit down for the second part.

EVELYN. Oh, no! Don't tell me you have to take that off?

RITA. No, it's nothing like that. (*Pause*) It's serious business, Evelyn. (*Pause*) They're coming.

EVELYN. Who?

RITA. My children.

EVELYN. Your children?

RITA. Yes, they're coming to see me.

EVELYN. To see you?

RITA. Yes.

EVELYN. In the play?

RITA. No, not exactly. They're coming to spend the weekend with me. A year ago, Charlie died. So they don't want me to be alone. Now here I am opening in this play in the Village. My first part in a play—my acting debut!

EVELYN. And what a debut! You can't let them see you. Why, it's a sin that you're doing this. Now I always thought you shouldn't be acting. But no, you insisted. So I thought, all right, you'll keep busy. Maybe it's for the best. But look what you're going to be in. You could be arrested wearing that . . . and on this of all weekends!

RITA. No, I won't be arrested. There's nothing wrong with how I look or with what I'm doing. It's a perfectly good avant-garde play.

EVELYN. But it's outrageous! To do it, on the first anniversary of your husband's death.

RITA. Let's not keep going over that, Evelyn. I've made up my mind to go through with this. And we've got to think of what to do.

EVELYN. What did you tell your children?

RITA. I told them they didn't have to come here. I said I would have company, I wouldn't be alone. But they insisted. What could I say?

EVELYN. Nothing. And you'll have to stay home with them, right here where you belong.

RITA. Evelyn!

EVELYN. That's right.

RITA. But I'm going to be busy—with run-throughs during the day. I won't have much time to spend with them.

EVELYN. This is a solemn time, Rita. How can you think of that play? The play doesn't matter. Lots of times, those things never go on.

RITA. Oh, but this will. The show must go on even if it's in a loft.

EVELYN. But what about Charlie's memory?

RITA. I've mourned him long enough. The days I spent crying—the endless nights—empty. It's a year.

EVELYN. That's too soon, Rita.

RITA. Only I can decide that, Evelyn. (*Pause*) You're old-fashioned.

EVELYN. Maybe, but you're crazy to be doing this at all . . . After Charlie died, you went wacko . . . Took up acting . . . You're nearly seventy!

RITA. I only do it as a hobby. I don't want to be a star. What's wrong with doing it for enjoyment?

EVELYN. It's crazy!

RITA. I always wanted to be an actress. (*Pause*) In high school I played in all the shows . . . Oh, you should have seen me . . . Then what did I do afterwards? Get married. Isn't that what everybody did then? Take care of a husband, raise children, take care of a house . . . be a caretaker . . . My dream died . . . slowly . . . Now my children are grown—my husband is dead . . . But I'm alive . . . My dream is coming back.

EVELYN. But so are your children this weekend. Don't you think you have a responsibility towards them?

RITA. To them?

EVELYN. Yes, they want to be with you on the anniversary of your husband's death . . . And you're going to be prancing around on a stage in that.

RITA. I have my own life to lead now.

EVELYN. But they're coming to see you, be with you.

RITA. Yes, but I don't want them to. I don't need them now. I have my own life and they have theirs.

EVELYN. You act like you're disowned or something. They send you things, cheeses, baskets of fruits, from time to time. And look at the interest they're showing.

RITA. Yes, now.

EVELYN. In a way, it's more than my children. I *still* don't know why they moved so far away—to Iceland. It's like another planet. If I hear from them twice a year, I'm lucky. Sometimes I think my children are senile.

RITA. That may very well be, Evelyn. But it's more than that. Our grown children have gone their own ways.

EVELYN. But your children—

RITA. All I'm saying is that I feel separate from my children now.

EVELYN. What a selfish woman you've become.

RITA. Maybe. But my problem all my life has been that I've been too giving—to everyone—my children, my husband. Now I want time for myself.

EVELYN. But not this weekend. Call up the theater, I mean the loft. Have somebody else do your part. Look, you're not getting any money for it.

RITA. I don't know if I can tell them that.

EVELYN. If you're not taking my advice, Rita, how can I help you?

RITA. You can help me by calling my children.

EVELYN. What?

RITA. Yes, calling them and telling them that you and George will be with me this weekend. If they hear it from you, maybe they'll change their minds.

EVELYN. No, no! I'm not going to lie, especially on the first anniversary of your husband's death.

RITA. Don't be so moralistic, Evelyn. Surely you can do me this favor.

EVELYN. Why don't I call that loft—tell them the situation?

RITA. No, call my children, Evelyn.

EVELYN. I can't.

RITA. For me, for our friendship of twenty-five years.

EVELYN. I just don't want to be involved in this. You'll just have to invite them to see the play when they're here.

RITA. But I can't let them see the play. Not that there's anything vulgar about it—there isn't. It's just the idea, Evelyn . . . I'm sure they'll be hurt and won't understand.

EVELYN. I don't blame them. They have a right to be. (*Pause*) No, I won't do it.

RITA (*whirling around; British accent*). I am sixty-eight years young. I eat Barricini chocolates. (*Begins blowing bubbles*)

EVELYN. I can't bear it!

RITA. What I can't bear is your attitude. After all these years, I find out that I have no friends. (*Pause*) Not one who comes through when you really need her.

(*Pause*)

EVELYN. I suppose a good friend would do it for another good friend. After all, we've been friends for ages.

RITA. Oh, thank you. I knew you'd come through. Good old Evelyn. I knew I could count on you.

(*Pause*)

EVELYN (*sniffing*). I never thought you'd come to this, Rita. (*Pause*) Because I am your real and best friend, I'm going to save you the embarrassment, the shame . . . Give me Carolyn's number.

RITA (*hands it to her*). Here.

EVELYN (*dialing*). Your daughter first . . . All right . . . (*Pause*) Hello . . . Carolyn . . . This is Mrs. Kane . . . Evelyn Kane . . . Yes, your mother's next door neighbor . . . Yes, I'm fine . . . Everything is all right . . . Listen, Carolyn . . . Your mother doesn't know I'm calling you—but she mentioned you were thinking of coming this weekend . . . I mean, planning . . . yes . . . Well, George and I were going to be with her . . . You see, we had it all planned. A visit to the cemetery . . . A quiet weekend . . . I'm just saying that she won't be alone . . . Oh, I see . . . Everything is packed? It's not necessary really . . . I understand . . . The memory of your father is sacred . . . And you should all be together at home quietly. (*Begins to sniff*) Just a cold, Carolyn . . . All right. Don't mention my call, please. I hope I see you . . . Good-bye. (*She hangs up*) Such a wonderful daughter—you should count your blessings.

RITA. A beautiful try, Evelyn, but it failed.

EVELYN. You really should be ashamed of yourself.

RITA. Please try Mark's number now . . . Maybe if you could convince him not to come, he can call Carolyn . . .

EVELYN. The whole thing is confusing.

RITA. No, please, Evelyn. Finish the job. (*Hands her the number*)

EVELYN (*dials the number; long pause*). No answer . . . (*Waits*)

RITA. Oh, hang up already. You can try later.

(EVELYN *puts phone back on hook.*)

EVELYN. No, it's all settled. They're coming. And you're going to be with them.

RITA. Who are you to tell me what to do?

EVELYN. How dare you speak to me that way? After doing you that big favor . . . By phoning I told a terrible lie.

RITA. Thanks for the favor. Don't worry, you'll still go to heaven even after that terrible lie.

EVELYN. I don't know what's wrong with you. Why don't you stop all this nonsense? First it was the part-time job, when your husband left you so well provided for. But it turned out that even that job wasn't enough.

RITA. It keeps me busy, but it's so unfulfilling. For it's only a job. I want to do something that matters. Why can't a woman do that? How many years do we have left to do what we want? Why dream of what we once wanted? Let's just do it!

EVELYN. Instead of taking up acting, you should take life easy, like George and I. We're happy.

RITA. Sitting like zombies in front of the television set?

EVELYN. We enjoy it.

RITA. When I come to your house and ask him what's happening in the news, he looks at me like I'm crazy. He doesn't know.

EVELYN. The news and TV make him sleepy.

RITA. It's not a very productive kind of life.

EVELYN. He worked hard all his life. Doesn't he have the right to relax the way he wants to?

RITA. Yes, I suppose he does.

EVELYN. We take vacations—a week or two in the country, take in the sunshine—fresh air—what else is there? When you're old. After a lifetime of working, just breathe the clean air—enjoy the pleasures of retirement.

RITA. It makes me sad to think of the way Charlie killed himself to make a living—working, working, working, no enjoyment . . . Always planning for the day when he'd retire. Oh, he had great dreams . . . A farm house with a horse or two . . . ducks, geese, sheep, chickens . . . and we'd sit on the porch . . . in the clear air . . . But then he died before he had a chance to make it happen . . . Ironic, isn't it? But that wasn't *my* dream . . . (*Pause*) Now it's time for myself. I want to fulfill myself—my own being. (*Pause*) You can't help it if your life is so ungratifying.

EVELYN. Ungratifying? I go with George for walks. He loves the parks. Even though they're all filthy now and covered with dog—you know what. And then he loves to listen to Barry Gray so I stay up at night and hear him call in and talk with him. Every time Barry Gray gives him fifteen minutes. George loves to reminisce about the good old days. Then we go to Roseland because we met there and our names are on those plaques on the wall. George loves to see it.

RITA. Why live through him? Everything for him. Do you stop to think of what makes *you* happy? What *you* want to do?

EVELYN. I want to make him happy, so I'll be happy.

RITA. But surely you have interests?

EVELYN. Interests?

RITA. Interests. Things you enjoy doing. Hobbies, pastimes.

EVELYN. Oh, one time I wanted to be an artist. Go to Paris, live a Bohemian life. But didn't every woman want to be something at one time?

RITA. Who says you can't paint now?

EVELYN. Now? Paint? Are you crazy?

RITA. You have the time. Just buy the paints.

EVELYN. George is allergic to paints. He sneezes.

RITA. Come and paint in my house.

EVELYN. I can't. My hands are arthritic . . . I'm happy with my life, Rita. I'm taking it easy . . . What are you trying to stir up?

RITA. I'm just trying to make you realize that you're not fulfilled. You're not doing anything.

EVELYN. There's nothing I want to do.

RITA. So you're going to sit around till you die? (*Pause*) Now we have some time. How much, we don't know. That's why we've got to seize it now. Don't let it rush by us. (*She begins jogging slowly around the room.*)

EVELYN. Do you think you're having a breakdown?

RITA. No.

EVELYN. I do . . . look at you . . . and this whole thing about your children and you not wanting to see them. (*Pause*) And you do the strangest things lately.

RITA. Like what? (*She is now doing simple calisthenics.*)

EVELYN. Like thinking you're an athlete.

RITA. I'm exercising. It's good for me. (*She continues exercises.*)

EVELYN. And you even ride a bicycle!

RITA. That's even better exercise.

EVELYN. An old woman on a bicycle?

RITA. I want to keep in shape. I'm sixty-eight years young! (*She stretches on toes and stretches her arms in the air.*)

EVELYN. Ha!

RITA. I had to get in shape physically for acting.

EVELYN. And then all those vitamins with that horrible-looking granola. I don't understand it.

RITA. I want to be healthy. It all helped me prepare for the stage. (*She does breathing exercises.*)

EVELYN. You're really bit by this acting bug only it seems to have stung your brain.

RITA (*relaxed, in a meditative position*). Do you know the moment I love best? When everybody is seated, the house is dark. And then slowly the lights go up. Like magic time. And it's a whole new world.

EVELYN. But to be at that world at your age—

RITA. I know I can do it now. I want it. (*Pause*) I remember when Charlie and I used to reminisce about our childhood, to see how far we could remember. He could remember colors, the color of his crib, his underwear. And do you know what I remembered—pictures in books of ladies with pinafores, gentlemen with high-buttoned shoes, singing, dancing . . . And I remembered what I wanted to be. . . . Once Charlie said, "Do you really think you would have been an actress if you didn't get married, raise a family?"

EVELYN. And what did you say?

RITA. I said, I don't know. How does anybody know? If such and such was—if this was that way—why think about it?—torment yourself about it? I spent the major portion of my life as a housewife. Fifty years.

EVELYN. That's half a century.

RITA. Yes. Half a century of doing for others.

EVELYN. I've put in close to half a century.

RITA. All the years . . . They pass so quickly. (*Pause*) Sometimes I think about the people who grew old with me . . . They retired to warm climates, the Southeast, the Southwest. . . . I get postcards every so often. . . . The husband with a golf stick in his hand smiling, his wife waving . . . surrounded by green grass . . . then the ones in mobile homes in the West, living out their lives . . . the ones who are dead and buried somewhere . . .

EVELYN. Yes.

RITA. That's why you have to spend the rest of your life doing what you want. It's my last chance to fulfill the dream of a lifetime.

(*Pause*)

EVELYN. Look in the mirror. What do you see?

RITA. I see a woman—an older woman trying to begin her life again.

EVELYN. No. Let me tell you what I see. An old woman thinking she's sweet sixteen.

RITA. Don't make fun of me. Inside I still feel sweet sixteen.

EVELYN. Rita, I know you for twenty-five years. I know what's good for you. This isn't. (*Pause*) What you need is a man.

RITA. No. Men are not my answer right now.

EVELYN. You joined a women's lib group? I heard they have them for old women now.

RITA. I have not joined a women's lib group! I've come to my senses—my feelings.

EVELYN. But isn't it lonely without a steady man around? Admit it.

RITA. Sometimes, but I've gone with other men since Charlie died. To this social, that social. They talk about their security, their pensions, their men's clubs—when they chased bears down mountains—

EVELYN. You don't want to give to them. You're shut off in your own world.

RITA. Evelyn, maybe you should go back to your apartment. You're making me nervous.

EVELYN. Well, George is reading the newspaper and watching TV. He doesn't talk much when he does that.

RITA. So why don't you start to do something? For yourself. You always said you liked working with your hands.

EVELYN. My hands?

RITA. Yes.

EVELYN. I always did like working with my hands. ***(She begins arranging*** RITA's ***flower bowl.)***

RITA. You always arrange them so well. Flower arranging is an art. Maybe you should start doing that.

EVELYN. Oh, look, Rita. I'm not about to start *anything* now. I don't think much of this old age. It's something that happens. You get pains, here and there, this hurts, that hurts. You don't know when it's going to be over . . .

RITA. We have opportunities, but you don't see them. Look how long we've lived. We have knowledge, wisdom, those things youth can never have . . . You make us sound like we're all invalids to be cast aside. We have strengths.

EVELYN. Strengths. What strengths?

(*Pause*)

RITA. I'll tell you a story about strength. A ninety-year-old woman learned wood carving.

EVELYN. Ninety years old? She should be resting at her age.

RITA. According to you. Evelyn, that woman is alive and so are we!

EVELYN. Alive?

RITA. Yes, alive! Why does everybody think of old age as a time to freeze, a time to die? To be dumped like scrap iron? People in beds, motionless, waiting for their eyes to finally close? No, this is a time for our freedom!

EVELYN. Those vitamins you take must have dope in them.

RITA. You should take some. They'll pep you up.

EVELYN. Vitamins at my age? I've never taken any. No reason to start now.

RITA. That's your problem. Your whole life is set. A routine, the same pattern, it never changes. Never try anything new—even if it's a small thing like a vitamin.

EVELYN. I can't wait for your children to get here and pull you back to your senses.

RITA. I'm fine. I'm just trying to get through to you. (*Pause*) Sometimes I see you walking with George. Following him. You go where *he* goes.

EVELYN. So?

RITA. So? Can't you understand? Don't you want to explore for yourself?

EVELYN. Explore, Rita? Please! This conversation is going in circles. I'm getting dizzy. (*Pause*) Why not forget about this play? Why don't we go out tonight? Look, we'll have a good time . . . I'll drag him away from the paper and the TV. We'll have dinner and then go to Roseland. We'll have fun, a lot of laughs. George is a riot when he wants to be. When he talks about the way the streets used to be paved . . . a place where he used to work where waiters sang and danced Irish jigs . . .

RITA. What do *you* remember, Evelyn?

EVELYN. Me?

RITA. Yes.

(*Pause*)

EVELYN. Well, I never gave it much thought, but . . . let's see . . . (*Pause*) On every Sunday in June, oh, it was years ago, they were such bright Sundays . . . there would be lots of cars going by . . . They had posters which said, "Just Married." And old beat-up shoes and tin cans were tied to the cars. And the tin cans made so much noise as they rode along. I think all the young women picked a Sunday in June to get married . . . (*Pause*) Come on, Rita, we'll all go out and reminisce . . .

RITA. No, I can't. I want to go over the script again.

EVELYN. So you really intend to go through with it? Not caring about anyone but yourself? (*Pause*) Did you ever stop to think that you're about to make a fool of yourself?

RITA. A fool of myself?

EVELYN. Yes. Your first time on the stage in over forty years, no fifty years, right? It's been ages.

RITA. Yes, but I'm confident that everything will be all right. Nothing will happen.

EVELYN. What if you forget your lines?

RITA. My part is mostly pantomime.

EVELYN. How will it feel to be the laughingstock in front of a lot of people?

RITA. Why should I be the laughingstock?

EVELYN. I can just hear everybody asking, who does she think she is, somebody so old thinking they can act and wearing that leotard . . . Let's face it, your figure isn't what it used to be.

RITA. That may be true. But people aren't that cruel. I'm old, but I'm still a person and deserve to be treated with respect.

EVELYN. The way old people are treated? They're laughed at or pitied.

RITA. No, Evelyn.

EVELYN. Yes, Rita. I'm telling you for your own good. Come on, take that off. Put on a dress. Throw away that script. (*Pause*) Besides you were probably cast because that director felt sorry for you.

RITA. No, the director liked me very much. He said, "For a woman your age, you certainly have a magnetism."

EVELYN. Sure, it's like people giving old people seats on trains and buses, they feel sorry for them, because they feel they might die any second.

RITA. Why do you think he pitied me?

EVELYN. Well, it just seems funny to me that he'd pick someone with no experience for the part. He's not paying you, is he?

RITA. No, as a matter of fact I offered to make a contribution to the theater group for . . . (*She stops, she has slipped.*)

EVELYN. Now I see everything, old girl!

RITA. I don't know what you're talking about!

EVELYN. Come on, Rita, I'm not a fool and neither are you.

RITA. I won't listen to your nonsense, Evelyn! My small donation to the theater was only—only a gesture—a gesture of goodwill.

EVELYN. Well, I'm sure it meant a great deal. Those crazy theaters have nothing. They were probably very grateful for your "goodwill." Face it, Rita. They needed your money!

RITA (*after a long moment*). Maybe you're right. Give the old hag a chance, he thought, out of pity . . . out of a need for my money.

EVELYN. You finally see the light?

RITA. The cast probably talked about me. Who's that crazy old woman? (*She takes script and throws it on the floor.*)

EVELYN. That's where it belongs.

RITA. Take a look at me! You're right. The audience will howl. (*Puts caftan back on*) Every audition I've gone to, they've all been young. I stuck out like a sore thumb. Old women don't take up acting.

EVELYN. Oh, honey, don't torment yourself now.

RITA. He cast me for the *money,* Evelyn! I've been such a fool!

EVELYN. Oh, Rita, just think of having a good time tonight. Look, I've got to start talking George into—

RITA. Going? Dragging him away from his routine?

EVELYN. Oh, he'll love it. He likes you.

RITA. He hardly says a word to me. Just nods.

EVELYN. George is a wonderful dancer.

RITA. He never dances. Just stands around looking into space as though he were remembering something he lost fifty years ago.

EVELYN. Come on, don't take it out on George. Think of the great time we'll all have tonight. In a few days, the mourning begins, silence . . . remembrance . . . with your children.

RITA. Yes . . . You're right . . .

EVELYN. At last you've come around to my way of thinking. I knew I could talk some sense into you. Well, I'm going to give George a buzz. (*Dials phone*) Hello . . . George . . . Yes, Evelyn, who else? George, let's all go to Roseland tonight with Rita . . . All three of us . . . It'll be such fun . . . Her children are coming this weekend . . . Yes, her children . . . Carolyn and Mark . . . To commemorate Charlie's death . . . Charlie . . . her husband . . . Dead one year . . . They'll all be staying at home . . . to be with her . . . So I thought why not go out tonight . . . a few days before . . . cheer her up a bit . . . Oh, don't be that way . . . Think of —Oh, all right . . . Look, when Carolyn and Mark come . . . Rita's children . . . Carolyn and Mark . . . we'll all get together for coffee and discuss things—current events. (*Slowly hangs up*) He's watching the news and reading the paper. I suppose I should be in there with him.

RITA. I don't know why he watches the news and reads the paper at the same time. He just stares at them both . . . like sleeping with his eyes open.

EVELYN. I know. He doesn't want to go to Roseland tonight but maybe some other night, Rita?

RITA. We'll see.

EVELYN. Oh, I wish you'd say yes. You wanted to tonight. Look, we'll make it up to you. (*Pause*) I better go in now . . . Or he gets mad . . . He doesn't talk to me as it is . . . Oh, well, you know how men are . . . But he was excited to hear that your children were coming. And he thought it was only proper that you spend the weekend quietly with them.

RITA. Did he say that?

EVELYN. Well, not exactly in those words, but he meant it anyway.

RITA. I got the feeling that he didn't know who my children were. You had to keep repeating their names.

EVELYN. Oh, no. He knew who they were. Well, when Carolyn and Mark come we'll all get together . . .

RITA. I don't know how much time I'll have. It's so limited this weekend.

EVELYN. But you won't be in the play . . .

RITA. I don't know . . .

EVELYN. Rita, this get-together with your children on this sacred occasion is the only thing that matters this weekend . . . Don't you want to share Charlie's memory with them? Think of what it's going to feel like to be with them again.

RITA. But then what? What about all the silences? So much distance and time between us . . .

EVELYN. But this weekend you'll be reunited! That's the way it should be. What kind of mother thinks only of herself?

RITA. I suppose my time should be theirs this weekend. (*Pause*) So my life has to stop for them.

EVELYN. You act like it's the end of the world. You have nothing to do.

RITA. How can you say that? I have something important to do, something *very* important to me!

EVELYN. Are you still talking about that play? You're not going on in that play . . .

RITA (*suddenly picking up script from floor*). Yes! Yes, I am! (*Takes off caftan*) I guess I let all the old fears take over! I was cast because the director thought *I could do it.* He believed in me . . .

EVELYN. But what you said before—?

RITA. You were forcing me to say it! It doesn't matter *how* I got the part. The most important thing is that *I can handle it!*

EVELYN. But what about your children?

(*Pause*)

RITA. I won't tell them about the play.

EVELYN. Thank heavens for that!

RITA. When they call I'll just tell them that I'm going to be busy this weekend. But there'll be time for us to go to the cemetery. Put flowers on his grave. Lilacs. He loved lilacs.

EVELYN. That's the least you could do.

RITA. And we'll all cry. . . . He really was a wonderful man. I think he'd be happy to know that I was acting in a play. (*Pause*) And then on with the course of living . . . We'll all have lunch . . . Then the rest of the time is my own.

EVELYN. Think it over. You may lose your children forever. If they find out, they won't forgive you.

RITA. You might be right. But how can I hide it? I guess I'll have to find the courage to tell them and pray they understand.

(*Pause*)

EVELYN. Well, I've tried my best. (*She is about to start*) Good luck, Rita, you'll need it!

RITA. Thanks, Evelyn. ***(But* EVELYN *lingers on, looks at the flowers, then rearranges one or two.)*** That looks nice.

EVELYN. I guess I *do* have a knack with my hands.

RITA. Yes, you do.

EVELYN. Crazy at this age to have a knack with your hands. Oh, well, what are you going to do? I've got to go in and watch the news with him.

RITA. And I guess I'll practice my part. (*Pause*) You will come to the play, won't you, Evelyn?

EVELYN. Rita, I wouldn't miss it for the world!

(*They hug warmly.*)

Curtain

Chapter 24
Chamber Theater

The second type of group interpretation is Chamber Theater. This method of presenting narratives, usually prose, combines interpretation techniques and acting. It may be defined as a way of dramatizing point of view in a piece of narration.

You will remember our discussion of point of view for the narrator in Chapter 5. The presence and use of the narrator is basic to Chamber Theater and thus the technique is different from Readers' Theater, where there is no intervening narrator between the characters and the audience.

Many stories and novels work very well in Chamber Theater. They are especially compatible when the narrator is involved with the characters and can respond with them. Look at the selections at the end of Chapter 5. Some of them would make interesting Chamber Theater performances.

Adapting a Story

The first thing to decide then in arranging a narrative for Chamber Theater is the function and degree of involvement for the narrator. He or she supplies important information to us, and more importantly, directs our responses to everything that goes on in the story, because he or she is the one the author has used to tell us the details. We need to know both about the action and more important about the thoughts and inner responses of the characters.

Care must be taken to use the narrator—whatever the degree of involvement in plot and action—exactly as the author has. The tense in which he or she speaks of the action and the use of first, second, or third person should be kept as it is written.

When the narrator is expressing an objective point of view—observing and reporting without sharing the thoughts and responses of any of the characters—there might well be close physical positioning in some scenes as they are reported to us. At other times, the narrator might work as far away as outside a proscenium or down in the audience area as transitions and descriptions of further action are reported. It is sometimes effective to have the narrator allow a scene to run its full course without interruption as he or she and the audience watch.

In the case of close relationship with a single character only, the narrator might well work physically close to that character. In dual-character point of view, that is when the narrator enters into the minds of two characters, he or she might be in close proximity to both, especially when they are engaged in a scene together, making visible the link between them. If the point of view is strictly objective, and we are not taken into the inner life of any of the characters, the narrator would probably work from outside the "acting area," perhaps moving closer to describe actions as the "actors" suggest them in pantomimes. The narrator can act as stage manager and shift properties for bridging changes in locale and time. There are as many variations of a narrator's active physical involvement as there are stories, and good taste and effectiveness are the final tests.

When we talked about narration in Chapter 5, we mentioned the handling of direct and indirect discourse. This is the next consideration in adapting a story for Chamber Theater. Sections which are heavy with dialogue (direct discourse) are said to be "in scene." This is your clue as to how to handle them. They are staged with specific action and the characters play to each other, rather than to the audience.

Indirect discourse is the next consideration in adapting a story. In the story the narrator handles all the reporting of thoughts and reactions. In Chamber Theater many of these may be given to the character involved. For example, in "A Visit of Charity" (page 279) the narrator would probably handle the entire first paragraph as the little girl enters from offstage. She would possibly circle the stage once and then pantomime the business of putting down the flower pot and opening the heavy door. If she is not a blonde and dressed to suggest the outfit the narrator tells us about, it would be better to cut that description. She would then approach a table, perhaps at upstage center, behind which the nurse would be sitting. The narrator must give her plenty of time for this to make it effective, and could watch her—or even follow her—as she goes. The nurse could be reading her magazine or working on a record of some kind. We would then move into "in scene" and the script might be arranged as follows:

Marian . . .	"I'm a Campfire Girl. . . . I have to pay a visit to some old lady," she told the nurse at the desk.
Narrator . . .	This was a woman in a white uniform who looked as if she were cold; she had close-cut hair which stood up on the very top of her head exactly like a sea wave.
Marian . . .	Marian, the little girl did not tell her that this visit would give her a minimum of only three points in her score.

These three speeches clearly establish the identity of the two characters involved. After this, some of the speech tags, such as "said the nurse" and so forth, could be cut or given to the narrator or retained by the speaker, as we have done with "she told the nurse at the desk." Giving all the speech tags to the narrator would tend to chop up some of the scenes. It is perfectly legitimate for a character to speak in the third person in Chamber Theater. Sections of the narration can be given to the characters whenever it is something they are aware of thinking or knowing. For instance, Marian is aware she isn't telling the nurse about her "minimum of three points." A few paragraphs farther on, she is certainly aware of feeling "as if she were walking on waves," although she probably is not aware that the feeling is caused by the fact that the linoleum is loose and bulging. Consequently, the speeches might be arranged like this:

Narrator . . .	There was loose, bulging linoleum on the floor
Marian . . .	Marian felt as if she were walking on waves,
Narrator . . .	but the nurse paid no attention to it.

Be careful, though, that you don't let the whole script get so divided into small segments that you lose the continuity.

The two old ladies would probably be on stage during the first part of the story but possibly seated with their backs to the audience in their own separate area. The narrator may move from one area to another as he or she comments on the "in scene" units or may stay at one side throughout. The old lady in the bed need not be actually in a bed. She might be curled up in a large chair or a reclining chair and covered with a blanket. There should be a rocking chair for the other old lady and a wicker chair for Marian. If Marian brings in an actual pot of flowers, which she certainly may, there should be a tall wardrobe for the first old lady to put it on. If she has merely pantomimed the pot of flowers, then the old lady may do the same.

The above paragraph touches on one of the problems of Chamber Theater. There is always the temptation to add one more specific property to the scenes. Once you start with a real pot of flowers, you must have some place to put it. If you have several scene changes, this could get quite complicated. It is better to eliminate everything you can, using only what must be there to allow for the "in scene" action. If you make the scene on stage and the costumes too specific, you destroy the need for the audience's imaginations. Then, when the narrator intrudes to speak directly to them, they must shift their whole concept for a moment. In all phases of interpretation performances, the golden rule might be "less is more" as far as specific, exterior delineation is concerned.

Chamber Theater, then, allows for a great deal of flexibility in its method. But like all forms of interpretation, it must be based on a clear understanding of the principles involved in that particular mode of presentation and careful analysis of the author's achievement. It is *not* making a novel into a play. It is the presentation of a piece of fiction on stage *as it was written,* with the narrator fulfilling the proper function so that point of view is made to operate vividly as it controls action and response.

Selection for Chamber Theater Interpretation

A Visit of Charity

by Eudora Welty

It was mid-morning—a very cold, bright day. Holding a potted plant before her, a girl of fourteen jumped off the bus in front of the Old Ladies' Home, on the outskirts of town. She wore a red coat, and her straight yellow hair was hanging down loose from the pointed white cap all the little girls were wearing that year. She stopped for a moment beside one of the prickly dark shrubs with which the city had beautified the Home, and then proceeded slowly toward the building, which was of whitewashed brick and reflected the winter sunlight like a block of ice. As she walked vaguely up the steps she shifted the small pot from hand to hand; then she had to set it down and remove her mittens before she could open the heavy door.

"I'm a Campfire Girl. . . . I have to pay a visit to some old lady," she told the nurse at the desk. This was a woman in a white uniform who looked as if she were cold; she had close-cut hair which stood up on the very top of her head exactly like a sea wave. Marian, the little girl, did not tell her that this visit would give her a minimum of only three points in her score.

"Acquainted with any of our residents?" asked the nurse. She lifted one eyebrow and spoke like a man.

"With any old ladies? No—but—that is, any of them will do," Marian stammered. With her free hand she pushed her hair behind her ears, as she did when it was time to study Science.

The nurse shrugged and rose. "You have a nice *multiflora cineraria* there," she remarked as she walked ahead down the hall of closed doors to pick out an old lady.

There was loose, bulging linoleum on the floor. Marian felt as if she were walking on the waves, but the nurse paid no attention to it. There was a smell in the hall like the interior of a clock. Everything was silent until, behind one of the doors, an old lady of some kind cleared her throat like a sheep bleating. This decided the nurse. Stopping in her tracks, she first extended her arm, bent her elbow, and leaned forward from the hips—all to examine the watch strapped to her wrist; then she gave a loud double-rap on the door.

"There are two in each room," the nurse remarked over her shoulder.

"Two what?" asked Marian without thinking. The sound like a sheep's bleating almost made her turn around and run back.

One old woman was pulling the door open in short, gradual jerks, and when she saw the nurse a strange smile forced her old face dangerously awry. Marian, suddenly propelled by the strong, impatient arm of the nurse, saw next the side-face of another old woman, even older, who was lying flat in bed with a cap on and a counterpane drawn up to her chin.

"Visitor," said the nurse, and after one more shove she was off up the hall.

Marian stood tongue-tied; both hands held the potted plant. The old woman, still with that terrible, square smile (which was a smile of welcome) stamped on her bony face, was waiting. . . . Perhaps she said something. The old woman in bed said nothing at all, and she did not look around.

Suddenly Marian saw a hand, quick as a bird claw, reach up in the air and pluck the white cap off her head. At the same time, another claw to match drew her all the way into the room, and the next moment the door closed behind her.

"My, my, my," said the old lady at her side.

Marian stood enclosed by a bed, a washstand and a chair; the tiny room had altogether too much furniture. Everything smelled wet—even the bare floor. She held onto the back of the chair, which was wicker and felt soft and damp. Her heart beat more and more slowly, her hands got colder and colder, and she could not hear whether the old women were saying anything or not. She could not see them very clearly. How dark it was! The window shade was down, and the only door was shut. Marian looked at the ceiling. . . . It was like being caught in a robbers' cave, just before one was murdered.

"Did you come to be our little girl for a while?" the first robber asked.

Then something was snatched from Marian's hand—the little potted plant.

"Flowers!" screamed the old woman. She stood holding the pot in an undecided way. "Pretty flowers," she added.

Then the old woman in bed cleared her throat and spoke. "They are not pretty," she said, still without looking around, but very distinctly.

Marian suddenly pitched against the chair and sat down in it.

"Pretty flowers," the first old woman insisted. "Pretty—pretty . . ."

Marian wished she had the little pot back for just a moment—she had forgotten to look at the plant herself before giving it away. What did it look like?

"Stinkweeds," said the other old woman sharply. She had a bunchy white forehead and red eyes like a sheep. Now she turned them toward Marian. The fogginess seemed to rise in her throat again, and she bleated, "Who—are—you?"

To her surprise, Marian could not remember her name. "I'm a Campfire Girl," she said finally.

"Watch out for the germs," said the old woman like a sheep, not addressing anyone.

"One came out last month to see us," said the first old woman.

A sheep or a germ? wondered Marian dreamily, holding onto the chair.

"Did not!" cried the other old woman.

"Did so! Read to us out of the Bible, and we enjoyed it!" screamed the first.

"Who enjoyed it!" said the woman in bed. Her mouth was unexpectedly small and sorrowful, like a pet's.

"We enjoyed it," insisted the other. "You enjoyed it—I enjoyed it."

"We all enjoyed it," said Marian, without realizing that she had said a word.

The first old woman had just finished putting the potted plant high, high on the top of the wardrobe, where it could hardly be seen from below. Marian wondered how she had ever succeeded in placing it there, how she could ever have reached so high.

"You mustn't pay any attention to old Addie," she now said to the little girl. "She's ailing today."

"Will you shut your mouth?" said the woman in bed. "I am not."

"You're a story."

"I can't stay but a minute—really, I can't," said Marian suddenly. She looked down at the wet floor and thought that if she were sick in here they would have to let her go.

With much to-do the first old woman sat down in a rocking chair—still another piece of furniture!—and began to rock. With the fingers of one hand she touched a very dirty cameo pin on her chest. "What do you do at school?" she asked.

"I don't know . . ." said Marian. She tried to think but she could not.

"Oh, but the flowers are beautiful," the old woman whispered. She seemed to rock faster and faster; Marian did not see how anyone could rock so fast.

"Ugly," said the woman in bed.

"If we bring flowers—" Marian began, and then fell silent. She had almost said that if Campfire Girls brought flowers to the Old Ladies' Home, the visit would count one extra point, and if they took a Bible with them on the bus and read it to the old ladies, it counted double. But the old woman had not listened, anyway; she was rocking and watching the other one, who watched back from the bed.

"Poor Addie is ailing. She has to take medicine—see?" she said, pointing a horny finger at a row of bottles on the table, and rocking so high that her black comfort shoes lifted off the floor like a little child's.

"I am no more sick than you are," said the woman in bed.

"Oh, yes you are!"

"I just got more sense than you have, that's all," said the other old woman, nodding her head.

"That's only the contrary way she talks when *you all* come," said the first old lady with sudden intimacy. She stopped the rocker with a neat pat of her feet and leaned toward Marian. Her hand reached over—it felt like a petunia leaf, clinging and just a little sticky.

"Will you hush! Will you hush!" cried the other one.

Marian leaned back rigidly in her chair.

"When I was a little girl like you, I went to school and all," said the old woman in the same intimate, menacing voice. "Not here—another town. . . ."

"Hush!" said the sick woman. "You never went to school. You never came and you never went. You never were anything—only here. You never were born! You don't know anything. Your head is empty, your heart and hands and your old black purse are all empty, even that little old box that you brought with you you brought empty—you showed it to me. And yet you talk, talk, talk, talk, talk all the time until I think I'm losing my mind! Who are you? You're a stranger—a perfect stranger! Don't you know you're a stranger? Is it possible that they have actually done a thing like this to anyone—sent them in a stranger to talk, and rock, and tell away her whole long rigmarole? Do they seriously suppose that I'll be able to keep it up, day in, day out, night in, night out, living in the same room with a terrible old woman—forever?"

Marian saw the old woman's eyes grow bright and turn toward her. This old woman was looking at her with despair and calculation in her face. Her small lips suddenly dropped apart, and exposed a half circle of false teeth with tan gums.

"Come here, I want to tell you something," she whispered. "Come here!"

Marian was trembling, and her heart nearly stopped beating altogether for a moment.

"Now, now, Addie," said the first old woman. "That's not polite. Do you know what's really the matter with old Addie today?" She, too, looked at Marian; one of her eyelids drooped low.

"The matter?" the child repeated stupidly. "What's the matter with her?"

"Why, she's mad because it's her birthday!" said the first old woman, beginning to rock again and giving a little crow as though she had answered her own riddle.

"It is not, it is not!" screamed the old woman in bed. "It is not my birthday, no one knows when that is but myself, and will you please be quiet and say nothing more, or I'll go straight out of my mind!" She turned her eyes toward Marian again, and presently she said in the soft, foggy voice, "When the worst comes to the worst, I ring this bell, and the nurse comes." One of her hands was drawn out from under the patched counterpane—a thin little hand with enormous black freckles. With a finger which would not hold still she pointed to a little bell on the table among the bottles.

"How old are you?" Marian breathed. Now she could see the old woman in bed very closely and plainly, and very abruptly, from all sides, as in dreams. She wondered about her—she wondered for a moment as though there was nothing else in the world to wonder about. It was the first time such a thing had happened to Marian.

"I won't tell!"

The old face on the pillow, where Marian was bending over it, slowly gathered and collapsed. Soft whimpers came out of the small open mouth. It was a sheep that she sounded like—a little lamb. Marian's face drew very close, the yellow hair hung forward.

"She's crying!" She turned a bright, burning face up to the first old woman.

"That's Addie for you," the old woman said spitefully.

Marian jumped up and moved toward the door. For the second time, the claw almost touched her hair, but it was not quick enough. The little girl put her cap on.

"Well, it was a real visit," said the old woman, following Marian through the doorway and all the way out into the hall. Then from behind she suddenly clutched the child with her sharp little fingers. In an affected, high-pitched whine she cried, "Oh, little girl, have you a penny to spare for a poor old woman that's not got anything of her own? We don't have a thing in the world—not a penny for candy—not a thing! Little girl, just a nickel—a penny—"

Marian pulled violently against the old hands for a moment before she was free. Then she ran down the hall, without looking behind her and without looking at the nurse, who was reading *Field & Stream* at her desk. The nurse, after another triple motion to consult her wrist watch, asked automatically the question put to visitors in all institutions: "Won't you stay and have dinner with *us?"*

Marian never replied. She pushed the heavy door open into the cold air and ran down the steps.

Under the prickly shrub she stooped and quickly, without being seen, retrieved a red apple she had hidden there.

Her yellow hair under the white cap, her scarlet coat, her bare knees all flashed in the sunlight as she ran to meet the big bus rocketing through the street.

"Wait for me!" she shouted. As though at an imperial command, the bus ground to a stop.

She jumped on and took a big bite out of the apple.

Chapter 25
Choric Interpretation

A third type of group performance is Choric Interpretation. It is directly descended from the classic Greek Theater.

Choric interpretation is a part of interpretation and is governed by the same rules and methods as individual interpretation. The difference lies in the use of many voices, bodies, and minds working together. Good choric interpretation is more than just a group of people saying the same words at the same time and starting and stopping together. Precision is important, of course, because without it the audience cannot understand what is being said. However, the techniques of choric interpretation are always a means to an end, never an end in themselves. And that end is sharing an experience in literature. Your attention to the emotional content and all the other aspects you have learned to look for in analysis must be complete.

Selection of Material

The range of material you may use for choric interpretation is far wider than is sometimes supposed. The first consideration is the author's intent. If the writing is intended to share an extremely individual and private experience, it is probably better for a single interpreter. If the selection speaks for many people, even though expressed in the single voice of the writer, it is suitable for a choir. "The End of the World," which we looked at in Chapter 7, for instance, would be appropriate. A love sonnet that implies one person speaking to or of another person would be less safe. But all literature that uses the personal pronoun *I* need not be avoided. You will find some first-person-singular suggestions at the end of this chapter.

Another factor in selecting material is the kind of climaxes the writing contains and the way they are achieved. Material that depends on sharp contrasts or on accumulation for the climaxes often is most effective with many voices.

The richness and importance of the sound pattern are important considerations. Tone color and all the subtle aspects of rhythm can sometimes be brought out more effectively by a group with different voice qualities and levels of pitch than by a single interpreter.

Many of the selections from previous chapters would work very well chorically. You may use prose as well as poetry, although poetry usually gives you more opportunity for sound values.

Responsibilities of the Individual in a Choric Group

Your director or the class itself may divide the material into various units, and the voice group you are in may not speak the entire selection. Nevertheless, *you are responsible for the whole selection* so you and your unit will fit smoothly into the total effect. That is why your early rehearsals will be done in unison.

Follow the same general process of analysis you use when you are going to perform alone. You must discover each separate element in the selection so you know what you have to work with. Then put the material together again. Much of this will be done during discussion with the group, but you must know from individual study the denotation and connotation of each word, the method of organization, and all the details you have learned to study.

Critics of choric interpretation claim that the individual must give up his or her own ideas to work with a group. Sometimes this happens, but we know that good writing gives unmistakable clues to all who do a thorough job of analysis.

If there is disagreement as to meaning, the group must reexamine the piece together and arrive at a common response. If you let the author lead the way, you are almost certain to work toward the same effect. Until the entire group reaches agreement, you will discuss and analyze as you rehearse, because the audience must receive a unified total effect.

Individual analysis remains the first step in choric interpretation. After you have completed this analysis, work on your techniques of voice and body to achieve the best possible communication of all the parts that make up the whole. A group is only as effective as each individual member working in it. You will soon learn to hear the others in relation to yourself and blend your vocal techniques with theirs. Don't be afraid to speak out and make use of all you have learned. Your director would rather tone down a group than try to force life into one that is tentative, with everyone waiting for someone else to speak out. How much you work alone between group rehearsals will make all the difference.

As you begin to work aloud on the selection, pay particular attention to your enunciation. Each word must be clear and distinct. This is even more important with a group than with a single reader because a slurred vowel or muffled consonant, multiplied by the number in the group, makes a choric reading unintelligible to the audience. Remember, controlled volume and a good firm tone are the result of proper breathing.

Voice Divisions

Your material may be done in unison or divided into units, with various voice groups speaking only specific parts of the whole selection.

There are many ways of arranging any selection. The decision will depend on the size of the group and the quality of the available voices, so it is never satisfactory to try to use someone else's arrangements. What worked for ten people may not do for thirty.

The clues for the voice arrangement will come from the demands of the material. There may be lines or sections that call for strong voices, while others will need a lighter touch. The decision will be based on tone color and connotation and on the emotion you wish to arouse.

The type of climax may be a determining factor in the arrangement. Climaxes are built in numerous ways. If you build a cumulative one, you may wish to add voices as the tension builds. This is one arrangement suggested for "The Negro Speaks of Rivers" at the end of this chapter. Or you may prefer to use unison and simply to increase volume as the tension builds. If the climax is sudden and depends on sharp contrast, you may want an abrupt change in voices to emphasize it. If the selection diminishes after the climax, you may want to decrease the number of voices to enhance this effect.

Ask yourself how a particular unit was meant to sound. Then decide whether the effect can best be attained by a single voice, by unison, by two, three, or any number of voices blended for a particular quality, or by a clear division between light and dark voices.

Light and Dark Voices

The term *light and dark voices* may need some explanation. The difference is not in pitch but in resonance. Light does not mean high, but refers to a voice having fewer overtones and undertones than a darker voice. The difference is like that between a violin and a cello. Both can produce the same musical note, but the resonance is different.

The classification of voices within any group can only be relative. There may not be any voice that is undeniably light or dark within your choir. But by comparison, some are darker than others. Never push your voice up or down from its natural range. If you do, the result will be artificial and violates one of the basic rules of good interpretation by calling attention to the performers and away from the literature. Just be sure there is good breath support and that your throat is relaxed so that you are using your natural voice properly.

Rehearsal Suggestions

After preliminary discussions, you begin to work aloud in group rehearsals. It is wise to work in unison until everyone has a sense of the entire selection. If all of you have done a thorough job in your individual analyses, you will soon move from unison to whatever voice division you decided on.

Mark your manuscript clearly so you remember all directions. The simplest method is to mark each unit as you go along, using **LV** for light voices, **DV** for dark voices, and **U** for unison. When you work alone, read the entire selection several times, and then work in detail on your assigned units. If you are blending selected light and dark voices for a particular effect, you will find it convenient to designate them as group 1, group 2, and so forth. In any case, mark the entire arrangement on your copy and underline those units you will speak. But keep your concentration on the whole poem so that you do not break the unity.

Keeping the Selection Together

Whenever a selection is divided into separate voice divisions, there is danger of losing the unity. It is your responsibility to see that this does not happen. When you are not speaking, continue to concentrate on the whole selection. Your unit or units must fit into and become a functioning part of the total poem.

An opposite problem that sometimes develops during rehearsals is that undue attention is given to the quality of the sound at the expense of the content. This may result in overemphasis of the rhythm. Or the tone color may be so tempting in a certain section that the choir soars into an orchestration of beautiful sounds signifying nothing. If this happens, recall the first steps in your analysis, especially of the organization of content and the location of climaxes.

Every detail must relate to every other detail for the total effect, and no one aspect of your interpretation should call attention to itself.

A few readings with the group speaking in unison as they did in early rehearsals should also help.

Bodily Action in Choric Interpretation

It is a common error to think of choric interpretation in terms of voices alone. As we know, the voice and body must work together to communicate what the mind has learned. Whenever the audience sees the choir of interpreters, bodily action must be considered, because it can add or detract from the effect of the communication. Posture and muscle tone must be as alert and vital for group work as for an individual performance. Be sure you respond to all the imagery and emotional elements during your rehearsals and use this response when you are with the group.

A choir may use gestures just as an individual interpreter does. It is a safe rule that gestures should not describe an object. A group of adults with their arms stretched out to look like trees is distracting, to put it mildly. Gestures should come from the way the object *makes you feel.* Empathy is the key.

Timing the Gestures

When your group uses gestures, they must be carefully worked out so their timing is perfect. Hands flying up and down at various intervals are totally ineffective. All the palms should be turned the same way, and the pace and extent of each gesture should be the same for every member of the group. It is better to understate than overstate any big gesture, but don't be afraid to use one when it is appropriate and has been carefully rehearsed and timed with the group.

As we already know, bodily action may range from a subtle change in muscle tone to dance movements, depending on the requirements of the selection and ability of the group. Choric interpretation coordinates beautifully with dance for appropriate material and occasions.

The arrangement of the choir on stage can suggest the mood of the selection. There are many ways of grouping people so they present an interesting and appropriate picture. At the end of the chapter are some suggested groupings. They are only suggestions and may need to be changed, depending on the size of your group and the purpose of the performance.

The Director's Role

Your group will need direction during rehearsals. It is a wise director, however, who works as far back in the room as possible so the group becomes accustomed to projecting past the edge of the platform. As you get used to working together, keeping your attention concentrated on the material, and sharing it with the audience, your director can step aside. In the last phases of rehearsal, he or she will probably not need to do more than give an occasional corrective signal. The most that needs to be done during performance is to give an unobtrusive starting signal from wherever the director is seated in the auditorium. Or the starting signal may come as a slight lift of the head by someone chosen from within the group.

If a director stands in front of the choir during performance, the attention of the group and of the audience is focused on him or her. This results in loss of mental contact and lack of directness for both audience and group. A director does not stand at the footlights and "conduct" the performance of a play. If the choir is ready for performance, it is ready to work without the waving arms and mouthed syllables of the director. His or her obtrusive physical presence during performance violates two basic rules of good interpretation. It calls attention to the mechanics of the art and detracts from the sharing of the selection.

Suggestions for Performance

You have the same responsibilities during a group performance as in a single performance, but, in addition, you must blend your voice to achieve the effect needed for the sound patterns, and discipline and time your bodily actions so they are in harmony with the others and do not break the total effect.

It is the responsibility of each member of the choir to keep constant mental contact with the audience. Just because there are twenty-nine other people is no reason for one to drift off into his or her own little dream world. A choir is only as effective as each member chooses to make it.

Miscellaneous Suggestions

Whether or not you memorize your selections depends on personal preference and some practical considerations. A group often feels more secure with manuscripts, especially if rehearsal time has been limited. If typed papers are used, they should be uniformly bound or mounted on stiff paper for appearance and ease in handling.

Black loose-leaf notebooks are practical. Every member of the group must be sufficiently free of dependence on the page to ensure directness and holding the attention of the audience.

Depending on the mood and degree of dramatic elements in the material, a choir may stand or sit or assume varying positions on the stage. Steps and platforms are effective for grouping a large choir in a limited amount of space.

It is often effective to change the grouping during a single selection when it is long enough to sustain such a variation. When a change of position is used within a selection, the timing and extent of the movement must be in harmony with the mood and emotional tone of the lines. Remember that the positions of your hands and feet, as well as general posture, are important.

If your group is giving a public performance, you will need to rehearse moving on and off stage. It is important that you look as if you know where you are going and are ready for the performance. If there are changes of grouping between numbers, this, too, must be rehearsed so there are no traffic jams. All changes should be accomplished as quickly and quietly as possible. Remember everything your audience can see or hear is a part of the performance.

In general, the simpler the dress, the less obtrusive the individual members of the choir will be and the more easily the audience will accept them as a single instrument. Many groups use dark trousers and white shirts open at the neck for the men, and dark skirts or slacks and long-sleeved white blouses for the women. Black and white gives enough contrast to look interesting, and the uniformity is pleasing. Choir robes or academic gowns are effective, although they may not be easy to obtain, and they tend to give an appearance of formality which may not be right for your material. Leotards are also very adaptable. It is wise to keep the clothing nondescriptive so it will be appropriate for a wide variety of selections.

The decision not to use *specific,* theatrical costumes is a practical and an aesthetic one. If the program includes several selections, there is danger that costume changes may take longer than the performance. More important is the aesthetic consideration. All members of a choir should blend into a single unit. The choir, like the individual interpreter, is not asking the audience to believe they are a specific group of characters. They are trying to create images in the minds of the listeners by suggestion. An exception is when a choir is part of a staged play, as in Greek tragedies or T. S. Eliot's *Murder in the Cathedral.*

The same reasoning should govern the use of makeup. Enough makeup to highlight the eyes and mouth is helpful. The amount depends on the stage lighting and the size of the auditorium. Descriptive makeup is dangerous and unnecessary unless the choir is part of a play cast.

The use of special lighting effects must be dictated by the material. At times mood lighting may be appropriate if the selection is long and dramatic enough for such effects to be helpful rather than obtrusive. In general, a choir group does not use extensive lighting because, like the individual interpreter, they wish to suggest—not be specific in—setting and exterior details.

Selections for Choric Interpretation

This poem tells the history of the black race. It is very effective when done in unison. Division into voices tends to emphasize the separate sentences in the second stanza and break the unity. However, if great care is used, the unity can be preserved. Two arrangements using different voice divisions are suggested below. You will notice there are no solo lines. You do not wish the audience to identify with *one* speaker but with the race of speakers.

The Negro Speaks of Rivers

by Langston Hughes

I	or II	
Unison	Unison	I've known rivers:
LV	DV	I've known rivers ancient as the world
		and older than the flow of human
		blood in human veins.
DV	Unison	My soul has grown deep like the rivers.
LV	LV	I bathed in the Euphrates when dawns
		were young.
DV	DV	I built my hut near the Congo and it
		lulled me to sleep.
$\frac{1}{2}$LV + $\frac{1}{2}$DV	LV	I looked upon the Nile and raised the
		pyramids above it.
Unison	DV	I heard the singing of the Mississippi
		When Abe Lincoln went down to
		New Orleans,
Unison	Unison	and I've seen its muddy
		bosom turn all golden in the sunset.
Unison	Unison	I've known rivers:
Unison	LV	Ancient
Unison	DV	dusky rivers.
Unison	Unison	My soul has grown deep like the rivers.

This poem depends for much of its effectiveness on careful attention to pace and timing. It would be fun to use solo voices for all the lines except the last eight. The first two, of course, should stay together. Cues must be picked up promptly and brightly. Hector thinks the conglomeration is wonderful! Let the sounds help keep it lively. The speed could pick up somewhat as you move along until you reach the last eight lines. These should be slower because your audience will be whirling by that time, and, more importantly, you will need to prepare for the turn on the repetition and the final four words.

Hector the Collector

by Shel Silverstein

	Hector the Collector
	Collected bits of string,
	Collected dolls with broken heads
	And rusty bells that would not ring.
	Pieces out of picture puzzles,
	Bent-up nails and ice-cream sticks,
	Twists of wires, worn-out tires,
	Paper bags and broken bricks.
	Old chipped vases, half shoelaces,
	Gatlin' guns that wouldn't shoot,
	Leaky boats that wouldn't float
	And stopped-up horns that wouldn't toot.
	Butter knives that had no handles,
	Copper keys that fit no locks,
	Rings that were too small for fingers,
	Dried-up leaves and patched-up socks.
	Worn-out belts that had no buckles,
	'Lectric trains that had no tracks,
	Airplane models, broken bottles,
	Three-legged chairs and cups with cracks.
Unison	Hector the Collector
	Loved these things with all his soul—
LV	Loved them more than shining diamonds,
DV	Loved them more than glistenin' gold.
Unison	Hector called to all the people,
	"Come and share my treasure trunk!"
	And all the silly sightless people
	Came and looked . . . and called it junk.

There is much fun in this "lesson on wise behavior." And a problem or two as well. You will have noticed that every line ends with the same rhyme. Use them fully but don't pound them. You will not need to. Also, the poet controls them with the numerous enjambment lines which will need only a barely perceptible suspension pause to set them off. The rhythm is somewhat relaxed so that the poem does not sound like a nursery rhyme.

To Kate, Skating Better Than Her Date

by David Daiches

Unison	Wait, Kate! You skate at such a rate
	You leave behind your skating mate.
	Your splendid speed won't you abate?
	He's lagging far behind you, Kate.
LV	He brought you on this skating date
	His shy affection thus to state,
	But you on skating concentrate
	And leave him with a woeful weight
	Pressed on his heart. Oh, what a state
DV	A man gets into, how irate
	He's bound to be with life and fate
	If, when he tries to promulgate
	His love, the loved one turns to skate
	Far, far ahead to demonstrate
	Superior speed and skill. Oh, hate
Unison	Is sure to come of love, dear Kate,
	If you so treat your skating mate.
LV	Turn again, Kate, or simply wait
	Until he comes, then him berate
	(Coyly) for catching up so late.
DV	For, Kate, he *knows* your skating's great,
LV	He's *seen* your splendid figure eight,
DV	He is not here to contemplate
	Your supersonic skating rate—
	That is not why he made the date.
LV	He's anxious to expatiate
	On how he wants you for his mate.
Unison	And don't you want to hear him, Kate?

This is a very strong poem about the flight of black slaves before the Emancipation Proclamation. This strength must be evident in your voices and in your muscles. The rhythm shifts into that of a spiritual from time to time. Make full use of it. Be sure you keep it together despite the numerous voice divisions.

Runagate Runagate

by Robert Hayden

	I.
Solo I	Runs falls rises stumbles on from darkness into darkness and the darkness thicketed with shapes of terror and the hunters pursuing and the hounds pursuing and the night cold and the night long and the river to cross and the jack-muh-lanterns beckoning beckoning and blackness ahead and when shall I reach that somewhere morning and keep on going and never turn back and keep on going
LV	Runagate
DV	Runagate
Unison	Runagate
Unison	Many thousands rise and go many thousands crossing over
Unison	O mythic North O star-shaped yonder Bible city
Solo II	Some go weeping and some rejoicing
Solo III	some in coffins and some in carriages
Solo IV	some in silks and some in shackles
Unison	Rise and go or fare you well
Solo I	No more auction block for me no more driver's lash for me

Solo V — If you see my Pompey, 30 yrs of age,
new breeches, plain stockings, negro shoes;

Solo VI — if you see my Anna, likely young mulatto
branded E on the right cheek, R on the left,
catch them if you can and notify subscriber.

All solos in unison — Catch them if you can, but it won't be easy.
They'll dart underground when you try to catch them,
plunge into quicksand, whirlpools, mazes,
turn into scorpions when you try to catch them.

Solo VII — And before I'll be a slave
I'll be buried in my grave

Solo VIII — North star and bonanza gold
I'm bound for the freedom, freedom-bound
and oh Susyanna don't you cry for me

Unison — Runagate

Unison — Runagate

II.

Solo IX — Rises from their anguish and their power,

Solo IX — Harriet Tubman,

Solo IX — woman of earth, whipscarred,
a summoning, a shining

Solo IX — Mean to be free

Solo IX — And this way the way of it, brethren brethren,
way we journeyed from Can't to Can.
Moon so bright and no place to hide,
the cry up and the patterollers riding,
hound dogs belling in bladed air.

/Unison — And fear starts a-murbling, /Never make it,

Unison/Solo IX — we'll never make it. /*Hush that now,*

Unison — and she's turned upon us, levelled pistol
glinting in the moonlight:

Solo IX — Dead folks can't jaybird-talk, she says;
you keep on going now or die, she says.

continued

Unison	Wanted Harriet Tubman alias The General alias Moses Stealer of Slaves
	In league with Garrison Alcott Emerson Garrett Douglass Thoreau John Brown
Unison	Armed and known to be Dangerous
	Wanted Reward Dead or Alive
Unison	Tell me, Ezekiel, oh tell me do you see mailed Jehovah coming to deliver me?
DV	Hoot-owl calling in the ghosted air, five times calling to the hants in the air.
LV	Shadow of a face in the scary leaves, shadow of a voice in the talking leaves:
Unison	Come ride-a my train
	Oh that train, ghost-story train through swamp and savanna movering movering, over trestles of dew, through caves of the wish, Midnight Special on a sabre track movering movering, first stop Mercy and the last Hallelujah.
	Come ride-a my train
	Mean mean mean to be free.

Enjoy the obvious rhymes in this poem. It allows for considerable muscle response to implement the "agony" of the experience.

Waiting for the Birdie

by Ogden Nash

1/2 Group/1/2 Group	Some hate broccoli,/some hate bacon,
Unison	I hate having my picture taken.
	How can your family claim to love you
	And then demand a picture of you?
	The electric chair is a queasy chair,
	But I know an equally comfortless pair;
1/2 Group	One is the dentist's, my good sirs,
1/2 Group	And the other is the photographer's.
Unison	Oh, the fly in all domestic ointments
	Is affectionate people who make appointments
	To have your teeth filled left and right,
	Or your face reproduced in black and white.
	You open the door and you enter the studio,
	And you feel less cheerio than nudio.
	The hard light shines like seventy suns,
	And you know that your features are foolish ones.
	The photographer says, Natural, please,
1/2 Group/1/2 Group	And you cross your knees/and uncross your knees.
Unison	Like a duke in a high society chronicle
	The camera glares at you through its monocle
	And you feel ashamed of your best attire,
1/3 Group	Your nose itches,
1/2 Group	your palms perspire,
1/3 Group	Your muscles stiffen,
Unison	and all the while
	You smile and smile and smile and smile.
	It's over;
1/2 Group	you weakly grope for the door;
Unison	It's not;
1/2 Group	the photographer wants one more.
Unison	And if this experience you survive,
	Wait, just wait till the proofs arrive.
	You look like a drawing by Thurber or Bab,
	Or a gangster stretched on a marble slab.
	And all your dear ones, including your wife,
	Say There he is, that's him to the life!
1/2 Group/1/2 Group	Some hate broccoli,/some hate bacon,
Unison	But I hate having my picture taken.

Unit VII
Interpretation Outside the Classroom

CHAPTER 26
Contests

CHAPTER 27
Festivals

CHAPTER 28
Program Building

Chapter 26
Contests

One of the most popular extracurricular activities in the field of speech is contest work. It is often called forensics, and includes debate and public address as well as interpretation and sometimes acting. Contests can be exciting and stimulating, exhausting and nerve racking, satisfying and frustrating, all at the same time. They always involve competition.

The attitude with which you enter a contest makes all the difference between its being an enriching experience for you or merely "bringing home the hardware" . . . or not bringing it home when you think you should have! Of course you want to win. Everybody does. But the important thing is the amount of performance experience you receive and the new contacts you make with both people and selections.

Contests are strictly regulated within the separate states although the rules do not vary that much from one to another. These rules are established by a state organization through the Department of Education and must be adhered to by all contestants. You will be given a maximum and minimum time limit for your performance. Take it seriously; you can be eliminated on that point alone. Areas of performance are designated by categories such as "dramatic," "humorous," "poetry," and so forth. There may also be group interpretation and duo-acting. Check these categories carefully in selecting your material. You are probably safest preparing a scene or two from a play for "dramatic" although the rules will usually make this clear.

The disadvantages of these categories is immediately evident. There are a great many things that are certainly worth working on which, technically, do not quite fit into such tight classifications. Choose something you enjoy and that you know is well enough written to hold up, because if you are successful you will be doing it over and over. If a selection fails to excite you after repeated readings, your performance is likely to become mechanical. The understandable temptation is to choose something for a contest that you already know you do well, but this certainly does not help you grow and become more versatile. It is not necessarily wise to use something that won last year, partly because no two readers handle any selection *exactly* the same way and partly because the judges will have already heard it and will either have a preconceived notion of how it must be done (which may not be right, after all) or they will have heard it

so often that they are bored with it. Whatever you choose must be analyzed carefully and thoroughly so that you know where it is going and how it gets there.

The first contest is usually on a local level. The winner, or sometimes the top two or three, then go on to district, state, regional, and even national meets.

One disadvantage of contests is the human quality of the judges. On the local and district levels the instructors or coaches of the contestants are often used as judges for groups in which their students are not involved. Sometimes local clergy or lawyers or business men and women help out as well. They are always dedicated and knowledgeable people doing their best to judge according to the rules. Nevertheless, anyone's response to literature and to any performance is bound to be somewhat subjective. If you have not met their criteria, do not be discouraged. Pay attention to their criticism and comments if they are willing to discuss your selection and material with you. Consider their comments carefully but don't try to change what *you know* the material demands. Put a loss down to experience and hope for better luck next time. You may, of course, ask the judge questions but never do you quibble or complain about the decision except perhaps to your instructor after it is all over. Take the criticism and try to learn from it but do not read to please a judge. You are reading to share the experience of the literature as you have discovered it through careful study.

One of the problems of contest work is keeping the selection and your performance fresh and alive. You will have done it so often you may substitute exterior or set actions for interior response. This in turn leads to exaggeration and lack of directness with your audience. When you begin to grow stale, go back to some of your earlier preparation. Concentrate on your empathic response and on the sense imagery. Revitalize your visualization of characters and scene. Remind yourself of the important steps in organization of plot or of the subtle contributions of the sound pattern in a poem. Most of all remember that you are responsible to your audience. They have not heard your performance or perhaps even your selection before. Concentrate on involving them in the literature and be sure you are using your techniques to support that literature rather than to show your skill in voice and body. Be a good showman!

Chapter 27
Festivals

Festivals are noncompetitive, interpretative events. Their real purpose is to get together to enjoy a day or more of interpretation and to learn from each other and the critic judges. The categories and whatever rules there may be are established by the school hosting the event and the practical consideration of keeping the schedule running smoothly. Sometimes a festival will have a theme or concentrate on a few selected authors or regional writers, or the program may be all poetry or all prose or all drama. Usually, however, you have considerable freedom of selection within the necessary time limits. The whole

atmosphere is much more relaxed than that of contest work.

A critic judge differs from a contest judge. He or she schedules some time at the close of each session to talk with the performer individually as well as in a group. There are no rankings. Nobody wins or loses a festival. Usually the critic judge makes written comments on the performances which are given to the participants after they are shared with the group involved.

Some festivals schedule a preliminary round of readings in small groups and end with a general program which everyone attends. A single reader for this final program is chosen by each group with which they worked in the preliminary round. The selection chosen need not be the best performance but rather one that had some interesting problems which may or may not have been completely solved. Festivals are great for experimental material.

At the final meeting a critic judge, if possible one who has not been involved in the earlier round, hears the selected performers and then spends some time giving his or her own critique of those performances, explaining why some things seemed to work and some did not and even asking that some portions be read again to try another approach. This is a very valuable session for all the participants because there is no strain of winning or losing. There is always an opportunity for questions and comments from the audience. The final critic judge should be chosen with care because the session can be a wonderfully rich learning experience if it is tactfully handled with no hint of competitive ranking.

Festivals range from very simple ones to elaborate ones. But they are always enjoyable and worth doing. Any school may host a festival. If you would like to

try one, here are a few suggestions to help you set one up. It is a fine project for your class or for your speech club.

The first thing to do, as far ahead as possible, is to clear a date with your principal and with the state organization which is in charge of contests. You do not need that organization's permission, of course, but you will want to avoid dates when neighboring schools will be busy with contests. Be sure to check, too, various vacations for the schools you plan to invite. When your date has been approved, the next question the principal will ask (or maybe even the first one), will be "How much will it cost?" A small simple festival can be handled for very little expense, especially if it is a one-day affair.

The next step is to contact the speech teachers and/or English teachers in the schools you plan to invite either by phone or by double postcard with a place to mark whether or not they are interested in further information. It is wise to ask that that information be returned by a specific date so you do not waste time and money sending a second mailing if they cannot plan to come. Be sure to include date and time and place; and make it sound like an invitation, not just an announcement. Send it to the Speech or English teacher rather than to the school. People are not too careful about passing on mail that isn't addressed to anybody in particular.

If your festival is to be a play festival or one which will include group performances, those planning to attend will want to know:

the approximate size of your stage so that they can plan grouping,

the time limit for each group,

what is available by way of properties, especially stools and platforms,

whether or not scenes from longer plays are acceptable with an appropriate introduction,

what lighting and sound effects you can provide,

what time they may have for rehearsal before performance in order to get used to the stage.

All of this should be included in your second letter which makes the final arrangements. If the group plans to bring their own properties, you will need to provide a space to store them.

Contact your critic judge for the final program as early as possible. A nearby college may have someone you would like to have come or perhaps your instructor knows someone who would be good. A personal letter is important. It should give all the information of time and place as well as what the judge's duties will be. He or she should be offered a fee to at least cover expenses and the fee should be as generous as you can manage. Critiquing is hard work and will take a whole day of his or her time. In academic circles the fee is called an *honorarium* which really means "It isn't what we know you are worth but it is all we have!"

If there are enough places near your school where your visitors can eat, you need not worry about providing them with lunch. If not, arrange to have the school cafeteria available. This, of course, entails lunch tickets which are a nuisance. Many groups like bringing a bag lunch and buying soft drinks, especially if the weather is likely to be good. It is pleasant to have coffee and donuts ready when visitors arrive in the morning or punch and cookies for an afternoon break, or both. The cost will vary with the number involved but it is a good way to become acquainted. You will need a committee to be in charge of this. The cookies or donuts can be donated if your parents are cooperative! Arrangements for lunch and the day's schedule should be included in your first letter which should go out several weeks in advance.

You will need several committees, some of them small ones.

Mailing committee: for the first announcements and follow-up letters;
Food committee: for lunch arrangements, morning coffee, and afternoon break;
Hospitality committee: to be sure someone is there to greet the guests when they arrive and to see that each group has at least one person to act as its host or hostess all day;
Finance committee: although much of this will be handled by the school office;
Rooms committee: to schedule and assign rooms for all the events and see that the rooms are left in good order at the end of the day.

There should be someone responsible for the critic judge to be sure he or she is provided with note paper, luncheon company, and any other little thing which might be required. You will need one or two people at a desk in the front hall to answer questions and check the list as the guests arrive.

Don't forget to arrange with the custodian to have the building open and rooms unlocked, lights and heat on, and the building locked at the end of the day. The school office will probably do this for you but people have been known to forget.

This will all be quite simple if there has been advance planning. The key is to keep everything running smoothly and ON TIME. And to make the participants feel like welcome special guests. Start small and well ahead of time. You'll have a great day and so will your guests and next year they may invite *you.*

Chapter 28
Program Building

In almost every community there are many opportunities to present programs outside the classroom. This is exciting to do and gives you a wide range of experience with different kinds of audiences. There may be opportunities to perform for school groups at your own or neighboring schools, local clubs, church groups, hospitals, retirement homes, or public libraries to mention only a few. Program chairpersons and recreation directors would be delighted to hear you are available.

Until you have had some experience giving such programs, you might feel more comfortable if two or more of you did the programs together. Group performances—choric readings, short plays, a Readers' Theater performance—would also be ideal. No matter how many people are involved, the program must be carefully rehearsed so that there is some continuity and everyone knows when he or she is reading and what kind of material precedes his or her selection. There should be some attention to the arrangement of selections so that they balance and complement each other instead of being just a collection of miscellaneous things strung together.

The first consideration in deciding which selections you will do is, as always, their literary worth. Do not perform something you know is inferior because you think your audience will not accept something better. It is your job to present your selection so well that it will not seem difficult. Never underestimate your potential audience. They are often more sophisticated and better read than you may think.

It is helpful if your program has a unifying theme. Often the purpose of the organization, the time of year, such as a holiday or a patriotic celebration, will suggest a theme. A program can be built on something as simple as people or places. It may also be—and most often is—determined by personal preference. In any case the whole program should have some discernible unity with enough variety to keep it interesting.

Working toward a unified program is important but it may not be the place to begin your consideration of selections. It is often more practical to begin with what you like to read and what you have ready or will have time to get ready. Then see what thematic thread you can find and plan transitions from one selection to the next which will follow this thematic thread.

Considering Your Audience

When you do a performance in the classroom, you know you have an audience whose interests are very like your own. This allows you a great deal of freedom in choice of selections. When you do a program outside the classroom, you must give some thought to what will be appropriate for that specific audience. You cannot, of course, know for sure what will interest everyone but it is possible to make some generalizations.

The first consideration, as always, is the literary worth of what you choose.

The second consideration is what your audience expects of you; they expect you to be young, skilled, intelligent, attractive, and interesting. Otherwise they would not have asked you to perform for them. But young does not mean childish or even childlike. It means vital and fresh. Four-letter words and risqué dialogue are not compatible with their image of you. You are an artist in their eyes and they expect you to be poised and well prepared. They have invited you because you can do something they cannot do as well. Use your intelligence and education but do not flaunt them.

Age is sometimes an important consideration in audience adaptation. In general, a young audience is more open to experimentation and a wider range of

subject matter than an older one. The very elderly, as in a retirement home, usually want at least some traditional familiar material. They want to be reminded of happier times and that there is still beauty and gentleness in the world. They are not interested in material on old age and death and illness. They want encouragement and diversion. If the group includes a wide age spread, try to have something for everyone, if possible. Such a program may be a little difficult to unify but it can be done. If you have any doubts about the suitability of a selection, it is better to omit it than risk offense. You are their guest performer.

Children are a wonderful audience. They like material about people, animals, clouds, birds, and everything they can visualize whether real or imaginary. Do not talk down to them. They are more sophisticated about the attitude of adults than we sometimes think. Be yourself and trust your selections. Selections should be relatively short and the transitions should be carefully handled to connect the literature with what the children already know about. Stories, of course, are great favorites and children enjoy having the story characters made vivid by more explicit vocal and physical characterization than might be appropriate for a more mature group. Children also love poetry which has "fun" sounds and rhythms.

The introduction which you use and the transitions which take you and your audience from one selection to the next are vitally important. They should not be long and elaborate. The introduction, as you know, will set the tone of the whole program. It is courteous to begin with an expression of pleasure at being with the group if it can be done briefly and gracefully. Keep it short. If there are to be several readers and you are not the first, the introduction to your portion of the program should form a bridge from the previous performer's selections, to the mood and train of thought that you wish to establish.

The transitions between selections should allow the audience a few seconds to complete their emotional response to the one you have just finished. Then lead them subtly and economically into the mood and area of response of the one to follow. This is the way to unify a program of diverse selections.

If you have established a theme, no matter how general, for the whole performance, it will help with the introduction and transitions as well as with the arrangement of selections.

Timing the Program

Only a rank beginner or an egotist allows the final program to run longer than the time agreed upon. Audiences become ill at ease if you go on longer than they expected you to. It is always better to have them wish there had been more time than to risk the sigh of relief and the hurried exit.

Time the program at frequent intervals during preparation. You will probably take more time as your preparation progresses. It is safe to add from eight to ten minutes to your early performance time of an hour's performance. Don't forget to allow for time for applause between selections. That is a phenomenon no performer wishes to prevent!

A Few Practical Details

It is always wise to get in touch with the program chairperson well in advance to be sure of time and location. You should always arrive at least fifteen minutes early. If you need stools or any special equipment, be sure to check whether such things are available. The chairperson will usually be able to provide a reading stand.

Once you have agreed to do a performance nothing short of a serious emergency should prevent you from being there on time, appropriately dressed and fully prepared.

It is helpful for publicity if you can think of a title for the program. It should be

brief and should suggest the theme without telling too much about the selections themselves. It should contain only three or four words, and if it is easy to remember, so much the better.

Out-of-classroom performances take effort, time, intelligence, imagination and a willingness to do a great deal of research to find the right selections. Even so, the experience of sharing good literature with an audience is rewarding and exciting.

Your audience will differ slightly from your classroom audience. They will expect you to be professional and, most important, they are there because they want to be. They want to enjoy themselves. They will feel no need to be critics. They will be completely responsive and receptive. The experience of elation and challenge which we talked about in the first chapter of this unit will be heightened and their response will make all your time and effort well worthwhile.

Unit VIII
History of Performance

EXIT
EXIT

In most ancient societies, the performer acted in two different roles. Beside a campfire or in the village square, he told stories, composed and recited poems, and passed on the myths and history of his people. He also participated in pageants and religious ceremonies in which events of history and daily life or mythology were acted out for the community. Then he, along with others, put on costume and makeup or masks and in song, dance, and mime depicted events that were important to a tribe or village. Traces of this kind of performance still linger in Native American dance ceremonies, tribal rituals of many African societies, religious pageants, and even Mardi Gras parades.

As communities grew larger and society more complex, it was awkward and often impossible for everyone to participate actively in a performance. Gradually most community members became onlookers instead of participants. Live theater takes its form from the ways in which it attempts to reunite performer and audience.

Audience and performer are even more widely separated in today's technological age. But whether we view a film as part of an audience, or watch electronic drama by ourselves at home, the performers' purposes are basically the same—to create believable, dramatic characters using all the skills and techniques available to them. In this, they are not very different from the earliest performers on earth.

Chapter 29
The Greeks

Greek drama grew out of religious ceremonies performed at festivals in honor of the Greek god of fertility and wine, Dionysus.[1] As part of the festivals, choral songs were chanted or sung to honor the god. Sometime during the sixth century B.C., the dancers and singers at these festivals ceased to perform extemporaneously, however. Not only did their performance become more regularized but legend has it that at one of these festivals a man named Thespis stepped out of his role as a leader of the chorus and became a character who spoke different lines and reacted to the chorus. In other words, dialogue was born.

Eventually a drama competition was held as part of the yearly, spring Dionysian festival. Each playwright who competed presented three tragedies, usually on the same theme, and then ended with a satyr play, a grotesque comic parody of the theme of the tragedies. Plays were performed all day long for several days, and prizes were awarded to the best playwright.

These religious events became concentrated in Athens, a city with thousands

1. **Dionysus** (dī″ə nī′səs).

Theatre at Epidaurus, c. 325 B.C.

Herodes Atticus Theatre, Athens

of people. As a result, not everyone could be included in a pageant or festival as had been done earlier in the villages. Those people who could no longer participate directly in a performance became the audience.

Plays written for these festivals retold the history or religious myths of the Greeks. They told stories of mortals interacting with gods and goddesses, of kings and queens, of battles, and of the family relationships of important historical characters.

The plays were performed in an enormous outdoor theater. This open-air theater was at the base of a hill, with audience seated up the sides of the incline in a horseshoe seating arrangement. In the center of the horseshoe was a large, flat space for dancing and choral movement called the *orchestra* where the chorus performed. At the back of this was a platform on which the actors stood, with a narrow building behind them which served as the scenery for all the plays. This was called the *skene,*[2] which is the source for our words *scenery* and *proscenium,* as well as *scene.*

Since the actors were far away from the audience and needed help to be seen and heard, they wore larger-than-life masks, really three-dimensional heads made of linen, wood, or cork with openings for eyes and mouth. These

2. **skene** (skān′ē).

masks helped the audience distinguish among the various characters each actor played. Since women did not act on the Greek stage and female characters were played by men, masks further aided the audience in character identification. The mouth opening in the masks apparently operated like a megaphone to help the actor project to the upper rows. Actors also often wore platform shoes which, though they restricted movement, somewhat balanced the effect of the large mask.

These conditions, and the fact that the plays grew out of the choruses of religious festivals, meant that playwrights concentrated on relatively simple plots with little physical action and long, dramatic poetry.

The most powerful Greek plays were the tragedies, serious plays that retold legend and history and explained how well-known people met their fates at the hands of the gods. The best of these are still regarded as some of the most moving drama in all theatrical history. Although texts of many of the plays have disappeared, some of the plays of three of the most important playwrights, Aeschylus, Sophocles, and Euripides[3] still survive.

One of the most powerful works, the *Oresteia*[4] trilogy (a group of three related plays), was written by Aeschylus (525-456 B.C.). The trilogy deals with the hero Agamemnon's murder and the revenge of that murder by his children Electra and Orestes.[5] The crowning achievement of Sophocles (495-406? B.C.), was the *Oedipus*[6] trilogy. Euripides (485?-406 B.C.) stressed the human characteristics of all his characters in such plays as *The Trojan Women, Medea,* and *Hippolytus.*[7]

The most famous of the comic playwrights was Aristophanes (448?-385 B.C.)[8] His broadly satirical plays made fun of local, well-known people and historical characters. Many of his comedies still survive and are performed today. These include *The Frogs, The Birds, The Clouds,* and *The Wasps.*

Near the end of the fourth century B.C., a new kind of comedy represented by the plays of Menander (342-292 B.C.) began to appear. In this so-called New Comedy, plot became more important than before, and satire began to disappear. Other traditions of the Greek theater were fading as well. These New Comedies eliminated choruses and long speeches and began to be produced more for entertainment alone than as part of a religious celebration.

The Romans invaded and conquered Greece in the second and first centuries B.C. and though they adopted the forms of the plays in their own literature, the strong social and religious foundations that inspired the Greeks were missing. As a result, they never succeeded in duplicating the brilliance of the original.

---

3. **Aeschylus** (es′ kə ləs), **Sophocles** (sof′ə klēz″), and **Euripides** (yů rip′ə dēz″).

4. ***Oresteia*** (ôr″e stē′ə).

5. **Agamemnon** (ag″ə mem′non), the leader of the Greeks in the Trojan War; **Electra** (i lek′tra); **Orestes** (ô-res′tēz).

6. **Oedipus** (ed′ə pəs).

7. ***Medea*** (mi dē′ə) and ***Hippolytus*** (hi pol′i təs).

8. **Aristophanes** (ar″ə stof′ə nēz″).

Activities

1. Select a scene from Unit III that you have already done. Perform it again in masks. Make the masks from paper sacks large enough to comfortably cover your head. Cut eyeholes and a hole to speak through. Draw the features of your character in the scene onto the mask with marking pens, but do not overdo the features. The idea is to exaggerate to make the features bigger than life but not to make them purposely funny-looking.

Compare the scene in the two performances. How did you have to change your acting when you were wearing the mask? How did this affect the tempo of the scene? Did you physically express emotions with your face even though it could not be seen? How did the audience react? What did the audience see that they had not seen in the performance without masks?

2. Try the same scene in a large performing space. If possible, use your football stadium or practice field. If weather or schedule will not permit this, use the cafeteria or other large room in the school. Play your scene so that persons sitting as far away as possible can still see and hear the scene.

What kind of adjustments did you have to make in your performance? How did this affect the tempo of the scene? How did this affect the subtlety of your expression?

Scene from *Oedipus Rex,* with Douglas Campbell, directed by Tyrone Guthrie (1955)

These two exercises should help to give some idea of performers' problems in ancient Greek theaters. Keeping what you have learned from them in mind, try the two following scenes. Do them each with masks and without, and both in the classroom and in a larger space.

In this scene from Sophocles' *Antigone* (an′tig″ə nē), the Chorus is a group of townspeople. Most of the class can be included in the Chorus. Creon is the king who has taken power after a civil war. Antigone is a young woman whose brother was killed. Against Creon's orders, she has buried her brother, Polynices (pol″ə nī′sēz) and Creon has ordered her to be sealed alive in a tomb. In this scene, she is preparing herself for the fate that awaits her.

from *Antigone*
by Sophocles
translated by E. F. Watling

CHORUS. But glory and praise go with you, lady,
To your resting place. You go with your beauty
Unmarred by the hand of consuming sickness,
Untouched by the sword, living and free,
As none other that ever died before you.
ANTIGONE. The daughter of Tantalus,[9] a Phrygian maid,
Was doomed to a piteous death on the rock
Of Sipylus, which embraced and imprisoned her,
Merciless as the ivy; rain and snow
Beat down upon her, mingled with her tears,
As she wasted and died. Such was her story,
And such is the sleep that I shall go to.
CHORUS. She was a goddess of immortal birth,
And we are mortals; the greater the glory,
To share the fate of a god-born maiden,
A living death, but a name undying.
ANTIGONE. Mockery, mockery![10] By the gods of our fathers,
Must you make me a laughingstock while I yet live?

---

9. The daughter of Tantalus, Niobe (nī′ō bē). To punish her for her excessive pride, the gods slew Niobe's children. Overcome by grief, she turned into a stone from which tears flowed. A whirlwind carried the stone to Mount Sipylus (si′pi ləs) in Phrygia (frij′i ə), the kingdom of Niobe's father.

10. mockery. Antigone mistakenly thinks that the Chorus is making fun of her.

O lordly sons of my city! O Thebes!
Your valleys of rivers, your chariots and horses!
No friend to weep at my banishment
To a rock-hewn chamber of endless durance,
In a strange cold tomb alone to linger
Lost between life and death for ever.
CHORUS. My child, you have gone your way
To the outermost limit of daring
And have stumbled against Law enthroned.
This is the expiation
You must make for the sin of your father.
ANTIGONE. My father—the thought that sears my soul—
The unending burden of the house of Labdacus.
Monstrous marriage of mother and son . . .
My father . . . my parents . . . O hideous shame!
Whom now I follow, unwed, curse-ridden,
Doomed to this death by the ill-starred marriage
That marred my brother's life.
CHORUS. An act of homage is good in itself, my daughter;
But authority cannot afford to connive at disobedience.
You are the victim of your own self-will.
ANTIGONE. And must go the way that lies before me.
No funeral hymn; no marriage music;
No sun from this day forth, no light,
No friend to weep at my departing.
(*Enter* CREON.)
CREON. Weeping and wailing at the door of death!
There'd be no end of it, if it had force
To buy death off. Away with her at once.
And close her up in her rock-vaulted tomb.
Leave her and let her die, if die she must,
Or live within her dungeon. Though on earth
Her life is ended from this day, her blood
Will not be on our hands.
ANTIGONE. So to my grave,
My bridal bower, my everlasting prison,
I go, to join those many of my kinsmen
Who dwell in the mansions of Persephone,
Last and unhappiest, before my time.
Yet I believe my father will be there
To welcome me, my mother greet me gladly,

And you, my brother, gladly see me come.
Each one of you my hands have laid to rest,
Pouring the due libations on your graves.
It was by this service to your dear body, Polynices,
I earned the punishment which now I suffer,
Though all good people know it was for your honour.

In this scene from *Electra* by Euripides, the dialogue is on a more personal level than it is in *Antigone.* Electra and Orestes are brother and sister. Their mother has murdered their father with the help of Aegisthus (i jis′thəs), and they are preparing to avenge the act. Orestes will have to do the actual killing, but he is hesitating because the act is so horrible to him. Electra is trying to prod him into action. Phoebus and Apollo, mentioned in this scene, are two different names for the Greek god of the sun. An oracle is an answer to a question believed to be given by a god through a priest or priestess. It often had a hidden meaning that was hard to understand.

from ***Electra***
by Euripides
translated by E. T. Vermeule

ELECTRA. Enough now. Women, take his body out of sight, conceal it well in darkness so that when she comes my mother sees no corpses till her throat is cut.

(The corpse is carried into the cottage.)

ORESTES. Hold off a little; we might find another plan.
ELECTRA. What's there? I see some allies racing from Mycenae.
ORESTES. Not allies. You are looking at my mother who bore me.
ELECTRA. How beautifully she marches straight into our net; see how grandly she rides with chariot and escort.
ORESTES. What—what is our action now toward Mother? Do we kill?
ELECTRA. Don't tell me pity catches you at the sight of her.

ORESTES. O god! How can I kill her when she brought me up and bore me?
ELECTRA. Kill her just the way she killed my father. And yours.
ORESTES. O Phoebus, your holy word was brute and ignorant.
ELECTRA. Where Apollo is ignorant shall men be wise?
ORESTES. He said to kill my mother, whom I must not kill.
ELECTRA. Nothing will hurt you. You are only avenging Father.
ORESTES. As matricide I must stand trial. I was clean before.
ELECTRA. Not clean before the gods, if you neglect your father.
ORESTES. I know—but will I not be judged for killing Mother?
ELECTRA. And will you not be judged for quitting Father's service?
ORESTES. A polluted demon spoke it in the shape of god—
ELECTRA. Throned on the holy tripod? I shall not believe you.
ORESTES. And I shall not believe those oracles were pure.
ELECTRA. You may not play the coward now and fall to weakness. Go in. I will bait her a trap as she once baited one which sprang at Aegisthus' touch and killed her lawful husband.
ORESTES. I am going in. I walk a cliff-edge in a sea of evil, and evil I will do. If the gods approve, let it be so. This game of death is bitter, and sweet.

(ORESTES *goes slowly into the house with* PYLADES[11], *without looking back.*)

11. **Pylades** (pil′ə dēz), a friend of Orestes.

Chapter 30
The Renaissance in Italy

During the time of the Roman Empire, which at its height stretched from Britain to the Red Sea, the theater never had the kind of public function it had in Greece. Most Roman playwrights imitated the Greeks, but only as a mark of their own education and sophistication. Many of the Roman plays we now know, such as those of Seneca (4? B.C.-A.D. 65), were probably never performed in public.

The performer did not disappear, however. In Rome itself, the capital of the Roman Empire, all literature was performed. Poets recited their works, as had the Greek poets. Because all books had to be copied by hand, writers "published" their works by giving them public readings. Storytellers, singers, dancers, and mimes traveled from town to town, performing their works wherever they could find a crowd. For a few years, Plautus (254?-184 B.C.) was able to have his comedies performed with great public success, but after he died, the formal comic theater disappeared as well.

After the Roman Empire declined in the fourth century, even the imitations of Greek plays and poems disappeared. The kind of performances common in prehistoric times returned to Europe: local storytellers passed on histories and legends, while traveling poets and troubadours brought tales of the outside world to village and castle.

Gradually the Christian Church, which had been strongly opposed to theatrical performances of any kind, began itself to depict biblical events in its religious services. Eventually, many communities in Europe began to hold parades and pageants on religious themes. These pageants developed into religious plays, called mystery plays and miracle plays, some of which were written down and saved.

By the fifteenth century, a major change in society had begun to occur, starting in the towns of northern Italy and gradually spreading across all of Europe. This change, called the Renaissance (literally, a rebirth of learning), was a time in which people began to rediscover and use the literature and learning of ancient Greece and Rome. As the ancient literature was rediscovered and its ideas spread, small troupes of wandering singers, acrobats, and comedians who had been traveling from village to village, became aware of the plays of Plautus. Although the plays themselves were not performed because society had changed so much in the 1500 years since he wrote them, the characters in those plays provided a foundation in Italy on which to build a new kind of theater. This new theater was called *commedia dell'arte.*[1]

Earlier, Plautus had built his plays around types of characters rather than specific, individualized persons. These character types reappeared in play after play under various names. We can recognize many of these characters because we still use them in comedy today. The hen-pecked husband, the naive young man or young woman, the miser, the bragging soldier who is a coward underneath, and the clever servant are just a few of the stock characters Plautus used in his works.

The performers of the *commedia* adopted these character types, gave them new Italian names, invented unique costumes, and made new plays for them to perform in.

Another invention passed on from Plautus (although it was begun in the Greek New Comedy) was the boy-meets-girl plot. The *commedia* used this as a simple framework and invented hundreds of variations of comic complications before the boy and girl finally got together at the end.

1. **commedia dell'arte** (kə mā′dē ə del är′tē).

The Triumph of Isabella by Van Alsloot (1615)

The most famous *commedia* characters are still referred to today. One of these was Arlecchino (Harlequin in French), the foolish servant with his dark mask and checkerboard costume. This acrobatic comic always got into outrageous situations and engineered comic plots. The other famous character was Pantalone, an old man who was identified by his costume of red breeches and stockings. He was a foolish, pompous old man who stood in the way of the lovers, sometimes as the father and sometimes as a competitor for the hand of the young woman. He was usually a businessman and miser, although he was often tricked by any number of schemes that made him look foolish.

With a basic plot and a set of permanent stock characters, *commedia* performers could make hundreds of plays, and they did. Each performer played the same stock character, no matter what the play. Each performance was improvised. The actors would agree on a plot and a general outline showing which characters did what and when; then they would invent their lines and stage business as they went along, depending on how the audience reacted and how the play seemed to be going. Since each stock character was expected to be true to type, and each performer had his own kind of jokes and comic business,

Harlequino

the actors did not really need lines, and the plays were not written down until years later.

When the *commedia* began, no town was large enough to support a full-time set of actors. To make a living, the players had to travel, just as earlier actors had done. In one town they might set up a platform in the town square; in another they might be in the courtyard of an inn; in another they would be at a fair; and at another they might be in a prince's court or banquet hall. Everything about the performance had to be flexible enough to fit any occasion and audience.

Most of the performances were outdoors. To help the audiences recognize the characters, performers often wore masks as well as unique, stylized costumes. The masks were different from the Greek masks because the distances between performers and audience were not nearly so great and because the comedies required a great deal of physical activity. Masks usually covered only the upper half of the face, exaggerated the eyes and nose for comic effect, and left the mouth and head free for talking and action.

Pantalone

As cities grew larger and indoor theaters were developed in the seventeenth century, *commedia* troupes began to settle in one place. Since audiences attended the theater more often and expected more and different plots, playwrights began to write plays for the troupes. By the middle of the eighteenth century, the traveling troupes had disappeared except in the most provincial parts of Europe.

Most *commedia* characters had a collection of jokes and comic physical business which they used as needed in different performances. These were called *lazzi* (lät′zē). The following scene from a modern play written in the style of the *commedia* contains a good example of *lazzi.*

Arlecchino and Pedrolino are both bumbling, comic servants. They meet on a street in the middle of the afternoon. Notice how the routine makes a simple piece of plot information more interesting to the audience.

Il Capitano

from ***A Gap in Generations***
by Jerry Blunt

(ARLECCHINO *enters* DR, PEDROLINO DL. *At a brisk pace they pass at* C.)

BOTH. Good day. (*After passing they simultaneously stop at* R *and* L, *see* *where they are, and cross back to confront each other at* C.) I was just coming to your house. (*Both laugh.*) You first. (*Both laugh.*)

ARLECCHINO. You.

PEDROLINO. I was just coming to your house.

ARLECCHINO. I was just coming to your house.

PEDROLINO. That's what I said.

ARLECCHINO. That's what I said.

PEDROLINO. Oh, that's where I heard it. (*Satisfied, both turn as though the meeting were ended and cross to exit. Again they stop simultaneously at* R *and* L, *turn, and come together again at* C.)

BOTH. Your master and family are to come to our house. (*Both laugh.*) You first. (*Both laugh.*)

PEDROLINO. You.

ARLECCHINO. Your master and family are to come to our house.

PEDROLINO. No, your master and family are to come to our house, because my master is dying—again.

ARLECCHINO. So is mine. (*Both laugh.*)

PEDROLINO. My master can't possibly travel to your house.

ARLECCHINO. My master can't possibly come to your house; the journey would kill him.

PEDROLINO. What are we to do? (*Both think. An idea comes simultaneously.*)

ARLECCHINO. If my master can't go to your house—

PEDROLINO. And my master can't go to your house—

ARLECCHINO. And this is half way between—

BOTH. Why don't we both come here? Ah! (*They shake. Still holding hands, they start to exit in their respective directions, but the handclasp causes each to circle and head the wrong way out. They stop simultaneously, turn, put right hand behind the back, and using other hand and forefinger in a cautionary gesture, they give each other a wide berth as they go out the correct exits. A little catch-step and heel kick punctuate the exit.*)

A good *commedia* troupe had hundreds of these routines, each designed to fit specific characters and specific situations. Once the plot was worked out, performers could select the ones that fit and add more at places where the audience laughed or skip some when they weren't working well with the audience.

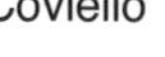

Coviello

Colombine

La Ballerina

Activities

1. Observe comic characters in television or in films. When they play characters or character types who appear several weeks in a row or in several similar films, they often develop routines like the one in *A Gap in Generations.* Identify as many of these as you can.

2. Make you own *lazzi.* Find a funny, interesting way to do each of the following activities: **(a)** putting on your shoes **(b)** eating a doughnut **(c)** picking up your books **(d)** putting on your coat.

Try these out individually. Then combine them into a scene in which you are trying to get to school in the morning.

3. Make up and try out *lazzi* for a number of situations. Write each of those situations on a piece of paper. Then have a partner choose one, and both of you improvise a scene. Use your *lazzi* when the chance arises. The partner should be the "straight man" in the scene.

4. Repeat Activity 3 with the partner now preparing his or her *lazzi* for the same scene. When you both improvise the scene, try to use your *lazzi* without destroying the other person's comic business.

5. Play the following scene from *A Gap in Generations.*
Pantalone is a middle-aged businessman who is bossy and miserly. Arlecchino is the same servant from the previous scene. Antonio and Lucia are servants in Signor Pantalone di Besignosi's house (sē′nyōr pant ə lō′ nē dē be sē nyō′ sē).

from ***A Gap in Generations***
by Jerry Blunt

ARLECCHINO. This is my master's house, Signor Pantalone di Besignosi. It is a very fine house, with exquisite furniture and hangings. (*He pantomimes the non-existent items.*) There are damask draperies, expensive paintings, done in oil, just like that fellow Titian does, and very special chairs and divans, marvelously constructed. If you see only one piece here now, it is because those fellows haven't had time to bring the rest on. But now you know the stuff is there—(*pointing offstage*)—and nobody is cheating you, it's all right, eh? So—we begin! But watch out, even in this fine house things go wrong. You are about to hear some fearful sounds. (*He crosses up into the set.*)

PANTALONE (*off* L). Oh, help me! help me! Arlecchino, you zanny, quick, quick. Do you hear me?

ARLECCHINO. Yes, Master, I hear you. I'm coming immediately, sooner or later. (*Runs* L, *stops, turns back to* C, *points to something in the air.*) Oh, a spider.

PANTALONE. Oh, what a spasm! What a pain! Oh, help me.

ARLECCHINO (*to audience*). A lit-t-tle spider.

PANTALONE. Someone, anyone, help!

ARLECCHINO (*still on spider in mid-air*). He's unwinding.

PANTALONE. Antonio, Lucia—help me!

ARLECCHINO (*calling off* R, *loudly*). Antonio, Lucia—Master calls!

PANTALONE. Help, help! (ANTONIO *and* LUCIA *enter* R.)

ANTONIO and **LUCIA.** Yes, yes, what is it? Yes, yes, who's calling?

ARLECCHINO. Run to the Master, quickly. We must all help him.

ANTONIO and **LUCIA** (*crossing* L *and out*). Be easy, Master. Here we are, don't strain. We are coming, Master, as fast as we can.

PANTALONE. You rogues, you zannies! Quick, take me in.

ANTONIO and **LUCIA** (*together, as they bring him in*). Master, do not bend over so, you'll die of the cramps. . . . Here, take my arm, rest on me. (PANTALONE *enters* L, *assisted by the servants.*)

PANTALONE (*stopping and bending*). Oh, what a twist this is. I'm all in knots. The devil will have me before the day is over.

ANTONIO and **LUCIA.** Easy, Master, take care. Quiet, let us help you.

PANTALONE (*seeing* ARLECCHINO *dangling the spider*). Ah, there's the scoundrel. I'll teach you to desert me in my dying hour. (*Swings cane.* ARLECCHINO *ducks,* PANTALONE *does a full circle, but when his cane comes to* ARLECCHINO *again the latter grabs it, does a full turn himself and ends with the cane striking the master in the stomach.*) Oh, you've killed me.

ARLECCHINO. I'm just giving you your cane, Master.

PANTALONE. Oh, thank you, Arlecchino. (*Realizes.*) Oh, you son of a coal miner. (*Starts to strike again but is stopped by another cramp.*) Help, help me down.

6. Identify from television, film, or the plays you have read as many stock character types as you can find. List the things that identify each character as a type (costumes, makeup, vocal habits, or physical routines). With a partner, pick one of these types to play. Think about the way your character acts and thinks. For example, sooner or later a miser always thinks about his money. When you feel that you understand how the character will act, improvise a scene with your partner in which the two characters meet.

Imagine that these two types are trapped together someplace, such as in an elevator. Improvise a scene between them. (One of the most popular plays in American history was put together exactly this way. Neil Simon's *The Odd Couple* is two hours of material about what happens when the world's biggest slob has to live with the world's neatest man.) If you feel adventurous, try the improvisation with three or four people.

7. Here is a very simple version of a *commedia* plot. Using your character types and *lazzi,* improvise an entire performance of the play. It should be about twenty minutes long.

Cast

FLAVIO, a young man
PANTALONE, Flavio's father, a businessman
ISABELLA, a young girl
LAURA, Isabella's mother
ARLECCHINO, Pantalone's servant
THE DOCTOR
THE CAPTAIN
SERVANTS and **TOWNSPEOPLE**

Argument of the Play

Flavio, Pantalone, and servants come to a strange town. By accident, after adventures with unusual townspeople, they arrive at their inn. Across the street live Laura and Isabella, whom they see walking together. Flavio immediately falls in love with Isabella. Pantalone also falls in love with Isabella, but Flavio thinks his father is in love with Laura, Isabella's widowed mother.

Both Flavio and Pantalone try to enlist Arlecchino's help in winning Isabella's hand in marriage.

The Captain, a military man, is engaged to Isabella, but she does not like him. He comes to claim her as his bride. She falls in love with Flavio and asks Arlecchino to help her escape the Captain. Laura wants to marry Pantalone because he is rich. She also tries to enlist Arlecchino's help.

Arlecchino tries to get the Doctor to declare Laura's house under quarantine, but this fails. He arranges things so that the Captain then frightens off Pantalone. Then with the help of some townspeople disguised as ghosts, he frightens the Captain away so that Flavio and Isabella are united, and Laura is free to pursue Pantalone.

Although this play seems complicated, it is really very short. If the performers can make it more complicated, they should. A *commedia* troupe would have added several more characters and had a number of *lazzi.* Such a play would have lasted two or three hours.

Remember as you perform the improvisation that what each character does must be logical. Arlecchino must find a way to get the Captain and Pantalone together, for example; they can't just meet and run away as soon as they see each other.

If this works and you become interested, try the same plot again with different character types in the roles. Compare the two performances, and discuss the variety of possibilities you found.

Chapter 31
The Renaissance in England and Spain

In those countries farthest from Italy, the *commedia dell'arte* had less influence. In England and Spain in particular, the rediscoveries of ancient literature produced quite different results.

There were traveling troupes of performers in both England and Spain during the sixteenth century. However, by the end of the century, Madrid and London were large enough to support actors who stayed in the city for most of the year. London had about 160,000 people when the first permanent theater was built in 1574. Many of these people did not go to the theater, of course, but to keep playgoers happy, acting troupes had to provide a variety of plays. By chance, England and Spain produced major playwrights who provided those plays.

Of the many plays Lope de Vega[1] (1562-1635) wrote for the actors of Madrid, more than 400 survive. He wrote tragedies, histories, and popular types of plays called cape-and-sword plays whose plots, though differing, centered around the theme of the highly developed Spanish sense of honor. The most popular of his plays today is *Fuente Ovejuna.*[2] Calderón de la Barca[3] (1600-1681) wrote about two hundred plays of many types, including a number of lyrical religious plays. Two other important Spanish playwrights of the period were Tirso de Molina[4] (1584-1648), who wrote the first Don Juan play, and Miguel de Cervantes (1547-1616), who also wrote the novel *Don Quixote.*[5]

In England, the playwrights of the time were overshadowed by one man, William Shakespeare (1564-1616). His thirty-eight plays were written in about twenty years while he was also acting and managing a theater in London. His tragedies include *Hamlet, Macbeth,* and *Romeo and Juliet;* his comedies include *As You Like It, A Midsummer Night's Dream,* and *The Taming of the Shrew;* his history plays include *Richard III* and the plays about Henry IV and his friend Falstaff.

Other prominent English playwrights of the period were Ben Jonson (1572-

1. **Lope de Vega** (lō′pā dā bā′gä).
2. ***Fuente Ovejuna*** (fwen′tā ō bā hün′ä), *The Sheep Well.*
3. **Calderón de la Barca** (käl′dər on dā lä bär′kä).
4. **Tirso de Molina** (tir′sō dā mō lēn′ä).
5. **Miguel de Cervantes . . . *Don Quixote*** (mig wel′ dā sər vän′tēz″ . . . don kē hō′tē *or* kwik′sət).

Engraving of a scene from *A Midsummer Night's Dream* c. 1800

1637), whose comedies *Volpone* and *The Alchemist* satirized society in ways that make the plays amusing today; Christopher Marlowe (1564-1593), whose tragedies such as *Dr. Faustus* revealed his talent for writing blank verse; and Thomas Dekker (1572?-1632?), who wrote a number of popular comedies like *The Shoemaker's Holiday.*

In both Spain and England, the first permanent theaters were different from those in the rest of Europe because they were adapted from the traditions of the traveling players. Formerly, actors had played wherever they could find a place, usually the courtyard of an inn where travelers stayed and where the local people came for drink and entertainment. The inns were usually horseshoe-shaped, with a courtyard in the middle. Actors set up platforms in the courtyard where they could charge admission and control who entered. When theaters were built, many of the features of the courtyard were retained.

In England most public theaters were square or octagonal. In the middle was a platform which extended from one side, a thrust stage. Audience surrounded the actors on three sides. Around the stage were balconies. Admission to the balconies cost more than admission to the ground floor, or pit, where the audience stood to watch the show. Actors made their entrances from doors in the back wall and played most of their scenes on the platform with little or no scenery. Some theaters had balconies over the stage which were used in parts of some plays. Spanish stages, called *corrales,*[6] were almost the same, except that more scenery was used at the back of the stage area. Many of the theaters had no roof so that plays could be performed in daylight.

In larger theaters 1500 or more people crowded into the audience space, many standing, some sitting in the balconies; sometimes a wealthy few sat on the stage itself.

Since in public theaters, the audience was varied—rich and poor, sophisticated and illiterate—actors and plays needed to be full of life and variety to hold everyone's attention. Audiences were enthusiastic and quick to show approval or disapproval of performers.

The thrust stage did not allow for much scenery, so playwrights incorporated information about shifts in time and place into the play itself. Both comic and tragic scenes were present in the same play and actors had to be versatile in their abilities since many kinds of plays were produced every year.

Women did not act on the stage in England, and women's parts were played by boys. In Spain, however, as in the Italian *commedia,* acting companies included women.

In England and Spain, despite the popularity of the theater with the general public, the sixteenth century was not always an easy time for actors or the theater.

The actor was never completely at home with society in general, and moralists in particular. Officials worried not only about the possibilities of disease being spread among audiences; the theater and actors and actresses were thought by some to be immoral influences. In England Thomas White neatly summed up the case against theaters:

> Looke but vppon the common playes of London, and
> see the multitude that flocketh to them and fol-
> loweth them: beholde the sumptuous Theater houses,
> a continuall monument of London prodigalitie and
> folly, But I vnderstande they are now forbidden
> bycause of the plague. I like the pollicye well
> if it hold still, for a disease is but bodged or
> patched vp that is not cured in the cause, and the
> cause of plagues is sinne, if you looke to it well:
> and the cause of sinne are playes: therefore the
> cause of plagues are playes.
>
> (from *A Sermon preached at Paules Cross . . . in the time of the Plague, 1578.)*

As a result of Puritan objections, the theaters in London were closed altogether from 1642 to 1660, and many were torn down.

6. ***corrales*** (kôr äl′ēs).

Activities

1. Your library will have most of the plays of Shakespeare. With the help of your teacher, select a short scene for use in class.

2. A great deal of research has been done on sixteenth-century theaters, especially the Globe, which was Shakespeare's theater. Find a picture of the Globe in a library and make a model of the Globe Theater. Bring it to class and explain how the stage works.

3. Select one of the scenes from Unit III which you have already performed. Arrange the class in a horseshoe shape and perform that scene again in the middle of that horseshoe. What changes did you have to make in the way you originally did the scene?

Try the same scene out-of-doors with the audience standing up. What other changes in performance have to be made?

The Stratford Festival Stage, Stratford, Ontario, Canada

Chapter 32
The Proscenium Stage

At the time that the *commedia* and the Shakespeare plays were at their peak of popularity, several innovations, begun principally in the private theaters of the Italian nobility, were destined to change all theater.

The first of these was a new form of performance. During the Renaissance, scholars noted that, in part, Greek tragedies were probably sung. When new tragedies were written, some playwrights experimented with music. Almost by accident they invented opera. By 1607 when the Italian composer, Claudio Monteverdi[1] (1567-1643) produced *Orfeo,* there was more music than dialogue in some plays. At first, only wealthy Italians paid for the privilege of seeing and hearing beautiful music combined with extravagant scenic effects. But in 1637 the first public opera house opened in Venice, and opera became so popular that more opera houses were soon built, not only in Italy, but in Paris and other cities in Europe.

The second innovation led to a new way of staging those performances. During the Italian Renaissance, artists gradually developed the principles of perspective painting. These are based on the observation that objects further away look smaller and that parallel lines appear to converge in the distance. Thus, painters found a way to make a flat painting look three-dimensional. As the public accepted this type of painting, audiences began to demand similar painting in the spectacle of the stage performances. Operas used lavish spectacular scenic effects, supported by the wealth of the audience, and painters gradually began to use perspective techniques to make those effects more realistic.

However, perspective painting is effective only when viewed from one angle, directly in front of the stage. Also, if scenery is to be changed, offstage areas have to be hidden from the audience. Producers developed the *proscenium* arch, which made a frame around the stage. The frame hid the scenery offstage and completed the illusion of the perspective painting on the scenery.

Eventually, producers looked for even more spectacular ways to utilize and alter scenery. What we call the *wing and border* setting was developed. In this type of setting, flats were constructed along each side of the stage, near the wings, and parallel to the front of the stage. A narrow strip of canvas, called

1. **Monteverdi** (mon″tə ver′dē).

Scene from *Twelfth Night*

a *border,* was hung from overhead and stretched horizontally from flat to flat. It was painted to blend with the flats on either side. For example, if the setting was an outdoor one, flats might be painted as trees or buildings and the border would depict sky or clouds. Another piece of painted canvas, called a *drop,* was then suspended from the ceiling to the stage floor at the back. All of these pieces were painted in perspective so that, from the audience, the set looked three-dimensional. To change the scene, stagehands slid off one set of flats and raised the border and drop into the space above the proscenium to reveal the next painted set. Perspective settings were quickly adopted elsewhere, and by the beginning of the eighteenth century, almost every theater in Europe had a proscenium stage.

Of course, the scenery had now become too complicated and expensive to risk in outdoor performance, so more theaters were closed in and plays were performed by candlelight. Not only did this cause audience complaints about the smoke obscuring the view of the stage, but it also forced major changes in audiences, the style of acting, and playwriting.

First, fewer people could be accommodated in an indoor theater. Second, scenery effects were expensive, so prices went up as well, which drove many of the poorer and less dedicated theater-goers away. Finally, the dim lighting and the problems of perspective eliminated much of the physical action of earlier plays by forcing the actors to stay in a limited area at the downstage edge of the stage. This in turn led to a verbal kind of play in which the actors stood

A Perspective setting

still for long periods and spoke long speeches. Since audiences were more uniformly educated and were members of the upper class, playwrights were able to concentrate on wit, style, and beauty of expression.

Because English theaters had been closed by the Puritans at this time, the French led the way in this new kind of play. Pierre Corneille[2] (1606-1684) led many French writers in trying to reproduce the ancient Greek tragedies in French verse. They even established a strict set of rules for the writing of plays. The tragic plays reached their peak in the works of Jean Racine[3] (1639-1699), who tried to turn interest to complex characters in simple plots. For the most part, however, playwrights emphasized plot over character for the next two hundred years.

One of the greatest of all comic playwrights was Molière[4] (1622-1673). An actor who had toured with an acting company, Molière managed a theatrical company, acted, and produced his own comedies. Many of his plays were based on *commedia*-style characters and plots but were more subtle and sophisticated than their models. Many of his plays are still performed, including *The Miser, Tartuffe,*[5] *The Misanthrope,* and *The Imaginary Invalid.*

---

2. **Corneille** (kôr nā′ *or* kôr ne′yə).
3. **Racine** (ra sēn′).
4. **Molière** (mō lyer′).
5. **Tartuffe** (tär tüf′).

Theatre Royal, Paris. Seventeenth century actors, Moliere at far left.

After English theaters reopened in 1660, with the restoration of the king, the proscenium style of the French playhouses was adopted. The witty, cynical comedies of William Congreve (1670-1729), William Wycherly (1604?-1716), and George Farquhar (1678-1707), and the tragedies of John Dryden (1631-1700) entertained the new, sophisticated audiences of the time.

Throughout the eighteenth century, fashions in play content changed as society changed, but the proscenium style of staging gradually became the only acceptable way to produce a play. It spread throughout all of Europe and to America.

Playwrights of talent and influence appeared in many countries. Oliver Goldsmith's popular *She Stoops to Conquer* (1773), first produced in London, and Richard Brinsley Sheridan's *The Rivals* (1775) and *The School for Scandal* (1777) rank with the best comedies of any era, as do the comedies of the French writer Beaumarchais[6] (1732-1799). Later, German playwrights such as Lessing (1729-1781), Goethe[7] (1749-1832), and Schiller (1759-1805) intro-

6. **Beaumarchais** (bō mar shā′).
7. **Goethe** (gā′tə).

duced the emotionalism that would become dominant in nineteenth-century plays.

That emotionalism was encouraged by the gradual return of larger audiences to the theater. These audiences were first encouraged by the development of the *pantomime* in the eighteenth century. Pantomimes were spectacular entertainments that combined mime, music, and lavish scenery. They were developed in response to a complicated set of licensing laws which were not repealed until the early nineteenth century. When that happened, the older theaters combined the Romantic emotionalism with the music and spectacle of the pantomimes into what we call *melodrama.*

The development of oil lamps, then limelight, and then gaslight made it possible for theaters to be illuminated more brightly, and the size of theaters could be increased once again. Mass audiences, many of whom were nearly illiterate, demanded spectacle. Increasingly greater emphasis was put on the scenery, so that it became essential to the action of the show. Melodramas included horse races, train wrecks, battles at sea, and dramatic rescues from raging streams. Characters became simplified, with the clearly defined heroes, villains, and maidens in distress (recognizable as *commedia* stock characters) who appear in films and television of the present day.

Activity

Perform the following scene from Act V of the comedy *She Stoops to Conquer.* This is the first scene in this unit in which scenery is essential and it cannot be performed without the tree. However, in class you may substitute a chair or anything similar to hide behind.

As you prepare the scene, decide where the most dramatic moment occurs. Tony Lumpkin, a "good old country boy" of his time, is Mrs. Hardcastle's son by her first husband. Mrs. Hardcastle wants Tony to marry Constance, a wealthy sophisticated young lady, but since neither Tony nor Constance are interested, Tony decides to help Constance win the young man she does want. To do this, Tony tricks his mother into taking a journey, then drives her in circles all night in her carriage on her own estate. He even runs the carriage through the pond, which is why she is soaking wet when she appears in this scene. Mr. Hardcastle, a kindly man, is her husband and Tony's stepfather, although the term "father-in-law" is used in the scene.

Tony is directed to speak once in an *aside.* This is a convention in which the actor or actress speaks directly to the audience, but no other characters on stage are supposed to hear what is said. When he says, "hem," he is probably clearing his throat very loudly. Tony's first line is spoken to the man with whom Constance is in love and who has just exited.

from ***She Stoops to Conquer***
by Oliver Goldsmith

TONY. Here she comes. Vanish. She's got from the pond, and draggled up to the waist like a mermaid.

Enter MRS. HARDCASTLE.

MRS. HARDCASTLE. Oh, Tony, I'm killed. Shook. Battered to death. I shall never survive it. That last jolt that laid us against the quickset hedge has done my business.

TONY. Alack, mamma, it was all your own fault. You would be for running away by night, without knowing one inch of the way.

MRS. HARDCASTLE. I wish we were at home again. I never met so many accidents in so short a journey. Drenched in the mud, overturned in a ditch, stuck fast in a slough, jolted to a jelly, and at last to lose our way! Whereabouts do you think we are, Tony?

TONY. By my guess we should be upon Crackskull Common, about forty miles from home.

MRS. HARDCASTLE. O lud! O lud! the most-notorious spot in all the country. We only want a robbery to make a complete night on't.

TONY. Don't be afraid, mamma, don't be afraid. Two of the five that kept here are hanged, and the other three may not find us. Don't be afraid. Is that a man that's galloping behind us? No; it's only a tree. Don't be afraid.

MRS. HARDCASTLE. The fright will certainly kill me.

TONY. Do you see anything like a black hat moving behind the thicket?

MRS. HARDCASTLE. O death!

TONY. No, it's only a cow. Don't be afraid, mamma, don't be afraid.

MRS. HARDCASTLE. As I'm alive, Tony, I see a man coming towards us. Ah! I'm sure on't. If he perceives us, we are undone.

TONY (*aside*). Father-in-law, by all that's unlucky, come to take one of his night walks. (*To her*) Ah, it's a highwayman, with pistols as long as my arm. An ill-looking fellow.

MRS. HARDCASTLE. Good heaven defend us! He approaches.

TONY. Do you hide yourself in that thicket, and leave me to manage him. If there be any danger I'll cough and cry hem. When I cough be sure to keep close. (MRS. HARDCASTLE *hides behind a tree in the back scene.*)

Enter HARDCASTLE.

HARDCASTLE. I'm mistaken, or I heard voices of people in want of help. Oh, Tony, is that you? I did not expect you so soon back. Are your mother and her charge in safety?

TONY. Very safe, sir, at my aunt Pedigree's. Hem.

MRS. HARDCASTLE (*from behind*). Ah! I find there's danger.

Tony Lumpkin and Mrs. Hardcastle

HARDCASTLE. Forty miles in three hours; sure, that's too much, my youngster.

TONY. Stout horses and willing minds make short journeys, as they say. Hem.

MRS. HARDCASTLE (*from behind*). Sure he'll do the dear boy no harm.

HARDCASTLE. But I heard a voice here; I should be glad to know from whence it came.

TONY. It was I, sir, talking to myself, sir. I was saying that forty miles in four hours was very good going. Hem. As to be sure it was. Hem. I have got a sort of cold by being out in the air. We'll go in if you please. Hem.

HARDCASTLE. But if you talked to yourself, you did not answer yourself. I am certain I heard two voices, and am resolved (*Raising his voice*) to find the other out.

MRS. HARDCASTLE (*from behind*). Oh! he's coming to find me out. Oh!

TONY. What need you go, sir, if I tell you? Hem. I'll lay down my life for the truth—hem—I'll tell you all sir. (*Detaining him*)

HARDCASTLE. I tell you I will not be detained. I insist on seeing. It's in vain to expect I'll believe you.

MRS. HARDCASTLE (*running forward from behind*). O lud, he'll murder my poor boy, my darling. Here, good gentleman, whet your rage upon me. Take my money, my life, but spare that young gentleman, spare my child, if you have any mercy.

HARDCASTLE. My wife! as I'm a Christian. From whence can she come, or what does she mean?

MRS. HARDCASTLE (*kneeling*). Take compassion on us, good Mr. Highwayman. Take our money, our watches, all we have, but spare our lives. We will never bring you to justice, indeed we won't, good Mr. Highwayman.

HARDCASTLE. I believe the woman's out of her senses. What, Dorothy, don't you know *me?*

MRS. HARDCASTLE. Mr. Hardcastle, as I'm alive! My fears blinded me. But who, my dear, could have expected to meet you here, in this frightful place, so far from home. What has brought you to follow us?

HARDCASTLE. Sure, Dorothy, you have not lost your wits! So far from home, when you are within forty yards of your own door! (*To him*) This is one of your old tricks, you graceless rogue, you! (*To her*) Don't you know the gate, and the mulberry-tree; and don't you remember the horsepond, my dear?

MRS. HARDCASTLE. Yes, I shall remember the horsepond as long as I live; I have caught my death in it. (*To Tony*) And is it to you, you graceless varlet, I owe all this? I'll teach you to abuse your mother, I will.

TONY. Mother, all the parish says you have spoiled me, and so you may take the fruits on't.

MRS. HARDCASTLE. I'll spoil you, I will.

(*Follows him off the stage. Exit*)

HARDCASTLE. There's morality, however, in his reply.

(*Exit*)

At its height in the nineteenth century, the melodrama, as you will see from this excerpt from *The Octoroon* (1859) by Dion Boucicault (dī′on bü′sē kâlt), was spectacular.

In this scene, McClosky, the villain, has murdered a friend of Wahnotee, an Indian, and has been captured on a steamboat.

from ***The Octoroon***
by Dion Boucicault

(*Fire seen.*)

JACKSON (*re-entering*). We are catching fire forward: quick, cut free from the shore.

Treadmills: one of the many kinds of stage machinery used for producing optical effects.

RATTS. All hands aboard there—cut the starn ropes—give her headway!
ALL. Ay, ay! (*A cry of "Fire" heard–steam whistle noise*.)
RATTS. Cut all away, for'ard—overboard with every bale afire.
(*The Steamer moves off with the fire still blazing.*)
(M'CLOSKY *re-enters, swimming*.)
M'CLOSKY. Ha! have I fixed ye? Burn! burn! that's right. You thought you had cornered me, did ye? As I swam down, I thought I heard something in the water, as if pursuing me—one of them darned alligators, I suppose—they swarm hereabout—may they crunch every limb of ye. (*Exit*.)
(WAHNOTEE *is seen swimming. He finds trail and follows* M'CLOSKY. *The Steamer floats on at back, burning*.)

SCENE 2. (*In a Cane-brake Bayou, on a bank, with a canoe near by,* M'CLOSKY *is seen asleep.*)
M'CLOSKY. Burn, burn! blaze away! How the flames crack. I'm not guilty; would ye murder me? Cut, cut the rope—I choke—choke!—Ah! (*Waking.*) Hello! where am I? Why, I was dreaming—curse it! I can never sleep now without dreaming. Hush! I thought I heard the sound of a paddle in the water. All night, as I fled through the canebrake, I heard footsteps behind me. I lost them in the cedar swamp—again they haunted my path down the bayou, moving as I moved, resting when I rested—hush! there again!—no; it was only the wind over the canes. The sun is rising. I must launch my dug-out, and put for the bay, and in a few hours I shall be safe from pursuit on board of one of the coasting schooners that run from Galveston to Matagorda. In a

little time this darned business will blow over, and I can show again. Hark! there's that noise again! If it was the ghost of that murdered boy haunting me! Well—I didn't mean to kill him, did I? Well, then, what has my all-cowardly heart got to skeer me so for?

(*He gets in canoe and rows off*. WAHNOTEE *appears in another canoe. He gets out and finds trail and paddles off after* M'CLOSKY.)

Activity

Prepare a report for the class explaining how special effects were created for melodramas. A number of theater history books should help you in your research; your teacher will be able to give you some specific advice about where to look.

Not all plays of the early- and middle-nineteenth century were built around spectacular effects. Many comedies and simple, sentimental dramas were popular. In this scene from *Rip Van Winkle*, Rip has awakened and come home after being under a spell for twenty years. He is sitting at the village inn when he sees Gretchen, his wife, and Derrick, the greedy villain of the piece. Meenie is Rip's daughter, whom he hasn't seen since she was a baby.

The American actor Joseph Jefferson was so successful in this role that he toured the country in it for more than twenty years. Notice how the asides are used to increase the sentimentality and emotion of the scene. As you play the scene be sure to use them as the playwright has directed.

from ***Rip Van Winkle***
by Dion Boucicault

(*Enter* DERRICK, *followed by* GRETCHEN.)

DERRICK. So you have come to that conclusion, have you?

GRETCHEN. I cannot accept this sacrifice.

RIP (*starting from his reverie, and turning to look at her*). Why, that is Gretchen's voice. (*As he recognizes her, and sees how aged she is.*) My, my! Is that my wife?

DERRICK. Oh, you can't accept! Won't you kindly allow me a word on the subject?

RIP (*aside, humorously*). No, indeed, she will not. Now, my friend, you are going to cotch it.

GRETCHEN. There is a limit even to my patience. Don't drive me to it.

RIP (*aside, drolly*). Take care, my friend; take care.

DERRICK. Look you, woman; Meenie has consented to marry my nephew. She has pledged her word to do so on condition that I settle an annuity on you.

GRETCHEN. I won't allow my child to break her heart.

DERRICK. You won't allow? Dare to raise your voice, dare but to speak except as I command you, you shall repent it to the last hour of your life.

RIP (*expectantly*). Now she'll knock him down, flat as a flounder.

DERRICK (*sneeringly*). You won't allow? This is something new. Who are you; do you think you are dealing with your first husband?

GRETCHEN. Alas, no; I wish I was.

RIP (*lost in wonderment*). My, my, if Rip was alive, he never would have believed it!

DERRICK. So you thought to get the upper hand of me, when you married me; didn't you?

GRETCHEN. I thought to get a home for my little girl—shelter, and food; want drove me to your door, and I married you for a meal's victuals for my sick child.

DERRICK. So you came to me as if I was a poor-house, eh? Then you can't complain of the treatment you received. You sacrificed yourself for Meenie, and the least she can do now, is to do the same for you. In an hour, the deeds will be ready. Now, just you take care that no insolent interference of yours spoils my plans; do you hear?

GRETCHEN. Yes, sir.

DERRICK. Why can't you be kind and affectionate to her, as I am to you. There, go and blubber over her; that's your way. You are always pretending to be miserable.

GRETCHEN. Alas, no sir! I am always pretending to be happy.

DERRICK. Don't cry. I won't have it; come now, none of that. If you come home today with red eyes, and streaky cheeks, I'll give you something to cry for; now you know what's for supper.

(*Exit*.)

RIP (*still amazed*). Well, if I hadn't seen it, I never would have believed it!

GRETCHEN (*absorbed in her grief*). Oh, wretch that I am, I must consent, or that man will surely thrust her out of doors to starve, to beg, and to become—(*Seeing* RIP.) Yes, to become a thing of rags and misery, like that poor soul.

RIP. She always drived the beggars away; I suppose I must go. (*Getting up, and starting to go*.)

GRETCHEN (*taking penny from her pocket*). Here, my poor man, take this. It is only a penny; but take it, and may God bless you, poor wanderer, so old, so helpless. Why do you come to this strange place, so far from home?

RIP (*keeping his face turned away from her*). She don't know me; she don't know me!

GRETCHEN. Are you alone in the world?

RIP (*trying to bring himself to look directly at* GRETCHEN). My wife asks me if I'm alone.

GRETCHEN. Come with me. How feeble he is; there, lean on me. Come to yonder house, and there you shall rest your limbs by the fire. (GRETCHEN *takes his arm, and puts it in her own. As they move towards her house,* RIP *stops, and, with an effort, turns and looks her full in the face, with a penetrating gaze, as if imploring recognition, but there is none; and, sadly shaking his head, he shrinks into himself, and allows her to lead him tottering off.*)

Chapter 33
The Rise of Realism

By about 1900, a new style of acting had appeared, generally called *realistic*. This was encouraged by the literary theories of the time and made possible by a number of inventions.

Formerly, actors' facial expressions were not nearly so important as bodily movement. Any subtlety in movement or gesture was lost on the audience. By the turn of the century most theaters had electric lights, which made it possible for actors to modify exaggerated gestures and to express emotion through facial expression rather than flamboyant action.

The invention of greasepaint by Ludwig Leichner in 1865 also made it possible for actors to give more realistic performances. Before that, most makeup was a heavy powder, often with a lead base, which either melted away in performance or solidified to produce a masklike appearance. Greasepaint was not only more reliable, it allowed for more subtle and realistic makeups.

With the development of the *box set,* more realistic settings were possible. Flats were arranged to form three walls, and a ceiling replaced the borders. Formerly, doors, windows, and even some furniture were merely painted onto a flat. With the use of the box set, actual doors and windows were built into the flats, and the use of real furniture became more common.

After the invention of the motion-picture camera, oppotunities for spectacle, variety, and physical humor expanded, and the audiences who had once filled the melodrama theaters shifted to the movie theaters. After sound films were successfully established in 1927, the live theater once more began to cater to a more select, wealthier, and better educated audience for its support.

The development of realistic writing, of novels of social criticism, and of plays that explored the lives of ordinary people with the problems of ordinary life rather than melodramatic heroes or the wealthy and titled, began about the middle of the nineteenth century. But this trend did not really affect the stage until the plays of Henrik Ibsen (1828-1906), appeared. In plays like *A Doll's House*, *The Wild Duck,* and *An Enemy of the People*, he not only challenged many of the social conventions of his time, but he developed complicated characters rather than complicated plots. George Bernard Shaw (1856-1950), with plays such as *Arms and the Man* (1894), Eugene Brieux in France, and Gerhart Hauptmann in Germany broadened the range of realistic topics and characters,

Scene from *The Little Foxes* performed at Sacred Heart Elementary School, Winnetka, Illinois by the Tower Players

a movement that was to continue into the twentieth century.

The person who had the most influence on the theater, however was not a playwright but a Russian actor and director named Konstantin Stanislavski (1863-1938). He developed a completely new method of training actors. His theories, called the Stanislavski Method, or just The Method in America, concentrated on training the actor to use his own emotion and imagination rather than any predetermined set of gestures or intonations. "What we need are simple, expressive actions with an inner content," he declared. He developed exercises and rehearsal techniques that were designed to produce the inner content that made the actions genuine in performance. He introduced the ideas of goals and subtexts which are a basic part of all actors' training today and which are introduced in Unit III.

Stanislavski found the perfect playwright to provide the plays for his theater and newly trained actors. Anton Chekhov (1860-1904) wrote only four major plays, but all four became classics. *The Sea Gull*, *Uncle Vanya*, *Three Sisters*, and *The Cherry Orchard* all depicted the fading of the landowner class in Russia and did so through a detailed study of people living through small, everyday events. These events were dramatic and emotionally important, but the characters did not directly express that emotion.

The most striking use of the Stanislavski approach has been in film acting. When a face is apt to be as much as twenty feet tall on a movie screen, the actors have to be absolutely relaxed and natural looking. They can also be

Kate Redi as Mme. Ranevskaya and Douglas Campbell as Lopahin in *The Cherry Orchard,* directed by Brian Jackson, Stratford, Ontario, Canada 1965

extremely subtle; many screen actors do their most expressive work with their eyes and small facial expressions, all of which stem from the realistic acting techniques first popularized by Stanislavski.

One of the most unusual aspects of realistic plays is that emotions are not actually expressed in the words spoken, or if they are, they are purposely expressed very poorly. Odd as it seems, in a realistic play the focus is often not so much on what is said as on what is not said. In almost all types of plays before this time, an emotional moment produced a long speech, sometimes in poetry. You can detect this difference in the two scenes that follow.

Activities

1. The following scene from *The Cherry Orchard* by Chekhov occurs in the last act of the play; it is one of the most moving moments in the play. Lopahin is a young businessman who has bought a country estate from a family who has lost its money. Varya is about 24, the adopted daughter of the family. They are ready to leave the estate, and Lopahin is waiting to take over the house. Play the scene with that information in mind.

As you work on the scene, several questions should occur to you. For example, why does Varya suddenly break into tears? Why does Lopahin start to talk about the weather? Why are there so many pauses? What is Varya looking for? Why is she looking for it just now? Why has Lopahin been waiting for the off-stage call? Supply logical answers for these questions, and use them to achieve your goals when you play the scene.

from ***The Cherry Orchard***
by Anton Chekhov
translated by Robert Corrigan

VARYA. That's strange, I can't find it. . . .

LOPAHIN. What are you looking for?

VARYA. I packed it myself, and I can't remember . . . (*A pause.*)

LOPAHIN. Where are you going to now, Varvara Mihailovna?

VARYA. I? To the Rogulins. I've taken a job as their housekeeper.

LOPAHIN. That's in Yashnevo, isn't it? Almost seventy miles from here. (*A pause.*) So this is the end of life in this house. . . .

VARYA (*still fussing with the luggage*). Where could it be? Perhaps I put it in the trunk? Yes, life in this house has come to an end . . . there won't be any more. . . .

LOPAHIN. And I'm going to Kharkov. . . . On the next train. I've got a lot of work to do there. I'm leaving Epihodov here. . . . I've hired him.

VARYA. Really! . . .

LOPAHIN. Remember, last year at this time it was snowing already, but now it's still so bright and sunny. Though it's cold . . . Three degrees of frost.

VARYA. I haven't looked. (A *pause*.) Besides, our thermometer's broken. . . .

(A *pause. A voice is heard from outside the door*.)

VOICE. Yermolay Alexeyevich!

LOPAHIN (*as if he had been waiting for it*). I'm coming! Right away! (*Goes out quickly*.)

(**VARYA** *sits on the floor, with her head on a bundle of clothes, crying quietly.)*

2. Play the Chekhov scene again, with the added knowledge that you didn't know the first time: When the scene occurs in the play, everyone knows that Lopahin is in love with Varya, and Varya is in love with Lopahin. Just before her entrance, her mother has convinced Lopahin that, if he will only ask her, Varya will agree to marry him. She has sent Varya into the room and told her that he is finally going to propose. Neither of them has ever had the courage to tell the other of his or her feelings. If they do not get together now, they will never see each other again.

How does this information affect the answers to the questions you asked in Activity 2? Try to use this new information in your performance. The characters' emotions should be conveyed by voice, action, and facial expression.

3. Many realistic scenes depend on the use of properties to give the appearance of reality and to help express emotions. With one or more partners, try one of the following scenes. Use real props. Do not speak a word; try to express the relationships only by the way you use the properties.

(a) Two teenagers have had an argument. One of their parents has calmed it down long enough to start dinner but has not solved the problem yet.

(b) A girl and a boy are studying in a library and decide they would like to get to know each other better.

(c) A boy and a girl who have just broken up their romance find themselves studying at the same table in a library.

(d) Use the same situations as **(b)** or **(c)** except that two friends at the table are watching and trying to help.

4. As you probably noticed in the scene from *The Cherry Orchard*, stage directions are important in many realistic plays. In the following scene, almost everything that happens is in the stage directions, so pay careful attention to them.

Vera and Dennis are married. Marjorie is his mother, who is living with them. Pam and Neil are friends who have come for a small birthday celebration for Dennis. Marjorie thinks that Vera is an unsuitable wife for her son and has frequently made it a point to let her know that. Vera is beginning to break under the strain.

The important thing to remember when playing this scene is the way Marjorie and Vera understand what lies under the relatively innocent lines. If you play Marjorie, do not worry about showing her age; play her goal. Everything takes place around a table set up on the patio. Marjorie is sitting off to one side, away from the table, to be out of the draft.

from ***Just Between Ourselves***
by Alan Ayckbourn

VERA *resumes pouring tea, this time* NEIL's *cup. As she starts this—*

MARJORIE (*suddenly*). Where's his cake?

VERA. What?

MARJORIE. Where's Dennis's cake?

DENNIS. Ah . . . (*He rises expectantly*)

PAM *and* NEIL *also look more or less expectant*

VERA. We didn't make one this year, Mother, did we?

MARJORIE. Dennis always has a cake.

VERA. Yes, but you've been ill, Mother, remember.

MARJORIE. You could have made him a cake, Vera. (VERA *gives* NEIL *his tea.)*

DENNIS (*mouthing,* sotto-voce *across to* MARJORIE). It doesn't matter, Mother.

MARJORIE (*mouthing likewise*). She could have made you a cake.

VERA *becomes aware of this silent conversation.* DENNIS *and* MARJORIE *continue mouthing and gesturing until* DENNIS *becomes aware of* VERA's *gaze.* VERA *leans forward to take two more cups.* DENNIS *passes them to her, then sits and gives a final gesture to silence his mother.*

VERA (*pouring* DENNIS's *tea*). You know what I'm like with cakes. And I can't do all that icing like you do. I just get it all over everything. We should have asked Mrs. Mandlesham . . .

MARJORIE. You don't need to ask anyone how to ice a cake.

VERA. Well, I can't do it.

PAM. Nor can I.

DENNIS. It's all right, mother, it's all right.

VERA *gives* DENNIS *his tea. She offers* DENNIS *a cucumber sandwich. He takes one. She offers* NEIL *who declines. She offers* PAM.

PAM. What about your mother? (PAM *takes the plate from* VERA, *rises, and goes and offers the sandwiches to* MARJORIE. VERA *pours her own tea*.)

MARJORIE (*unaware of* PAM). Ever since he was a little boy, he's always had his cake. Even when your father was dying, Dennis, I still made you your cake.

PAM *gives up proffering the plate, waves it at* MARJORIE *somewhat 'V' sign-like and replaces it on the table, then sits again.*

DENNIS. Yes, marvellous they were too, mother. Marvellous.

A long silence. VERA *counts the cups, then reaches for the hot water jug. She catches the sugar spoon with her wrist, sending sugar high in the air.* VERA *attempts to ignore this. The others concentrate their attentions elsewhere. Shakily,* VERA *replenishes the teapot with hot water. The others find this, despite themselves, compulsory viewing. She returns hot water jug to the table, as it happens close to* NEIL's *place.* NEIL, *nervous, shifts his legs. Having safely negotiated this,* VERA *smiles round. Everyone looks away.* VERA *reaches for the remaining empty cup and saucer. She rattles it dangerously but places it in front of her. She puts milk in the cup. She starts pouring tea.* MARJORIE's *voice suddenly breaks the silence.*

MARJORIE. Remember when you were in the army. (VERA's *tea-pouring experiences a hiccup*.) I parcelled them up and and I sent them to you overseas.

VERA. Yes, well, I'm very sorry. (*She rises with the cup, preparing to take it across to* MARJORIE.)

MARJORIE. I think the least you could have done, Vera, is to make him a cake. It was really very thoughtless to forget . . .

The teacup begins to vibrate uncontrollably in VERA's *hand*.

VERA (*through gritted teeth*). Will someone take this cup, please. Will someone take this cup from me.

PAM (*rising and taking the cup from her*). Here. Here, all right.

PAM *takes cup to* MARJORIE. VERA *sits.* NEIL *rises, takes a couple of sandwiches, puts them on a sideplate and takes them over to* MARJORIE.

NEIL. Would you like a sandwich, Mrs . . .

PAM *returns and sits.*

MARJORIE. Yes, I might as well have a sandwich. NEIL *returns and sits. Pause.* Seeing as she hasn't made a cake.

VERA (*spilling a cup and saucer*). Oh.

Tea pours all over the table, running down between the slats. NEIL *and* PAM *rise hastily.* DENNIS, *still seated, suppresses his mirth.*

Chapter 34
Artistic Reactions to Realism

Almost as soon as realistic plays were introduced, many playwrights and directors reacted against them. Some of those who rejected realism were inspired instead by modern movements in painting, sculpture, poetry, and music. These people were sometimes known as the *avant-garde,* a French term for those who are ahead of their time in creating new methods or ideas. Still others continued to be inspired by popular vaudeville—entertainment featuring a variety of acts, such as songs, dances, and skits; the old pantomimes; and the ballad-operas of the eighteenth century, which combined satirical text with songs.

The avant-gardists, after about 1920, tried a number of different experiments and ideas. The best-known of these included several "isms."

The aim of *expressionism* was to use all the parts of a play—scenery, cos-

Set by Lee Simonson for *The Adding Machine* 1923

tume, and acting—to express an emotional state or feeling. This feeling was often in the mind of a central character, and the plays were like the character's dreams (or nightmares). The movement began in Germany about 1910 with plays by Georg Kaiser, and was exemplified in a number of American plays in the 1920s. The most successful of these were *The Adding Machine* by Elmer Rice (1892-1967) and *The Hairy Ape* and *The Emperor Jones* by Eugene O'Neill (1888-1953).

Symbolism was an outgrowth of the work begun by a number of French poets, who used characters and setting to stand for mental states. These techniques were applied to the theater by the Belgian playwright Maurice Maeterlinck (1862-1949) and used by many different writers for many different purposes. Reality was suspended, and realistic characters found themselves in unusual places and situations chosen to make a symbolic point rather than to depict ordinary events of life. A number of playwrights in many countries tried at least one play in this style, but the most successful and popular was probably *The Skin of Our Teeth* by the American playwright, Thornton Wilder (1897-1975).

Absurdism began from the philosophical idea that life in the modern world is irrational and pointless. The movement began in France and had a major influence throughout Europe and America. In a typical absurdist play, characters speak in pointless, often amusing, exchanges and are involved in a series of actions that seem to be completely arbitrary. The most widely performed of

Scene from *Waiting for Godot*

Set from *Leonce and Lena,* staged by the Rumanian director Liviu Ciulei

these plays include *Waiting for Godot* by Samuel Beckett (1906-) and *The Bald Soprano* by Eugene Ionesco (1912-).

Since all of these trends were against realism, actors and actresses were expected to be nonrealistic in performance. Moods and attitudes were to be exaggerated for artistic effect. Performers might even be expected to use techniques drawn from imitations of machines or animals or even puppets.

Realistic theater and acting which aimed at duplicating and interpreting the "real" world had little use for the techniques of opera or the dance. There was an audience, however, for a theater that included all the elements of performance. In America, the response to this audience was the musical comedy, the most popular form of theater for the last fifty years. During the twenties and thirties, most musicals had meager, silly plots and depended on music only for their success. The opening in 1943 of *Oklahoma* by Richard Rodgers and Oscar Hammerstein, II, proved, however, that it was possible to integrate music, dance, characters, and a strong plot into a dramatic whole. During the next thirty years, many playwrights, lyricists, and composers created the popular musical-comedy classics which are regularly performed by professionals and amateurs alike across America.

The musical is never completely realistic. Although many realistic techniques of acting are used, most of the performance revolves around music in some way. Dialogue is short and crisp, and characters are sharply drawn. The performer must work quickly and broadly to establish character. Because musicals are expensive to produce and must therefore play in big theaters, the performer must work with a bold emphasis. The use of microphones in most theaters makes it possible for the performer to be understood without resorting to the old melodramatic acting techniques, however.

In Europe, one man in particular tried to combine all of the various styles of twentieth-century theater into a single approach. Bertolt Brecht (1898-1956) was a poet, playwright, and director in Germany. In the twenties, he developed a type of theater which he called the *epic theater.* This combined realistic and nonrealistic acting in the same performance; actors involved in a realistic scene might sing a song or spout a political commentary. Many of his plays used music, but they were never quite musicals the way American productions were. The scenery combined many different elements, some realistic, some symbolic and expressionistic. Often, signs were lowered from the ceiling or large photos appeared as a comment on what was happening on stage. Many of his plays had political as well as social messages, and they had a major influence on writers and producers in many countries. These included the *Three-penny Opera* with music by Kurt Weill, *The Caucasian Chalk Circle,* and *Mother Courage,* which have become modern classics.

Bubbling Brown Sugar with (from the left) Cecelia Norfleet, Cab Calloway, Jean DuShon and Bobby Hill. May, 1980, Paramount Arts Centre, Aurora, Illinois

In the United States in the last two decades, all these influences have combined to produce an extremely varied theatrical environment. Many of the avant-garde plays could not draw the big audiences they needed to fill the Broadway theaters, so they moved to small theaters in converted buildings all over the country. Often in these new theaters, the thrust stage and the arena stage were utilized, and actors began to learn to work in these spaces.

In these smaller theaters, playwrights tried new themes and new styles, and found new audiences as well. Minority playwrights found theaters to perform their works, and they attracted audiences who had not formerly been a part of the regular theater audience. Plays by black playwrights, *A Raisin in the Sun* by Lorraine Hansberry or *No Place to Be Somebody* by Charles Godone, expressed the minority experience in vivid, realistic terms. Other groups soon began to contribute to the American stage. In recent years, many theaters have concentrated on the works of women writers and the experiences of women in modern America. Some groups do improvisational plays, while others are rediscovering the values of intensely realistic plays and performances. Musicals continue to be popular, and many theaters produce classics from all periods to growing and approving audiences.

The actor who wishes to work professionally in America today has to be aware of and to be able to work in an enormous number of different situations. There is no longer any one type of play or any one way to do a performance. Performers may play in theaters with audience capacity ranging from 40 to 3000. They must learn to adjust to movie and television cameras as well. In one show, performers may be required to sing and dance, in another to use mime and improvisation, in a third to be as natural and realistic as possible, and in a fourth to speak Shakespearean verse with clarity and ease.

The modern theater is a world of great variety and challenge. For performers and audiences, it offers insights and experiences drawn from all nations and the history of the last 2500 years. In schools and community theaters, in professional theaters, and through the film and television media, the beginning performer today is fortunate to have access to the world's greatest dramatists and performers.

Activities

1. In your library, find photographs of one of the plays mentioned in this chapter. Show the photos to the class and report what you have found out about how the play looked in performance.

2. Play the scene from *The Bald Soprano.* In some ways, this scene is extreme realism. The more realistically and sincerely you play the scene, the funnier and more absurd it becomes. The scene is also often performed with the Smiths and Martins simplified so that they become caricatures of middle-aged, middle-class people. Try it both ways when you work on it in class.

In this scene from *The Bald Soprano,* one of the most famous of the absurdist plays, Mr. and Mrs. Smith are a middle-aged couple, and Mr. and Mrs. Martin are another similar couple who are guests of the Smiths. The two couples are having a little talk before dinner. Ionesco has called this an "antiplay," and this scene demonstrates some of the reasons why. Things start with promise but never go anywhere, which is one of the playwright's ways of showing the absurdity of the characters and also of the theatrical conventions that make the audience expect something interesting and logical to happen.

from *The Bald Soprano*

by Eugene Ionesco

MRS. SMITH (*to the Martins*). Since you travel so much, you must have many interesting things to tell us.

MR. MARTIN (*to his wife*). My dear, tell us what you've seen today.

MRS. MARTIN. It's scarcely worth the trouble, for no one would believe me.

MR. SMITH. We're not going to question your sincerity!

MRS. SMITH. You will offend us if you think that.

MR. MARTIN (*to his wife*). You will offend them, my dear, if you think that . . .

MRS. MARTIN (*graciously*). Oh well, today I witnessed something extraordinary. Something really incredible.

MR. MARTIN. Tell us quickly, my dear.

MR. SMITH. Oh, this is going to be amusing.

MRS. SMITH. At last.

MRS. MARTIN. Well, today, when I went shopping to buy some vegetables, which are getting to be dearer and dearer . . .

MRS. SMITH. Where is it all going to end!

MR. SMITH. You shouldn't interrupt, my dear, it's very rude.

MRS. MARTIN. In the street, near a café, I saw a man, properly dressed, about fifty years old, or not even that, who . . .

MR. SMITH. Who, what?

MRS. SMITH. Who, what?

MR. SMITH (*to his wife*). Don't interrupt, my dear, you're disgusting.

MRS. SMITH. My dear, it is you who interrupted first, you boor.

MR. SMITH (*to his wife*). Hush. (*To* MRS. MARTIN) What was this man doing?

MRS. MARTIN. Well, I'm sure you'll say that I'm making it up—he was down on one knee and he was bent over.

MR. MARTIN, MR. SMITH, MRS. SMITH. Oh!

MRS. MARTIN. Yes, bent over.

MR. SMITH. Not possible.

MRS. MARTIN. Yes, bent over. I went near him to see what he was doing . . .

MR. SMITH. And?

MRS. MARTIN. He was tying his shoe lace which had come undone.

MR. MARTIN, MR. SMITH, MRS. SMITH. Fantastic!

MR. SMITH. If someone else had told me this, I'd not believe it.

MR. MARTIN. Why not? One sees things even more extraordinary every day, when one walks around. For instance, today in the Underground[1] I myself saw a man, quietly sitting on a seat, reading his newspaper.

MRS. SMITH. What a character!

MR. SMITH. Perhaps it was the same man!

(*The doorbell rings.*)

MR. SMITH. Goodness, someone is ringing.

MRS. SMITH. There must be somebody there. I'll go and see. (*She goes to see, she opens the door and closes it, and comes back.*) Nobody. (*She sits down again.*)

MR. MARTIN. I'm going to give you another example . . .

(*Doorbell rings again.*)

MR. SMITH. Goodness, someone is ringing.

MRS. SMITH. There must be somebody there. I'll go and see. (*She goes to see, opens the door, and comes back.*) No one. (*She sits down again.*)

MR. MARTIN (*who has forgotten where he was*). Uh . . .

MRS. MARTIN. You were saying that you were going to give us another example.

MR. MARTIN. Oh, yes . . .

(*Doorbell rings again.*)

MR. SMITH. Goodness, someone is ringing.

MRS. SMITH. I'm not going to open the door again.

---

1. **Underground,** subway.

Glossary of Interpretation and Theater Terms

Ad-lib: an unwritten line made up by the actor.
Allusion: indirect reference to a person, place, or thing.
Anti-pro: hanging position of lighting instruments in front of the proscenium arch.
Apron: part of the stage in front of the main curtain on a proscenium stage.
Area: (1) an imaginary division of the stage floor (see page 182); (2) part of the stage where a lighting instrument is aimed.
Arena: a performing space with audience on all sides.
Aside: a line spoken directly to the audience which is assumed the other characters on stage cannot hear; most common in plays written before 1900.

Backstage: any parts of the theater which the audience will not see.
Barn doors: a set of metal flaps placed in front of lighting instruments that can be folded to cut off part of the light.
Base: the foundation color of a makeup used for the primary skin color.
Batten: a pipe or wood strip from which lighting instruments or scenery can be hung.
Blackout: to make the stage completely dark.
Blocking: when and where the characters move on stage.
Border: another name for a teaser.
Border lights: another term for the trays.
Box set: set in which flats with built-in doors and windows form the walls and a ceiling replaces borders.
Brace cleat: a metal plate drilled with holes; used with a stage brace and stage screw to brace scenery.
Business: physical activity done by the actor, other than the blocking.

Cable: extension cords and visible electrical wiring on the stage.
Call: the time when you are expected to be present for rehearsal or performance.
Clown white: a strong white greasepaint used as a base for most clown and mime makeup.
Conservatory: school devoted to dramatic arts or one of the other fine arts.
Cross: to move from one place on stage to another.
Cue: (1) a signal for something to happen; (2) the line or business on which this signal is given.
Curtain: a drape on stage which covers the full stage opening.
Curtain call: the time at the end of a show when all the actors reappear to receive and acknowledge the audience's applause.
Cut: (1) stop whatever you are doing; (2) to eliminate from the script or the show.
Cyclorama: a large, smooth drape at the rear of a proscenium stage used for special lighting effects, usually as sky.

Dim: to make the lighting less bright.
Dimmer: an electrical control system which allows you to control the amount of power used in a lighting instrument, and thus the amount of light produced by that instrument.
Direct discourse: the exact quotation of a character's words.
Double: to play two or more characters in the same show.
Dramatic monologue: selection in which there is a single speaker who addresses other characters who do not speak.
Dress rehearsal: a rehearsal with all parts of the show except the audience.
Drop: a large piece of scenery which may be lowered from overhead.
Dry brush: painting technique in which a brush having a small quantity of paint is lightly dragged across a surface.
Dutchman: a thin strip of scenery material used to cover cracks or spaces in scenery pieces.

Ellipsoidal spotlight: a lighting instrument with an ellipsoidal reflector (see page 236).
Empathy: the interaction of emotional and physical response to a selection or situation.
Enjambment line: a line of poetry whose thought straddles over into the next line without any punctuation; also called straddling or run-on line.

Feminine line ending: a line of poetry which ends on a light stress.
Flat: a flat piece of scenery constructed of cloth stretched across a wooden frame (see page 229).
Floor plan: a scale drawing of the stage as seen from overhead, showing where all scenery and props are placed.
Flood: unfocused, general lighting.
Follow spot: a spotlight which can be moved during a show to follow a performer in action.
Footlights: strip lights placed at the front of the apron which shine upward from the floor.
Fresnel: a lighting instrument with a step lens (see page 236).
Fulcrum: the place that a poem turns (see page 100).

Gel: (1) a piece of colored medium placed in front of the lens of a lighting instrument to change the color of the light; (2) to put a gel in place.
Gel frame: a metal frame which holds a gel in place.
Greasepaint: stage makeup made with an oil or cream base.
Ground cloth: large piece of canvas laid on the stage floor, usually painted to act as a floor for the set.

Highlight: the light color used in makeup and painting to suggest three dimensions (see page 219).
Hot spot: the brightest part or the center of a lighting area.
House: the audience portion of the theater.

Improv: short for improvisation; a scene which is improvised.
Indirect discourse: reported conversation.
Instrument: a unit of lighting equipment on the stage.
Intermission: a break in the action of a play or interpretative performance during which the actors or performers do not appear and the audience may leave their seats.

Jack: a triangular brace which holds up a flat.

Kinesthetic imagery: the bodily response of muscles tensing and relaxing.
Kinetic imagery: indicates overt physical activity.

Lamp: a light bulb used in stage lighting instruments.
Lamp housing: casing that holds the lamp socket.
Latex: a rubber or rubber-like material used to build flexible, three-dimensional makeup pieces, which can be glued to the actor's skin and covered with normal makeup materials.
Leg: a tall, narrow drape used to mask the wings on a proscenium stage.
Leko: another name used for ellipsoidal spots.
Lens: a shaped piece of glass used in lighting instruments, through which the light passes and is focused.
Level: another name for a platform.
Light plot: the chart showing where the instruments should be hung and the directions for plugging and focusing them.
Lines: (1) the speeches the actors say; (2) ropes used on stage.
Loose-pin hinge: hinge designed especially for joining flats; the pins can be easily removed to separate flats (see illustrations, page 229).

Mask: to hide from the view of the audience.

Mat knife: a cutting tool with either a razor or razorlike blade, used for cutting cardboard and stiff paper.
Melodrama: a type of drama with emphasis on exaggerated appeal to the emotions and usually having a happy ending.
Mime: (1) a performer who works without speech or props; (2) to act without physical properties, usually with stylized makeup and costumes.

Pancake: another name for cake makeup used by some manufacturers.
Pantomime: (1) to pretend to use props which are not there—often used in rehearsals before scenery and props arrive; (2) any acting of normal activity without props or scenery pieces; (3) a special type of play, usually English, with spectacular scenery, very much like American musicals but usually on plots from children's stories; (4) any scene done without speech—sometimes these scenes will have real props and scenery, but still be called pantomime because they are silent.
P.A.R.: parabolic aluminized reflector; a commercial name for a lamp which has its reflector built in and which usually screws into normal household lamp sockets.
Patch: to connect the lighting circuits to the dimmer circuits.
Patch board: a panel with either movable connectors or with a set of plugs which is used to connect the lighting circuits to the dimmer board circuits.
Persona (ae): the speaker of a poem or other literary work, not necessarily identical to the author.
Pin connector: a type of stage electrical plug with round, brass plugs.
Pit: the part of the house directly against the edge of the apron of a proscenium stage; often this is lower than the floor of the seating section and is used for the orchestra in musicals.
Platform: a weight-bearing raised structure that may be varied in height by attaching different sets of supporting legs.
Playing across the room: the interpreter's rehearsal technique of placing characters out across the audience.
Plot: (1) the story of the play or narrative; (2) a chart showing where lighting instruments are placed and focused; (3) a chart showing where scenery pieces are placed, stored, or hung.
Practical: a piece of scenery, props, or lighting equipment which the actors use in the set and which actually works, such as a window that opens or a table lamp that turns on and off.
Pre-set: (1) scenery, props, or lighting cues set before the house opens; (2) a type of dimmer system with two or more complete control panels.
Production book: the copy of the script kept by the Stage Manager which contains all the information for running the show.
Project: to speak loudly and clearly enough to be heard in the audience.
Prompt: to give lines to the actors when they miss or forget them.
Prop: short for properties, all the items carried or moved by the actors and decorative parts of the set, usually including all furniture.
Proscenium: the wall which separates the house from the stage and backstage areas, and the type of stage which has a proscenium.
Prosody: the study of the structure of poetry.

Repertory company: a theatrical company that performs several plays regularly and in alternate sequence.
Rhyme: in poetry, the correspondence of sounds in the final syllables of two or more lines.
Rhyme scheme: the pattern of rhyme sounds in a poem.
Role: an actor's character, lines, and actions in a play.
Rouge: reddish makeup materials.

Royalty: the fee paid to the playwright or holder of the copyright in return for the right to perform the work in public.
Run-through: a rehearsal of a scene, act, or entire show done without a stop for changes, corrections, or notes.

Scale: a drawing or model made at a fixed ratio of items shown to their full-size versions; for example, at a scale of 1/2″—1′, 1/2″ on the drawing will be 1′ in the finished set piece.
Scansion: the marking off of lines of poetry into feet.
Scene: (1) a place where the action of a play occurs; (2) a division of the play script which takes place in one place and one time unit.
Scoop: a lighting instrument without a lens, used to provide flood lighting over a large, general area.
Scrim: a piece of loosely woven scenery material which looks solid when light shines directly on its surface but which is transparent if light is shown on something behind it.
Script: the written version of the play.
Scumbling: modifying the color or tone of a painted surface by overlaying parts of the surface with an opaque or semiopaque color.
Set: all the scenery and property pieces used in a scene.
Shadow: the dark color used in makeup and painting to suggest three dimensions (see page 219).
Soliloquy: a long speech by a character alone on the stage.
Stage brace: metal loops that hold two overlapping lengths of hardwood that can be adjusted in length and locked into position with a thumb screw. The top end of the brace is fitted with a double hook and the bottom with an angular or curved foot iron (see illustration, page 230).
Stage screw: large steel screw with a handle instead of a head that can be driven into the floor by hand turning.
Straddle lines: see enjambment.
Stress: the relative loudness given a syllable or word in a sound pattern.
Strike: to remove from the stage.
Strip lights: another name for the trays.
Suspension pause: in poetry, a slight pause where the thought straddles the line.

Teaser: a long, narrow drape which masks the overhead areas of a proscenium stage, usually hanging in front of each lighting batten to mask the instruments.
Tech rehearsal: a rehearsal in which technical cues are established and practiced.
Terminal pause: in poetry, an end-of-the-thought pause.
Tone color: the poet's manipulation of vowels and consonants to reinforce meaning and mood.
Top hat: a metal funnel which is placed in front of the lens of a lighting instrument to make the beam of light smaller.
Tormentor: another name for a leg.
Trays: strips of small lamps in a long metal tray that give a general, unfocused light.
Twist lock: a type of stage electrical plug which must be inserted and then twisted to lock in place before a connection will be made.

Wagon: a platform on wheels.
Walk-through: a rehearsal in which the actors do all the blocking and business but do not say all the lines.
Wings: the backstage space on either side of a proscenium stage.
Work light: a general lighting used for rehearsals or technical work which does not go through the dimmer board.

Index